Reimagining Irish Studies for the Twenty-First Century

Reimagining Ireland

Volume 100

Edited by Dr Eamon Maher,
Technological University Dublin – Tallaght Campus

PETER LANG
Oxford • Bern • Berlin • Bruxelles • New York • Wien

Reimagining Irish Studies for the Twenty-First Century

Eamon Maher and Eugene O'Brien (eds)

PETER LANG
Oxford • Bern • Berlin • Bruxelles • New York • Wien

Bibliographic information published by Die Deutsche Nationalbibliothek. Die Deutsche Nationalbibliothek lists this publication in the Deutsche Nationalbibliografie; detailed bibliographic data is available on the Internet at http://dnb.d-nb.de.

A catalogue record for this book is available from the British Library.

Library of Congress Cataloging-in-Publication Data

Names: Maher, Eamon, editor. | O'Brien, Eugene, 1958- editor.
Title: Reimagining Irish Studies for the twenty-first century / Eamon Maher, Eugene O'Brien.
Description: Oxford ; New York : Peter Lang, [2021] | Series: Reimagining Ireland, 1662-9094 ; Vol. 100 | Includes bibliographical references and index.
Identifiers: LCCN 2020054346 (print) | LCCN 2020054347 (ebook) | ISBN 9781800791916 (paperback) | ISBN 9781800791923 (ebook) | ISBN 9781800791930 (epub) | ISBN 9781800791947 (mobi)
Subjects: LCSH: Ireland--Civilization--Study and teaching. | Ireland--Social life and customs--Study and teaching. | Ireland--Historiography.
Classification: LCC DA910 .R45 2021 (print) | LCC DA910 (ebook) | DDC 941.50072--dc23
LC record available at https://lccn.loc.gov/2020054346
LC ebook record available at https://lccn.loc.gov/2020054347

ISSN 1662-9094
ISBN 978-1-80079-191-6 (print) • ISBN 978-1-80079-192-3 (ePDF)
ISBN 978-1-80079-193-0 (ePub) • ISBN 978-1-80079-194-7 (mobi)

Cover photograph by Paul Butler

© Peter Lang Group AG 2021

Published by Peter Lang Ltd, International Academic Publishers, 52 St Giles, Oxford, OX1 3LU, United Kingdom oxford@peterlang.com, www.peterlang.com

Eamon Maher and Eugene O'Brien have asserted their rights under the Copyright, Designs and Patents Act, 1988, to be identified as Editors of this Work.

All rights reserved.
All parts of this publication are protected by copyright. Any utilisation outside the strict limits of the copyright law,
without the permission of the publisher, is forbidden and liable to prosecution. This applies in particular to reproductions, translations, microfilming,
and storage and processing in electronic retrieval systems.

This publication has been peer reviewed.

To the highly talented and supportive Irish Studies community who make it such a vibrant space in which to work.

Eugene would also like to dedicate this book to Áine, Eoin, Sinéad and Dara who keep me grounded and supported through everything.

Message from the Series Editor

As we reach the landmark 100th volume in the *Reimagining Ireland* series, it would be remiss of me not to make reference to a number of people who have contributed majorly to the success of the project.

There have been three Commissioning Editors to date, each of whom has left a positive imprint. When Joe Armstrong first approached me with the idea of setting up a series in Irish Studies, I was immediately inspired by his infectious enthusiasm for, and belief in, what he envisioned. It did not take long to convince me to take on the role of General Editor. When Joe left, Christabel Scaife joined the team and her formidable editing skills, empathetic personality and encouragement of authors brought the series to a level that exceeded even Joe's and my own expectations. After Christabel's departure, Tony Mason took over at the helm. Tony was known to me from his work with Manchester University Press and he brought an extensive knowledge of academic publishing, and of Irish Studies in particular, which, combined with a larger than life and enabling personality, have made him an invaluable asset. These three people are owed a great debt of gratitude for their energy, vision and hard work which have made *Reimagining Ireland* the significant series that it has become and will hopefully remain.

The technical staff at Peter Lang, Oxford, have been a pleasure to work with. They are too numerous to be named individually, but they have shown great efficiency and courtesy in their dealings with me and with authors. The books are always attractively produced and the quick turnaround from manuscript stage to publication is something that marks us out from our competitors. I would also like to thank the various peer reviewers for giving so freely of their time to assess book projects and supply invaluable feedback so that we can stand over the academic quality of our books.

Without the several hundred authors, editors and contributors, there would be no series and so I would like to express my gratitude to them for choosing *Reimagining Ireland* as the home for their work. Some of these people have done multiple books with us, which proves that their experience has been a positive one. Working with such talented academics is a genuine privilege and a source of pride to me.

Although it is invidious to single out people, I do have to make special mention of Eugene O'Brien, whose *'Kicking Bishop Brennan up the Arse': Negotiating Texts and Contexts in Contemporary Irish Studies* is the first book in the series, and who has worked with me on a number of subsequent collections, including this special 100th volume. Eugene is an unbelievable source of support and inspiration, and his massive contribution to *Reimagining Ireland* is just one of the many ways in which he has shown himself to be an invaluable collaborator and friend.

As we look to the future of Irish Studies in this collection, I can but hope that I am blessed with the same talented authors, collaborators and friends for the next 100 volumes of *Reimagining Ireland* as I have been for the first 100. Success in a project like this is built on people coming together and working towards a common goal. The ever-growing *Reimagining Ireland* community is an excellent example of what can be achieved when you get that mix right. Long may it continue.

EAMON MAHER

Table of Contents

List of Figures   xiii

DECLAN KIBERD
Foreword: Future Perfect   xv

Acknowledgements   xxi

EAMON MAHER
Introduction: Reimagining Irish Studies for the Twenty-First Century   1

MÁIRTÍN MAC CON IOMAIRE
1 Applying a Food Studies Perspective to Irish Studies   19

BARRY HOULIHAN
2 Archives in Irish Studies: Locating Memory and the Archival Space   39

KATY HAYWARD
3 Between Britain and Europe Once More: The Significance of Brexit for the Reimagination of Ireland   59

MARY S. PIERSE
4 Catching the Mood: George Moore's *Fin-de-Siècle* Involvements   73

BRIAN MURPHY
5 Drinking Spaces in Strange Places: New Directions in Irish Beverage Research   91

EÓIN FLANNERY
6   Ecotheory and Criticism   111

GRACE NEVILLE
7   Poverty-Trapped: French Traveller Accounts of Poverty in
    Ireland over the Centuries   125

EAMONN WALL
8   Irish Studies in North America: Reflections   143

MAUREEN O'CONNOR
9   Irish Women's Writing   157

HARRY WHITE
10 'Monuments of Its Own Magnificence': Musicology within
    Irish Studies   169

ELKE D'HOKER
11 New Directions in Short Fiction   183

SYLVIE MIKOWSKI
12 No Country for Young Girls?: Representations of
    Gender-Based Violence in Some Recent Fiction by Irish
    Women Writers   193

COLIN COULTER AND PETER SHIRLOW
13 Northern Ireland's Future(s)   209

JOHN WALSH
14 'Real' Language Policy in a Time of Crisis: Covid-19, the
    State and the Irish Language   229

Contents

RUTH BARTON
15 Reimagining Irish Film Studies for the Twenty-First Century   247

CATHERINE MAIGNANT
16 Religion in Irish Studies   255

PAUL ROUSE
17 Sport and the Irish   271

EUGENE O'BRIEN
18 The Dawning of Difference: Literary and Cultural Theory
    in Irish Studies   283

MARGUÉRITE CORPORAAL
19 'The Words Will Come': Today's Legacies of the Great Irish
    Famine   301

MICHAEL CRONIN
20 Language, Time and the Improbable in Contemporary Ireland   319

DEREK HAND
21 'What Would I Say, if I Had a Voice?': The Irish Novel and
    the Articulation of Modernity   331

Notes on Contributors   343

Figures

Figure 2.1.	Wedding dress designed by Joe Vaněk for actress Holly Hunter as Hester Swane. *By the Bog of Cats*. San José Rep production. Joe Vaněk Archive, NUI Galway.	49
Figure 2.2.	Research photographs taken by Joe Vaněk, boglands in County Offaly. Joe Vaněk Archive, NUI Galway.	51
Figure 2.3.	Aerial photograph of the Pigeon House Power Station and Lab, 1951. E.S.B. Archives.	53
Figure 2.4.	Amy McElhatton in *The Sin Eaters*. ANU Productions. Photo © Pat Redmond.	56
Figure 5.1.	Beverage spaces and Irish retail: Penny's Coffee Cart Mary Street, Dublin. Photo by Brian Murphy, 2019.	105
Figure 5.2.	Beverage spaces and Irish Corporate Culture: O Barnaby's Pub, Fifth Floor Qualtrics, Dublin. Killian Woods, 2017.	106
Figure 5.3.	Beverage spaces and the pub with no beer: The Virgin Mary, Capel Street, Dublin. Photograph: Tom Honan, *The Irish Times*.	107
Figure 5.4.	Beverage spaces and Cycling Cafes: The Old Hardware, Narraghmore. Photo by Brian Murphy, 2020.	108
Figure 19.1.	Still from Lance Daly, *Black '47* (2018).	309
Figure 19.2.	*Bridget O'Donnell and Children* (1849). *Illustrated London News*, 22 December 1849. Engraving. High resolution image of Ireland's Great Hunger Museum, Quinnipiac University, Hamden, Connecticut.	310

Figure 19.3. *Village of Moveen* from *The Illustrated London News* of 22 December 1849. High resolution image courtesy of Ireland's Great Hunger Museum, Hamden, Connecticut. 312

Figure 19.4. James Mahoney, *Woman Begging at Clonakilty*. *Illustrated London News*, 13 February 1847. Engraving. High resolution image courtesy of Ireland's Great Hunger Museum, Quinnipiac University, Hamden, Connecticut. 315

DECLAN KIBERD

Foreword: Future Perfect

This will have been a happy day

– Samuel Beckett

There was a time – within the living memory of some contributors to this excellent volume – when there was no such thing as Irish Studies. If you wanted to buy a novel by Kate O'Brien or Ben Kiely, you sought them out in the general fiction section of a good bookshop. If you wished to read about Parnell, you would as like as not find the desired book on shelves headed 'biography' or 'history'.

All that changed with the foundation in the 1960s of special chairs devoted to Anglo-Irish Literature or Irish History and Political Science. Slowly, other sub-categories emerged: anthropology, sociology, geography and musicology. Some disciplines are still nascent: for years, certain people denied that there was a distinctive Irish cuisine, and, though you can hardly cross a major city now without passing an Irish pub, it will be some time yet before the texts produced by Alison Armstrong, Darina Allen, Máirtín Mac Con Iomaire or Rhona Kenneally generate a clearly themed range of Irish restaurants, not to mention a set of university examination papers interrogating the provenance and meaning of Irish food.

I am – like the contributors to all hundred volumes of this fine series – speaking solely of curricular university study. However, there is a deeper sense in which many of us were practising Irish Studies from the moment we entered primary school; there were times when, in the first five decades of the new state, with all the hours devoted to the Irish language, history, religious past, geography, folk and culinary traditions, we seemed to study little else. Even the syllabus of the English language was a sort of crash-course in Anglo-Irish poetry from William Allingham to Aubrey de Vere and the younger W. B. Yeats.

I can still recall John McGahern urging a class of solemn 8-year-old boys to 'put a bit more jizz' into a recital of 'Up the Airy Mountain' – and following it with a discourse on the Halloween rituals of rural Ireland. That was in 1959. Nowadays, university students in South Bend and Kyoto study these matters. So, my mother wasn't wholly wrong when, on being asked what she thought of my book *Inventing Ireland*, she giggled and said: 'Ireland always existed, Declan – you know that'.

Doubtless, the decades preceding and following independence witnessed a tremendous intensification of Irish Studies in the nation's primary and secondary schools. The leaders of the cultural revival made a point of familiarising themselves with a set of codes that seemed to be dying and being reborn at one and the same time: to such an extent that one Aran Islander told a visitor that the native language could never die: 'Believe me, Mr Synge, there are few rich men in the world who are not studying the Irish'.

This process – mostly internal to Ireland itself between the 1890s and 1960s – seemed to go global thereafter. The decades of national revival had prompted overseas intellectuals to take an interest in the lore of the island: from Heinrich Zimmer and Kuno Meyer, through Simone Téry and L. Paul-Dubois, to Langston Hughes and other exponents of the Harlem Renaissance. But these were for the most part exceptional individuals, who sought in Ireland some deeply personal qualities which connected them to their inmost psychic needs. It was only in and after the 1960s that Irish Studies emerged as a widespread global practice, taken by many as a test-case of the modernising world – for the French, a process of secularisation; for Irish-Americans, a myth of self-explanation; for South Americans, a repository of magic realism; and for almost everyone, an early example of that postcolonialism suddenly manifest to academics in works by Senghor, Cesaire, CLR James and so on. As far back as Edmund Spenser's disquisitions, and much later in those of Matthew Arnold, the curricular study of Irish texts in overseas universities has been a crisis-driven discipline, designed to explain (especially to the English) the strange psychology and even stranger politics of a baffling peripheral people; but once the Troubles erupted in a new form after the civil rights agitation of

1968, Ireland became a fashionable subject for commentators as different as Gayatri Spivak and Edward Said.

There had always been intrepid individual scholars whose deep interest in, for example, Jonathan Swift, had led them to a wider engagement with the matter of Ireland. At the US university of Notre Dame in the early 1980s, Christopher Fox was one of the first commentators to notice how Swift had portrayed Ireland as a martyr to malformed theories of development and modernisation. In Fox's view, that army of writers who thought that Swift could be explained outside his Irish contexts was missing the main point. They took Swift, as similar critics take today's anti-colonial insurgents, as a study in the pathology of a sick person rather than as a symptom of a distressed society.

Such naïve critics often missed the fact that Swift was, with his strong sense of the future, not only one of the founders of Anglo-Irish Literature, but also an early satirist of those methods of quantification which not only immiserated his Dublin but now threaten also the very future of humanistic studies across the globe. Ireland was indeed interesting as a laboratory in which deranged futuristic experiments could be tried out. It was a victim of the crazy theories of the Penal Laws – Sir William Petty thought it useful in the 1690s to calculate the amount of lands confiscated from Catholics; but it also became a testing-ground for all kinds of decolonial theories in the 1960s. As one of Beckett's monologists wearily observed: 'Extraordinary how mathematics helps you to know yourself'.

In many third-level colleges across the world, after the 1960s, charismatic individual teachers of Irish subjects such as history, literature or sociology, began to build wider multidisciplinary projects, as the number of students expanded and 'theory' took hold to feed their desire for a course which would somehow integrate all those disparate subjects. Once a victim of misplaced theory, Ireland for a few years became a beneficiary of smarter theorists. It offered a knowable community to idealistic visitors – strife-torn, yes (which made it doubly interesting), but also friendly, studiable and eloquent.

Some who analysed the island's conflicted nature did not always recognise how unstable their own countries of origin were, though the shrewder among them must have seen in Ireland's 'quaking sod' a fore-image of what might happen in the wider world, under the predations of a casino capitalism after the crash of 2008.

In general, however, those scholars who visited and studied the country had a tonic effect on the practices of academia in Ireland. Even after the liberations of the 1960s, many professors had prosecuted intense turf wars to defend the 'integrity' of their particular discipline, fearing that it could be destroyed by the promiscuity of a multidisciplinary approach. Yet it was becoming ever more clear that the great intellectual advances in, say, economic history or studies of folk environment, had been made by multilingual scholars such as Cormac Ó Gráda or Angela Bourke, just as literature departments awoke suddenly to the sheer fecundity of bilingual writers from Samuel Beckett to Nuala Ní Dhomhnaill. It became a matter of some urgency to take the various disciplines out of their self-imposed quarantines. Yet what Edward Said had once observed of Arabic Studies was also true of Irish Studies; they often emerged earlier, and in more developed form, in overseas locations rather than in their homelands; and frequently as a way of responding to a political crisis that was often deeply cultural in its sources.

It would be as naïve now, as it was in 1921, to announce that the political crises of Ireland have been resolved. The implications of Brexit alone would make a mockery of such a contention. One irony has been the vast alteration in the position taken by once-leading scourges of nationalist tradition. As soon as the current peace seemed to have been secured, many of them took starring roles in the 1916 commemorations at the National Concert Hall; and some went on to issue scathing denunciations of the Brexiteers, as if those very English in whom they had invested their fondest hopes, during the period when John Bull's interventions in Irish affairs were recast as 'a shared experience', had now contrived to let the side down. Meanwhile, the more level-headed leaders of Irish opinion have quietly abandoned many nationalist nostra, as they seek further integration into the European Union and a sensible working arrangement with a less insular Britain (in which both Scotland and Wales often look to Ireland as a model). Perhaps the real meaning of Brexit in 2016 was that England at last confronted a long-deferred national question, which the Irish had faced exactly 100 years earlier.

Nationalism had begun to fade slowly in the Irish Republic with the negotiated accession to the European Union in the early 1970s. What little opposition there was to that accession came less from narrow-gauge nationalists than from worried socialists such as Michael D. Higgins, who has long since anyway become an ardent Europhile and a comrade of its social democrats. The final evidence of this fading was the withdrawal of the historical claim on the six northern counties by a huge majority vote in 1998.

But nature abhors a vacuum; and, even in its most militant form, nationalism has usually been a secondary formation through which a frustrated cultural identity seeks expression. With traditional religiosity also in free fall, it may well be that culture will become the site and stake of future Irish debates – albeit in globalised versions of the novel and drama, or in assertions of the civil rights of Irish speakers alongside those of other ethnic groups who have enriched the tapestry of the contemporary island. As the short stories of Dubliners are rewritten by young Polish immigrants in a contemporary idiom, or as the transatlantic novel or pan African lyric reappear in an Irish mode, we can be sure that fusion food and fusion music point the way forward. Ever since *Gulliver's Travels*, a gift for cultural comparison has characterised Irish writing. There may be no such thing as an Irish mind but, as Conor Cruise O'Brien once said, there has long been an Irish condition, productive of common and recurring characteristics in those caught up in it.

The heroic phase of Irish Studies in universities is probably winding down, but the post-Ireland of which artists write is under the sway of forces which may clarify themselves only in the future. In a primary school on the edge of Balbriggan, a Romanian child may already be narrating a new, unexampled version of the story of Cuchulain, under the amused eye of a teacher who could be the next John McGahern. There is an ideological and emotional surplus in all present moments which suggests that there will always be unfinished business, a future exciting to precisely the extent that it is unknown.

So, we beat on, boats against the current, on a journey with no destination, to continue our study of a people who never quite knew home or how to stay in it, searching for something, as the great Scott Fitzgerald said, commensurate with our capacity for wonder. Whether we are tenth-generation natives of Carraroe, readers of Joyce in Trieste, or that Romanian child pondering Cuchulain in Balbriggan, we are all embarked on the search for a version of this country which none of our ancestors had ever known.

Declan Kiberd
Clontarf, Dublin
16 November 2020.

Acknowledgements

The editors are infinitely grateful to Professor Declan Kiberd for agreeing to write the Foreword to this landmark publication. Having the leading Irish Studies scholar endorsing the book is a wonderful boost.

Professor Victor Merriman offered us invaluable advice when we were planning the collection and suggested topics and authors that enhanced the final version immensely.

We would also like to express our heartfelt thanks to the specialist authors for agreeing to be involved in the project. In spite of the huge stress and anxiety occasioned by the effects of the coronavirus, they succeeded in producing what are, by any standards, superb contributions to the mapping out of possible developments within Irish Studies in the twenty-first century.

We wish to thank Tony Mason and all the staff at Peter Lang, Oxford, for their enthusiasm and support with regard to the series, and to the 100th volume in particular.

Finally, Paul Butler has provided a stunning image to adorn the cover of the book for which we are greatly indebted.

EAMON MAHER

Introduction: – Reimagining Irish Studies for the Twenty-First Century

To mark the milestone 100th book in *Reimagining Ireland*, Peter Lang commissioned a special volume offering both a retrospective on what has been achieved to date in the series, and an outline of future possibilities. Clearly, Irish Studies is a discipline that has blossomed over the past number of decades. This flowering was assisted greatly by the emergence in the 1960s and 1970s of 'area studies', or area-based programmes, which emphasised that knowledge of the literature, culture, history and diversity that shape and mould various specialisms should be an essential ingredient of university courses. Hence, French Studies, Peace Studies, Women's Studies, European Studies, and Postcolonial Studies, to cite but a few examples, all came to the fore and proposed a broader menu for exploration than had heretofore been the norm. In one of the first attempts to define this new phenomenon in 1988, the editors of *Irish Studies: A General Introduction* noted a 'quickening of interest in Irish Studies as an integrated, multi-disciplinary programme of learning' from the 1960s onwards, particularly in the United States.[1]

The term 'Irish Studies' covers a multitude: literature (in Irish and Hiberno-English), the postcolonial experience (only valid for the twenty six counties that currently constitute the Republic of Ireland), the Irish diaspora, religion, politics, sociology. As the editors of the collection mentioned above remarked: 'The nature of Irish Studies remains a subject of debate and its limits are fluid rather than fixed'.[2] Taking the 'fluid' rather

---

1   Thomas Bartlett, Chris Curtin, Riana O'Dwyer and Gearóid Ó Tuthaigh (eds), *Irish Studies: A General Introduction* (Dublin: Gill and Macmillan, 1988), 1.
2   Ibid., 6.

than the 'fixed' view on board, this collection appreciates that the task it has set itself is not a simple one, mainly because of the vastness of the topic. But the aim was never to provide an exhaustive encyclopaedic overview of Irish Studies. Rather, the idea was to provide a 'forward look' (as opposed to what Frank O'Connor once called the 'backward look') at how Irish Studies might develop in the twenty-first century.

The fact that there are now 100+ volumes in *Reimagining Ireland*, a series that published its first book in 2009, shows the rude good health of the field. And it is far from being alone in this regard. There are several university presses that also publish Irish titles, most notably Cambridge University Press, where there is obvious strength in literary and cultural studies; Cork, with a *Books of Irish interest* series, featuring most notably the *Atlas of the Irish Revolution* – they also have responsibility for the *Irish Review*; Edinburgh, which brings out the *Irish University Review* and has recently announced the establishment of *Irish Studies Now*, a series that will be edited by Emilie Pine; Liverpool, which has a long track record in the area, and whose *Reappraisals in Irish History* and *Studies in Irish Literature* series are gaining traction; Manchester, a significant player that has brought out many titles concentrating in the main on sociology, history and politics; Oxford, which has no designated Irish Studies list, but which regularly publishes books of Irish interest; Syracuse, whose *Irish Studies* series is probably the longest-running in the area; and UCD Press, which publishes various monographs and has the *Classics of Irish History* series.

Independent publishers continue to produce academic books with an Irish Studies slant. At the start of the third millennium, Eugene O'Brien's *Irish Writers and Filmmakers*, with the Liffey Press, brought a real energy and impetus to Irish Studies scholarship with twelve titles, all of which were widely reviewed. Liffey also published *The Irish Book Review*, again under the editorial direction of O'Brien, that reviewed books of Irish interest. Other notable publishers in this regard are Four Courts Press, whose *Classics of Irish History* series is highly esteemed; Irish Academic Press, newly aligned to Merrion Press, noted mainly for its history titles; Edward Everett Root Publishers, whose *Studies in Irish Literature, Cinema and Culture* series is edited by Pilar Villar Argaïz, as well as the *Key Irish Women Writers* series and *Irish Women Writers: Texts and Contexts*, edited by Kathryn Laing and Sinéad Mooney; and Palgrave Macmillan, which is becoming more active in the area and which has in the past been particularly associated with drama. Most recently, Routledge has initiated a *Studies in Irish Literature* series, with Eugene O'Brien at the helm, which aims to employ a number of theoretical frameworks to offer fresh insights into Irish writing.

No serious discussion of publishing in the area of Irish Studies can fail to take account of Field Day, which has played a central role in the development of Irish Studies as an academic discipline worthy of respect. Originally a theatre company, founded in 1980 in Derry by Seamus Deane, the actor Stephen Rea and playwright Brian Friel in order to stage the latter's play, *Translations*, it gradually moved into many different areas. Others to join the theatre company as codirectors were Seamus Heaney, Tom Paulin, Thomas Kilroy and David Hammond. Joe Cleary comments on how, largely as a result of Deane's energy and vision, Field Day gradually extended its operations outside of theatre by publishing pamphlets on the Troubles, a three-volume anthology of Irish writing (1990), followed by a two-volume annex for women writers eleven years later, a Field Day Critical Conditions series consisting of fifteen monographs (in association with Cork and Notre Dame University Presses). In 2005, Deane launched Field Day Publications and, with Brendán Mac Suibhne, the annual *Field Day Review*, which received the financial backing of the Irish American CEO of Coca Cola, Donald Keough.[3] The controversy surrounding the initial three volumes of *The Field Day Anthology of Irish Writing* when it was published in 1991 was mainly attributable to the dearth of women writers, but this was compounded by the accusation that the anthology had a strong nationalist bias, a contention that Cleary finds is not backed up by the facts.[4] Field Day is undoubtedly a project to which Irish Studies

---

3 For an excellent overview of the Field Day project and Seamus Deane's role in same, see Joe Cleary, 'Dark Fields of the Republic: Seamus Deane's Sundered Provinces', *Boundary 2* (Summer 2010), 1–68; also, Adrian Frazier, 'In the Field of Vision', review of *Field Day Review*, vol. 1, *The Irish Times*, 28 May 2005.

4 Cleary quotes from Deane's own 'General Introduction' to the *Anthology* which avows the reductionist notion that 'Nationalism, cultural or political, is no more than an inverted image of the colonialism it seeks to replace', Cleary, *Boundary 2*, 37.

is seriously indebted because of the seriousness, academic rigour and attention at home and abroad that it brought to the discipline.

Irish Studies demands a mastery and understanding of a number of specialisms and how they impact on, and interact with one another. In *Ireland Beyond Boundaries: Mapping Irish Studies in the Twenty-First Century*, a collection he co-edited with Yvonne Whelan in 2007, Liam Harte remarked that one of the distinguishing features of Irish Studies is 'self-reflexivity'. He continued: 'Contemporary Irish Studies is perhaps best understood as a discipline – however contested its constitution as such – in a continual state of deconstruction….'[5] We have seen how the hybrid nature of Irish Studies makes it difficult to define in exact terms the epistemological status of the discipline. For some, it is primarily an offshoot of postcolonial studies, with particular reference to history and literature. However, it also has a foothold in area studies, cultural theory, feminism, sociology, political science and anthropology. In many ways, Ireland serves as a sort of case-study on which various theories can be gainfully tested and explored, an interpretation which coincides with the view of Declan Kiberd who noted (with a strong ironic inflection) that, 'through many centuries, Ireland was pressed into service as a foil to set off English virtues, as a laboratory in which to conduct experiments, and as a fantasy-land in which to meet fairies and monsters'.[6] It is certainly no longer the case that Ireland's bitter colonial struggle with its nearest neighbour, and its sometimes romantic, or romanticised past, is the main aspect that attracts scholarly interest. Indeed, Kiberd himself has been instrumental in demythologising Irish Studies through his masterly application of postcolonial theory and its impact on the literatures of Ireland in English and in Irish.

---

5   Liam Harte, 'Introduction', in *Ireland Beyond Boundaries: Mapping Irish Studies in the Twenty-First Century*, edited by Liam Harte and Yvonne Whelan (London: Pluto, 2007), 2. Colin Graham's *Deconstructing Ireland* made the same case in 2001, a year before Claire Connolly's ground-breaking collection *Theorizing Ireland* was published by Palgrave Macmillan, with essays by many of the main figures of the 'first wave' of Irish Studies such as Angela Bourke, Patricia Coughlan, Joe Cleary, Seamus Deane, Luke Gibbons, David Lloyd and Connolly herself.
6   Declan Kiberd, *Inventing Ireland: The Literature of the Modern Nation* (Cambridge, MA: Harvard University Press, 1970), 1.

Writing in 2004, Linda Connolly, while acknowledging that history was the foremost humanities discipline in Irish academia for much of the twentieth century, detects a transformation during the 1980s: ' "Postcolonial" theorists have focused much of their energies in Irish Studies on contesting the long-standing hegemony of history and historians'.[7] For Connolly, postcolonial critics and criticism, 'are not the beginning and end of Irish Studies as a discipline', and she goes on to argue quite forcefully that this form of methodology (or ideology), particularly as represented in the Field Day writings and 'associated polemics', for example, were not embraced by all working in the area. She concludes: 'In addition, a suspected fusion of postcolonial criticism with "nationalist" politics (and/or republicanism) has generated acrimony across the field'.[8] As should be the case within any healthy discipline, Irish Studies would appear to be a contested space, with a lot of 'self-reflexivity' and debate about what its defining characteristics should be.

Irish Studies currently has a strong presence in a large number of countries around the world.[9] But there are no grounds for complacency, once more according to Harte: '[t]he picture that emerges is of a subject in process, its boundaries and topography being reshaped by a plethora of competing forces, its future within the academy by no means secure'.[10] Obviously the market forces that control universities, and the difficulties caused by the interdisciplinarity that is at the heart of Irish Studies, mean that there is as great a need as ever for imagination and flexibility when it comes to mapping a viable future. And there are encouraging signs that this is happening. For example, in Europe alone, EFACIS (European Federation

---

7   Linda Connolly, 'The Limits of "Irish Studies": Historicism, Culturalism, Postcolonialism', *Irish Studies Review* 12, no. 2 (2004), 139–162, 139.
8   Connolly, 'The Limits of "Irish Studies" ', 141.
9   At this juncture, I draw the readers' attention to the Golden Jubilee edition of the *Irish University Review* (Volume 50, Number 1), Spring/Summer 2020, edited by Emilie Pine. In addition to contributions by a number of former editors of the journal, it also contains essays on Irish Studies in Australia and New Zealand (Dianne Hall and Ronan McDonald); Japan (Andrew Fitzsimons); Continental Europe (Ondřj Pilný) and South America (Beatriz Kopschitz Bastos).
10 Harte, 'Introduction', 12.

of Associations and Centres of Irish Studies) has fifty registered Centres, and that is far from representing the full number currently in existence. In addition to conferences and publications, EFACIS has also been responsible for two important initiatives: the Irish Itinerary, which began during Ireland's Presidency of the EU in 2013 and which facilitates Irish writers' and artists' attendance at co-ordinated events hosted by Irish Studies centres across Europe, and the PhD seminars at the Irish College in Leuven, which, since 2015, allow graduate students in Irish Studies to attend master classes and workshops. There are national associations of Irish Studies in almost every European country at this point.

IASIL (International Association for the Study of Irish Literatures) has a presence in thirty five different countries. ACIS (American Conference of Irish Studies) is very strong in the United States, and was instrumental in lending weight and credibility to Irish Studies as a discrete academic discipline when it was set up in the 1980s[11] – in the past it would have been a subset of English Literature or History faculties. CAIS (Canadian Association of Irish Studies), the long-established SOFEIR, the French umbrella organisation for Irish Studies, BAIS (British Association of Irish Studies), ISAANZ (Irish Studies Association of Australia and New Zealand), AEDEI in Spain, ABEI (Brazilian Association of Irish Studies), AFIS (Association of Franco-Irish Studies), which is based in TU Dublin, and NEICN (North-East Irish Culture Network, UK), are just a few of the better-known associations which are active in terms of conference organisation and publications.

In addition, there are several highly regarded Irish Studies journals, many of which have links to the aforementioned associations. Journals are indispensable platforms for the dissemination of scholarship in the field and they add academic credibility to the discipline. Some of the main Irish Studies journals include the *Irish University Review* (IASIL), *Études Irlandaises* (SOFEIR), the *Canadian Journal of Irish Studies* (CAIS), *Irish Studies Review* (BAIS), *New Hibernia Review*, *Éire-Ireland*, *Irish Review*, *Studies: An Irish Quarterly Review*, *Estudios Irlandeses* (AEDEI), *ABEI Journal* (ABEI), *The Irish Literary Supplement* (biennial journal/newspaper

---

11   See Eamonn Wall's chapter in this volume for a more detailed discussion of ACIS.

of ACIS), *RISE (Review of Irish Studies in Europe), American Journal of Irish Studies* (Glucksman Ireland House/New York University), *An Sionnach: A Journal of Literature, Culture and the Arts, Australian Journal of Irish Studies* (ISAANZ), *The Dublin Review of Books, Irish Political Studies, Irish Theatre Magazine, Irish Pages, Poetry Ireland, The Stinging Fly, History Ireland*, and others that have a more tenuous link to the area. These journals reveal once more the scope and variety of Irish Studies and its strongly established presence within academia. In her Introduction to the Golden Jubilee edition of the *Irish University Review*, Emilie Pine remarked: 'Irish Studies has no founding charter, no list of commandments, or global constitution. It emerges from the interests of individuals and groups, and it will always reflect the times, in terms of what it includes, and also what it excludes'.[12] This is an important point in that it underlines once more the fluid nature of Irish Studies, its inclusivity and openness to various academic disciplines. In a similar way, the *Irish University Review*, while it will inevitably be influenced by the particular interests of its editors, must look beyond vested interests and seek to represent diverse views as they reveal themselves at various points in time. Former editors of the journal acknowledge in the Jubilee issue what their ambition or focus was, some declaring a desire to bring about gender balance among the contributors and the topics covered, others a commitment to give more space to less canonical literary figures, and yet more to highlighting translations of Irish texts into English and other languages, and so on.

This brief survey reveals that publishing and other academic activities in the area of Irish Studies are impressive and wide-ranging, and this is the context within which the *Reimagining Ireland* series operates. It embodies the variety and scope of the discipline that have been traced through the various publications, journals and associations outlined above. *Reimagining Ireland* is a broad church, in that it looks at multiple areas, both those traditionally associated with Irish Studies and the new emerging directions within academic critique. In terms of offering an overview of the series to date, it is instantly clear that it is committed to a transdisciplinary approach and is open to proposals dealing with any relevant area of Irish Studies.

---

12   Emily Pine, 'Introduction', *Irish University Review* (Spring/Summer 2020), 1–9, 1.

Placing the volume number in brackets, one can see that the topic/area that features most frequently is literary studies of one form or another. There are monographs on canonical figures such as John McGahern (23); Colm Tóibín (44); Yeats (10, 18); John Banville (50), and a combined study of Bacon and Beckett (6). Paul Muldoon's 'poetics of place' is covered by Anne Karhio (77) and the series also published the first book-length study of Frank McCourt (78). There are nine essay collections devoted to specific writers: Mary Leadbeater and Dorothea Herbert (13); Colum McCann (17); Marina Carr (20); Thomas Moore (24); George Moore (51, 69); John McGahern (56); Joseph Sheridan Le Fanu (76) and Mary O'Donnell (88).

Among the literary topics covered are culture wars and the Abbey theatre (29); varying issues associated with women writers such as the animal/species (19), the cultural present (25), new critical perspectives (40), women novelists in Britain (62); literary representations of Catholicism (36); critical reception of Irish plays in the London theatre (41); urban and rural landscapes in modern Irish literature and culture (43); literary and cultural representations of the Irish family (47); fictions of the Land War (58); dance in contemporary Irish drama (61); the short story (63); the year 1798 in twentieth-century fiction and drama (64); Irish literature and the First World War (72); literature and culture in the new Ireland (73); theatre environments (84); writing slums (86); theatre and popular song (85), and theatre archives (87). A number of collections also contain essays on literary figures, in particular the majority of comparative studies and the books that grapple with modernism (14) and 1950s Ireland (46).

Matters connected to the Irish language are dealt with in four books (3, 15, 32 and 65), and these elicited a good response in terms of sales. In fact, John Walsh's *Contests and Contexts: The Irish Language and Ireland's Socio-Economic Development* (15), which challenges the commonly held view that the Irish language is an obstacle to Ireland's economic development, was by far the bestseller of the first fifty volumes of *Reimagining Ireland* (perhaps illustrating indirectly the validity of the position adopted by the author). The stated ambition of Walsh's book was to ground its argument 'in theoretical perspectives from sociolinguistics, political economy and development theory', in order to suggest 'a new theoretical framework for understanding the relationship between language and development'. This is an approach that exemplifies the broader desire of *Reimagining Ireland* to employ different methodological tools, and to expand the potential of Irish Studies to move into areas that tended to be somewhat occluded previously, especially in mainstream publications. Clearly, literature written in Irish has long been a core interest of many Irish Studies scholars, but this socio-economic inflection definitely broke new ground, as did Irene Luchitti's study of the hidden life of Tomás O'Crohan (3), Mairéad Conneely's examination of writing the Aran Islands (32) and B. Mairéad Pratschke's treatment of Gael Linn's *Amharc Éireann* film series (65).

Among the other main clusters one finds are books that place Ireland in parallel to other societies and cultures. Chief among these comparators would be France (28, 55, 66, 68 and 69), a preference that undoubtedly is linked to the General Editor's close involvement with Franco-Irish Studies; Argentina (81, 90); the Czech Lands and West to East (49, 52); Scotland (38); Poland (39); Germany (75); Spain (82); and the Nordic Countries (91). In terms of Northern Ireland, there are monographs devoted to Northern Irish Fiction (26, 59) and community politics and the Peace Process in contemporary Northern Irish drama (31), whereas *Ireland and The North* (91) uses 'North' to refer to both the Nordic countries and the Six Counties that constitute Northern Ireland.[13] Film and cinema account for four books (16, 21, 27, 67) – Zélie Asava's monograph on representing black and mixed race identities in Irish film (16) being the recipient of the 2011 Peter Lang Young Scholars Competition in Irish Studies, while Jeannine Woods's postcolonial study of Irish and Indian cinema (21) offers some illuminating insights on this intriguing topic. Advertising is the subject of two monographs (22, 95), one dealing with culture and Irishness, while the other looks at the iconic brand that is Guinness.

---

13 *Ireland and the North* is significant in how it employs areas as diverse as art history, literary history and theory, archaeology, antiquarianism and media studies, in addition to political analysis, to examine Ireland's relationship with the Nordic countries. The description on the back page concludes: 'With three sections on Material Culture, Political Culture and Print Culture, the book moves beyond the predominant literary paradigm in Irish Studies to make a significant contribution to expanding and developing the field'. We will see later in the Introduction how this conforms perfectly to the thrust and ambition of *Reimagining Ireland*.

Single subject studies include cultural identity within and beyond Ireland (2); cultural perspectives on globalisation and Ireland (5); autobiography, stories of self in the narrative of a nation (7); a history of Irish ballet, 1927–1963 (8); revolution and evolution (12); back to the future of Irish studies, a festschrift to Tadgh Foley (30); southern Ireland and the Liberation of France (33); literary anthologies in the 'Library of Ireland' (34); the Irish diaspora (37); encounters across cultures (42); Ireland and victims (45); Ireland and the world of the 1950s (46); visual culture (48); the crossings of art in Ireland (53); Ireland and popular culture (54); global legacies of the Great Irish Famine (60); authority and crisis (70); the Fenian invasion of Canada in 1886 (71); new perspectives on Irish TV series (74); Irish Studies and the dynamics of memory (79); reimagining Irish folklore (80); the Great Irish Famine and social class (89); the life and work of the liturgical artist Richard King (92); trauma and identity in contemporary Irish culture (94); contemporary arts, culture and politics in Ireland (96); travel narratives of the Irish Famine (98); and memorialising the Magdalene Laundries (101).

The first title in the series, Eugene O'Brien's *'Kicking Bishop Brennan Up the Arse': Negotiating Texts and Contexts in Contemporary Irish Studies*, was chosen specifically to set the tone for what was to follow. This was a collection of previously published essays on canonical literary figures such as Yeats, Joyce, O'Faoláin and Heaney, along with examples from public culture in the form of the hugely successful *Father Ted* TV series (the title is borrowed from one of the most famous episodes in the series), globalisation and Guinness advertising. O'Brien's stated ambition to reconsider Irish Studies 'through the medium of literary and cultural theory' was one that chimed with the desire of the series to 'reimagine' the concepts of Ireland and 'Irishness' through as many lenses as possible. In the essays on literature, O'Brien concentrated on the 'the nature and development of literary theory as a discipline, tracing the cultural milieu of Derrida, Lacan and Foucault' which he applied to the Irish context. He then provided a deconstructive reading of how *Father Ted* prefigured the massive decline of the authority and status of the Catholic Church in 'the symbolic order of contemporary Ireland', and, by undertaking a 'reading across the borders of the literary, the social and the filmic' (he used the example of the 1999 award-winning

American Beauty), he elucidated the ability of popular culture to capture the pulse of society and to poke gentle fun at the once powerful clerical caste and other elites. This approach was extended to exploring the 'societal haunting of Ireland by its globalised other', by showing how advertising of the iconic Guinness brand 'has followed, paralleled and at times anticipated, socio-cultural trends in contemporary Irish society'. O'Brien's essays fitted neatly, therefore, into the stated desire of *Reimagining Ireland* to examine the past and present and to suggest possibilities for the future, 'by looking at Ireland's literature, culture and history and subjecting them to the most up-to-date critical appraisals'. In the Introduction to his own series on Irish writers and filmmakers, O'Brien underscored the value of understanding 'the transformative potential of the work of the artist in the context of the ongoing redefinition of society and culture', an ambition that *Reimagining Ireland* sought to extend beyond literature and film onto the extremely wide tapestry that Irish Studies comprises at present.

Finally, two other collections in the series that merit special mention are volume 57, *'Tickling the Palate': Gastronomy in Irish Literature and Culture*, and volume 93, *Recalling the Celtic Tiger*. The first, co-edited by Máirtín Mac Con Iomaire and Eamon Maher, was inspired by the inaugural Dublin Gastronomy Symposium that was held in Cathal Brugha Street in 2012. In her Foreword, food expert and academic Darra Goldstein welcomed the 'nuanced literary, cultural and sociological interpretations of Ireland and its food' and hailed the first academic study of Irish gastronomy, which she hoped would inspire many other volumes on the same subject.[14] The popularity of this book is undoubtedly linked to the huge interest currently among the general public for anything related to food. Celebrity chefs have their own TV programmes and newspaper columns, conceivably as a result of Ireland having become a nation of 'foodies' in the past few decades. This book brings together chapters on writers' depictions of food and drink, a description of fine dining in the Dublin restaurants at the turn of the twentieth century, which contrasts with the discussion

---

14   Darra Goldstein, 'Foreword', in *'Tickling the Palate': Gastronomy in Irish Literature and Culture*, edited by Máirtín Mac Con Iomaire and Eamon Maher (Oxford: Peter Lang, 2014), xvi.

of how housewives in the tenements were forced to 'manage' food as best they could in times of extreme economic hardship. There are also contributions on gastronomic nationalism, beer consumption in elite houses in eighteenth-century Ireland, the Irish pub abroad and Arthur's Day, all of which shows the potential of gastronomy to tell a different type of story than the one that is normally narrated within Irish Studies.[15]

Recalling the Celtic Tiger, edited by Brian Lucey, Eamon Maher and Eugene O'Brien, was described by Fintan O'Toole in his *Irish Times* review as, 'the best overview of the excitement and madness we are likely to get for quite some time. And it might help us not to do it all over again'.[16] Containing 123 separate entries on a sample of the main actors, features, events and consequences of the Celtic Tiger period, this collection sought to reach out to a more general readership than what is normally achieved by an academic title.

In brief then, *Reimagining Ireland* brings together monographs and edited collections covering an extensive canvas. Indeed, many of the books in the series tend to cross over generic boundaries and the interdisciplinary, transdisciplinary and multidisciplinary opportunities that research in Irish Studies affords, which is possibly one of its most attractive features. In spite of its breadth, it is becoming obvious that a 'Reimagining Ireland' book must have a few distinguishing features: firstly, it should bring a fresh and original perspective to the subject it covers; ideally it would employ a number of methodological tools to achieve its stated objective (from whence the transdisciplinarity); and finally it must demonstrate an awareness that any book accepted will be part of a series and hence should comply with the tone, style and stated aims and objectives of that series. Whereas other book series have dealt with, and continue to cover, certain aspects of Irish Studies, none has attempted in the same way to accommodate the ever-expanding nature of the discipline under the one roof. There is no favouring of postcolonialism over history, religion over cultural studies,

---

15 See Declan Kiberd's Foreword on this subject and Máirtín Mac Con Iomaire's chapter in this collection dealing with the importance of food studies within Irish Studies.

16 Fintan O'Toole, 'The Rise and Fall of a Great Delusion', review of *Recalling the Celtic Tiger*, in *The Irish Times The Ticket* (4 January 2020), 14–15.

politics over literature, nationalism over revisionism, film over sociology and so on. The series' remit is deliberately wide, because that is what Irish Studies demands.

Indeed, scholars in the Irish Studies domain can occasionally come up against obstacles to career progression by dint of the tendency to trade in so many disciplines. They also encounter prejudice or downright ignorance at times. Cheryl Herr describes her experience of applying for tenure in an American university in 1983, and having her suggestion of including some Irish academics as external assessors rejected by the Chair of Faculty with the comment: 'I don't think we need the word of a drunken Irishman in this case'. Such blatant stereotyping and anti-Irish rhetoric was not confined to the Faculty Chair either, according to Herr, who noted that people working in transnational diasporic programmes were equally 'resistant to including Irish Studies as a legitimate colonial or postcolonial field of inquiry'.[17] The fact that Irish Studies courses were popular with students in North American universities at the time might well have sparked rancour among certain colleagues who were not working in the area, but what is significant in this instance is the difficulty encountered by Irish Studies scholars in justifying their specialism in North America during the 1980s.

The experience in other countries with a long track record in Irish Studies such as France bears this out. Topics related to Ireland usually featured as a subset of English or modern languages faculties in French third-level institutions, and it took time to convince university authorities in places like Caen, Lille, Rennes and the Sorbonne (which were the pioneers in the area) that Irish Studies needed its own space and could justify its own faculty of experts. At the time of writing, many Irish Studies scholars in France still face serious challenges when it comes to charting a career path. Ondřj Pilný offers an excellent summary of what is happening in several universities in continental Europe at present in relation to Irish Studies:

> In the current atmosphere of marginalization of the humanities by technocrats and populist politicians alike, which has brought about an often critical lack of funding and precariousness of jobs in academia and non-applied research, focus on allegedly

---

17   Cheryl Herr, ' "Re-imagining Ireland," "Rethinking" Irish Studies', *New Hibernia Review* 7, no. 4 (January 2003), 123–135, 123.

> marginal areas such as Ireland is often discouraged; for instance, many English departments treat an Irish specialism – or are made to by university management – as one of those unnecessary frills that should be shed whenever there is need to cut, since students really need to focus on the English language and the main Anglophone cultures, that is to say English and American, only. Irish Studies experts thus have to justify their existence by bringing in funding and producing 'measurable' outputs in the form of international projects and publications – and professional Irish Studies networks have played a seminal role in this effort.[18]

This is a challenge that is facing specialists in the Irish Studies area all around the globe: the need to justify what it is we do and to highlight its 'utilitarian' potential. It is interesting that Pilný points to the importance of international networks in foregrounding the importance of what scholars achieve in the area, often with little or no institutional support.

Herr compares two significant Irish Studies events that were organised in Charlottesville by Andrew Wyndham of the Virginia Foundation for the Humanities. The first, 'Irish Film: A Mirror up to Culture', which took place in 1996, was attended by the then Minister for Arts, Culture and the Gaeltacht, Michael D. Higgins, who gave a stirring opening address. For Herr, this meeting produced a stimulating and highly effective exchange between various producers, actors and others involved in the area of Irish and American film, along with academics and the general public. The second gathering in 2003, entitled 'Re-Imagining Ireland' (which is of obvious interest to us in this instance), was a much bigger affair which set out to be a 'town meeting of Ireland, out of Ireland' that would 'discuss the past and the present, and build bridges to the future'.[19] The event was attended by writers, journalists (foremost among whom was Fintan O'Toole), and Irish Studies experts from Ireland and North America, representatives of Irish American business and the diaspora. President Mary McAleese was present, and the various panels discussed issues such as 'the impact of the global economy on Irish national politics and on traditional culture, especially after September 11; population migrations worldwide and Ireland's

---

18 Ondřj Pilný, 'Irish Studies in Continental Europe', *Irish University Review* (Spring/Summer 2020), 215–220, 217–218.
19 Conference website, available online: <https://irishamerica.com/2003/04/re-imagining-ireland-conference/> [accessed 1 May 2020].

place in the EU; religious and political identities in Ireland'.[20] Herr felt that the 'Re-Imagining Ireland' gathering confirmed the adage that 'lightning rarely strikes twice' and that 'more is not necessarily better'. She noted that 'the announced project was too amorphous and too multidimensional for much progress to be made on any front'.[21] Could it be argued perhaps that the task of reimagining Ireland requires far more than a three-day conference to achieve anything worthwhile, that maybe a book series is necessary to come close to fulfilling such a momentous remit?

Herr argues that Ireland is constantly reimagining the past: 'Our novels, films, songs, paintings, and histories are made of those sometimes incompatible and always complicated, always emotional, revisions. The stories we tell each other function therapeutically as well as ideologically'. She concludes: 'It is more difficult to imagine the future than it is to re-imagine the past'.[22] This Introduction would argue that it is equally difficult to do either of these things, and that is why *Reimagining Ireland* represents such an important contribution to Ireland's understanding of its past and present, as well as to supplying signposts and indications of what the future may bring. In his preface to *The Reimagining Ireland Reader*, a selection of material taken from the first 50 volumes in the series, David Lloyd notes that 'to reimagine Ireland is at one and the same time to bring forward what was already there but occluded by the official narratives in play at any moment'.[23] According to Lloyd, Ireland in the past had a great capacity to supply the works that others would theorise. Such a role relegates the country to the colonial periphery, 'the ragged western edge' of that particular world. But, he added: 'It has been the work of the last decades, however, and the work of *Reimagining Ireland* as a series, to theorise Ireland from our own location'.[24] Bringing Irish Studies back to Ireland was

---

20 Herr, 126.
21 *Ibid.*, 129.
22 *Ibid.*, 135.
23 David Lloyd, Preface, *The Reimagining Ireland Reader: Examining Our Past, Shaping Our Future* (Oxford: Peter Lang, 2018), xi.
24 Lloyd, Preface, xiii.

one of the features of the series that was also commended by Luke Gibbons, who added that it is 'at the cutting edge of what it means to be Ireland'.[25]

The titles published in *Reimagining Ireland*, while showing a high concentration on the more traditional areas such as literature and cultural theory, are also providing a platform for other fields of interest which are coming to the fore on a regular basis. Indeed, the series is alive to the importance of not being associated with any one specialism. The centenary celebrations of the War of Independence, the Civil War and the partition of the country under the Government of Ireland Act, will call for a reappraisal and reimagining of the whole concept of Irishness in the third millennium. Sinn Féin's spectacular gains in the 2020 General Election in the Republic show that the political weather vane has moved, and that many voters are prepared to forget the party's well-known links to the IRA and terrorist activity if they can deliver improvements in the three 'H's: health, housing and homelessness. The grand coalition of the two main political opponents and fierce adversaries since the Civil War, Fianna Fáil and Fine Gael, illustrates that former enmities can be jettisoned when the country is faced with a global pandemic, the consequences of which will be felt for many years, and perhaps decades, to come. (The two parties went into a coalition government with the Greens on the 26 June 2020).

The fact that Brexit did not really feature as a burning issue in the 2020 election, in spite of its probable harmful consequences for Ireland's economy due to its strong dependence on its nearest and most important trading partner, indicates a certain disconnect between the electorate and the traditional political elite.[26] There has been increasing debate about the possibility of a united Ireland in the wake of Brexit, a topic that certainly could, and perhaps should, be reimagined in the series also.[27] As the fallout from the Covid-19 virus is affecting every country around the globe, bringing with it a huge disruption in social and economic terms, and, more importantly, hundreds of thousands of deaths, one wonders

---

25 Luke Gibbons' assessment of the series, available online: <https://www.peterlang.com/view/serial/REIR> [accessed 8 May 2020].
26 See Katy Hayward's chapter on Brexit for a detailed discussion of its potential impact.
27 This is covered in Colin Coulter and Peter Shirlow's chapter on Northern Ireland.

how Ireland will be changed by it. The series has already grappled with the legacy of the Great Famine and the Celtic Tiger, two very important events in Ireland's history, because it seeks to learn from past lessons in order to prepare better for the future. There will undoubtedly be due consideration given to these important events in *Reimagining Ireland*, because it is the role of the series, and of Irish Studies as a discipline, to be alert to what has happened, is happening and will happen to Irish society and culture, and to how people adjust to crucial events.

This special collection, in line with the stated ambition of the series in which it appears, will therefore seek to explain the importance of Irish Studies across the globe, while tentatively sketching out what the prospects of the discipline might be in the coming century. The editors are hugely indebted to the contributors for agreeing to write on areas wherein they have a proven track record, and for making this such a special initiative. Obviously, not every aspect of Irish Studies could be discussed and some may well regret the absence of their own preferences or specialisms. Nevertheless, we believe that there is more enough between the covers of the book to at least outline tentatively the direction, or, more accurately, directions, Irish Studies may be headed in the twenty-first century. It looks like an exciting future and we are happy to have the opportunity to chart and predict some of its main features.

MÁIRTÍN MAC CON IOMAIRE

1 Applying a Food Studies Perspective to Irish Studies

Food studies and Irish Studies stem from the same 'studies' phenomena and share many similarities in their journeys from the margins to becoming established academic disciplines. A common feature of the new academic studies movement, whether French, gender, postcolonial, cinematic, African, Irish or food is their interdisciplinary or transdisciplinary nature. They become more than any one discipline and scholars within these new fields continuously investigate from various angles, often adopting 'self-reflexivity' as an approach.[1] Stereotypical postcolonial notions of the drunken[2] or 'stage Irishman', or food's association with the quotidian domestic, and therefore, feminine, led some academics up until relatively recently to dismiss either as worthy of any form of serious study.[3] However, with the advent of the cultural turn in the 1970s, whether you were interested in medicine, literature, poverty or religion, each could be studied by applying either an Irish or a food lens. Moreover, recent research has argued that a food studies lens could be insightful to the field of Irish Studies and that a

---

1   Liam Harte, 'Introduction', in *Ireland Beyond Boundaries: Mapping Irish Studies in the Twenty-First Century*, edited by Liam Harte and Yvonne Whelan (London/ Dublin/ Ann Arbor: Pluto, 2007), 2.
2   For examples of this anti-Irish prejudice in academia, mentioned in Eamon Maher's Introduction to this volume, see Cheryl Herr, ' "Re-imagining Ireland," "Rethinking" Irish Studies', *New Hibernia Review* 7, no. 4 (January 2003), 123–135; 123.
3   For food studies examples of this phenomenon, see Warren Belasco, *Food: The Key Concepts* (New York: Berg, 2008), 1; also mentioned in Brian Murphy's chapter in this volume.

'gastrocritical'[4] reading of canonical writers such as Seamus Heaney[5] or Maria Edgeworth[6] might prove revelatory.

This chapter will compare the journey by Irish Studies and food studies to becoming established disciplines, discussing the key figures, journals, courses, conferences and encyclopaedias associated with both. It will identify early outliers of food themes within the Irish Studies canon in addition to traditional sources, track the growth of food studies in Ireland, particularly in the last decade, and make suggestions where future Irish Studies scholars might adopt a food studies lens. One early crossover between the two disciplines was an exploration of food-related placenames in Ireland[7] which melded gastro-topography and *dinnseanchas*,[8] with Brian Friel's play *Translations*, the staging of which was the origin of Field Day[9] in 1980. Two terms are used interchangeably in this chapter, 'gastronomy'[10] and 'food

---

4   Anke Klitzing, '"My Palate Hung with Starlight" – A Gastrocritical Reading of Seamus Heaney's Poetry', *East-West Cultural Passage* 19, no. 2 (2019), available online: <https://doi.org/10.2478/ewcp-2019-0010> [accessed 4 October 2020].

5   Eugene O'Brien, '"Sunk Past Its Gleam in the Meal Bin": The Kitchen as *Locus Amoenus* in the Poetry of Seamus Heaney', *Canadian Journal of Irish Studies* 41 (2018), 270–289.

6   Dorothy Cashman, '"That Delicate Sweetmeat, the Irish Plum": The Culinary World of Maria Edgeworth (1768–1849)', in *'Tickling the Palate': Gastronomy in Irish Literature and Culture*, edited by Máirtín Mac Con Iomaire and Eamon Maher (Oxford: Peter Lang, 2014), 15–34.

7   Máirtín Mac Con Iomaire, 'Gastro-Topography: Exploring Food-Related Placenames in Ireland', *Canadian Journal of Irish Studies* 38, no. 1/2 (2014), 127–158.

8   'Dinnseanchas' is a class of onomastic text in early Irish literature, recounting the origins of placenames.

9   The importance of Field Day to Irish Studies and its subsequent debates and controversies is covered by Eamon Maher's Introduction to this volume.

10 Gastronomy stems from the Greek word 'gastro' (stomach) and 'nomos' (law). The French philosopher, Brillat-Savarin, noted that gastronomy is the 'reasoned knowledge of everything connected with the nourishment of man'. Priscilla Parkhurst Ferguson expanded on this to include texts, defining gastronomy as 'a set of structured culinary practices and texts uniting producer and consumer'. Noting the subtitle of Brillat-Savarin's book, 'Meditations on Transcendental Gastronomy – An Up-to-Date Theoretical and Historical Work', Ferguson argues that gastronomy is both comprehensive and foundational, as it draws on the natural sciences (physics, chemistry and physiology) and on every sort of learning including cuisine,

studies',[11] the former being a more European concept which incorporates food history, while the latter stems from the United States and is firmly influenced by the 'studies' phenomenon.[12] Both terms were employed when the MA in Gastronomy and Food Studies, the first postgraduate Masters programme in Ireland concerning food in its broader socio-cultural and historic contexts, was developed at the Dublin Institute of Technology in 2017.

When Liam Harte and Yvonne Whelan mapped Irish Studies in the twenty-first century in their 2007 *Ireland Beyond Boundaries* (2007), they included chapters on intellectual criticism, historiography, religion, gender, media, geography, music, sports and Irish culture, but made no mention of food. In 2014, this lacuna began to be filled with the publication of *'Tickling the Palate': Gastronomy in Irish Literature and Culture*, volume 57 of the *Reimagining Ireland* series which we are celebrating in this publication. Further food-related chapters appeared in a number of other edited volumes within this series (cf. volumes 55, 66, 68 and 93), and in volumes 9 and 14 of the *Studies in Franco-Irish Relations* (SFIR) series, also published by Peter Lang.[13] A notable sign of food history's acceptance as a discipline in Ireland was the *Proceedings of the Royal Irish Academy Section C* special issue on food and drink in Ireland, published in 2015.[14]

---

commerce, politics, literature and medicine. Cf. Jean-Anthelme Brillat-Savarin, *Physiology of Taste*, translated by Ann Drayton (London: Penguin, 1994); Priscilla Parkhurst Ferguson, 'A Cultural Field in the Making: Gastronomy in 19th Century France', *American Journal of Sociology* 104, no. 3 (1998), 597–641, 603.

11 Marion Nestle and William A. McIntosh, 'Writing the Food Studies Movement', *Food, Culture and Society* 13, no. 2 (2010), 159–179.

12 However, it is the broader definition of gastronomy as 'the study of food and beverages and their impact on culture and society', coined by Joseph Hegarty, that was embraced on gastronomy and culinary programmes in the Dublin Institute of Technology from the late 1990s.

13 Frank Healy and Brigitte Bastiat (eds), *Voyages between France and Ireland: Culture, Tourism and Sport* (Oxford: Peter Lang, 2017); Eamon Maher and Eugene O'Brien (eds), *Patrimoine/Cultural Heritage in France and Ireland* (Oxford: Peter Lang, 2019).

14 Elizabeth FitzPatrick and James Kelly (eds), *Proceedings of the Royal Irish Academy, Section C* (*Special Issue, Food and Drink in Ireland*), 115 (2015). This special issue was later published as a book in 2016.

The special 'Food Issue'[15] of the *Canadian Journal of Irish Studies* in 2018 further championed the importance of food in Irish scholarship, bringing it towards the mainstream. In 2018, *The Routledge Companion to Literature and Food* married aspects of the two disciplines and Ireland was suitably represented.[16] A further omen of the gradual awareness and appreciation of food studies within the Irish Studies arena is Field Day Podcast No. 31, recorded during the Covid lockdown in Spring 2020, titled Irish Culinary History with Dorothy Cashman.[17] When the next milestone review of Irish Studies appears in future years, it is hoped that food will be considered an obvious lens through which to interrogate developments within Irish society both at home and abroad.

The Studies Phenomenon

As Eamon Maher notes in the Introduction to this volume, Irish Studies emerged in the 1960s and 1970s, influenced by the 'area studies' movement. Area studies was a post-Second World War, principally American, phenomenon which was strongly tied to the Cold War and the need for

---

15   Rhona Richman Kenneally and Máirtín Mac Con Iomaire (eds), *Canadian Journal of Irish Studies* (The Food Issue), 41 (2018).
16   Máirtín Mac Con Iomaire, 'The Food Trope in Literature, Poetry, and Songs from the Irish Tradition', in *The Routledge Companion to Literature and Food*, edited by Lorna Piatti-Farnell, Donna Lee Brien (New York: Routledge, 2018), 364–378.
17   Available online: <https://fieldday.ie/field-day-podcast/>. In Podcast no. 31 Dorothy Cashman reads the long-forgotten recipe books of Irish country houses, and inserts them into the history of the country and the world. In her analysis of one recipe book from Kilkenny, she gives a fascinating portrait of a network of women and food culture, just as Ireland transitioned from the Georgian era to the Victorian; in Podcast no. 26, Cooperative movements and political changes in Ireland, historian Patrick Doyle opens his account of the Irish cooperatives with a description of a simple but revolutionary machine – the cream separator – and shows how it connected the butter-producing Irish farm to the grand technological enterprises of British imperialism and international trade [accessed 4 October 2020].

a better understanding of Russia and China, in addition to dealing with the fallout from the decolonisation of Africa and Asia. From a food perspective, courses on domestic economy, nutrition or culinary arts precede the later emergence of food studies. However, it is the interdisciplinarity of the post-war studies movement which marks the paradigm shift in this new form of scholarship.

Food Studies

Gastronomy and food studies are described as being interdisciplinary, multidisciplinary and even transdisciplinary. The reason for this is that many of the early scholars came from the disciplines of anthropology (Sidney Mintz, Claude Levi-Strauss, Mary Douglas, Jack Goody), sociology (Fernand Braudel, Norbert Elias, Stephen Mennell, Priscilla Parkhurst Ferguson), history (Jean-Louis Flandrin, Massimo Montinari, Hans J. Teuteberg, Reay Tannahill), art history (Roy Strong, Barbara Ketchum Wheaton, Claudia Roden), philosophy (Carolyn Krosmeyer, Elizabeth Telfer), psychology (Paul Rozin) and English literature (Harold McGee). Gastronomy and food history are terms more associated with European countries, whereas the term 'food studies' is predominantly an American phenomenon.

One of the earliest programmes in food studies in the United States was the Master of Liberal Arts (MLA) in Gastronomy at Boston University in the early 1990s. The fact that it was called 'Gastronomy' no doubt reflects the French background of its two collaborative founders, Jacques Pépin and Julia Child. However, when Marion Nestle launched her Masters in Food Studies in 1996 at New York University, she was drawing firmly from the similar 'studies' programmes already in NYU (Africana, cinema, French, gender, etc.), although she conceived food studies to include foodways, gastronomy and culinary history as well as critical approaches to studying other food-related issues in society.[18] In 2000, a Master of Arts in Gastronomy was

18   Nestle and McIntosh, 'Writing the Food Studies Movement'.

established at the University of Adelaide in conjunction with their Research Centre for the History of Food and Drink and *Le Cordon Bleu*. One of the first Irish students to complete this programme, by distance learning, was John Mulcahy – his Masters' dissertation[19] subsequently formed the basis of the food tourism policy so successfully pursued by Fáilte Ireland, where he worked for many years.[20]

In Europe, there were a number of organisations involved in studying European food history such as the *Institut Européen d'Histoire et des Cultures de l'Alimentation* (IEHCA) and the International Commission for Research into European Food History (ICREFH). Key individuals included Peter Scholliers, Hans J. Teuteberg, Marc Jacobs, Claude Fischler, Massimo Montanari, Jean-Louis Flandrin and Fabio Parasecoli. Established in 2004 and inspired by the Slow Food Movement, the University of Gastronomic Sciences opened in Pollenzo, Italy and provided several Masters programmes in the gastronomy field. In Britain, a Masters in the Anthropology of Food is offered in the School of Oriental and African Studies (SOAS) in London: one of its former course leaders, Harry West, has recently set up a Masters in Food Studies at the University of Exeter. In Scotland, a Masters in Gastronomy was established in Queen Margaret's University in Edinburgh.[21]

---

19   John D. Mulcahy, *Making the Case for a Viable, Sustainable Gastronomic Tourism Industry in Ireland* (Unpublished Masters Dissertation, University of Adelaide, 2009).

20   For an exploratory review of food tourism policy in Ireland see Ketty Quigley, Margaret Connolly, Elaine Mahon and Máirtín Mac Con Iomaire, 'Insight from Insiders: A Phenomenological Study for Exploring Food Tourism Policy in Ireland 2009-2019', *Advances in Hospitality and Tourism Research* 7, no. 2 (2019), available online: <https://dergipark.org.tr/en/download/article-file/884620> [accessed 7 October 2020]; also see John Mulcahy, 'A Nexus of Food, Tourism, and Education in Ireland – at the Margins or the Centre? An Autoethnographic Perspective', in *Margins and Marginalities in Ireland and France: A Socio-Cultural Perspective*, edited by Catherine Maignant, Sylvain Tondeur and Déborah Vandewoude (Oxford: Peter Lang, 2021), 155–172.

21   It is interesting to note the origin of Queen Margaret's University was the Edinburgh School of Cookery and Domestic Economy, Atholl Crescent.

Gastronomy has been gaining attention in European circles for a number of decades. In 2005, *An Post*, the Irish postal service, issued two stamps designed by Ross Lewis, Chef Patron of Chapter One Restaurant, to celebrate European Gastronomy. The stamps depicted oysters and a modern interpretation of Irish stew. That same year, a book entitled the *Culinary Cultures of Europe: Identity, Diversity and Dialogue* was published by the Council of Europe, with chapters written on every member-state, including Ireland.[22] Gastronomy moved into the postgraduate realm in Ireland as a module on the MSc in Culinary Innovation and New Product Development at the Dublin Institute of Technology in 2007 and with the graduation of the first PhD in Food History in 2009.[23] Other doctoral candidates have since successfully completed their Irish-themed food studies-related dissertations, both in Ireland and abroad, on subjects ranging from wine and beverages,[24] Irish 'foodies',[25] the impact of Italian foodways on Irish food habits,[26] Irish culinary manuscripts,[27] Guinness advertising,[28] Irish diplomatic dining,[29] the meaning of food and foodways in Ireland

22   Regina Sexton, 'Ireland: Simplicity and Integration, Continuity and Change', in *Culinary Cultures of Europe: Identity, Diversity and Dialogue*, edited by Darra Goldstein, Kathrin Merkle, Fabio Parasecoli, and Stephen Mennell (Strasbourg: Council of Europe, 2005), 227–240.

23   Máirtín Mac Con Iomaire, *The Emergence, Development and Influence of French Haute Cuisine on Public Dining in Dublin Restaurants 1900-2000: An Oral History* (PhD thesis, DIT, 2009), available online: <https://doi.org/10.21427/D79K7H> [accessed 4 October 2020].

24   Brian Murphy, *Changing Identities in a Homogenised World: The Role of 'Place and Story' in Modern Perceptions of French wine Culture* (PhD Thesis, QQI/Institute of Technology Tallaght, 2013).

25   Marjorie Deleuze, *La Dimension Identitaire des Pratiques, des Habitudes et des Symboliques Alimentaires de l'Irlande Contemporaine* (PhD thesis, Université de Lille III, 2015).

26   Déirdre D'Auria, *The Impact of Italian Foodways on Irish Food Habits in the Twentieth Century* (PhD dissertation, UCD, 2012).

27   Dorothy Cashman, *An Investigation of Irish Culinary History through Manuscript Cookbooks, with Particular Reference to the Gentry of County Kilkenny (1714-1830)* (PhD Thesis, TU Dublin, 2016).

28   Patricia Medcalf, *Advertising the Black Stuff in Ireland 1959-1999: Increments of Change* (Oxford: Peter Lang, 2020).

29   Elaine Mahon, *Irish Diplomatic Dining 1922-1963* (PhD Thesis, TU Dublin, 2019).

1922–1973,[30] gender inequality in professional kitchens,[31] Irish food tourism policy[32] and the social meaning of claret in Georgian Ireland.[33]

A key event bringing gastronomy and food studies into the mainstream in Ireland was the establishment of the inaugural biennial Dublin Gastronomy Symposium (DGS) in May 2012, a collaborative project between the Dublin Institute of Technology and the Institute of Technology Tallaght. This event connected interested stakeholders from Ireland's catering colleges and universities with international scholars and enthusiasts. It was also one of the first collaborative projects that foresaw and predated the merger of the two institutes to become Ireland's first Technological University. The first keynote address was given by Professor Darra Goldstein, editor of *Gastronomica: The Journal of Critical Food Studies*. The DGS received sponsorship from Fáilte Ireland which, as previously mentioned, was developing a Food Tourism team and policy strategy under the stewardship of John Mulcahy. Relationships and trust established in 2012 led to the first gastronomy-themed parallel session at the Association of Franco-Irish Studies (AFIS) conference in Limerick in 2013, which resulted in the inclusion of three gastronomy-related chapters in Volume 55 of the REIR series.[34] Brian Murphy has highlighted the importance of the Dublin Gastronomy

---

30   Marzena Keating, Bain Sult as do Bhéile: *In Search of Irish Culinary Culture. The Meaning of Food and Foodways in Ireland in 1922–1973* (PhD Thesis, SWPS University of Social Sciences and Humanities, Warsaw, 2019).

31   Mary Farrell, *A Critical Analysis of Gender Inequality in the Chef Profession in Ireland* (PhD Thesis, TU Dublin, 2020).

32   John Mulcahy, *Recognising the Place of Food Tourism in Ireland: An Autoethnographic Perspective* (PhD Thesis, TU Dublin, 2020).

33   Tara McConnell, *The Social Meaning of Claret in the Lives of Georgian Ireland's Elite* (PhD Thesis, TU Dublin, 2021).

34   Dorothy Cashman, 'French Boobys and Good English Cooks: The Relationship with French Culinary Influence in Eighteenth- and Nineteenth-Century Ireland', in *France and Ireland in the Public Imagination*, edited by Benjamin Keatinge and Mary Pierse (Oxford: Peter Lang, 2014), 207–222; Tara McConnell, 'Ireland in the Georgian Era: Was There Any Kingdom in Europe So Good a Customer at Bordeaux?', in Keatinge and Pierse, 223–240; Brian Murphy, 'Exporting a 'Sense of Place': Establishment of Regional Gastronomic Identity Beyond National Borders', in Keatinge and Pierse, 241–257.

Symposium to his research in his chapter in this volume. Despite the success of the DGS,[35] it would take another five years to witness the commencement in 2017 of the first Master of Arts Degree in Gastronomy and Food Studies in Ireland.[36] The wait, however, was serendipitous, as fresh energy and new blood had by then joined the Masters' teaching team with qualifications from both Irish and European universities.

Food Scholarship in Ireland

Culinary history, food history, gastronomy and food studies are relatively new disciplines, with the core texts emerging within the last half-century. One of the drivers towards moving food, domesticity and the history of everyday life to the fore in academia was the French concept, 'histoire des mentalités', which described a particular way of researching and writing history principally associated with the Annales School. Although the French have long studied 'histoire des mentalités', Irish historians have concentrated more on high politics, focusing on archival documents left by the 'winners of conflicts'. In Ireland, 'tradition' – how ordinary people remember things (including language, food and much of our heritage) – has been left to the folklorists,[37] and is often disseminated via the oral tradition.[38] The

---

35 For more information, see: <https://arrow.tudublin.ie/dgs/> [accessed 28 October 2020].

36 Information on MA Gastronomy and Food Studies is available online at: <https://www.tudublin.ie/study/postgraduate/courses/gastronomy-and-food-studies/> [accessed 26 October 2020].

37 In volume 80 of the REIR series, *New Crops, Old Fields: Reimagining Irish Folklore*, edited by Conor Caldwell and Eamon Byers, focus is placed on the second life of folklore, the variety of ways in which traditions have been reused and recycled in other contexts by politicians, poets, visual artists, sportsmen, tourism officers, museum curators, writers and musicians.

38 Máirtín Mac Con Iomaire, 'Recognizing Food as Part of Ireland's Intangible Cultural Heritage', *Folk Life* 56, no. 2 (2018), 93–115.

ground-breaking work of folklorists in Ireland on food must therefore be acknowledged.[39]

The establishment of a new liberal / vocational paradigm with the inauguration of the BA (Hons) in Culinary Arts in the Dublin Institute of Technology in the 1999/2000 academic year is suggested to have played a pivotal role in moving gastronomy and food studies into the spotlight in Ireland.[40] For over a decade now, scholars in Ireland have been studying gastronomy and food history at both Masters and Doctoral level, which has provided a more nuanced perspective on Ireland's culinary heritage.[41] An argument has been made for recognising food as part of Ireland's intangible cultural heritage, and for the importance of researchers engaging with primary sources in the Irish language to gain a more complete picture of the country's gastronomic heritage.[42] In bolstering this call, recent scholarship has adopted the concepts of Arjun Appadurai and Igor Kopytoff[43]

39 Henry H. Glassie, *Passing the Time in Ballymenone: Culture and History of an Ulster Community* (Philadelphia: University of Pennsylvania Press, 1982); Kevin Danaher, *Hearth and Stool and All!: Irish Rural Households* (Dublin: Mercier Press, 1985). The Irish Folklore Collection at University College Dublin has comprehensive holdings of Danaher's work. Brid Mahon, *Land of Milk and Honey: The Story of Traditional Irish Food & Drink* (Dublin: Poolbeg Press, 1991); Patricia Lysaght, 'Bealtaine: Women, Milk, and Magic at the Boundary Festival of May', in *Milk and Milk Products from Medieval to Modern Times*, edited by Patricia Lysaght (Edinburgh: Canongate Academic, 1994), 208–229; Patricia Lysaght, 'Food-Provision Strategies on the Great Blasket Island: Sea-Bird Fowling', in *Food from Nature: Attitudes, Strategies and Culinary Practices*, edited by Patricia Lysaght (Uppsala: Royal Gustavus Adolphus Academy for Swedish Folk Culture, 2000), 333–363; Patricia Lysaght, 'Seabirds and their Eggs', in *Encyclopedia of Food and Culture*, edited by S. H. Katz (New York: Scribner, 2003), 3, 243–245.

40 For a detailed overview of the development of gastronomy, food studies and culinary education in Ireland, see Máirtín Mac Con Iomaire, 'From the Dark Margins to the Spotlight: The Evolution of Gastronomy and Food Studies in Ireland', in *Margins and Marginalities in Ireland and France: A Socio-Cultural Perspective*, 129–153.

41 For examples of this scholarship, see Kenneally and Mac Con Iomaire, *Canadian Journal*; and Mac Con Iomaire and Maher, *'Tickling the Palate'*.

42 Mac Con Iomaire, 'Recognizing Food'.

43 Arjun Appadurai, 'The Social Life of Things', in *The Social Life of Things: Commodities in Cultural Perspective*, edited by Arjun Appadurai (Cambridge: Cambridge

to the iconic dish 'Irish stew'[44] to present a biography of a recipe, tracing the origins of the dish from archaeological potsherds, oral sources, through manuscript sources to printed cookbooks. The Food Cult[45] project, funded by the European Union, brings together history, archaeology, science and information technology to explore the diet and foodways of diverse communities in early modern Ireland, which might serve as a model for future comparative and interdisciplinary work in the field of historical food studies. Each of the individual research projects,[46] both completed and currently under study, reveal tesserae in the larger mosaic of Irish food culture. A broader understanding of this particular aspect of Irish culture can possibly illuminate other elements of Irish Studies scholarship for a clearer understanding of our shared cultural past and present. It is evident that we are standing on the shoulders of giants, but who then, were the early researchers who paved the way for the current generation of Irish food studies scholars?

Elements of a Discipline

Whether Irish Studies or food studies, there are certain elements required to establish an academic discipline. First come the trailblazers, who clear the ground, often unaware of the influence their labours will have on the future field. Then come the seminal texts[47] which enrich the ground upon

---

University Press, 1986), 3–63; Igor Kopytoff, 'The Cultural Biography of Things', in *The Social Life of Things*, 64–91.

44   Dorothy Cashman and John Farrelly, '"Is Irish Stew the Only Kind of Stew We Can Afford to Make, Mother?" The History of a Recipe'. *Folk Life* 59, no. 1 (2021). Forthcoming.

45   The Principal Investigator on this project is Dr Susan Flavin, available online: <https://foodcult.eu/> [accessed 4 October 2020].

46   This includes beverage projects outlined in Brian Murphy's chapter in this volume.

47   Maher notes authors such as Declan Kiberd, Colin Graham, Angela Bourke, Patricia Coughlan, Joe Cleary, Seamus Deane, Luke Gibbons, David Lloyd and Claire Connolly among the 'first wave' of Irish Studies scholars. Seminal texts by Joe Lee and Terence Browne could be added to the list, as could the scholarship of

which the seeds for modules or courses can be sown. With time, and a number of successful harvests (graduates), come the encyclopaedias/companions which (attempt to) codify the discipline. The conferences/symposia may be conceptualised as hiring fairs or agricultural shows, where ideas and best practices are disseminated, debated and networks are built. In the Introduction to this book, Eamon Maher has charted the trajectory that Irish Studies has taken from early beginnings to its current global reach as a discipline, citing the journals, conferences, national bodies and canonical publications which underpin the discipline. Arguably, *Studies: An Irish Quarterly Review*, the Jesuit journal founded in 1912, pre-imagined the discipline in both name and interdisciplinary scope. Other publications that predate the establishment of Irish Studies as a discipline include *The Bell* (1940–1954)[48] and *The Capuchin Annual* (1930–1977),[49] both of which exerted a significant influence on a generation of Irish intellectuals, with the latter having an international circulation.

Within food studies, the influence of the Annales school[50] has previously been noted. The oldest and longest-running conference is the Oxford Symposium on Food and Cookery[51] (1979–present), founded and co-chaired by Alan Davidson, retired diplomat, food historian and editor of

---

    the late Margaret McCurtain, who chose to focus on the previously neglected area of women's history.

48 From a food historian's perspective, the first comprehensive description of eating out in Dublin during the Emergency comes from an article in *The Bell*, ranging from dock workers' cafés, chophouses, an Indian restaurant on Baggot Street, to the Unicorn and Jammet's, and back down the social scale to fish and chip shops where the vinegar bottles were chained to the tables. See Micheal Burke, 'Eating in Dublin', *The Bell* 2, no. 3 (1941), 12–20.

49 The complete collection of *The Capuchin Annual* is now freely available online to scholars: <http://www.capuchinfranciscans.ie/capuchin-annual-1930-1977/>.

50 Robert Forster and Orest Ranum (eds), *Food and Drink in History: Selections from the Annales, Economies, Sociétés, Civilisations*, Volume 5 (Baltimore: John Hopkins University Press, 1979).

51 Available online: <https://www.oxfordsymposium.org.uk/0-how-we-began/> [accessed 28 October 2020].

The Oxford Companion to Food,[52] and social historian Dr Theodore Zeldin.[53] The journal *Petits Propos Culinaires* and the publishing house Prospect Books emerged from the Davidson and Oxford Symposium network. In the United States, the Association for the Study of Food in Society[54] (ASFS) was founded in 1985, with the goal of promoting the interdisciplinary study of food and society. The Association's annual meetings, which commenced in 1987, have since 1992 been held jointly with the Agriculture, Food and Human Values Society. The ASFS publishes the journal *Food, Culture and Society: An International Journal of Multidisciplinary Research*.[55] Despite Warren Belasco's reservations[56] in 2008 regarding the lack of seriousness attributed to the discipline,[57] food studies, by 2020, has its own canon,[58] edited collections,[59] thematic readers, guiding authors,[60] peer-reviewed

52 Alan Davidson, *The Oxford Companion to Food* (New York: Oxford University Press, 1999).
53 Theodore Zeldin, *Eating and Drinking in France 1848-1845, Volume 2. Intellect, Taste and Anxiety* (Oxford: Clarendon Press, 1977).
54 Available online: <https://www.food-culture.org/> [accessed 28 October 2020].
55 Available online: <https://www.tandfonline.com/toc/rffc20/current> [accessed 28 October 2020].
56 Belasco's statement is available in Brian Murphy's chapter of this volume.
57 See Footnote 2.
58 Examples include: Kenneth Kipple and Kriemhild Coneè Ornelas, *The Cambridge World History of Food, Volumes 1 & 2* (Cambridge: Cambridge University Press, 2000); Jean-Louis Flandrin and Massimo Montanari, *Food: A Cultural History from Antiquity to the Present* (New York: Columbia University Press, 1999); Stephen Mennell, *All Manners of Food: Eating and Taste in England and France from the Middle Ages to the Present*, 3rd ed. (Chicago: University of Illinois Press, 1996).
59 Examples include: Ken Albala, *Routledge International Handbook of Food Studies* (New York: Routledge, 2013); Fabio Parasecoli and Peter Scholliers, *A Cultural History of Food, Vols. 1-6* (London: Bloomsbury Academic, 2016).
60 Examples include: Rachel Laudan, *Cuisine and Empire: Cooking in World History* (Berkeley: University of California Press, 2013); Massimo Montanari, *Food Is Culture* (New York: Columbia University Press, 2006); Priscilla Parkhurst Ferguson, *Accounting for Taste: The Triumph of French Cuisine* (Chicago: University of Chicago Press, 2006); Sidney Mintz, *Tasting Food, Tasting Freedom: Excursions into Eating, Culture, and the Past* (Boston: Beacon Press, 1986); Sidney Mintz, *Sweetness and Power: The Place of Sugar in Modern History* (New York: Viking

journals,[61] symposia and postgraduate degrees available for those who wish to pursue the topic at an academic level. Christopher Kissane recently observed that, 'we are long past the days when food was not given serious attention by historians. But that does not mean we have figured out how to approach such a vast subject'.[62]

Food Studies in Ireland Past, Present and Future

Doctoral research within the food studies field in Ireland is growing steadily, albeit from a low base. Dorothy Cashman[63] describes various appellations, noting that food history is seen as encompassing culinary history, somewhat in the manner of Russian dolls, both further falling under the umbrella term of food studies. With Brian Murphy's chapter on beverage research in this volume, the further Russian doll of beverage studies is comprehensively charted and championed. The most comprehensive overview of Irish food history sources to date is provided by Cashman's dissertation, with McConnell filling any gaps from the perspective of the history of wine from the pre-Christian era through to the Georgian period.

An early seminal text[64] of Irish food studies is Anthony Lucas's 1960 paper, 'Irish food before the potato', which noted that Irish food displayed a

Penguin, 1985); Barbara Ketchum Wheaton, *Savouring the Past: The French Kitchen and Table from 1300-1789* (London: Chatto & Windus, 1983).

61   Examples include: *Food & History*, edited by Francis Chevrier, Brepols, 2007–present; *Food and Foodways, Explorations in the History and Culture of Human Nourishment*, edited by Carole Counihan (Routledge, 1985–present); *Food Studies: An Interdisciplinary Journal*, edited by Courtney Thomas, Common Ground Research Network, 2011–present.

62   Christopher Kissane, *Food, Religion and Communities in Early Modern Europe* (London: Bloomsbury, 2018), 9.

63   Cashman, *An Investigation of Irish Culinary History through Manuscript Cookbooks*, op. cit.

64   Very early trailblazers might include Eugene O'Curry for his series of lectures on the manners and customs of the Ancient Irish, or Kuno Meyer, whose works on

remarkable continuity of tradition, 'from the time of the earliest documentary evidence down to the widespread adoption of the potato in the late 17th century'.[65] Lucas's scholarship was re-assessed in 2013 by Liam Downey and Ingelise Stuijts in light of new archaeological findings and found to be relatively accurate, apart from the claim that consumption of beef was rare in ancient Ireland.[66] Another early text of note to food studies scholars is Katherine Simms, 'Guesting and Feasting in Gaelic Society', which outlines the various obligations of hospitality contained within the Brehon Laws.[67] The first modern history book to allocate two chapters to food was Louis Cullen's[68] *The Emergence of Modern Ireland*.[69] Leslie Clarkson and Margaret Crawford's history of food and nutrition in Ireland is comprehensive, although they are at pains to point out that their book 'is not a history of cooking in Ireland'.[70] The folklorists' contribution to preserving Irish food traditions has been acknowledged earlier in this chapter and Bríd Mahon's *The Land of Milk and Honey* is particularly worth noting. Other key figures in charting Irish food ways in the mid-twentieth century include Florence Irwin and Maura Laverty. For a few years prior to

---

the twelfth-century food odyssey Aisling Meic Con Glinne are key. Also, of note is Fergus Kelly, *Early Irish Farming* (Dublin: DIAS, 1997).

65 Anthony T. Lucas, 'Irish Food Before the Potato', *Gwerin: A Half Yearly Journal of Folk Life* 3, no. 2 (1960–1962), available online: <https://doi.org/10.1179/gwr.1960.009> [accessed 28 October 2020].

66 Liam Downey and Ingelise Stuijts, 'Overview of Historical Irish Food Products- A.T. Lucas (1960-2) Revisited', *The Journal of Irish Archaeology* XXII (2013), 111–126.

67 Katharine Simms, 'Guesting and Feasting in Gaelic Society', *Journal of Royal Society of Antiquaries of Ireland* 108 (1978), 67–100.

68 Louis Cullen's contribution to Irish food studies was marked in 2016 with the inaugural Dublin Gastronomy Symposium Fellowship Award.

69 Louis Michael Cullen, *The Emergence of Modern Ireland 1600-1900* (London: Batsford Academic and Educational Ltd., 1981). Cullen also researched the Irish wine trade with Bordeaux.

70 Leslie A. Clarkson and Margaret E. Crawford, *Feast and Famine: Food and Nutrition in Ireland 1500-1900* (Oxford, 2001), 8.

the dawn of the twenty-first century, and influenced by Alan Davidson, Regina Sexton[71] appeared to be the sole researcher exploring food history in Ireland although Patricia Lysaght[72] was publishing on food contemporaneously in the folklore field. Increased levels of research in the new millennium into Ireland's culinary heritage, culture and food history has assisted in revealing a more balanced and nuanced story about our ancestors' dining habits and foodways,[73] negating some postcolonial impressions of

71 Regina Sexton, "I'd Ate It Like Chocolate!': The Disappearing Offal Food Traditions of Cork City', in *Disappearing Foods: Studies in Foods and Dishes at Risk: Proceedings of the Oxford Symposium on Food and Cookery 1994*, edited by Harlan Walker (Totnes, Devon: Prospect Books, 1995), 172–188; *A Little History of Irish Food* (Dublin, 1998); 'Porridges, Gruels and Breads: The Cereal Foodstuffs of Early Medieval Ireland', in *Early Medieval Munster: Archaeology, History and Society*, edited by Mick Monk and J. Sheehan (Cork: Cork University Press, 1998), 76–86; 'Irish Food, Thirteenth to Seventeenth Centuries', in *The Encyclopedia of Ireland*, edited by Brian Lalor (Dublin: Gill and Macmillan, 2003).

72 Patricia Lysaght's contribution to Irish food studies was marked in 2020 with the Dublin Gastronomy Symposium Fellowship Award. For the citation, see: <https://arrow.tudublin.ie/dgs/dgs_fellowships.pdf> [accessed 28 October 2020].

73 Máirtín Mac Con Iomaire and Pádraic Óg Gallagher, 'The Potato in Irish Cuisine and Culture', *Journal of Culinary Science and Technology* 7, no. 2–3 (2009), 152–167; Máirtín Mac Con Iomaire and Pádraic Óg Gallagher, 'Irish Corned Beef: A Culinary History', *Journal of Culinary Science & Technology* 9, no. 1 (2011), 27–43; Máirtín Mac Con Iomaire, 'The Changing Geography and Fortunes of Dublin's Haute Cuisine Restaurants 1958-2008', *Food Culture & Society* 14, no. 4 (2011), 525–545; Helen O'Connell, ' "A Raking Pot of Tea": Consumption and Excess in Early Nineteenth-Century Ireland', *Literature & History* 21, no. 2 (2012); Máirtín Mac Con Iomaire, 'Public Dining in Dublin: The History and Evolution of Gastronomy and Commercial Dining 1700-1900', *International Journal of Contemporary Hospitality Management* 25, no. 2 (2013), 227–246; Susan Flavin, *Consumption and Culture in Sixteenth-Century Ireland* (Woodbridge, Suffolk: Boydell Press, 2014); Madeline Shanahan, *Manuscript Recipe Books as Archaeological Objects: Food and Text in the Early Modern World* (Maryland: Lexington Books, 2014); Rhona Richman-Kenneally, 'Tastes of Home in Mid-Twentieth-Century Ireland: Food, Design, and the Refrigerator', *Food and Foodways* 23, no. 1–2) (2015), 80–103; Cashman, *An Investigation of Irish Culinary History through Manuscript Cookbooks'*; *Food and Drink in Ireland*; James Kelly, *Food Rioting in Ireland in the Eighteenth and Nineteenth Centuries: The "Moral Economy" and the Irish Crowd*, edited by Elizabeth FitzPatrick and James Kelly (Dublin: Four Courts Press, 2017); *Canadian Journal of Irish Studies* (The Food Issue) 41 (2018); See also the work of Caitríona

barbarity and uncivilised 'otherness' represented by some foreign visitors and diarists. Toby Barnard observed a particular phenomenon in relation to commentary on Ireland, 'scrupulous observers told what they had seen, but saw what they had been told to expect'.[74] Sources familiar to Irish studies scholars, such as the diary of Humphrey O'Sullivan, the letters of Bishop Synge, Dorothea Herbert's 'Retrospections', or the writings of John Gamble reveal the level of sophistication among the upper and middling sorts in pre-Famine Ireland.[75]

More recent research, that may be of interest to Irish Studies scholars, has explored various food studies topics, such as the influence of Italian foodways on Irish food habits,[76] the influence of the court at Dublin Castle,[77] food and fellowship among Franciscan friars,[78] food representation in Irish

---

Clear, for example, Caitríona Clear, *Women of the House: Women's Household Work in Ireland, 1922–1961: Discourses, Experiences, Memories* (Dublin: Irish Academic Press, 2000); '"We Will Again, Please God": Maura Laverty, Irish Tradition, and Optimism', in *The Past in the Present: A Multidisciplinary Approach*, edited by Fabio Mugnaini, Padraig O. Healai and Tok Freeland Thompson (Esch-sur-Alzette: editpress, 2006), 41–52.

[74] Toby Barnard, 'The Gentrification of Eighteenth-Century Ireland', *Eighteenth-Century Ireland/Iris an dá chultúr* 12 (1997), 137–155, 141.

[75] c.f. Tomás de Bhaldraithe, *Cín Lae Amhlaoibh* (Baile Átha Cliath: An Clóchomhar Tta., 1970); Marie-Louise Legge (ed.), *The Diary of Nicholas Peacock 1740–1751* (Dublin: Four Courts Press, 2005); Marie-Louise Legge (ed.), *Synge Letters: Bishop Edward Synge to His Daughter Alicia. Roscommon to Dublin 1746–1752* (Dublin: Lilliput Press, 1996); Dorothea Herbert, *Retrospections* (Dublin: Town House, 2004 [1929]); John Gamble, *Society and Manners in Early Nineteenth-Century Ireland* (Dublin: Field Day, 2011).

[76] D'Auria, *The Impact of Italian Foodways on Irish Food Habits in the Twentieth Century*.

[77] Máirtín Mac Con Iomaire and Tara Kellaghan, 'Royal Pomp: Viceregal Celebrations in Georgian Dublin', in *Celebrations*, edited by Helen Saberi (Devon: Prospect Books, 2012).

[78] Dorothy Cashman, '"To a Little Girl for Keeping the Poultry Last Year": Food and Fellowship in a Franciscan Community in Georgian Ireland', *Dublin Gastronomy Symposium* 2018, available online: <https://arrow.tudublin.ie/cgi/viewcontent.cgi?article=1134&context=dgs> [accessed 4 October 2020].

women's magazines,[79] restaurant criticism in Irish newspapers,[80] Polish migrants foodways in Cork,[81] cuisine and culinary heritage in Seamus Heaney's poetry,[82] the food trope in Irish literature,[83] to Irish women making home in Coventry.[84] So, as previously mentioned, whether researching aspects of medicine, literature, poverty or religion, each can be studied by applying either an Irish or a food lens.

Conclusions

From place names to mythology, storytelling to poetry and songs, food and hospitality is a vibrant theme that runs through Ireland's past.[85] However, when the topic of food is discussed within the historiography of Ireland, the focus tends to be on the consequences of the Great Irish Famine

---

79   Marzena Keating and Máirtín Mac Con Iomaire, 'Tradition and Novelty: Food Representations in Irish Women's Magazines 1922-1973', *Food, Culture and Society* 21, no. 4 (2018), 488–504.

80   Claire O'Mahony, *The Development of Newspaper Restaurant Criticism in Ireland, 1988–2008* (MA thesis, TU Dublin, 2018), available online: <https://arrow.tudublin.ie/tfschcafdis/4/> [accessed 7 October 2020].

81   Linda Coakley, 'Polish Encounters with the Irish Foodscape: An Examination of the Losses and Gains of Migrant Foodways', *Food and Foodways* 20, no. 3–4 (2012), 307–325.

82   Anke Klitzing, '"Gilded Gravel in the Bowl": Ireland's Cuisine and Culinary Heritage in the Poetry of Seamus Heaney', *Folk Life*. Forthcoming.

83   Mac Con Iomaire, 'The Food Trope', op. cit.

84   Moya Kneafsey and Rosie Cox, 'Food, Gender and Irishness – How Irish Women in Coventry Make Home', *Irish Geography* 35, no. 1 (2002), 6–15.

85   Hospitality is a theme that underpinned Gaelic society, and stemming from as early as Aisling Meic Con Glinne, satire is a trope used by poets to call out skinflints who refused traditional hospitality. See Mac Con Iomaire, 'The Food Trope'; Discussing Séamus Dall Mac Cuarta's *Tithe Chonn an Chait*, Declan Kiberd noted: 'The Protestant ethic now taking hold brought with it the spirit of capitalism to the detriment of the poets who suffered due to their ambiguous class position'. See Kiberd, *Irish Classics* (London: Granta Books, 2000), 57.

(1845–1852). Darra Goldstein points out that Ireland has suffered twice for its famines and food shortages: 'First due to very real deprivations; and second because these deprivations present an obstacle to the exploration of Irish food. All too often the story begins and ends with potatoes or famine'.[86] There has also been a tendency among commentators (particularly travellers' accounts) to present discussions about food in Ireland before the Famine in a binary fashion (wealthy or poor).[87] Against this, Tomás de Bhaldraithe in his introduction to *Cín Lae Amhlaoibh* notes the vivid descriptions in Humphrey O'Sullivan's diary of the fine meals of the middle classes that disproves claims that the Irish-speaking natives did not have a varied diet or were not proficient in the art of cookery.[88] Scholars from diverse disciplines (archaeology, history, sociology, folklore, linguistics, literature, architecture, drama, business, art and design) are currently engaging in research on Ireland's food heritage, culture and history, which highlights the transdisciplinary nature of gastronomy and food studies.

This chapter celebrates the role Eamon Maher, as series editor of both the REIR and SFIR series, and as past president of AFIS, has played in championing gastronomy and food studies within the Irish Studies field in Ireland and abroad. It identifies the *Canadian Journal of Irish Studies* under the editorship of Rhona Richman Kenneally as playing a pivotal role in mainstreaming food in Irish Studies. Significantly also, in 2019, the *Irish University Review* had a special issue on Food, Energy, Climate: Irish Culture and World Ecology.[89] Now that food studies in

---

86   Darra Goldstein, 'Foreword' to *'Tickling the Palate'*, xii.
87   For such claims see Daniel Corkery, *The Hidden Ireland* (Dublin: M.H. Gill and Son, 1956), 10; Vincent Morley, *The Popular Mind in Eighteenth-Century Ireland* (Cork: Cork University Press, 2017), highlights that 'there is no factual basis for Corkery's claims that a middle class did not exist in eighteenth-century Munster', 2.
88   de Bhaldraithe, *Cín Lae Amhlaoibh*, xxx. He writes: 'Tá cuntas inti ar bhéilí breátha an duine mheándeisiúil a bhréagníonn an té a deir nach raibh éagsúlacht beatha is ollúint in ealaín na cócaireachta ag na Gaeilgeoirí'.
89   Sharae Deckard, 'Introduction: Reading Ireland's Food, Energy and Climate', *Irish University Review* 49, no. 1, Special Issue – Food, Energy, Climate: Irish Culture and World Ecology (2019).

Ireland has its own canon, edited collections, symposia, postgraduate programmes and, with the launch in 2020 of the first volume of the *European Journal of Food, Drink and Society*,[90] its own journal, Irish Studies scholars may well be inspired to adopt the food lens and collectively interrogate this rich harvest.

---

90   Available online: <https://arrow.tudublin.ie/ejfds/> [accessed 4 October 2020].

BARRY HOULIHAN

2 Archives in Irish Studies: Locating Memory and the Archival Space[1]

On an early summer morning in May 2009, plastic sacks of confidential medical records were discovered buried in a former landfill site, near the village of Glounthaune in Co. Cork. The site was being unearthed as part of the then works to reopen the Cork-Midleton railway line. The medical records dated back to the 1970s and early 1980s, and contained sensitive personal information including patient names and addresses, of both adults and children, as well as detailed accounts of illness, treatments and other confidential information. The custodians of the records, the Health Service Executive (HSE) South, confirmed that the records originated from Cork University Hospital and St Finbarr's Hospital in the city. The act of such careless disposal of records was shocking, but it was not surprising. Fintan O'Toole wrote about the crisis of archives and archiving in Ireland in the wake of the records' discovery in the landfill. In such cases where personal and sensitive materials are discarded from the preserved record, 'the records of government and high diplomacy will probably survive. What gets lost are the vestiges of the lives of the ordinary, the anonymous and the vulnerable'.[2] As historian Margaret M. Scull points out: 'Modern Irish history, at times,

---

1   I am indebted to Tanya Keyes, Archivist, E.S.B. Archives and to Owen Boss of ANU Productions for their expertise and help in sourcing materials and images for this chapter.
2   Fintan O'Toole, 'Neglect of Archives Shows Contempt for Citizens', *Irish Times*, available online: <https://www.irishtimes.com/culture/tv-radio-web/neglect-of-archives-shows-contempt-for-citizens-1.650656> [accessed 25 July 2020].

remains trapped in the political, only surveying high politics through government archives'.[3]

This chapter will look at examples within contemporary Ireland and outline the risk of memory and the archival space as it pertains to Irish Studies broadly, and specifically to Irish literary, theatrical and cultural records. While addressing questions of digital memory, the spaces of performance in Irish theatre, as well as the facets for interrogating national social memory, an intangible archive, I explore these sites of memory that provide new meeting places for the cultural interrogation of the past.

Locating the Archival Space – Order and Records

The collection of poems, *Strange Museum*, by Tom Paulin, published in 2002, comprised a number of reflections on the presence of memory and the yet-absent past. Paulin's poems are populated by memories of time and places in the distant past, fragments of undocumented histories, ghostly people and the legacies of former presents. The 'Strange Museum' is a place of recovery as well as encounter. The metaphor of museum as a site of memory is realised by 'the strangeness' of it all, as Paulin outlines the disorientating effect of memory upon those who recall it: 'First I awoke in an upstairs drawing-room. / The curtains had been pulled back, but the house was empty. / A patriarch's monument'.[4]

Archives are ordered assemblages of the past, fragments which have defied both time and place to exist at a future temporal juncture, preserved, curated and accessible, though also of course not without risks of institutional privilege of access, official censoring (and alteration/tampering) and the drawing up of archival boundaries of acquisition upon lines of

---

3 Review by Margaret M. Scull, 'Guy Beiner, Forgetful Remembrance: Social Forgetting and Vernacular Historiography of a Rebellion in Ulster', *Journal of Contemporary History*, July 2020, available online: <https://doi.org/10.1177%2F00220094 20921295a> [accessed 7 September 2020].
4 Tom Paulin, *New Selected Poems* (London: Faber and Faber, 2014), 37.

gender, ethnicity, and class. In terms of gender, Melissa Sihra has argued that 'tilting the lens onto women's perspectives in Irish theatre reclaims previously closed-off paths, offering new routes for the present and the future'.[5] Michael Pierse[6] and Elizabeth Mannion[7] have uncovered histories and narratives of working-class and urban performance histories. Vukasin Nedeljkovic's *Asylum Archive* project intervenes in the documentation process as an activist archive of disclosure of those living and confined within the Direct Provision system in Ireland.[8]

It is necessary to consider the processes of memory and position of archives within Irish Studies. How are literary, cultural and social histories documented and in turn interrogated? How can such records then serve in the production of new knowledge in Irish Studies? If, in addressing this latter question, the records and sources made available to future generations merely reconstruct 'patriarchal monuments' within Irish Studies, as Paulin observes, then the risk surely remains in the maintaining of a 'strange museum' where archives and records of Irish literary and cultural production are obscured from objective scrutiny and study.

Writing in 2001, Claire Connolly identified the challenges already visible in national public memory and the archival space, in terms of social remembrance, public commemoration and cultural engagement in Irish historiography. Citing the Republic's 'current rage for commemoration', Connolly outlines the risks of desire for the 'discovery of a usable past',[9] a past to serve the present needs of the privileged and powerful.

---

5 Melissa Sihra, *Marina Carr, Pastures of the Unknown* (London: Palgrave MacMillan, 2018), 8.
6 Michael Pierse, *Writing Ireland's Working Class: Dublin after O'Casey* (London: Palgrave MacMillan, 2011).
7 Elizabeth Mannion: *The Urban Plays of the Early Abbey Theatre: Beyond O'Casey* (New York: Syracuse University Press, 2014).
8 Available online: <http://www.asylumarchive.com/> [accessed 28 August 2020].
9 Claire Connolly, 'Theorising Ireland', *Irish Studies Review* 9, no. 3 (2001), 311–312.

The Spaces of Irish Performance and Memory – Physical to Digital

In 2015, in advance of the centenary of the 1916 Rising taking place in April 2016, Sinn Féin proposed to present a 'visual spectacular' light show, projected nightly onto the façade of the General Post Office (GPO) on Dublin's O'Connell Street. Entitled *The Rising Son et Lumière 2016*, the event intended to show a narrative account of the events of 1916 as they unfolded and projected onto the GPO. The scenes depicted included the GPO coming under shellfire and erupting in flames, as well as the 1916 rebels' 'last stand' before the order of surrender was issued by Pádraig Pearse. The whole event was also intended to be broadcast online to a live worldwide audience. The GPO was, in this instance, to be used as a backdrop for 3D video-mapping projection, and the event would take place from 24–29 April 2016, the anniversary dates of the Rising, following a 'live' digital re-enacted nightly in line with how events unfolded a century before. In the official brochure of commemoration events planned by Sinn Féin for 2016, it was stated that the party has 'undertaken a Visual Arts project using modern technology that will not only provide a "must-see" event on O'Connell St but which will also reach a worldwide audience via the internet'.[10] The plans were eventually rejected by the management of An Post owing to the affiliation of the event to a political party.[11]

However, the digital (re)performance of the past, in this case the events of the 1916 Rising, was being utilised by Sinn Féin as a means of presenting and curating the physical layering of historical events onto the site and streetscape of Dublin city's main thoroughfare. The archive of nationalist memory in the form of the architecture of the GPO becoming a performance site through digital means incorporated an alternate retelling of Irish

---

[10] 'Sinn Féin National Launch 1916 Commemoration Events', available online: <https://www.sinnfein.ie/files/2015/SinnFein2016BrochureWeb.pdf> [accessed 28 July 2020].

[11] 'An Post Gives Cold Shoulder to Sinn Féin 2016 GPO Spectacular', available online: <https://www.irishtimes.com/news/politics/an-post-gives-cold-shoulder-to-sinn-f%C3%A9in-2016-gpo-spectacular-1.2383147> [accessed 12 August 2020].

history – an archive of memory made digital and global, but curated for political rather than historiographical interpretation.

The GPO had in the years previous to this also been subject to the planning of becoming a theatre in its own right. The further twinning of Irish nationalism and Irish theatre through the memory of performance was continued by the proposed moving of the Abbey Theatre from its current location to the site of the GPO in 2009. The idea was presented within the Fianna Fáil-Green party coalition Programme for Government, which prescribed 'the detailed assessment of the GPO complex with a view to locating the Abbey Theatre there'[12] and suggesting that the works would be completed in time for the centenary of the 1916 Rising in 2016. Willie White, then Artistic Director of the Project Arts Centre in Dublin, stated that the proposal to move the Abbey Theatre to the GPO site was 'not just bad for politics, it was bad for art. There needs to be an independence between cultural and political discourse in Ireland and the move would align the two ... it would also make the theatre a museum, and theatre is about the moment, the contemporary moment, not the past'.[13] The then Minister for Arts, Sports and Tourism, Martin Cullen, also commissioned multiple feasibility reports into the construction of a new purpose built theatre for the Abbey and which was to be located in the expanding docklands area at George's Dock. Over €600,000 was spent by the Government on reports and plans into the new theatre sites for the Abbey Theatre by the end of 2009. The planned move of the Abbey Theatre never materialised. These planned developments were symptomatic of the alignment of the embodied memory of physical space with the desire for political association and ownership of the archival memory of the formation of the Irish state. Echoes of the 'performance' of Irish nationalism through sites associated with its past were being equated with the revisionist historicism of Irish political

---

12 Proposed Programme for Government, 10 October 2009. Irish Election Manifestos Archive, available online: <https://tinyurl.com/y5aeeove> [accessed 24 August 2020].
13 'The Abbey and the GPO – An Improbable Alliance?', *The Irish Times*, 17 October 2009, available online: <https://www.irishtimes.com/news/the-abbey-and-the-gpo-an-improbable-alliance-1.758615> [accessed 4 August 2020].

parties. The culture of display, as defined by Georgina Guy,[14] becomes 'a staging of a staging' and reflects a meeting point of curatorial practice where records are selected, framed and presented as part of a viewpoint into the archival past, to serve a particular form of memory.

Exhibitions, Curation and Display: Archives and Making Visible

The recently opened Museum of Literature Ireland (MOLI) is a new partnership between the National Library of Ireland and University College Dublin. Located at the old Earlsfort Terrace on Dublin's St Stephen's Green, the museum states that it also allows both partners (UCD and NLI) to expand beyond their traditional physical spaces.[15] Within the museum, the space of curatorial physical display meets its digital counterpoint, where the museum becomes both library, educator as well as broadcaster, with the establishment of the 'Radio MOLI'. Branded as 'a digital radio station for Irish literature', Radio MOLI functions as a portal site for archived recordings of writer talks and interviews, lectures, as well as content from the Irish Poetry Reading Archive, based at Special Collections of UCD.

As well as its permanent exhibition on James Joyce, the other opening exhibition at MOLI was entitled *Kate O'Brien: Arrow to the Heart*,[16] and explored the works of the Limerick-born author and was curated by the author's grand-niece, actress Kathy Rose-O'Brien. The exhibition presented the tangible spaces of O'Brien's personal and intellectual worlds – her schooling, family life, travel and the influence of art upon her writing. Also

---

14 Georgina Guy, *Theatre, Exhibition, and Curation: Displayed and Performed* (London: Routledge, 2016), 30.
15 MOLI – About, available online: <https://moli.ie/about/ucd-national-library/> [accessed 12 August 2020].
16 *Kate O'Brien: Arrow to the Heart*, curated by Kathy Rose O'Brien, was exhibited at the Museum of Literature Ireland from September 2019 until 29 January 2020.

present in the exhibition is a detailed presentation on the pressures and censures of conservative Catholic Ireland of the early and mid-twentieth century upon the life and writing of O'Brien.

Anna Pilz and Whitney Standlee outline how 'exhibitions are a relatively new phenomenon in Irish women's literary history ... [and] remind scholars that there are additional and important works of literature to be revisited and explored'.[17] The significance of the exhibition lies in its making visible the tangible and intangible record; the archive of memory and of the unremembered; the presence of Kate O'Brien's resistance to enforced silence of Irish society's moral theocracy. The exhibition is an important act and document in itself. The personal and literary networks are crucial to the working against the gaps within the archival space of memory. *Arrow to the Heart* pivots this obscured record to clearly highlighting O'Brien, as Eibhear Walshe argues, as 'a central voice within Irish fiction of the twentieth century ... [who articulated] an Irish feminist sensibility'.[18]

The networks of the writer, such as that of O'Brien, as Tina O'Toole outlines, capture 'the fluid and transnational nature of queer kinship networks differs from the more static aspects of mainstream communities perhaps especially in Ireland where identities and relationships based on, and sharply delimited by, familial and fixed spatial contexts have tended to be paramount'.[19] These 'fixed spatial contexts' that O'Toole describes can be found within the archival space, the quiet interludes where relationships are formed and the imagination is allowed to echo. As Gaston Bachelard elaborates on the question of space and memory: 'The distant past resounds with echoes ... in this reverberation, the poetic image will

---

17 Anna Pilz and Witney Standlee, 'A Case for Editorial and Curatorial Interventions', Irish Women's Writing (1880–1920) Network Blog, available online: <https://irishwomenswritingnetwork.com/2020/07/30/a-case-for-editorial-and-curatorial-interventions/> [accessed 20 August 2020].

18 Eibhear Walsh, 'Kate O'Brien', *A History of Modern Irish Women's Literature*, edited by Heather Ingram and Clíona Ó Gallchoir (Cambridge: Cambridge University Press, 2018), 229–230.

19 Tina O'Toole, 'Cé Leis Tú? Queering Irish Migrant Literature', *Irish University Review* 43, no. 1 (Spring/Summer 2013), 131–145.

have a sonority of being. We are able to experience resonances, sentimental repercussions, reminders of our past'.[20]

The literary archive of such networks present evidence of conversations and intellectual exchange through series of letters, correspondence and related records and the concentric layering of archives within archives. Within the papers of the Lyric Theatre, Belfast, is the archive of the literary journal, *Threshold*, founded by Mary O'Malley in 1958.[21] Further to publishing the new literary journal, the Lyric also opened a new art gallery, which operated under the directorship of Austrian artist and designer, Alice Berger-Hammarshlag. Kate O'Brien officiated at the opening of this gallery on 22 April 1963. The policy of the gallery was to show works by artists of international stature and those of notable promise whose work has not been seen in Belfast before, thus setting a standard of high artistic quality comparable with that of any cosmopolitan gallery anywhere.[22]

In choosing O'Brien as the figure to launch such an ambitious artistic venture, O'Malley reinforced O'Brien's standing as an international writer as much as an Irish writer.[23] As the artistic figurehead of the launch, O'Brien was positioned as a public figure connected with the cosmopolitan and the idea of the European urban metropolis, where theatres, galleries and literary magazines regularly created spaces for artists to respond to the wider region and also to international artistic movements.

---

20   Gaston Bachelard, *The Poetics of Space* (Boston, MA: Beacon Press, 1994), xvi–xvii.
21   The Lyric Theatre filled the role of an Arts Centre for Belfast (and Northern Ireland) by publishing a literary journal, *Threshold*, for over four decades, beginning in 1958 and ceasing publication in 1990, as well as also founding an art gallery, craft shop, and a music and drama school. The full archive catalogue for the Lyric Theatre/O'Malley Archive at the Hardiman Library, NUI Galway can be viewed online: <https://tinyurl.com/yybvjldg> [accessed 12 August 2020].
22   Report of New Gallery, 1963, T4/970, Lyric Theatre/O'Malley Archive, Hardiman Library, NUI Galway.
23   For more on the archival correspondence between see Barry Houlihan, 'Letters and the Archive: Kate O'Brien and Mary O'Malley', Irish Women's Writers Network Blog, available online: <https://irishwomenswritingnetwork.com/2019/12/03/letters-and-the-archive-kate-obrien-and-mary-omalley/> [accessed 12 August 2020].

Design and Irish Performance – Tangible Memory of Embodied Histories

The archive of design is often a neglected record within the historiography of Irish performance. The scenographic record is documented to a limited extent with production photographs or descriptions by critics in reviews. This also been to the detriment of how design is approached, documented and preserved. Scholarly work by Elaine Sisson and Linda King have argued how Irish studies needs to be considered within a visual record of design activity in Ireland during the twentieth century.[24] Siobhán O'Gorman has also pointed out that 're-examining theatre practice of the past through the lens of scenography … allows us to acknowledge and explore contributions of other collaborators, such as designers and actors, in ways that promote more holistic theatre and performance histories'.[25]

The award-winning designer Joe Vaněk has worked for more than three decades in Ireland and is internationally recognised as one of the most significant designers in theatre and opera. The Joe Vaněk Archive of Theatre and Opera Design at NUI Galway is a richly detailed collection that charts the creation and population of Irish theatre spaces since the mid-1980s. Vaněk has been designing for most of the major theatre, opera and dance companies in Ireland since 1984. The archive comprises manuscripts, costume designs, drawings, research photographs, notebooks, letters and email, fabric samples and other materials.

By the Bog of Cats premiered at the Abbey Theatre, Dublin, in 1998, directed by Patrick Mason and starring Olwen Fouré as Hester Swane. The US premiere of the play came on 31 May 2001, staged at the Victory Gardens Theatre, presented by the Irish Repertory of Chicago. In September 2001,

---

24 Elaine Sisson and Linda King, 'Visual Shrapnel: Rethinking Irish Studies through Design and Popular Visual Culture', *The Canadian Journal of Irish Studies* 38, no. 1 (2014), 56–83.

25 Siobhán O'Gorman, 'Irish Theatre: A Designer's Theatre', in *The Palgrave Handbook of Contemporary Irish Theatre and Performance*, edited by Eamonn Jordan and Eric Weitz (London: Palgrave MacMillan, 2018), 354.

the San José Repertory Theatre staged the play with Holly Hunter in the role of Hester Swane. As Richard Russell writes, 'Hester Swane leads the ultimate unsettled life: she is a tinker, an itinerant who roams the bog'.[26] Within the study of Irish drama and its historiography, Melissa Sihra argues for 'a matriarchal lineage'. In recalibrating the historiographic and archival lens of Irish theatre away from a patriarchal canonical construct, Sihra outlines how 'women have long been denied a central position of meaning making in Irish theatre while men have been privileged within the narrative'.[27]

Vaněk's archive offers a further facet to the archive of design. Moving beyond photographic records of fixed moments of performance, access to the records of scenic development become possible through the designer's archive. Vaněk's research in advance of designing the San José Rep production of *By the Bog of Cats* comprises in itself an archive of landscape and an archive of memory entwined within the landscape. Sihra signifies the importance of landscape to Carr's plays. The bog offers 'a fecund doubleness that is both mundane and supernatural'.[28] Vaněk's manuscript design notebooks become a living record of collaboration within production – the costume designs are noted for the corporal habitation and embodiment of the actor in character, the movement of the actual body must be facilitated by the elements of the character ascribed by the playwright and as materialised by the designer.

---

26   Richard Russell, 'Talking with Ghosts of Irish Playwrights Past: Marina Carr's *By the Bog of Cats*', *Comparative Drama* 40, no. 2 (Summer 2006), 155–156.
27   Sihra, *Marina Carr: Pastures of the Unknown*, 4.
28   Ibid., 123.

Figure 2.1. Wedding dress designed by Joe Vaněk for actress Holly Hunter as Hester Swane. *By the Bog of Cats*. San José Rep production. Joe Vaněk Archive, NUI Galway.

The gestation of design traces through Vaněk's photographs of physical sites of the midlands and bogs of County Offaly, where he was accompanied by Marina Carr, seeking the threshold of the liminal space between recorded past and present being on the bogs. In his notes, Vaněk recounts how 'the mythic quality can come from the characters retreating further into the past'.[29] The present space is archived in a corporeal sense as is evidenced by Vaněk in his archive correspondence: 'Perhaps the sense of place – of the farm – is depicted more surrealistically? Walls fly out, world open up again'.[30] As the worlds 'open up' on stage, Vaněk simultaneously opens up landscapes and folklore, as his archive showcases photographs of boglands and the patterns of the opened landscape as the bog is cut. What the papers reveal is a landscape of memory, recording layers of habitation across time, homeplaces preserved within the bog.

29 *By the Bog of Cats*, Notebook, T26/20/1, Joe Vaněk Archive, Hardiman Library, NUI Galway.
30 *By the Bog of Cats*, Notebook, Act 1, Scene 6, T26/20/1, Joe Vaněk Archive, Hardiman Library, NUI Galway.

Figure 2.2. Research photographs taken by Joe Vaněk, boglands in County Offaly. Joe Vaněk Archive, NUI Galway.

Speaking at the Galway International Arts Festival in 2019, President Michael D. Higgins addressed a capacity audience at NUI Galway in a lecture on the theme of 'Home'. Higgins outlined that within an Irish context and consciousness, the structure of the house emerges as the home by becoming a site of intimacy and creativity, of memories and dreams.[31] Contemporary performance has also moved beyond the space of the homeplace in recent years and into other physical spaces of memory as a means to interrogate national archive and national memory.

Performing Archival Space – the Secrets of the State

ANU Productions are an award-winning theatre and performance company based in Dublin and founded by Louise Lowe and Owen Boss in 2009. ANU have created new forms of Irish drama that situate audiences within an immersive and site-specific world, cognisant of geo-temporal contexts and historical settings. The company has established a body of work that seeks out and breaks open the forced silences in Irish society as well as in the instruments of power which maintain those silences. It makes visible the documented and undocumented record of our physical, architectural, emotional and psychological histories. Brian Singleton outlines the significance of archival records and testimony, sources that are physical, oral or intangible, within the immersive site-specific and site-responsive work of ANU:

> Their chosen histories are of the marginalized in colonial or post-colonial contexts, characters that end up on the wrong side of history or on the negative side of narrative. Their engagement with history is often on the personal level of individuals who lived through historical moments but who have not been historicized. Their source materials are to be found equally in archives, but also in documented oral histories, as well as in the often undocumented remembrances of the past by ordinary local people.[32]

---

31 President Michael D. Higgins, 'Home', as part of the First Thought series of talks, 21 July, 2018. Galway International Arts Festival Archive, Hardiman Library, NUI Galway, available online: <https://digital.library.nuigalway.ie/islandora/object/islandora %3A6897> [accessed 14 August 2020].

32 Brian Singleton, *ANU Productions: The Monto Cycle* (London: Palgrave, 2016).

The Sin Eaters was a large-scale site-specific production by ANU as part of Dublin Theatre Festival in 2017.[33] It took place at Pigeon House Lab, Poolbeg, Dublin 4. Pigeon House was built in the late eighteenth century and acquired by the Electricity Supply Board (ESB) in 1929. According to ESB Archives, in 1965, the ESB built a new generating station on the site beside Pigeon House, known today as Poolbeg station, named after the Poolbeg lighthouse situated at the entrance to the Dublin port. Pigeon House was later decommissioned in 1976.[34]

Figure 2.3. Aerial photograph of the Pigeon House Power Station and Lab, 1951. E.S.B. Archives. I am grateful to Tanya Keyes, Archivist, E.S.B. Archives for her detailed help on sourcing this image.

33 Directed by Louise Lowe and designed by Owen Boss. Sound Design by Carl Kennedy. Costume Design by Niamh Lunny. Lighting Design by Paul Keoghan. Film work by Paddy Cahill. All female cast included – Neili Conroy, Katie Honan, Úna Kavanagh, Niamh McCann, Amy McElhatton, Rachel O'Byrne, Emma O'Kane and Amanda Coogan.
34 Pigeon House, Portfolio, ESB Archives Website, available online: <https://esbarchives.ie/portfolio /pigeon-house/> [accessed 12 August 2020].

In traditional folklore, a sin eater is a person who, through a ritual eating of bread from the breast of a corpse, takes on the sins of the dead person, thus absolving the soul and allowing that person to rest in peace. Though more common in folklore and in anthropological studies of Wales, instances of the practice of 'sin eating' have been documented in Ireland from studies published during the nineteenth century. One account noted how at funerals in Ireland a plate of snuff is placed upon the breast of the dead, or upon the coffin, and everyone who attends the funeral is expected to take a pinch.[35] Historian Anne Ridge also recounts how the laying in state of the body at the wake as part of an Irish funerary tradition as being 'a liminal period, between death and burial [that] was always looked upon as a danger zone, and people took different measures to protect themselves'.[36]

The choice of the Pigeon House site by ANU, with its interior laboratory spaces, was significant in that it challenges the enforced and systemic silencing of human voices and of documented testimony within the State. This production explored the process of 'collective sin eating' on part of the Irish people as a process to begin to absolve the social stigma inflicted upon those women who were systematically confined within an institutional network. The laboratory is traditionally a space of experiment, of rigorous testing of ideas and evidence, in pursuit of new knowledge. In ANU's production, the setting became a crucible for exploring the national conscious by giving voice to those forcibly obscured from public record.

At the edge of Dublin city audiences travelled through the building in an hour-long show that marked an inquiry into state, church and family.[37] ANU's production acted as a further conduit through the liminal position

---

35   E. Sidney Hartland, 'The Sin-Eater', *Folklore* 3, no. 2 (June 1892), 152.
36   Anne Ridge, *Death Customs on Rural Ireland: Traditional Funerary Rites in the Irish Midlands* (Galway: Arlen House, 2009), 60.
37   *The Sin Eaters*, Anu Productions Official website, available online: <http://anuproductions.ie/work/sin-eaters/#:~:text=A%20sin%20eater%20is%20a,events%20that%20have%20shaped%20Ireland> [accessed 18 July 2020].

of the Irish State undergoing a reckoning with its failings to its most vulnerable people who were institutionalised within systemic networks of confinement, stigmatisation and enforced labour. Early on in *The Sin Eaters*, the small group of audience members are brought through the building of the Pigeon House lab. Soil samples were tested at the lab for identifying elements of their composition, their fertility, their viability to power the land and the State, and are meticulously catalogued within a wooden drawer system, still intact in the lab. The audience is questioned by cast member Amy McElhatton, as they are physically surrounded by the incubation of the memory of Irish soil: 'Do you think places hold memories?' This raises the overarching issue of national memory– can memory be absolved from the physical land that has held the secrets and moments of past traumas? According to Miriam Haughton, the potency of ANU's work lies in 'its staging of testimonies and recovered histories in the very building where those experiences were acquired'.[38]

The treatment or perception of 'Sin', in particular by women, was common across the networks of Mother and Baby Homes, Magdalene Laundries, mental hospitals, institutional reform schools, among others, and used as a reason to physically and emotionally remove these individuals from society. By fracturing the identity of these women, their children and the others detained within these networks, the personal archive of existence within the State ceased to function. Birth certificates were altered, adoption records were forged, death certificates and burial records were falsified, and testimony made by and on behalf of victims and survivors to those in positions of authority or public office was often ignored. The archival record of systemic abuse in Ireland was being dismantled by those agents who profited most from its existence.

---

38 Miriam Haughton, 'From Laundries to Labour Camps: Staging Ireland's "Rule of Silence" in Anu Productions' Laundry', *Modern Drama* 57, no. 1 (Spring 2014), 69.

Figure 2.4. Amy McElhatton in *The Sin Eaters*. ANU Productions. Photo © Pat Redmond.

Úna Kavanagh presents a bloodied form, sustained on an intravenous line within a bare and soiled hospital ward, giving voice to the trauma experienced by women who were forced to travel from Ireland to seek medical care for abortion. The campaign to repeal the Eighth Amendment of the Irish constitution, as then still in place in Ireland in 2017, was a lingering presence of the power of archival documents in support of the State's policy on abortion treatment. In one particular scene, Katie Honan, dressed in school uniform, represents the tragic and unimaginable isolation of Ann Lovett, who died giving birth in secret at the site of the church grotto in Granard, Co. Longford, in 1984. Surrounded by filing cabinets and case files, the visible presence of official and legal record and also of inaction in response to evidence, become 'monuments of patriarchy' within the production.

In her programme note to *The Sin Eaters*, archivist Catriona Crowe outlines how

> *The Sin Eaters* will make formal accusation of the Irish state for inflicting trauma on our citizens, a practice which is still sadly prevalent – direct provision for refugees,

appalling housing conditions, neglect of vulnerable children, and the many journeys women with unwanted pregnancies are forced to make because of denial of their human rights, among many other things. This formal interrogation will provide the opportunity to reflect on trauma as a societal as well as a personal affliction, and to consider how this may be remedied.[39]

Crowe also comments on the site-specific but also geo-temporal specific memory that the production site of the Pigeon House labs and their hinterland present to local Dublin audiences and also the 'ghosted' or haunted memory of past emigrants who departed Ireland. For many, the last sight of their homeland would have been the Poolbeg chimney stacks, which, as physical monuments, [oversaw their] traumatic departures from Ireland.[40] As both signifiers of memory and as physical sites of encounter between citizen and the State, such sites as outlined within this chapter, from the G.P.O to the bogs of the midlands, our literary manuscripts and spaces of display and encounter, embody the actions and memories which cannot be so easily separated from the individual. They contain residual memory – a physical archive which empowers rather than silences those who are reflected within the national memory.

Conclusion

Lucy Collins points out that for literary and indeed for all archival collections, the role they play is shaping the critical futures of studies of Irish culture and is paramount:

> Any discussion of a literary archive needs to take into account the relationship between the recording of the creative past and the shaping of a critical future. Collections, rather than functioning purely as a source of materials, are rewarding subjects of study in their own right, and illuminate the construction of our literary heritage.[41]

39 Catriona Crowe, Programme Note, *The Sin Eaters*, Anu Productions, Dublin Theatre Festival, 2017.
40 Crowe, Programme Note.
41 Lucy Collins, 'Hidden Collections: The Value of Irish Literary Archives', *Irish University Review* 50, no. 1 (May 2020), 187.

For Irish society and for Irish Studies, these archival legacies need to be protected, resourced by physical and digital conservation, made accessible where it is ethically right to do so, and be studied, exhibited, and acknowledged by scholars and the public. The alternative is that we may once again find our records buried in plastic sacks in a landfill. The archive must reject its quality as a 'strange museum' and continue to be challenged, renewed and assessed on its ability to function fairly in service to the people of the State, to provide accountability and transparency in society and its governance, and ultimately, as a record of Irish identity and culture.

KATY HAYWARD

3 Between Britain and Europe Once More: The Significance of Brexit for the Reimagination of Ireland

When I began my PhD in University College Dublin in 1999, its working title was 'Ireland Reimagined'. That postgraduate flash of inspiration was hardly an original one. Even within the ensuing three years of my doctoral study, there were several eminent publications and conferences on that very theme. The turn of the millennium played its part in stimulating this notion, as did the juvenile Celtic Tiger, and the 'Boston or Berlin' debate.[1] But there is no doubt that it was the 1998 Good Friday (Belfast) Agreement that was the primary prompt for widespread recognition that Ireland had reached an historic moment of change. As it happened, my doctorate ended with a rather more circumspect thesis than the one I had set out with. Yes, 'Ireland' was being redefined in official discourse and, indeed, this was embodied in the Good Friday Agreement. But this was not a wholly radical 'reimagination'. In many ways, the concept of Irish nationhood underpinning it would have been remarkably familiar to Irish nationalists a hundred years beforehand. The Agreement states that the right to self-determination is held

1   On 21 July 2000, Tánaiste Mary Harney delivered a speech to the American Bar Association in the Law Society of Ireland in which she described the country as being 'closer to Boston than Berlin'. This was the first of a number of speeches by government ministers and TDs in which the EU was compared somewhat unfavourably to the USA as a partner for Ireland. Whilst for some, like Harney, this was about liberal economic policies (e.g. low tax, low regulation), for others, such as Síle de Valera and Éamonn Ó Cuív, it took the form of a modern version of Irish republicanism and mild Euroscepticism. Elements of this debate were present in the 'No' campaign and result in the referendum on the Nice Treaty in 2001.

by 'the people of the island of Ireland alone'.[2] And it confirms that it is the birthright of all people born on the island of Ireland (including Northern Ireland) to 'identify themselves and be accepted as Irish'.[3] As this chapter elucidates, it is what accompanies these statements that makes the 'Ireland' imagined at the start of the twentieth century quite different to that imagined in the twenty-first. And it is precisely this 'imagining' that is challenged by Brexit.

In a manner typical of his contemporaries, D. P. Moran described the historic quest for Irish independence in terms of 'a battle of two civilisations': the Irish versus the English.[4] But Moran's claim was that the development of 'Irish Ireland' had become impeded by seeing Irish civilisation only in terms of the English – be it English conventions and economics or English misgovernment and harm. At the start of the new century, he argued for a different approach. Moran wanted his generation to see the Irish nation in its own terms. He argued that Irish civilisation needed to grow 'from the roots of one of the oldest in Europe', 'relying on her own genius', and thus:

> Our master-passions will be wrapped up *in the construction of our own nation*, not in the destruction of another.[5]

Moran claimed that this inspiration was one that Henry Grattan had identified 120 years earlier, in a plea for Irish legislative independence made before the Irish Parliament. It is worth considering this in some of its original fullness, not least bearing in mind that Grattan's Irish patriotism melded comfortably with his Protestantism and loyalty to the British monarchy:

> And as anything less than liberty is inadequate to Ireland, so is it dangerous to Great Britain.

2 Agreement between the Government of the United Kingdom of Great Britain and Northern Ireland and the Government of Ireland, 10 April 1998, Article 1 (iv).
3 *Agreement*, Article 1 (vi).
4 D. P. Moran, *The Philosophy of Irish Ireland* (Dublin: James Duffy and Co., 1905 [1900]), 94–114.
5 Moran, *Irish Ireland*, 114. Italics added.

> *We are too near the British nation*, we are too conversant with her history, we are too much fired by her example, *to be anything less than her equal; anything less, we should be her bitterest enemies* – an enemy to that power which smote us with her mace, and to that Constitution from whose blessings we were excluded:
>
> To be ground as we have been by the British nation, bound by her Parliament, plundered by her Crown, threatened by her enemies, insulted with her protection, while we return thanks for her condescension, or a system of meanness and misery which has expired in our determination, as I hope it has in her magnanimity.[6]

As Grattan declared the rights of Ireland, numbers in the loyalist militia of the Irish Volunteers swelled to tens of thousands. It may interest present-day readers to recall that the Volunteers' demands for concessions included that of tariff-free movement of goods into Britain, as seen in their purported slogan, 'Free trade or a speedy revolution'.[7] This was not to be the last time when the movement of goods across the Irish Sea formed a bone of contention between the British government and loyalists in Ireland.

The 1801 Act of Union failed to quell turbulence in Ireland and arguably served to exacerbate the tragedy that befell the country in the nineteenth century. The population, through starvation and emigration, fell from over 8 million in 1841 to under 4.5 million in 1901. This devastating loss compared to England's population, which rose from 13.7 million to 30 million over the same time period. Apart from all else, proximity of government to the governed appeared to bring favourable outcomes. In this context, Moran's summation of Grattan's speech seems particularly striking in its ambition and its simple high-mindedness: 'As her equal, we shall be her sincerest friend'.[8]

[6] Henry Grattan, 'The Speech Which Introduced the Declaration of Rights, 19 April 1780', in *Speeches of the late Rt Hon Henry Grattan in the Irish Parliament in 1780 and 1782* (London: T. C. Hansard, 1821), 16. Italics added.

[7] Under the *Acts of Trade and Navigation* (originating in the mid-seventeenth century), goods from Britain could access Ireland freely, but Irish goods entering Britain were subject to tariffs. The original purpose of this militia was to defend Ireland from potential incursions from Europe whilst British military attention was focused on rebellion in America. See: Thomas Mac Nevin, *The History of the Irish Volunteers of 1782* (Dublin: James Duffy, 1845).

[8] Moran, *Irish Ireland*, 114.

In contemplating the prospect of equality, Moran and many of his peers envisaged the possibility of expunging British influence from the Irish nation. Finding it inconceivable to imagine that Protestants or Dissenters could be *as* Irish as Catholics, Moran's conception of Irish Ireland was deeply exclusivist and, ironically, one that came close to rationalising the territorial division of Ireland. After the Easter Rising and the War of Independence, the partition of Ireland by the Anglo-Irish Treaty in 1921 was seen by the majority as being the way in which the friction-filled legacies of British-Irish history could be relatively peaceably contained and managed for the time being. Based on the old district boundaries, the new border cut through some 1,400 landholdings and even individual buildings.[9] It divided villages, parishes and communities, and separated market towns from their traditional hinterlands. In both territories, partition left substantial minorities on the 'wrong' side of the border. Even at the time of partition, Catholics constituted over a third of the total population in Northern Ireland and Protestants around 10 percent of the population in the Irish Free State. Nevertheless, notions of the 'Protestant North' and the 'Catholic South' came into common parlance, blanking out an historic wealth of cultural diversity and complexity that would prove difficult to uncover and explain even just a few generations later.

The creation of 'Northern Ireland' was seen at the time as a temporary measure – one to be revisited and adjusted over time through a dedicated Boundary Commission (the failure of which was rapid and consequential).[10] But as tends to happen when boundary lines are drawn on a map, the Irish border soon began to take on a significance of its own. The development of official Irish nationalism in the Free State first centred upon the process of nation-building, that is to say, legitimising the state through its association with the Irish nation, and then on the process of state-building, in terms of consolidating the structures of the state.[11] Following its acceptance of

---

9   Peter Leary, *Unapproved Routes: Histories of the Irish Border, 1922–72* (Oxford: Oxford University Press, 2016).
10 Kieran J. Rankin, 'Deducing Rationales and Political Tactics in the Partitioning of Ireland, 1912–1925', *Political Geography* 26, no. 8 (2007), 909–933.
11 Katy Hayward, *Irish Nationalism and European Integration: The Official Redefinition of the Island of Ireland* (Manchester: Manchester University Press, 2009), 14–15.

the intergovernmental agreement on the boundary (December 1925), the Irish government could no longer present the border as a transitory and insignificant line. Official Irish nationalism had to define its nation in a way that was not merely territorial. The ethno-cultural nation that was subsequently fostered by the governmental elite drew upon narratives and concepts that were commonly shared by constitutional and republican nationalists. The twenty-six-county state had to embody this national identity even as it recognised its incompleteness.

The stronger the assertion of the unique characteristics of the Irish nation, the clearer their distinction from the characteristics of others became. Thus, as the Irish state became 'more Irish', so those outside its jurisdiction became *ipso facto* less so. This included Northern Ireland. Indeed, the more trenchantly Ireland was identified as Gaelic, Catholic and rural, so almost by default, Northern Ireland was seen as a land of the planter, Protestant and industrialised. The casual use of such indiscriminate markers (and the near invisibility of northern nationalists in much of this discourse) gave the new political boundary the status of an 'ethnic' divide. Although official Irish nationalism maintained irredentist ambitions, official discourse on both sides of the border magnified their differences.[12]

For their part – not having originally advocated for partition, but always preferring Union to Home Rule – unionists in Northern Ireland sought to find the grounds for the legitimacy of their Parliament too. In a debate in Stormont in 1934, Northern Ireland Prime Minister James Craig sought to answer the question as to whom his government serves:

> Since we took up office we have tried to be absolutely fair towards all the citizens of Northern Ireland. Actually, on an Orange platform, I, myself, laid down the principle, to which I still adhere: that I was prime minister not of one section of the community but of all, and that, as far as I possibly could, I was going to see that fair play was meted out to all classes and creeds without any favour whatsoever on my part.

When challenged on this, however, Craig spoke in an infamously blunt manner:

---

12   Hayward, *Irish Nationalism*, 99.

> In the South they boasted of a Catholic state. They still boast of Southern Ireland being a Catholic state. All I boast of is that we are a Protestant parliament and Protestant state. It would be rather interesting for historians of the future to compare a Catholic state launched in the South with a Protestant state launched in the North and to see which gets on the better and prospers the more.
>
> It is more interesting for me at the moment to watch how they are progressing. I am doing my best always to top the bill and be ahead of the South.[13]

The Protestant identity of Northern Ireland and its government was conceived in direct response to the Catholicism of the Irish state. The fact that partition seemed to allow direct *competition* between the two jurisdictions, as well as cultural opposition, was viewed with relish by some. 'Ireland' and 'Northern Ireland' were being imagined in near-choreographed contradistinction.

This was true among academic discourse (including in Irish Studies) as well as in public and political imagining. This is demonstrated by the Dutch geographer Heslinga, even as he criticised the practice:

> It would seem that there is among scholars in the Republic some reluctance – unconscious rather than conscious – to lay stress on the north-south contrasts which are as inherent in early Irish history, secular and ecclesiastical, as they are in modern history … *even if the ancient north-south divisions arise from different causes than the modern political conflict.*[14]

Heslinga takes as his starting point cultural commonalities of northern Britain (particularly the Protestantism of Scotland) and 'from this derives a somewhat deterministic rationale for the Irish-UK land border'.[15] Such retrospective justifications for the drawing of the Irish border were,

---

[13] James Craig, contribution in Northern Ireland Parliamentary Debates, 24 April 1934, quoted in: Jonathan Bardon, *A History of Ulster* (Belfast: The Blackstaff Press, 1992), 538–539.

[14] M. W. Heslinga, *The Irish Border as a Cultural Divide: A Contribution to the Study of Regionalism in the British Isles* (Assen: Van Gorcum and Co., 1971), 18–19. Italics added.

[15] Kevin Howard, 'Nationalist Myths: Revisiting Heslinga's "The Irish Border as a Cultural Divide"', *Mapping Frontiers, Plotting Pathways* working paper No. 16 (Dublin: University College Dublin, 2006), 12.

of course, also made by Ulster unionists.[16] The concept of 'ancient' differences within the island of Ireland makes it no different to any other territory in Europe. What is contestable, however, is the notion that the drawing of the border was an act of nationalistic recognition as distinct from one of imperialistic management. As Ruane and Todd explain, the decision to partition Ireland was not based on a response to the intrinsic Britishness of Northern Ireland so much as a reaction to the threat of armed rebellion against home rule by northern unionists.[17] What all this serves to show is that national and cultural identities may adjust to political and governmental realities. But the partition of Ireland is best understood in the context of the remapping of Europe after the First World War, in which the cartographic scalpel was wielded by 'those far from the ethnic and linguistic realities of the regions which were to be divided'.[18]

As it was drawn, so it became lived. The Irish border was not just a symbolic divide. Tensions between the British and Irish governments were often felt most acutely at that boundary line, and suffered most by residents of the border region. A good example of this was the Anglo-Irish Trade War in the mid-1930s, when each sought to land a blow on the other through the imposition of higher tariffs on a widening range of goods. It was the customs officials, small traders and citizens along the Irish border who suffered the most immediate and direct consequences. And, unsurprisingly, the emergence of the Troubles in the late 1960s had direct and devasting impact on the border communities. Alongside customs posts came the infrastructure, paraphernalia and restrictions associated with securitisation. Part of the British state's response to what they characterised as 'paramilitary incursions' from the southern side of the Irish border included the

---

16 Ian Adamson, *The Cruthin: A History of the Ulster Land and People* (Newtownards: Nosmada Books, 1974, 2nd edn).
17 Joseph Ruane and Jennifer Todd, 'Northern Ireland: Religion, Ethnic Conflict and Territoriality', in *The Territorial Management of Ethnic Conflict*, edited by John Coakley (London and Portland: Frank Cass, 2003, 2nd edn), 45–72, 48–49.
18 Eric Hobsbawm, *Age of Extremes: The Short Twentieth Century, 1914–91* (London: Abacus, 1995).

setting up of army checkpoints and the positioning of multiple military bases and watchtowers along the border itself.[19]

The escalation of security action along the border both reflected and contributed to further ratcheting up of political tensions between the two governments. It also led to a deepening alienation between communities within Northern Ireland and across the border. Those living in the border region itself could not help but also be affected, in practical, physical and emotional ways, by these tensions:

> Before the peace, it was a psychological iron curtain. We would go up [across the border] to visit family ... but there was a psychological dimension to it, that you avoided [crossing the border] otherwise.[20]

Perhaps one of the deepest cruelties of violence – direct violence and the violence of state policies on either side – was that it led to the hardening of the 'border of the mind' even among those whose lives and identities were, to all intents and purposes, cross-border. It should also be recognised that violence deepened the 'border in the mind' between Britain and Ireland too – and it became increasingly difficult to cross. The academic field of Border Studies shows us that borders are manifest not just at the edge of a state but in 'bordering practices' within it.[21] These bordering practices were very present within Britain during the Troubles, to the detriment of people from all parts of the island of Ireland.[22] It is likely that they will reemerge across these islands in new forms in the wake

---

19 Patrick Mulroe, *Bombs, Bullets and the Border: Policing Ireland's Frontier: Irish Security Policy, 1969-1978* (Newbridge, Co. Kildare: Irish Academic Press, 2017).

20 Participants in a focus group in the border village of Pettigo, cited in Hayward and Komarova, *The Border Into Brexit* (Belfast: Irish Central Border Area Network and Queen's University Belfast, 2019).

21 James Scott and Henk van Houtum, 'Reflections on EU Territoriality and the "Bordering" of Europe', *Political Geography* 28 (2009), 271–273. Tamara Vukov and Mimi Sheller, 'Border Work: Surveillant Assemblages, Virtual Fences, and Tactical Counter-Media', *Social Semiotics* 23 (2013).

22 Paddy Hillyard, *Suspect Community: People's Experience of the Prevention of Terrorism Acts in Britain* (London: Pluto Press, 1993).

of Brexit, as a new immigration regime comes into play in the United Kingdom.

Ireland's north/south and east/west relationships were transformed upon accession to the European Economy Community (EEC). Common EEC membership opened both the UK and Ireland to the processes and practices of European integration. This had a particular effect around the Irish border in terms of cross-border cooperation and a growing all-island economy, albeit an uneven one.[23] The introduction of EEC regulations on customs declarations in 1987 had immediate effect on the ease with which goods could be transported between north and south. Later, the creation of the Single Market (with its official entry into operation on 1 January 1993) erased many obstacles to cross-border trade and economic development.[24] In a very practical way, the context of European Union successfully enabled change in cross-border economic relationships in Ireland, as well as political ones.[25]

Common EEC/EU membership formed a vital context for moving away from British-Irish antagonism and mistrust towards a positive and productive intergovernmental relationship.[26] By 1985, the Anglo-Irish Hillsborough Agreement managed to coax out an unprecedented 'determination of both governments to develop close cooperation as partners in the European Community'. As the two governments became increasingly aware of matters of mutual interest, membership of EU made a bilateral approach to common issues – including the Northern Ireland conflict – increasingly plausible.[27] With a mix of 'inspiration', incentives and

---

23 James Goodman, *Single Europe, Single Ireland? Uneven Development in Process* (Dublin: Irish Academic Press, 2000).

24 Wolfgang Kowalsky, 'Past and Future of the EU Single Market', *European Review of Labour & Research* 16, no. 3 (2010), 437–441.

25 Katy Hayward and Mary C. Murphy, 'The EU's Influence on the Peace Process and Agreement in Northern Ireland in Light of Brexit', *Ethnopolitics* 17, no. 3 (2018), 276–291.

26 Elizabeth Meehan, '"Britain's Irish Question: Britain's European Question?": British-Irish Relations in the Context of the European Union and the Belfast Agreement', *Review of International Studies* 26, no. 1 (2000), 83–97.

27 Joseph Ruane and Jennifer Todd, *The Dynamics of Conflict in Northern Ireland: Power, Conflict, and Emancipation* (Cambridge: Cambridge University Press, 1996), 281.

opportunity, plus high-level diplomatic nudges and initiatives, EU membership created a new environment for the dynamics of the British-Irish relationship.[28] These were the conditions which enabled the 'reimagination' that transformed the British-Irish relationship at the end of the twentieth century.

At least in principle, EU membership was the best possible opportunity for Ireland and Britain to experience equality as (as D. P. Moran would have had it) 'the basis for sincerest friendship'. Equality is distinct from equity. As a large member-state, the UK had more influence in the European Parliament and European Council (when Qualified Majority Voting is applied) than Ireland, for instance. And, as one of the most substantial net contributors, the UK received special treatment with the rebate from the EU's budget. Indeed, so important was the UK to the EU that when, in 2015, Prime Minister David Cameron led a 'renegotiation' of the terms of its membership, it agreed considerable opt-outs for the UK. The resulting agreement was described as one which would 'secure Britain's *special status* in the EU'.[29] As we know, the British electorate was unconvinced, and Cameron failed in his effort to secure popular support for Remain in the subsequent referendum on the UK's membership of the EU (23 June 2016). Taoiseach Enda Kenny's response to the Brexit referendum result was not to downplay the significance but to assure people that the Irish Government had planned for the eventuality. He was unambiguous that whilst 'Ireland's strong and close relationship with the UK will remain', 'Ireland's future lies within the European Union':

> That is profoundly in our *national* interest.
>
> After more than 40 years of membership, we have built up *strong bonds of partnership* with all the other member states, and with the European institutions, that will

---

28 Mary E. Daly (ed.), *Brokering the Good Friday Agreement: The Untold Story* (Dublin: Royal Irish Academy, 2019), 139.

29 Press release on the conclusions of the European Council, 18–19 February 2016; available online: <https://www.consilium.europa.eu/en/meetings/european-council/2016/02/18-19/> [accessed 31 October 2020]. Italics added.

continue to serve us well. We must now begin a period of reflection and debate on *how we can renew the Union of 27* and equip it for the challenges ahead.[30]

Few (other than mainly British pro-Brexit commentators and politicians) seem surprised by Ireland's unwavering commitment to EU membership. Ireland has made the most of all mechanisms of influence within and through the EU, including those allowing small states to punch above their weight. The College of Commissioners, overseeing the executive branch of the EU, is constituted of members nominated by each national government. The Presidency of the Council rotates between all member-states. The comitology of the EU,[31] the wide range of agencies, the vast networks, the lobbying system, all offer opportunities to put forward the Irish point of view and to raise Ireland's profile.[32] Such mechanisms helped realise Ireland's genuine equality with the UK as a member-state. The UK's withdrawal from the European Union presented an enormous test of Ireland's influence and its standing as an EU member-state. This is obvious. What is less obvious is what it necessitates in terms of the 'reimagination' of Ireland after Brexit. That Ireland's *national interest* and its *future* lay in its *partnership* with the European Union is a statement that would be quite typical of Irish official discourse.[33] What is unfamiliar and unknown is the context in which this will have to be realised, for example, one in which such commitment to the EU will almost inevitably mean divergence from its nearest neighbour.

---

30 Enda Kenny, *Statement by an Taoiseach on the UK Vote to Leave the European Union*, 24 June 2016; available online: <https://merrionstreet.ie/en/News-Room/Speeches/Statement_by_An_Taoiseach_Enda_Kenny_TD_on_the_UK_Vote_to_Leave_the_European_Union.html> [accessed 31 October 2020]. Italics added.
31 The set of procedures through which EU member-states control how the European Commission implements EU law. Before detailed implementing measures for EU law is decided, the Commission must consult a committee where every EU country is represented, available online: <https://ec.europa.eu/transparency/comitology-register/screen/home> [accessed 31 October 2020].
32 Brigid Laffan and Jane O'Mahony, *Ireland and the European Union* (Basingstoke: Palgrave Macmillan, 2008).
33 Hayward, *Irish Nationalism*.

Perhaps now it is appropriate to turn to consider what was made possible in the 'reimagination' of Ireland at the turn of the century, and what it meant for Northern Ireland. The British-Irish Agreement reached on Good Friday 1998 was one in which Irishness was conceived as being compatible with Britishness [D. P. Moran be damned]. The Agreement confirmed the birthright of the people of Northern Ireland to be British as well as (or even instead of) Irish.[34] The self-determination of the people of the island of Ireland was to be 'between the two parts respectively'.[35] Most significantly – and with a previously unknown sense of hope and mutual respect – this recognition of the *Britishness and Irishness* of Northern Ireland came in the context of a common desire to make the British-Irish relationship closer:

> Wishing to develop still further the unique relationship between their peoples and the close co-operation between their countries as friendly neighbours and as partners in the European Union.[36]

Outwith the European Union, the neighbours may remain on friendly terms, but the development of relationships and close cooperation will be considerably more difficult, both in practice and (if we are not careful) in principle.

This is why Brexit is so significant – why it compels the reimagination of Ireland and why it necessitates an adjustment for Irish Studies. In this short chapter, we have recognised variety and change, and symbiosis, in conceptions of British and Irish on the island of Ireland. All this has occurred in the context of what we might loosely call 'Europe' but whose influence Irish Studies has definitively identified in cultural, intellectual, and philosophical terms as well as, for example, revolutionary, institutional and trade terms. We know from the drawing of the Irish border and the 'imagining' of Ireland that developed over the century that cultural and political identities are capable of changing radically – and of being radically changed. This should be borne in mind as we consider what Brexit might mean for Ireland and, indeed, for Irish Studies. The UK's withdrawal

---

34   *Agreement*, Article 1 (vi).
35   *Agreement*, Article 1 (ii).
36   *Agreement*, preamble.

from the European Union has already proven some things. Ireland is an effective, and respected, member-state. That protecting the 1998 Agreement and peace process was made one of the top three UK-EU priorities in the withdrawal negotiations is in no small part testament to this. Subsequently, the Protocol on Ireland/Northern Ireland in the final UK-EU Withdrawal Agreement (October 2019) was lauded as a triumph of Irish diplomacy. The fact that this same Protocol is criticised as a source of shame for the United Kingdom government encapsulates the difficulties that Brexit means for the British-Irish relationship.

The Protocol on Ireland/Northern Ireland is a compromise. It is a UK-EU compromise that will shape the future of relations across all three strands of the 1998 Agreement: unionist/nationalist, north/south and British/Irish. It is a compromise that creates new 'bordering practices' between the islands of Britain and Ireland, even as it seeks to avoid hardening the border across the island of Ireland.[37] Whether there will be tariff-free movement of goods across the Irish Sea has become a matter for UK-EU relations but which will have potentially devastating impact on traders and consumers in Ireland, north and south. Ireland finds itself once more between Britain and Europe. Northern Ireland is in a more vulnerable position still. *De jure* in the United Kingdom, its customs territory and internal market whilst *de facto* in the EU's customs union and single market for goods, the legal, political and economic environment for Northern Ireland look unnervingly full of ambiguities. This perhaps allows opportunities for new relationships and dynamics, but even the most creative political thinker or imaginative canny diplomat would struggle to forge these in an environment best described as 'unknown'. What has changed above all else is the pace and extent of change itself – and this is before we even consider the lasting impact of the Covid-19 pandemic that hit Europe just weeks after the UK left the EU at the end of January 2020. One Irish

---

37 Katy Hayward, 'The Revised Protocol on Ireland/Northern Ireland', *Queen's University Policy Engagement blog*, 19 November 2019; available online: <http://qpol.qub.ac.uk/the-revised-protocol-on-ireland-northern-ireland/> [accessed 31 October 2020].

diplomat described in simple terms the Brexit challenge for Ireland: 'There is no predictability. There has been a paradigm shift'.[38]

The existential shock will cause domestic wounds to Britain too. A new divide has been created in British politics that will take far longer to erase than it did to create. And the expectations (more than hopes) of Scottish nationalists and Irish nationalists, together with the centralising policies of Westminster, show intrinsic tensions in the Union that will be difficult to contain in a neo-imperial model of statehood.[39] Externally, because 'Brexit means Brexit', there has to be a recalibration of the British-Irish relationship. The Programme for Government of 2020 anticipates a 'strategic review' of the British-Irish relationship in 2021 – the centenary year of the Anglo-Irish Treaty. The lack of regular meetings between British and Irish ministers, the loss of networks between officials and the absence of British presence in the institutions of the EU will lead to decreasing familiarity between the two at all levels. Incredible as it may seem after decades of careful nurturing, close communication between British and Irish officials and relationships of trust between British and Irish politicians can no longer be assumed. What happens in these 'gaps of familiarity' is a matter of grave concern; and this is where, perhaps, the richness of Irish Studies can play a part. Brexit could all too easily create the conditions for a new 'battle of two civilizations'; there will be some on all sides who relish this prospect. But the imagination of the Good Friday Agreement requires the opposite. Brexit may mean Ireland Reimagined, but it should be one which unwaveringly recognises, and even cherishes, its Britishness as well as its Europeanness.

---

38   Tony Connelly, 'Brexit: The Slow Death of Chequers, or a Cliff Hanger Deal?' RTÉ News, 9 September 2018; available online: <https://www.rte.ie/news/analysis-and-comment/2018/0908/992329-brexit-chequers-may/> [accessed 31 October 2020].

39   John Coakley, Brigid Laffan and Jennifer Todd (eds), *Renovation or Revolution? New Territorial Politics in Ireland and the United Kingdom* (Dublin: UCD Press, 2005).

MARY S. PIERSE

4 Catching the Mood: George Moore's *Fin-de-Siècle* Involvements

In one short period of the *fin de siècle* era, in the time from publication of *Modern Painting* (1893) to that of *The Lake* (1905), George Moore (1852–1933) produced nine remarkably dissimilar works,[1] an assortment so diverse that it could easily be assumed that no one person was author of them all. The ability and versatility are notable in novels, short stories, critical essays and drama. This varied pattern would seem to chime with the unsettled atmosphere of a millennial epoch. However, it would be an error to assume that the disparate nature of the books is indicative of any authorial unease or millennial fever. This chapter will chart a course through Moore's publications in those years and will argue that his imagination and resourcefulness, allied to perceptive flair, allowed him to deliver starkly contrasting compositions that furnish intriguing glimpses into the milieux and atmospheres pertaining in the literary, artistic and political worlds of the time.

---

1   The nine were: *Modern Painting* (1893); *The Strike at Arlingford* (1893); *Esther Waters* (1894); *Celibates* (1895); *Evelyn Innes* (1898); *The Bending of the Bough* (1900); *Sister Teresa* (1901); *The Untilled Field* (1903); *The Lake* (1905). However, nine could be viewed as an underestimate since, in the same period, Moore also revised and rewrote some of those texts, including *Esther Waters*, *Evelyn Innes*, *Celibates* and *The Lake*. In addition, articles by him appeared in several newspapers such as *The Speaker*, and *The Pall Mall Gazette*.

The Literary Route

The divergent approaches taken by Moore are immediately evident in the course of one year, with a very significant difference apparent in style and genre between *Modern Painting* (1893) and *Esther Waters* (1894). The former is a collection of articles written by Moore as art critic of *The Speaker*, and the latter a bestselling novel that broke several Victorian taboos. *Modern Painting* is notable for its engaged and often-polemical style.[2] Here one encounters a flamboyant, opinionated Moore, projecting the image of an avant-garde art connoisseur, familiar with the prime movers and shakers of the artistic world, an intimate of leading impressionists, the expert who fearlessly champions the New English Art Club against the conservative hegemony of the academy and disparages the nature of established art education. The bad artistic taste of authorities, from the Royal family to municipal galleries, is excoriated. Moore is intent on enlightening the public and enlivening the discourse. This *modus operandi* differs from the tone and practice of *Parnell and His Island* (1887) and of *Confessions of a Young Man* (1888) in that, rather than blunt attacks that shock and draw attention to himself, GM now speaks as the educated and established specialist whose expertise gives licence to admonish, to contradict and to preach. This is ostensibly for the greater good, but with the collateral achievement of installing himself as professional in the field.

Reflected in his art criticism from 1890 onwards is Moore's discernment of the shifting sands of taste, of the emergence of resistance to conservative theory and practice, of the possibility of demolishing authoritarian diktat, and of doing so by more subtle methods than he had previously employed. This sensitivity to atmosphere and trends – whether or not they coincided with his own predilections – underpinned many of GM's creative works. In *Esther Waters* (1894), Moore set about creating depictions of the life of a servant and her difficulties in hostile environments.

---

2   George Moore had published similar art criticism in *The Hawk* from 1888 before becoming art critic at *The Speaker* in 1891.

To make a servant the central character in a novel was unprecedented, to allow her to voice her story, resist Victorian strictures and still survive was exceptional; to highlight manifestly unjust societal practice and prejudice constituted a challenge to the establishment. The novel was hugely successful, praised for different reasons (its highlighting of the ills of gambling, drinking and wife-beating, the courageous path taken by the heroine) and roundly condemned, being banned by W. H. Smith for mention of a lying-in hospital. As Esther battles on from one trauma to another, her bravery and pragmatism stand in contradistinction to the hypocrisy of clergy and of adherents to various religious codes. Unfairness in the judicial system is apparent, class snobbery is obvious and stereotyping is prevalent. It is noteworthy that those social issues feature as difficulties in Esther's life rather than being foregrounded from an authorial soapbox.

This literary treatment of contentious issues broke new ground in its disdain for existing English literary models as it eschewed the traditional pattern of rewards, punishments, and moral exhortations, and especially any 'happy ever after' conclusions. Moore zoned in on the ethically intolerable, presenting problematic facets of society without a concomitant and definite critique, and without deference towards privileged societal structures. Amongst the glaring examples of abuse in *Esther Waters*, there were two which would have garnered sympathy at a popular level and challenged religious precept: the denial of value to the life of an 'illegitimate' child by forcing the predatory purchase of its mother's milk; the victimisation of servants made pregnant by employers and their expulsion to penury in the name of preserving the sanctity of the employer's family. Moreover, the absence of closure drew the reader into the frame whether to protest and reject, to defend or to justify. Just as his art essays courted reaction, the twists and turns in the story of Esther enticed the reader into engagement.

Readers hoping for a similar novel to follow on immediately from the success of *Esther Waters* were not to be satisfied. The contrast between that book and Moore's volume *Celibates* (1895) is remarkable. Slums and sawdust, pubs and servant misery have vanished; the cast of *Celibates* is at home in drawing rooms, on tennis courts and at art classes in Paris. This change is paralleled by a transformation in form, style, tone, reference and focus. The umbrella title of *Celibates* shelters three separate stories whose eponymous central characters do not fit easily within the confines of Victorian gendering. Conflicts, entangled with religion, sexuality and education, are agonising for the particular individuals involved. John Norton, Mildred Lawson and Agnes Lahens are single persons whose life options are unduly restricted by their upbringing, by the expectations of an older generation and by societal norms. The institution of marriage is not an appealing one. In each story, society's persistent interest in establishing pairs is thwarted: the ambition of John's mother to generate an heir for the estate is unsuccessful; Mildred's brother wants to pass her to suitable male care and see her settled in marriage, but in her mind, marriage is what would befall her if she failed at art; Agnes is repelled by Mr Moulton's advances and particularly by old Lord Chislehurst who 'likes very young girls'.[3] The end of a family line is common to all three stories. The restlessness and discontent contest Victorian ideals of family and marriage and, in so doing, touch raw nerves in the context of ongoing concern with the condition of British manhood and womanhood, with the threat to patriarchal authority, with the New Woman and emergence of 'surplus' women, and with the vogue for religious and spiritual experience. In *Celibates*, a rich assembly of lightly sketched characters reflect those topical issues and refuse a certain future.

In yet another possibly unexpected turn, Moore had also involved himself in drama in 1893. Those focused on his stories might well have missed the publication in June 1893 of *The Strike at Arlingford*, a drama in three acts, which had been presented by the Independent Theatre Society at the Opera Comique in the Strand, London four months previously. Moore had been deeply concerned with promotion of the society, seeing it as modern in the mode of Ibsen and a positive development far removed from the prevalent melodramas. The play was not the first of Moore's several ventures into the theatre – it had been preceded by his involvement with Bernard Lopez on *Martin Luther* (1879) and by his cooperation with Augustus Moore in the translation of *Les Cloches de Corneville* (1883), and by *Le Sycomore* (1886), a translation (with Paul Alexis) of W. S. Gilbert's play *Sweethearts*. It would be followed by several solo and cooperative dramatic ventures, including *The Bending of the Bough* (1900) and *Diarmuid*

---

3   George Moore, *Celibates* (London: Walter Scott, 1895).

and Grania (1901). *The Strike at Arlingford* was not a success, although it might have been expected that its roman-à-clef traces would at least have given rise to some degree of comment.[4] Some critics allowed that it had literary merit but opined that Moore might be better to 'stick to his last' as a novelist, as he was one of the few writers to 'be seriously reckoned with'.[5] Looking back at Moore's previous interest in drama, and looking forward to his ongoing experiments with the genre – right up to *Aphrodite in Aulis* (1930) and *The Passing of the Essenes* (1930) – the subjects are very disparate. Moreover, it seems somewhat perplexing that he would persist with writing plays, despite his own 1911 admission to John Eglinton that, 'to press all the subtleties with which the subject is replete into dialogue seems to me a little beyond my talent'.[6] However, since he continued to strive for dramatic success and theatrical involvement, it suggests that this was another world where he wished to contribute, that he valued the immediacy of a stage presentation, and that drama was an additional vehicle through which he aspired to launch ideas, to challenge and to influence.

While Moore had been accused of inadequate acquaintance with, and insufficient research into, trade unions and socialism for *The Strike at Arlingford*, the same charges could not be levelled at his 1898 novel *Evelyn Innes* or at its linked novel *Sister Teresa* (1901). Often referred to as his music novels, and recognised for their psychological underpinning, their excellence was widely acclaimed, with praise coming for their erudition, for their accurate depiction of contemporary attitudes to early music and for the psychological understanding – 'treasures for the antiquarian and the connoisseur'.[7] The central character of *Evelyn Innes* moves from a sheltered

---

4   The central characters had much in common with Eleanor Marx and her then partner, Edward Aveling. Moore had been in contact with Marx since 1885.
5   That review in the *Academy* (February 893) also noted that the study was often penetrating and always fearless, 'of the kind of human nature it pleases Mr. Moore to be occupied with', even if it was thought that Moore was rather too pessimistic.
6   *Letters of George Moore* (Bournemouth: Sydenham & Co, 1942), 18. John Eglinton was the pseudonym of W. K. Magee, librarian at the National Library in Dublin and remained a long-term friend of Moore.
7   W. Wright Roberts, 'Musical Parlance in English Literature III', *Music & Letters* 6, no. 1 (January 1925), 3–4.

upbringing in a musical home devoted to early church music, to starring on operatic stages all over Europe, and then, torn by guilt and resultant unhappiness, she abandons lovers and moves temporarily to the convent of the Passionist Sisters. It is to that convent that Evelyn will return to be a nun in the subsequent volume *Sister Teresa*. The psychology underpinning her choices is rich. The story of Evelyn's life and loves reflects the dominant musical enthusiasms of the *fin de siècle*, whether the flourishing passions for Wagner, or the attractions of Italian opera, and it is counterpointed by the more esoteric return to the interests of her father: the earlier music of Palestrina, Vittoria and Ockeghem. Music forms a backdrop, echoes mood, functions as metaphor and meshes the sister arts in a mode appropriate to the synaesthetic fashion of the *fin de siècle*.[8]

Evelyn Innes is a novel that can be understood as a simple story of experience, sin and repentance,[9] or as commentary on the situation of a young female artiste who vacillates between lovers and the spiritual, between filial duty and career opportunity. It can be read as a depiction of well-known characters of the period with many discerning the figure of Yeats (and AE in later revisions) behind the character of Ulick Dean, and detecting a Moorian admixture of traits from the nature of acquaintances like William Eden and Lord Howard de Walden in constructing the character of Sir Owen Asher. *Evelyn Innes* may be construed through the lens of Wagnerian studies, both from the point of novelistic development in the period and in the light of prevailing Wagner mania. In Stoddard Martin's comprehensive analysis, the book is judged to be a 'loose chronological progress through all of Wagner's works, *Parsifal* finally having more to do with the heroine's progress from sex and the world to the Church than any other'.[10] Martin details the 'systematic paralleling' of Moore's novel with

---

8   For Moore's recourse to music right through his writing career see Mary S. Pierse, 'Moore's Music: Reading the Notes, Knowing the Score', in *George Moore: Influence and Collaboration*, edited by Ann Heilmann and Mark Lllewellyn (Delaware; London: University of Delaware Press, 2014), 53–67.

9   General critical interpretation at the time is neatly summarised by Jean C. Noël as 'une vulgaire intrigue amoureuse et l'histoire d'une conversion', Jean-C. Noël, *George Moore: l'homme et l'œuvre* (Paris: Marcel Didier, 1966), 279.

10 Stoddard Martin, *Wagner to 'The Waste Land'* (London; Basingstoke: Macmillan, 1982), 108.

Wagner's compositions, from *The Flying Dutchman*, to *Tannhauser*, *Parsifal*, *Lohengrin* and *Tristan und Isolde*.[11] Since both *Evelyn Innes* and *Sister Teresa* are saturated in Wagnerian atmosphere and reference, Moore's effective repudiation of the texts may surprise: in 1921, his verdict on *Evelyn Innes* and *Sister Teresa* was to refer to them as two of his most successful books but to also claim that, 'they do not correspond with my aestheticism'.[12] That denial of his literary compositions is thought-provoking. The change of mind is one possible key to his approach to creativity and, in addition, it may contribute towards explanation of what appears as his total disregard for establishing authorial recognition in the traditional manner.

A Deviation? An Interlude?

Moore may not have planned a divergence from novel to drama in 1899, but it was a digression that would soon enmesh him in a new Irish world from which would come some of his most remarkable fiction. That particular theatrical foray occurred between publication of *Evelyn Innes* and *Sister Teresa* and resulted from circumstances that saw him given ownership of Edward Martyn's play *The Tale of a Town*. It was Martyn who had enlisted Moore's help in preparing presentation of his own play, *The Heather Field*, and of Yeats's *The Countess Cathleen* in May 1899. Moore was perceived as the person amongst them with having most experience in drama. After many alterations to the text of *The Tale of a Town* – at Moore's suggestion and in collaboration with W. B. Yeats, AE, Lady Gregory and many others – Martyn refused to let his name feature as co-author with Moore. The play was renamed *The Bending of the Bough* and on its performance in the Gaiety Theatre in Dublin in February 1900 was deemed a public success. In that period, the Moore/Yeats partnership was also engaged in writing *Diarmuid and Grania*, a play performed at

---

11   *Ibid.*, 104–110.
12   George Moore, 'Preface to the New Edition of 1921', in *The Lake* (Gerrards Cross, Bucks: Colin Smythe, 1980), x–xi.

the same theatre in autumn 1901, in the third season of the Irish Literary Theatre. The fraught negotiations for all the plays were the stuff of real drama in their mélange of comedy, melodrama, wheeling and dealing, back-stabbing, factional disagreement, and conflicting ideologies. A parting of the ways of Yeats and Lady Gregory from Martyn and Moore was not long in coming and Moore was not invited to be part of the Irish National Theatre Society (1903) or the Abbey Theatre (1904). It was clear that while, 'the spirit of contagious creativity Moore generated [...] exhilarated Yeats',[13] they had reached a fork in the road on their aesthetic and political journeys, and the jealousy and envy of artistic rivalry fuelled degrees of mutual mistrust. Nonetheless, and in the short term, it did not prevent Moore from helping Yeats with *The Shadowy Waters* (first produced in January 1904)[14] and with a draft of the Cuchulainn story that subsequently became *On Baile's Strand*, (first performed at the official opening of the Abbey Theatre on 27 December 1904).[15]

On reading *The Bending of the Bough* and *The Tale of a Town*,[16] it is obvious that the final version retains much of Martyn and that it never became a truly Moore play. The concept was Martyn's, the *dramatis personae* and much of Martyn's dialogue remain although the characterisation has been enlivened and the resolution of painful choice is sharper. The options in crowd-pleasing one-liners differ. The final act of *The Bending of the Bough* has Kirwan advise Jasper Dean to join an antiquarian society since he has opted to marry English Millicent rather than stand by the nationalist cause. Kirwan also says that, 'The cause is not lost but the next opportunity will come to a new man'. The relevance of those judgements

---

13 Adrian Frazier, *George Moore 1852-1933* (New Haven; London: Yale University Press, 2000), 281.
14 Available online: <Irishplayography.com> [accessed 8 July 2020].
15 The Oxford Reference site credits Lady Gregory as co-author, available online: <https://www.oxfordreference.com/view/10.1093/oi/authority.20110803100249811> [accessed 8 July 2020]. However, Adrian Frazier quotes Gregory as saying that Moore had a hand in the process and was 'resolving himself into a syndicate for the re-writing of plays', Frazier, *George Moore*, 316.
16 The full text of both plays is provided in *Selected Plays of George Moore and Edward Martyn* (Gerrards Cross, Bucks: Colin Smythe, 1995).

was not lost on the audience. *Par contre*, in Act V of *The Tale of a Town*, Millicent only proposed 'congenial political activities' and a timid Jasper finds her suggestion 'a sympathetic way of putting things'. With the English national anthem sounding,[17] and the Town Hall cleaner waving a Union Jack, Kirwan bitterly concludes: 'For us, this is always the Tale of a Town'. In both versions, development of the story had appealing features which, in their final rendering, resonated with contemporary theatre-goers. However, in 1900 Moore was already refocusing, both on his return to finish *Sister Teresa* and on dealing with matter-in-hand, the provision of scenes for *Diarmuid and Grania*.

Moore was involved in direction of two other theatrical ventures in 1901 and 1902. The first was Douglas Hyde's *Casadh an tSúgáin* with amateur actors from the Gaelic League, including Hyde himself. The production was hailed by an animated audience which applauded it at the Gaiety Theatre on 21 October 1901. Moore then persuaded Hyde to write *The Tinker and the Fairy*, and organised its staging, *as Gaeilge*, as *AnTincéar agus an tSidheóg* before an invited audience of about 200 in his garden at Ely Place in May 1902. Moore, a relatively new campaigner for the Irish language, sought and valued the connection to Hyde who was joint founder with Eoin Mac Neill of the Gaelic League (Conradh na Gaeilge), and was its president for many years. Moore recognised the potential propaganda value to the League of theatre productions and pushed for more.[18] Adrian Frazier describes Moore's 'characteristically immoderate enthusiasm for a new idea'[19] and undoubtedly, his passionate articles on the importance of the Irish language exude the fervour of a new convert.[20] The title of one such article, 'A Plea for the Soul of the irish people', might stand as banner

---

17   The actual wording of the stage note is 'The English national anthem is heard on a band outside'.
18   Declan Kiberd, 'George Moore's Gaelic Lawn Party', in *The Way Back*, edited by Robert Welch (Dublin: Wolfhound Press, 1982), 13–27.
19   Frazier, *George Moore*, 284.
20   For instance, his essay 'The Irish Literary Renaissance and the Irish Language' in *New Ireland Review* (April 1900); his talk on 'Literature and the Irish Language', published in *Ideals in Ireland* (1901), edited by Lady Gregory; his 'A Plea for the Soul of the irish people', in *Nineteenth Century* (February 1901).

for his language crusade in 1901, but it has resonance and relevance too for his subsequent texts as he came to comprehend a reality of life in Ireland which undercut the fiction of a Gaelic renaissance and was light years away from his experience and expectation. As he settled into life in Dublin, it was from this new base that he embarked on publications that would break fresh literary ground on his own creative journey and supply fresh stimulus and example for others.

In Ireland – and at Home?

In terms of a swing from the Wagnerian vogue and the lengthy musings of *Evelyn Innes* and *Sister Teresa*, and from attention to the stage, the change to the pared prose of *The Untilled Field* (April 1903) is radical. A suggestion that GM might produce a collection of short stories, rather in the style of Turgenev's *Tales of a Sportsman*,[21] was the immediate spur, but ideas had been hatching in Moore's mind for a long time prior to his return to Ireland.[22] In late autumn of 1901, the task began and Moore's intentions were clear: 'The book is a perfect unity'; he did not want it seen 'as a collection of short stories'. He toyed with different titles, including *The Passing of the Gael*, and as early as June 1902, he could state that, 'every story tells how this country is going to pieces'.[23] He further elaborated: 'I am painting a portrait of my own country'.[24] As part of his crusade for Irish-language literature, his story of 'An Gúna Pósta' appeared in the *New*

---

21 Attributed to John Eglinton by Joseph Hone, *The Life of George Moore* (London: Victor Gollancz, 1936), 242. Richard Allan Cave credits Clara Christian with the idea. Richard Cave, *A Study of the Novels of George Moore* (New York: Irish Literary Studies/Barnes & Noble, 1978), 168.

22 George Moore, 'Turguenoff' in *Impressions and Opinions* (1891), 'an object, skillfully indicated, has a charm that a complete painting cannot have', 76; 'a bare narrative should possess the same intellectual charms as the psychological novel', 90.

23 Letter to Fisher Unwin, 7 February 1902. Reproduced in Helmut Gerber (ed.), *George Moore in Transition* (Detroit: Wayne State University Press, 1968).

24 *Ibid*. Letter to Fisher Unwin, 4 June 1902.

Ireland Review[25] and it was to be one of the six stories of *An tÚr-Ghort*, published under the name of Seorsa Ó Mordha in 1902, thus taking precedence over *The Untilled Field* some months later. There was no excited reaction to *An tÚr-Ghort*,[26] the sales were minimal, and the Gaelic League factions were not disposed to promote the book or to espouse Moore's idea of translating classics into Irish.[27] It cannot be said that such negativity affected composition of *The Untilled Field* since many of the stories had already been completed. Moore had ploughed that furrow, aware that there were many predisposed to dislike depictions of Ireland which were not safely contained in myth and legend.

Contemporary literary appraisals of *The Untilled Field* ranged widely. In the *Mercure de France*, the reviewer noted that GM's realism was exact, and that his sympathy and love for Ireland were charming. Sympathy was also the quality noted in the *Daily Chronicle*. *The Athenaeum* praised Moore's intuitive perception, vivid pictures and concluded it was a 'sound piece of work'. For *Das Literische Echo* (Berlin), the political statements seemed to be more important than the artistic pattern.[28] As 'a perfect unity', in a portrait of Ireland, *The Untilled Field* portrays only a rural Ireland – to which Joyce's *Dubliners* might be seen as an urban sequel and response – where poverty and bleakness are both compounded and relieved by individuals.

---

25 Letter to James Huneker, 11 July 1902, quoted by Gerber, *George Moore in Transition*, 253.

26 In January 1902, *The New Ireland Review* also published 'Tóir Mhic an Dhíomasuigh' (November 1902) and 'An Déirc' (December 1902). All were subsequently revised, re-translated and appeared in *The Untilled Field*. A review in *The Academy* (London on 2 August 1902, 'Mr George Moore done into Irish') said it was 'free from polemics and political ardour' and that Moore offered a new focus.

27 Padraigin Riggs provides detailed background to translation and reception in 'An tÚr-Ghort and The Untilled Field', in *George Moore: Artistic Visions and Literary Worlds*, edited by Mary Pierse, 130–141. Declan Kiberd points out that in the longer run, 'Moore's flirtation with the Gaelic movement proved surprisingly influential', since the Irish government sponsored a scheme from 1926 to translate the classics into Irish. Kiberd, op cit., 27.

28 All quotations are from 1903 reviews qtd. in Robert Langenfeld, *George Moore: An Annotated Secondary Bibliography of Writings about Him* (New York: AMS Press, 1987).

Moore would claim that *The Lake* was 'my landscape book',[29] but in the literary innovation of the themed and unified *The Untilled Field*, his minimalist locale paintings also constitute an effective medium for the message. The non-verbal images double the aesthetic force, the mindscape becomes a catalyst to reader reaction.

With yet another turn and development in his prose, Moore then produced *The Lake* (1905), the first English-language stream-of-consciousness novel, one interwoven with epistolary exchanges.[30] Symbolism is rich, rendering of thought and speech is extended, the sensory quality of the backdrop abounds in visual, tactile and aural elements, all combining subtly to accompany and convey the inner voyage of Fr Oliver Gogarty. The landscape can be dreamy and romantic. This is a novel that is musical, even as it is contemporary in its unobtrusive sprinkling of up-to-date references to trains, price of livestock, and industrial accident, and mixed with reference to an ancient Celtic heritage and continuing debate on dogma.[31] With a degree of superficial simplicity, Moore has created a complex work that is psychologically rich and artistically intricate and which, if his creative journey had halted at that point, would have constituted a triumphant climax for any authorial oeuvre.

A Moorian Plan?

One of the first things that must be realised about Moore's literary output in the *fin-de-siècle* period is that it cannot be viewed as the result of a comprehensive authorial roadmap, or even an outline plan. Its every disparate

---

29   George Moore, *Letters 1895-1933 to Lady Cunard*, edited by. Rupert Hart-Davis (London: 1957), 45. For further consideration of Moore's use of landscape, see Mary Pierse, 'Inside and outside the frame: landscape pictures and real debates in *The Untilled Field* (1903) and *The Lake* (1905)' in *Land and Landscape in Nineteenth-Century Ireland*, edited by Una Ní Bhroiméil and Glenn Hooper (Dublin: Four Courts Press, 2008), 145–155.

30   Frazier judges it to be a 'stylistic *tour de force*', 347.

31   Pierse, 'Inside and Outside the Frame', 145–155.

twist and turn of genre and style arose from deep-seated drive and enthusiasm, forces that did not diminish with time, and which propelled and fuelled his pioneering cultural activity. There are elements of the spirit of modernism within its urge to 'make it new', but the possibility of that achievement is less attributable to a literary programme and is infinitely more due to aspects of George Moore's own being: an inexorable and ongoing absorption in whatever world he found himself, combined with a judgement that was remarkably dispassionate, and the compulsion to translate his assessments and conclusions into the written word. Often, that transposition would be accomplished in innovatory fashion and incorporate the sister arts, it frequently displayed Moore's attachment to his birthplace and it always sought to promote freedom. Absorption, judgement, heritage, innovatory art and above all freedom were always present.

Artistic development can be marked by ability to change or modify style and in Moore's case, he appears to have been in perpetual motion at the end of the nineteenth century. If the reading and playgoing public registered protest or upset, it was because they were confronted (often gently) by a difficult present rather than allowed to bask in images of a safe future clothed in the clichéd beliefs, myths or party line of times past. Writing in *Hail and Farewell* about Édouard Manet, Moore declared: 'The work of the great artist is himself', and 'Art is a personal rethinking of life'.[32] Those opinions describe the essence of Moore and the supporting evidence is to be found in his writings where life is continuously re-assessed and reconsidered. Such texts display his artistic mode of intertwining the arts – in keeping with the reciprocity that was in the air – both in his use of techniques of the pictorial world and his interweaving of music, use of musical form and reference.[33] Apparent in his lines, there is patent sympathy, empathy, humanity, and a resultant determination to make manifest the injustices and inequalities that shackle body and soul. The concerns are always of the present, a time indicated by very contemporary issues, whether ideological, literary, philosophical, social or literary – and regardless of

32 George Moore, 'Vale', in *Hail and Farewell* (Gerrards Cross, Bucks: Colin Smythe, 1985), 532, 533.
33 Moore used symphonic form in the structure of *Esther Waters*.

whether they featured prominently in topical discussion. Indeed, public silence on such matters would appear to impel Moore into addressing them. The GM mode is to travel far from the classic forms of drama, epic, tragedy and to counteract a prevailing tendency to situate novels in the past. Certain closure is eschewed, and particularly that of the 'happy ending'. While essays on art advance strong opinions, and seek to educate, fiction can evince purposely inconclusive narrative that is rich in its suggestive power. What surfaced on the page was often painted with art, carefully shaped, a musical in form and notes.

Moore's Worlds

From the time of his birth at Moore Hall, Moore spent significant periods of his life living successively in London, Paris, London, Dublin and London. In and from each location, he absorbed atmosphere and attitudes and drew on various elements from those sojourns. His successive experiences flooded into prose on art (*Modern Painting*), into analysis of social structures and individual plights (*Esther Waters* and *The Untilled Field*), into psychology (*Celibates, Evelyn Innes, Sister Teresa*), into cultural movements (*The Untilled Field, The Lake*). Zola, Flaubert, Balzac, D'Annunzio and Dujardin loomed large in his list of literary personages who interested and influenced him. His Parisian interactions with painters, notably with Manet, Monet and Degas, but also with developing and fading fashions in style and beliefs, were to be invaluable. The vogue for Wagner provided Moore with a basis for *Evelyn Innes* – probably the first Wagnerian novel in English – wherein parallels between Evelyn's thoughts and situations, in addition to the opposing interpretations of Wagner by the characters Owen and Ulick, are soaked in Wagnerian opera. Similar Wagnerian shades and tone pervade and permeate *Sister Teresa*. Every Wagnerian encounter in France, London and Bayreuth bore literary fruit.

Then came zeal and zest for Ireland and its culture. As he wrote in 1900, 'you must live the subject'.[34] This was exactly what he had done

---

34   Letter to Nia Crawford, April 1900, Ms 2645, National Library of Ireland.

previously: he used his involvement with a travelling actor company when writing *A Mummer's Wife* (1885); his close observance of the cruel marriage market provided the material for *A Drama in Muslin* (1886); his Parisian friendships with artists gave further insight, allowing him to discern the academy-flouting nature of Impressionist art and apply the lessons to art criticism. Accordingly, he jumped right into promotion of Irish language, drama and literature, and even into searching for druids with AE at Newgrange. Yet, devotion to a cause did not blind his appraising eye or deter it from detecting idiosyncrasy, illogicality, abuse of power, inequality, pusillanimity. The unadorned prose of the *Untilled Field* lays bare many of those characteristics, as do the flowing, musical and perceptive paintings of *The Lake*.

Moore was not a Victorian didact, hence he chose different methods to expose what he saw as wrongs, be they employment conditions, poverty, imprisoning interpretations of religious precepts, crippling stereotypes that were limiting both to men and women, a loaded judicial system, or the blindness of the Big House class. Often recognised as a feminist – and justifiably so for his recognition of the restrictions imposed on women – he deserves plaudits too for pinpointing how lack of money disempowered men, since in terms of Victorian beliefs, it stripped them of status and power and thereby called male identity into question.[35] Moore showed marriage in various forms: happy marriages are notably absent in *Esther Waters* and women are the marital victims. In *Celibates*, Agnes, the lost child of a miserable marriage (an adulterous mother and a disempowered father), has neither positive model nor white knight to save her, so she refuses any marriage and retreats to a convent. In the same book, in the story 'John Norton', Moore undermines the Victorian code that attributed blame to rape victims as he enlists sympathy for the fate of raped Kitty.

John Eglinton (W. Magee) identified George Moore as 'a soul in contact with some perennial source of caustic insight and salutary disillusionment'.[36] In any consideration of Moore's *fin de siècle* literary work, it seems

---

35   In 'Agnes Lahens', the figure of Major Lahens is a case in point.
36   The description occurs in Eglinton's 'Introduction' to *Letters from George Moore to Ed. Dujardin 1886-1922* (New York: Crosby Gaige, 1929), 7. He repeats it in John Eglinton, *Irish Literary Portraits* (London: Macmillan, 1935), 86.

very obvious that he was a man of enthusiasms, some of them sequential, and all fired by a spirit that would not settle for limitation of freedom in personal or artistic terms. He believed that 'a man without allegiance is like a ball of thistledown'.[37] His own artistic contributions were considerably weightier than such flying seed bursts although, like thistledown, they flew in myriad directions and, ironically, rather than advertise the author's talent and versatility, their very dispersed diversity contributed to the ultimate diffusion of George Moore's own author recognition.

Et, en fin de compte?

George Moore's *fin de siècle* was a period of innovation and experiment and its interest continued, not just during his following, prolific years. A century later, the qualities of libertarianism, bravery and multifaceted artistry continue to resonate, and they have drawn a new readership for Moore's texts. The appreciative readers include students, academics and independent individuals from five continents. The past decade has seen ten international conferences, in Ireland, France, England, Monaco and Spain, each devoted to exploration of the Moore oeuvre and enjoyment of Moorian fun. Delegates have travelled from all corners of Europe, and from Japan, Australia, USA, Brazil, Argentina, Israel and Canada; the deliberations have resulted in several books[38] and numerous articles on a wide range of topics. A new George Moore Association has been formed, a very egalitarian group that houses Moore relatives, art aficionados, history buffs, teachers of English, drama enthusiasts, and it is open to all.

---

37   Letter to Maud Cunard, 9 January 1906 in *George Moore, Letters to Lady Cunard, 1895-1933*, 48.
38   Six books and many articles have already been published following the biennial conferences, and other publications are expected shortly.

Perhaps there should be no surprise that there is a twenty-first century Moorian world, one where Moore studies flourish and his significance is perceived and embraced. It is the diversity of genre, the breadth of vision, the 'caustic insight' that attract; it is Moore's ever-fresh honesty, individualism, tolerance and nonconformism that strike chords with a generation which appreciates his insights into multiple forms of sexuality, his support for gender equality and his unrelenting drive for freedom.

BRIAN MURPHY

5 Drinking Spaces in Strange Places: New Directions in Irish Beverage Research

The quotidian task of consuming beverage is something that appears remarkably simple and is part of normal activity for those of us lucky enough to live in a bountiful society. Like food, it is a necessary sustenance without which the human body cannot survive. And yet, down through the centuries the drinks we consume and the way in which we consume them have become cultural signifiers that can tell us much about who we are. Many research areas have their origins in the more practical and applied aspects of life and food studies is perhaps the most pertinent example of this. Despite recently becoming a field of study in its own right, it still struggles at times to be considered worthy of serious academic endeavour. Warren Belasco suggests that:

> Even now, with the rising interest in food studies, a serious analysis of family dinner rituals, cookbooks, or the appeal of fast food may still evoke surprise and even scorn. 'Do professors really study that?' your friends and family ask. 'If you're going to go around telling your colleagues you are a philosopher of food', philosopher Lisa Heldke writes, 'you better be prepared to develop a thick skin – and start a wisecrack collection'.[1]

As an important subset of food studies, beverage scholars have also been developing their own distinct research field; and this chapter posits that recent forays into beverage studies have the potential to play an important role in an Irish Studies context. A context that has reached far into many other interdisciplinary areas including sport, food and tourism. The developing role of beverage studies presents an interesting topic when

---

1   Warren Belasco, *Food: The Key Concepts* (New York: Berg, 2008), 1.

viewed through an epistemological lens. Its history lies in the applied arts of service and hospitality.

Down through the years, beverage as part of the dining experience became enhanced through the change from *service à la française* in the nineteenth century into *service à la russe*[2] which placed a focus on serving selected wines as opposed to guests choosing for themselves what to drink. In more recent times we have seen an increasing value placed upon cocktail, barista and sommelier skills with the global success of Netflix programmes such *Somm*, a proliferation of wine, spirit and coffee courses and opportunities for professionals and the general public to undertake formal beverage qualifications. In tandem with the rise of food studies and the emergence of a gastronomic cultural field in Ireland,[3] its as yet less renowned cousin beverage has started to emerge as an area worthy of academic study in its own right. There have also been considerable developments regarding the formal recognition of beverage qualifications in third-level institutions with the development of degrees in areas such as Beverage Management, Wine Studies, Brewing and Distilling. From an Irish research perspective, there has been notable beverage research output across a number of academic platforms including the biennial Dublin Gastronomy Symposium, the Association of Franco-Irish Studies, the Beverage Research Network and within the National Centre for Franco-Irish Studies, all of whom have endeavoured to include and promote beverage studies as part of their research output through annual conferences, seminars, publications and events.

Despite the prevalence of beverage in daily life, prior to the intervention of the aforementioned groups, it has traditionally remained in the wings when it comes to interpreting its value through an Irish academic lens. Areas of Irish Studies are broad and typically were closely aligned to

---

2   Prior to the nineteenth century, the meal experience consisted of a large number of dishes and drinks presented together at the same time for guests to help themselves. This was known a *service à la française*. With the development of *service à la russe*, guests began to choose their dishes from a formalised menu and waiting staff had a bigger role in serving particular wines with foods of choice.

3   Brian Murphy, 'A Hundred Thousand Welcomes: Food and Wine as Cultural Signifiers', in *From Prosperity to Austerity: A Socio-cultural Critique of the Celtic Tiger and its Aftermath*, edited by Eamon Maher and Eugene O' Brien (Manchester: Manchester University Press, 2014), 161–173.

postcolonial studies, literature and history at the start. This chapter argues for the consideration of beverage studies as part of the Irish Studies research agenda because of its importance as a backdrop for many cultural aspects of Irish life. Understanding beverage in Ireland means understanding its role in our history, the nature of beverage consumption spaces and their role in Irish commensality. Beverages have much to tell us about human nature and how we interact with others. Our beverage identity has been exported around the world through products like Guinness, Irish whiskey, Baileys and the ubiquitous Irish pub, which has also become a strong vehicle of cultural export.

This chapter is not confined to alcoholic beverages and considers the role of Ireland's emerging coffee culture, the rise of non-alcoholic products and their potential in shaping future generations of Irish people. The recent Covid-19 crisis has impacted on how we interact with drinking and our drinking spaces. In fact, this chapter was started on the 29 June 2020, the first day that restaurants and pubs that serve food were allowed to reopen following the unprecedented Covid lockdown in the months prior to that. The restrictions imposed have presented many with a vista of how our lives are changed when the social spaces, that up to now have been the fabric of many of our lives, are suddenly removed. The significant consequences of this removal have been amplified during this period and the reimagining of our drinking spaces has had significant implications sociologically. There are many examples down through our history where strong associations have been made between the abuse of alcohol and what it means to be Irish. However, more recently our relationship with our drinking spaces has started to change and it is this changed landscape that begs strong consideration when considering the role of beverage in Irish Studies.

Setting a Context

The area of beverage studies can be divided into three main categories. Firstly, we have the practical, more applied aspect of beverage studies populated by an ontology of drinks understanding, ingredients, methods and hospitality skills dominated by an extensive level of product knowledge and awareness among practitioners. This is a world populated by masters of wine, mixologists, sommeliers, restaurateurs, baristas and bar tenders. It is also an area that has been well serviced by further and higher education in Ireland in recent decades through a wide variety of practically focused programmes. Secondly, we have an area of academic discourse that deals primarily with beverage through the lens of business and science. This area explores topics such as the health impacts of beverage consumption, the societal effects of alcohol abuse and the economic consequences of the drinks industry. It is an area which frequently dominates political discourse and it can be argued that in some cases has led to a diminution of the importance of beverage culture in Irish society. The final category of beverage studies and the principal subject of this chapter concerns an area of academic study that explores other important aspects of the beverage world. Neither applied nor business focused, this category deals with issues including gastronomic identity, communication of *terroir*, the language and lexicon of drinks and the semiotics of drinks products. It explores the sociological history of drinks and the role beverage spaces can play in cultural expression. All three beverage categories intersect at various points and are interdependent on each other. They all have something to offer within a general cultural studies context, but it is the final one that most lends itself to an Irish Studies research agenda.

A Developing Literature

There have been considerable developments in beverage literature and although an exhaustive review is beyond the scope of this chapter there are a number of important sources that should be identified. Early forays in an Irish context focused on the wine world and both Renagh Holohan's *The Irish Chateaux*,[4] and T. P. Whelehan's *The Irish Wines of Bordeaux* (1990)[5]

4   Renagh Holohan, *The Irish Chateaux: In Search of the Wild Geese* (Dublin: Lilliput Press, 1989).
5   T. P. Whelehan, *The Irish Wines of Bordeaux* (Dublin: The Vine Press, 1990).

demonstrated interest in the field. In 1998, Elisabeth Malcolm explored the pub in both a cultural and historical context in an important chapter entitled 'The Rise of the Irish Pub: A study in the disciplining of popular culture' that featured in *Irish Popular Culture 1650-1850*.[6] In 1996, Kevin Kearns published *Dublin Pub Life and Lore: An Oral History*[7] which explored the pub's impact on Irish cultural life through the testimonies of publicans and barmen. Cian Molloy's 2003 book *The Story of the Irish Pub*[8] offered another key text exploring the history of the pub and the families that were key to its evolution. Ted Murphy's important and substantial tome *A Kingdom of Wine*[9] was first published in 2005, with a revised edition published in 2013, and it charts the drinking traditions, wine making and wine trading history of the Irish from pre-Christian times to the present day. There continued to be considerable interest in the study of the Irish Pub and following sociologist Perry Share's early incorporation of Oldenburg's 'Third Place' concept in the context of the Irish Pub,[10] 2008 saw the publication of Gwen Scarborough's PhD, *The Irish Pub as Third Place: A Sociological Exploration of People Place and Identity*.[11]

In terms of more technical books, the beverage education sector frequently relied on both UK and US texts. However, tourism organisations

---

6   Elisabeth Malcolm, 'The Rise of the Irish Pub: A Study in the Disciplining of Popular Culture', in *Irish Popular Culture 1650-1850*, edited by James S. Donnelly and Kerby A. Miller (Dublin: Irish Academic Press, 1998), 50–75.
7   Kevin C. Kearns, *Dublin Pub Life and Lore: An Oral History* (Dublin: Gill Books, 1996).
8   Cian Molloy, *The Story of the Irish Pub: An Intoxicating History of the Licensed Trade in Ireland* (Dublin: The Liffey Press, 2003).
9   Ted Murphy, *A Kingdom of Wine: A Celebration of Ireland's Winegeese* (Cork: Onstream Publications, 2005).
10 Perry Share, 'A Genuine "Third Place"? Towards an Understanding of the Pub in Contemporary Irish Society' (Sociological Association Ireland Conference, Cavan, 2003), available online: <https://nanopdf.com/download/third-place-institute-of-technology-sligo_pdf> [accessed 23 September 2020].
11 Gwen Scarborough, *The Irish Pub as a 'Third Place': A Sociological Exploration of People, Place and Identity* (PhD Thesis, Institute of Technology Sligo, 2008).

such as the Council for Education, Recruitment and Training (CERT) and industry bodies such as the Vintners Federation of Ireland (VFI) produced a number of useful trade manuals, texts and guides down through the years that helped with delivery on many beverage-related training courses. In 2013, James Murphy added two very important and comprehensive educational texts, *Principles and Practices of Bar and Beverage Management*,[12] and *Principles and Practices of Bar and Beverage Management: The Drinks Handbook*.[13] These books were a significant contribution to the beverage education canon and provided a much-needed Irish text for applied practitioners in the area. Ireland's pub culture again came to the fore in 2013, this time through a new medium with Alex Fegan's widely acclaimed film documentary *The Irish Pub*,[14] which was released to both cinema audiences and on DVD in 2013. It offered a unique historical and cultural insight into the role of the pub in Irish society. Among the many books published on Irish Whiskey and other drinks products, Fionnán O' Connor's 2015 book *A Glass Apart*[15] stands out as offering an erudite exploration of the historical importance Irish Single Pot Still Whiskey, the origins of Irish Whiskey in general and its important recent revival. Ireland's beverage culture crossed media boundaries once again with Susan Boyle's unique show *A Wine Goose Chase*.[16] The one-woman performance integrates wine tasting, history, music and drama and has been running at various locations and food festivals throughout Ireland since the show's inception at the Aboslut Dublin Fringe Festival in 2012. Kevin Martin's 2016 publication *Have You No*

---

12 James Murphy, *Principles and Practices of Bar and Beverage Management* (Oxford: Goodfellow Publisher, 2013).
13 James Murphy, *Principles and Practices of Bar and Beverage Management: The Drinks Handbook* (Oxford: Goodfellow Publisher, 2013).
14 Alex Fegan, *The Irish Pub* (Element Pictures Distribution, 2013).
15 Fionnán O'Connor, *A Glass Apart: Irish Single Pot Still Whiskey* (Mulgarve, Victoria: The Images Publishing Group, 2015).
16 Brian Murphy, 'A Wine Goose Chase Reviewed', *Canadian Journal of Irish Studies* 41 (2018), 292–294, available online: <https://www.jstor.org/stable/e26435216> [accessed 23 September 2020].

Homes to Go to[17] provided yet another excellent historical insight into the Irish pub and its role in Irish society. Finally, well-known Irish historian Diarmuid Ferriter has also written extensively on the country's historical association with drink and both his book *Nation of Extremes: Pioneers in Twentieth-century Ireland*[18] and the recent chapter, 'Drink and society in twentieth-century Ireland' in *Food and Drink in Ireland*[19] are important examples which examine and debate controversies and trends in relation to the consumption of alcoholic drink in twentieth-century Ireland and its role in stereotyping Irish identity.

There are also many wine writers and journalists who have contributed to Ireland's unique beverage culture. Names like John Wilson, Mary Dowey, Ernie Whalley and Mairtin Moran immediately spring to mind, but special mention must be made of the recently deceased Tomás Clancy, wine correspondent with the *Sunday Business Post*; his weekly articles frequently moved beyond wine writing and description and delved into the historical and cultural context of beverage and its engagement with Irish society. A keen supporter of beverage research in Ireland, Clancy was always available to lend an encouraging hand to those engaged in drinks research endeavours.

In addition to the beverage literature mentioned above, there are a variety of research projects currently underway in Irish beverage studies areas. These projects are housed in a number of research centres that have been at the forefront in promoting beverage research in recent years.

---

17   Kevin Martin, *Have You No Homes to Go to* (Cork Collins Press, 2016).
18   Diarmuid Ferriter, *Nation of Extremes: Pioneers in Twentieth-Century Ireland* (Dublin: Irish Academic Press, 1999).
19   Diarmuid Ferriter, 'Drink and Society in Twentieth-Century Ireland', in *Food and Drink in Ireland*, edited by Elisabeth Fitzpatrick and James Kelly (Dublin: The Royal Irish Academy, 2016).

The School of Culinary Arts and Food Technology

The School of Culinary Arts and Food Technology at Technological University Dublin (TU Dublin) has been at the heart of food and beverage education for over seventy five years. Based in Cathal Brugha Street, the School has long been recognised as a centre of excellence with a wide array of courses specific to the drinks industry from higher certificate to honours degree level. In more recent years the School has developed an extensive beverage research agenda and currently has a number of postgraduate projects exploring a diverse range of themes as follows:

Project Title	Author
Formal wine writing in Ireland (1975 – 2005)	Diarmuid Cawley
What's in a wash? The historical trajectories and contemporary potential of Irish Whiskey mash bills from 1779–1975	Fionnán O Connor
Irish country pubs as perceived and experienced through the lens of Irish publicans (1960–2022)	James McCauley
The social meaning of Claret in the lives of Georgian Ireland's elite	Tara McConnell

There have already been substantial research outputs from these projects including conference organisation, presentation and publications. Tara McConnell has recently published a chapter entitled 'The Social Meaning of Claret in Eighteenth Century Ireland' in *The Irish Community in Bordeaux in the Eighteenth Century: Contributions and Contexts*.[20] RTÉ's *Brainstorm*[21] is another important academic platform, and hosts

---

20 Tara McConnell, 'The Social Meaning of Claret in Eighteenth Century Ireland', in *The Irish Community in Bordeaux in the Eighteenth Century: Contributions and Contexts*, edited by Charles C. Luddington (New Haven: Yale University Press). Forthcoming.

21 RTÉ's *Brainstorm* is a partnership between RTÉ and Irish third level institutions, University College Cork, NUI Galway, University of Limerick, DCU, Technological University Dublin and Maynooth University. The Irish Research Council and Teagasc are also promoters of the online platform.

Diarmuid Cawley's pieces, 'All you ever wanted to know about natural wines'[22] and 'A nose for wine: all you need to know about sommeliers'.[23] James McCauley has also been published on *Brainstorm* with titles including 'The death of the Irish rural publican'[24] and 'What's next for the Irish pub?'[25]

The National Centre for Franco-Irish Studies

The National Centre for Franco-Irish Studies (NCFIS), under the direction of Dr Eamon Maher, is based in TU Dublin and provides another important Irish beverage research hub. Though historically focused on more traditional humanities research areas, it has recently encouraged and supported a number of gastronomic projects. Current post graduate research projects underway at the Centre include:

Project Title	Researcher
A study of the cultural representation of the Irish Pub	Aoife Carrigy
How theatre practice and performance shapes experiential engagements within the Irish beer and whiskey industry	Susan Boyle
Irish Whiskey and cultural identity: From the making to the commodification of a signifier of Irishness	Sylvain Tondeur

22   Diarmuid Cawley, 'All You Ever Wanted to Know about Natural Wines', available online: <hrrps://www.rte.ie/brainstorm/2018/0814/985019-guide-to-natural-wines/> [accessed 16 September 2020].
23   Diarmuid Cawley, 'A Nose for Wine: All You Need to Know about Sommeliers', available online: <https://www.rte.ie/brainstorm/2019/0314/1036356-a-nose-for-wine-all-you-need-to-know-about-sommeliers/> [accessed 16 September 2020].
24   James McCauley, 'The Death of the Irish Rural Publican', available online: <https://www.rte.ie/brainstorm/2019/0418/1043366-the-death-of-the-irish rural publican/> [accessed 16 October 2020].
25   James McCauley, 'What's Next for the Irish Pub?', available online: <https://www.rte.ie/brainstorm/2020/0507/1136959-pubs-ireland-future-coronavirus/> [accessed 17 October 2020].

Over the last ten years the NCFIS has also supported other projects where beverage culture and Irish Studies have been foregrounded, including *Exploring the Role of Place and Story in Perceptions of French Wine Culture*[26] and *Five Decades of Guinness Advertising in Ireland: Increments of Change.*[27] In addition, the Centre publishes the *Journal of Franco-Irish Studies*[28] and the recent sixth volume of this journal was entirely devoted to beverage culture.[29]

The Dublin Gastronomy Symposium

There have been a number of academic conferences in Ireland where beverage studies has found a willing platform in terms of both presentation and publication. Since its inaugural conference in 2012, the Dublin Gastronomy Symposium (DGS) has provided a unique forum for beverage research. Chaired by Dr Máirtín Mac Con Iomaire from TU Dublin and heavily focused on food studies, each of its biennial conferences has contained panels and papers on drinks. In addition, the DGS, in collaboration with the NCFIS, was core to the development of the Beverage Research Network which has organised beverage culture research seminars in 2015, 2017 and 2019. The DGS also provides an extensive academic resource in the form of the DGS Arrow portal.[30] Prominent beverage papers available on this online platform include, 'The Power of

---

26   Brian Murphy, PhD Thesis (2013).
27   Patricia Medcalf, PhD Thesis (2017).
28   *The Journal of Franco-Irish Studies* is a peer reviewed postgraduate online journal that seeks to explore relevant intersections and shared experiences between France and Ireland.
29   *JOFIS* Volume 6, available online: <https://arrow.tudublin.ie/jofis/> [accessed 10 October 2020].
30   The DGS hosts an extensive resource of its papers on the TU Dublin Arrow platform, available online: <https://arrow.tudublin.ie/dgs/> [accessed 10 October 2020].

Wine Language: Critics, Labels and Sexism',[31] 'Powerful Puzzles: Mapping the Symbiosis Between Two Great Signifiers of Irishness, The Writer and The Pub',[32] 'Claret: the preferred libation of Georgian Ireland's élite',[33] 'Shaken not Stirred – The Evolution of the Cocktail Shaker',[34] 'The Irish Whiskey Renaissance: A Revolution of Sorts?'[35] and 'Guinness and Food: Ingredients in an Unlikely Gastronomic Revolution'.[36]

The Association of Franco-Irish Studies

The Association of Franco-Irish Studies (AFIS) is an international collaborative network of institutions and scholars, formed in 2003 at the Institute of Technology Tallaght and hosts annual conferences on the links between Irish Studies in France and Ireland. The association is currently chaired by Dr Sarah Balen from the Dun Laoghaire Institute of Art, Design and Technology and has published a wide range of books

---

31 Diarmuid Cawley, 'The Power of Wine Language – Critics, Labels and Sexism', available online: <https://arrow.tudublin.ie/dgs/2018/may30/12/> [accessed 10 October 2020].

32 Aoife Carrigy, 'Powerful Puzzles: Mapping the Symbiosis between Two Great Signifiers of Irishness, The Writer and The Pub', available online: <https://arrow.tudublin.ie/dgs/2018/may30/11/> [accessed 6 September 2020].

33 Tara McConnell, 'Claret: The Preferred Libation of Georgian Ireland's Élite', available online: <https://arrow.tudublin.ie/dgs/2012/june612/3/> [accessed 6 September 2020].

34 James Murphy, 'Shaken not Stirred – The Evolution of the Cocktail Shaker', available online: <https://arrow.tudublin.ie/dgs/2012/june612/4/> [accessed 6 September 2020].

35 Sylvain Tondeur, 'The Irish Whiskey Renaissance: A Revolution of Sorts?', available online: <https://arrow.tudublin.ie/dgs/2016/June1/7/> [accessed 6 October 2020].

36 Patricia Medcalf, 'Guinness and Food: Ingredients in an Unlikely Gastronomic Revolution'. Food and Revolution. Dublin Gastronomy Symposium, Dublin, 1 June. Arrow@DIT, available online: <https://arrow.dit.ie/cgi/viewcontent.cgi?article=1084&context=dgs> [accessed 22 October 2020].

both in Ireland and in France over its seventeen-year history. These books have included many beverage chapters including, 'Using a 17th century Benedictine monk to convert myth into history in an effort to sell more fizz',[37] 'The Role of Revolution and Rioting in French Wine's relationship with Place',[38] 'Cognac, Scotch and Irish: Lessons in Gastronomic Identity',[39] and 'A New Phenomenon: Whiskey Tourism in Ireland',[40] 'Calling Time on Alcohol Advertising in Ireland'[41] and 'Irish Cultural Heritage through the Prism of Guinness's Ads in the 1980s'.[42]

The *Reimagining Ireland* Book Series

The *Reimagining Ireland* series began in 2003. Edited by Dr Eamon Maher, the series now boasts an impressive 100 volumes and covers a very wide range of diverse Irish Studies topics. The very first volume in the series was a monograph from cultural theorist Eugene O' Brien, which

---

37 Brian Murphy, 'Using a 17th Century Benedictine Monk to Convert Myth into History in an Effort to Sell More Fizz', in *Histoire et Mémoire en France et en Irlande/History and Memory in France and Ireland*, edited by Sylvie Mikowski (Reims: Épure, 2011), 291–308.

38 Brian Murphy, 'The Role of Revolution and Rioting in French Wine's Relationship with Place', in *France, Ireland and Rebellion*, edited by Yann Bévant, Anne Goarzin and Grace Neville (Rennes: Tir, 2011), 149–167.

39 Brian Murphy, 'Cognac, Scotch and Irish: Lessons in Gastronomic Identity', in *Voyages between France and Ireland: Culture, Tourism and Sport*, edited by Frank Healy and Brigitte Bastiat (Oxford: Peter Lang, 2017), 237–255.

40 Sylvain Tondeur, 'A New Phenomenon: Whiskey Tourism in Ireland', in *Voyages between France and Ireland: Culture, Tourism and Sport*, edited by Frank Healy and Brigitte Bastiat (Oxford: Peter Lang, 2017), 257–274.

41 Patricia Medcalf, 'Calling Time on Alcohol Advertising in Ireland', in *Margins and Marginalities in Ireland and France: A Socio-Cultural Perspective*, edited by Catherine Maignant, Sylain Tondeur and Déborah Vandewoude (Oxford: Peter Lang, 2020).

42 Patricia Medcalf, 'Irish Cultural Heritage through the Prism of Guinness's Ads in the 1980s', in *Patrimoine/Cultural Heritage in France and Ireland*, edited by Eamon Maher and Eugene O'Brien (Oxford: Peter Lang, 2018).

included a substantial chapter entitled, '"Tá Siad ag Teacht": Guinness as a Signifier of Irish Cultural Transformation'. This important contribution undoubtedly encouraged further exploration of other beverage-related topics in the series. Some of the topics covered include: 'Appellation "Éire" Contrôlée: Historical Links Between France's Wine Heritage and Ireland',[43] 'The Irish Pub Abroad: Lessons in the Commodification of Gastronomic Culture',[44] 'Wine and Music: An Emerging Cultural Relationship',[45] 'Thinking Beyond the Bottle: Traditional French Wine versus New Media'[46] and '"Brew as much as possible during the proper season": Beer Consumption in Elite Households in Eighteenth-Century Ireland'.[47] By far the most prominent beverage example of the series is Patricia Metcalf's monograph, *Advertising the Black Stuff in Ireland*,[48] which uses the story of Guinness to interpret Ireland's cultural history between the years 1959 to 1999. In a recent *Irish Times* review, John Fanning described Medcalf's contribution as 'ground-breaking'. Fanning's comments help to highlight the important role beverage studies can play in understanding Ireland's cultural landscape:

43 Brian Murphy, 'Appellation 'Éire' Contrôlée – Heritage Links between France's Wine Heritage and Ireland', in *Franco-Irish Connections in Space and Time: Peregrinations and Ruminations*, edited by Eamon Maher and Catherine Maignant (Oxford: Peter Lang, 2012), 117–132.
44 Brian Murphy, 'The Irish Pub Abroad: Lessons in the Commodification of Gastronomic Culture', in *'Tickling the Palate': Gastronomy in Irish Literature and Culture*, edited by Máirtín Mac Con Iomaire and Eamon Maher (Oxford: Peter Lang, 2014), 191–205.
45 Brian Murphy, 'Wine and Music: An Emerging Cultural Relationship', in *France and Ireland: Notes and Narratives*, edited by Una Hunt and Mary Pierce (Oxford: Peter Lang, 2015), 143–158.
46 Brian Murphy, 'Thinking beyond the Bottle: Traditional French Wine versus New Media', in *New Critical Perspectives on Franco-Irish Relations*, edited by Anne Goarzin (Oxford: Peter Lang, 2015), 159–180.
47 Tara Kellaghan, '"Brew as Much as Possible during the Proper Season": Beer Consumption in Elite Households in Eighteenth-Century Ireland', in *'Tickling the Palate': Gastronomy in Irish Literature and Culture*, edited by Máirtín Mac Con Iomaire and Eamon Maher (Oxford: Peter Lang, 2014), 177–190.
48 Patricia Medcalf, *Advertising the Black Stuff in Ireland 1959-1999: Increments of Change* (Oxford: Peter Lang, 2020).

I'm not suggesting that *Advertising the Black Stuff* should replace the collected works of Diarmuid Ferriter and Roy Foster, but it can augment what they have to say and hopefully it may inspire other academics to dip their toes into advertising's Aladdin's cave and add to our understanding of our collective times past and present.[49]

In addition to the material mentioned above, there have been other academic publications that are relevant in the field of Irish beverage studies. These include, 'The rise of whiskey tourism in Ireland: Developing a *terroir* engagement template', in the *Journal of Gastronomy and Tourism*,[50] 'In search of identity: an exploration of the relationship between Guinness's advertising and Ireland's social and economic evolution between 1959 and 1969',[51] and 'Advertising gastronomic identity in an epicurean world: the case for Irish Single Pot Still whiskey',[52] in *The Irish Communication Review*.[53] Although not exhaustive, the publications identified above suggest that beverage studies research has played a considerable role in Irish academic discourse over recent years and helps bolster the argument for it to be considered as an important part of Irish cultural studies.

49 John Fanning, 'Advertising the Black Stuff in Ireland 1959–1999: Through a Guinness Glass Brightly', in *The Irish Times*, 25 July 2020, available online: <https://www.irishtimes.com/culture/books/advertising-the-black-stuff-in-ireland-1959-1999-through-a-guinness-glass-brightly-1.4306112> [accessed 10 September 2020].

50 Brian Murphy, 'The Rise of Whiskey Tourism in Ireland: Developing a *Terroir* Engagement Template', in a special edition in the *Journal of Gastronomy and Tourism* 3, no. 2 (2018), 107–123, available online: <https://www.cognizantcommunication.com/journal-titles/journal-of-gastronomy-and-tourism> [accessed 10 September 2020].

51 Patricia Medcalf, 'In Search of Identity: An Exploration of the Relationship between Guinness's Advertising and Ireland's Social and Economic Evolution between 1959 and 1969', *Irish Communication Review* 15, no. 1, 3, available online: <https://arrow.dit.ie/cgi/viewcontent.cgi?article=1143&context=icr> [accessed 19 September 2020].

52 Brian Murphy, 'Advertising Gastronomic Identity in an Epicurean World: The Case for Irish Single Pot Still Whiskey', *Irish Communication Review* 15, no. 1 (2016), Article 7, available online: <http://arrow.dit.ie/icr/vol15/iss1/7> [accessed 18 September 2020].

53 Available online: <https://arrow.tudublin.ie/icr/vol15/iss1/> [accessed 18 September 2020].

Drinking Spaces in Strange Places

New Directions for Beverage Research

The physical spaces where beverage has been consumed have historically been quite limited and fixed by place and time. As such, beverage research tended to be centred on these spaces. For example, the Irish pub provided a key focal point for consideration of issues such as gender, music, story and performance. It acted as a refuge for artists and writers alike who used its muse-like influence for inspiration and sometimes solace to cope with frequent rejection. Drinking within the home was another source of subject material for playwrights and poets. In more recent times both beverages and the places associated with their consumption have changed, but their ability to contribute to the discourse on Irish cultural life is no less diminished. The following examples help demonstrate that beverage research remains contemporary and relevant in an Ireland that has changed considerably in terms of its drinking culture over recent years and suggest that new drinks and new drinking spaces will continue to act as important cultural signifiers.

Figure 5.1. Beverage spaces and Irish retail: Penny's Coffee Cart Mary Street, Dublin. Photo by Brian Murphy, 2019.

In 2018, Pennys unveiled their newest addition to the Irish retail market that 'basically guarantees we're never going to want to leave'.[54] The Primark Coffee Cart shown in Figure 5.1 is positioned in the middle of the shopping aisles in Penny's' flagship store in Mary Street, Dublin. Although coffee shops have long been associated with large retail stores this somewhat unique approach presents an incongruous picture of how beverage can be directly integrated into the on-floor shopping experience. Its introduction exemplifies Ireland's love affair with both coffee and retail and how the beverage has become synonymous with every aspect of our lives. This seemingly inconsequential example can provide substantial material for the exploration of modern Irish society, its mercantile nature, our desire for instant gratification, for cheap food and drink and for fast fashion. Identifying such a drinking space in such a strange location demonstrates the important role coffee plays in Irish culture and the rich vein of investigation it potentially facilitates.

Figure 5.2. Beverage spaces and Irish Corporate Culture: O Barnaby's Pub, Fifth Floor Qualtrics, Dublin. Killian Woods, 2017. Killian Woods 'Take a guided tour of ... the billion-dollar tech firm with an Irish pub in its office', available online: <https://www.thejournal.ie/office-tour-qualtrics-dublin-3-3447734-Jun2017/> [accessed May 18, 2020].

54 Kelley Ryan, 'Pennys' Newest Addition Basically Guarantees We're Never Going to Want to Leave', available online: <https://www.her.ie/food/pennys-newest-addition-basically-guarantees-never-going-want-leave-439546> [accessed 20 October 2020].

Drinking Spaces in Strange Places 107

There can be few more odd locations for a traditional Irish Pub than the fifth floor of the Dublin offices of Qualtrics, a billion-dollar market research firm based in the US. However, this is the location of O' Barnaby's Irish Pub, part of the staff facilities that Qualtrics makes available to their young workforce, along with games rooms, coffee shops and relaxing breakout spaces. According to Qualtrics EMEA chairman Dermot Costello, the pub 'opens on Thursday and Friday evenings for a few hours so staff can come, have a few drinks and catch up on the week'.[55]

Again, this presents an example of a new atypical drinking space that might be used to explore Irish cultural themes such as authenticity, globalisation, cultural appropriation and how Irish society is viewed both from within and without.

Figure 5.3. Beverage spaces and the pub with no beer: The Virgin Mary, Capel Street, Dublin. Photograph: Tom Honan, *The Irish Times*.

A third example of a somewhat atypical Irish drinking space and how it might be of value in a cultural studies context is Dublin's first non-alcoholic pub located in Capel Street. The opening of the Virgin Mary pub, shown in Figure 5.3, in May 2019 caused something of a stir at the

---

55 This is a quote from a video tour/interview that Dermot Costello did with the *Journal.ie* where he explained the working environment for the staff at Qualtrics Dublin offices.

time with considerable media attention noting the unusual nature of such a concept in Irish cultural life. Rory Carroll, Irish correspondent with *The Guardian*, noted at the time:

> The Irish writer Brendan Behan made a famous declaration that he drank only on two occasions. 'When I'm thirsty and when I'm not'. Many compatriots adopted the quip as a defiant motto, an embrace of the stereotype of the boozy Irishman swaying on a bar stool. But the image needs updating because Dublin is about to get a pub with a twist: no alcohol.[56]

The Virgin Mary's opening in the capital marks a significant departure in terms of the nation's perceived relationship with drinking. It encourages further exploration in terms of cultural tropes, inherent Irish attitudes to alcohol or even religious interpretations considering the pub's name. One can imagine the furore regarding the name if the pub had opened a pre-Celtic Tiger era.

Figure 5.4. Beverage spaces and Cycling Cafes: The Old Hardware, Narraghmore. Photo by Brian Murphy, 2020. Photo of The Old Hardware Community Café a newly designated Cycle Café, Narraghmore, Co Kildare (2020).

56 Rory Carroll, "Ireland Is Changing': Booze-Free Bar Opens in Dublin', *The Guardian*, 8 May 2019 available online: <https://www.theguardian.com/world/2019/may/08/ireland-is-changing-booze-free-bar-opens-in-dublin> [accessed 18 May 2020].

Drinking Spaces in Strange Places 109

Sport and fitness have become major pursuits in Ireland and while there have always been strong beverage links through GAA, rugby or golf clubs, some less obvious partnerships have developed as modern Ireland embraces a more active health and wellness culture. Cycling, in particular, has become a feature in many people's lives and there are emerging examples of beverage spaces becoming core to the experience. Rural coffee shops and community cafés have become synonymous with the Irish cycling community as long cycle routes are often informally structured around potential stop off points. A more formal engagement between such cafés and cycling enthusiasts is now under way with recent government allocations for the development of formal Cycling Cafés:

> Drive-through cinemas, 'cycle cafés', and outdoor seating and dining facilities are among the projects to be funded in a €2.8 million package to help rural communities adapt to the Covid-19 pandemic ... Funding will also go to supporting the establishment of cycle cafes – coffee stops for cyclists on greenways and other rural cycling routes.[57]

Historically, we may have considered a pub crawl on a Saturday night, an inevitable consequence of Irish drinking culture; now a 50 km cycle on a Sunday morning through rural Ireland on a route peppered with designated cycle cafés is considered a normal part of life.

Conclusion

Ireland has unique relationship with beverage. Though not always positive, it has nonetheless acted as a cultural backdrop for many aspects of our society. Just as food studies has become defined by a strong research agenda, this chapter argues that the field of Irish beverage studies deserves similar consideration. It posits that beverage can be considered a legitimate part of the Irish Studies research agenda and suggests that a

---

57 Marie O Halloran, 'Towns and Villages to Get €2.8m for "Cycle Cafes" and Outdoor Cinemas', *The Irish Times*, 3 August 2020, available online: <https://www.irishtimes.com/news/politics/towns-and-villages-to-get-2-8m-for-cycle-cafes-and-outdoor-cinemas-1.4320134> [accessed 21 August 2020].

new cohort of researcher is emerging in the field, one that comes from the more practical and applied side of the sector. Historians, sociologists and literature scholars will always have a keen interest in the topic, but this new cohort has the potential to complement more traditional approaches by focusing on new emerging areas of beverage and beverage spaces. Products such as coffee, tea and non-alcoholic alternatives are increasingly being foregrounded and deserve considerable attention as new Irish generations engage with beverage and the places of its consumption in previously inconceivable ways. Early on in the chapter we discussed how food studies is a relatively recent academic phenomenon and has been somewhat looked down upon by more traditional academic communities.[58] Experience tells us that the same premise applies to beverage studies. Anybody working in the area will recognise the refrain, 'Sure isn't that only about pulling pints?' Thankfully there have been substantial advances in how food studies is perceived in Ireland, much of it due to the hard work of the research communities described above. This chapter has argued that beverage studies, particularly in an Irish Studies context, deserves a similar academic fate, but only time will tell whether the valued research contribution it makes will ultimately be recognised.

---

58   Warren Belasco, *Food: The Key Concepts* (New York: Berg, 2008).

EÓIN FLANNERY

6 Ecotheory and Criticism

In a wide-ranging essay published over thirty years ago in *Irish University Review*, the late Pat Sheeran highlighted an inherent hypocrisy that he saw as characteristic of Irish attitudes to our vernacular landscapes. For Sheeran, the Irish are exceptionally proficient in retailing the depth of their attachment and commitment to locality and to 'place', yet when one confronts the material evidence, there is little to support the idea that we value our landscapes in any meaningful way. We might well term Sheeran's intervention as proto-ecocritical given the clarity and vehemence it brings to exposing the self-congratulatory mythologies that inform such hollowed-out species of Irish attachment to place. For Sheeran:

> [w]hat is immediately striking about the Irish preoccupation with place is that it has little or nothing to do with tending, cultivating, enhancing, or otherwise materially affecting the immediate environment. This is our first clue towards the resolution of a major discrepancy or paradox. For while we Irish credit ourselves with a strong sense of place, the places themselves are allowed to go to wrack and ruin.[1]

In a sense the landscapes that are identified with are abstractions, even touristic simulacra, of an historic Ireland, and certainly not a landscape that requires intensive labour or personal sacrifice. And in this respect, Sheeran catalogues the copious evidence against the widely propagated but utterly vacuous contention that the Irish harbour a particular affinity for landscape or place. At length, Sheeran details:

---

1 Patrick Sheeran, 'Genius Fabulae: The Irish Sense of Place', *Irish University Review* 18, no. 2 (Autumn, 1988), 192.

> The list of our sins of commission and omission with regard to the landscape (understood as the environment modified by the permanent presence of a group of people) is daunting, even if we omit the cardinal sin of pollution. Let us call them to mind: the destruction of field monuments (up to 60% in some areas), coniferization of marginal land, arterial drainage that flings up spoil heaps of raw earth, geometric forestry plantation on undulating hills, cavernous, corrugated steel farm outbuildings in glossy colours, the destruction of hedgerows and their replacement by brick walls, the use of bland asbestos on roofs rather than natural slate, litter and rubbish everywhere. Given all of this we might more properly speak of a sense of placelessness rather than a sense of place.[2]

Though writing in 1988, Sheeran could well be reflecting upon the social and geographical landscapes of Ireland a decade, or two decades, later such is the consistency of neglect and material exploitation visited upon swathes of Irish urban and rural landscapes. Considering the inventory of mistreatment listed above, there is clearly little transaction between abstract conceptions of landscape and place, and the impulses to extract maximum utility from the raw materialities of the actual landscapes of the country. There is a deep historical irony on display here; we are highly sensitised to the sufferings and wrongs of our colonial history, yet we do little to manage the well-being of the land reappropriated a century ago.

If Sheeran's analysis strikes ecocritical notes, the dominant theoretical debates at that time in Irish academia centred upon the politics of Irish postcolonial studies. Shadowed by the ongoing violence in Northern Ireland, much conversation within Irish literary and historical studies revolved around nationalist-postcolonialist and revisionist discords. One of the lingering, and limiting, problems with the development of postcolonial analysis in Ireland was that it became enmeshed in disputes on identity politics, and postcolonial theory had perceived roots in, and affiliations with, a republican-nationalist agenda. Yet if we return to the work of the founding figure of international postcolonial studies, we cannot but trace the early and necessary links between ecocriticism and postcolonial theory. In many ways postcolonial studies has always been attuned to the politics of space and place, and to the ecological traumas of exploitation. As Edward Said notes in *Culture and Imperialism*: 'Imperialism is after all

---

2   Sheeran, 'Genius Fabulae: The Irish Sense of Place', 194.

an act of geographical violence through which virtually every space in the world is explored, charted and finally brought under control'.[3] Said points to the incremental but relentless discursive objectification of human and non-human ecologies of the colonised world, processes under which landscapes, languages and cultures were catalogued and often sundered.[4] Thus the literary histories and cultural histories of what has become termed postcolonial ecocriticism provide telling reminders of the intrusive footprints of both the material realities and the signifying exercises of imperialism.[5]

Equally, in aggregating the critical tools of postcolonial criticism and ecocriticism, there is the potential for historically informed and theoretically sophisticated critiques of the material and discursive agents of power in the contemporary politico-economic conjuncture. With recent and ongoing work in Irish ecocriticism, we see a reorientation of Ireland's colonial history, as not simply a clash of political doctrines of tribal loyalties, but one founded upon, and sustained by, widespread and enduring environmental exploitation, devastation and profound social injustice. And, indeed there are tangible echoes of Sheeran's environmental indictment in the later work of international critics such as Graham Huggan, who frame their concern for the environment within a late imperial context. Aggregating the two fields, Huggan concludes that: 'Both are equally concerned with critically analysing the representational mechanisms that lend legitimacy to these practices [corporate expansionism and technological managerialism], demonstrating the power of culture to (re)shape the word, and through it, the world.'[6] In this extract, Huggan appears to confine his argument to the 'representational mechanisms' that underwrite global capitalist modernity, but elsewhere, with Helen Tiffin, he clarifies

---

3   Edward W. Said, *Culture and Imperialism* (London: Vintage, 1993), 271.
4   See Alfred W. Crosby, *Ecological Imperialism: The Biological Expansion of Europe, 900-1900* (Cambridge: Cambridge University Press, 1986).
5   On the relationship between postcolonialism and environmentalism see, Rob Nixon, 'Environmentalism and Postcolonialism', in *Postcolonial Studies and Beyond*, edited by Ania Loomba, Suvir Kaul, Matti Bunzl, Antoinette Burton and Jed Esty (Durham, NC and London: Duke University Press, 2005), 233–251.
6   Graham Huggan, 'Postcolonial Ecocriticism and the Limits of Green Romanticism', *Journal of Postcolonial Writing* 45, no. 1 (2009), 6.

his position on this point: 'Both postcolonialism and ecocriticism are [...] aimed at providing conceptual possibilities for a *material* transformation of the world [original emphasis]'.⁷ As an Irish genus of ecocriticism has taken shape in the past decade, we have seen pioneering work, particularly in analyses of the representational politics of our engagements with place, landscape and natural resources, together with the emergence of projects that go beyond the representational in their environmental analyses.

Contemporary Irish history, specifically that of the past twenty years, saw the nature of the relationship between people and land intensify dramatically and, in large part, detrimentally. There has been an approximate synchronicity between the Celtic Tiger 'boom' and 'bust', and the embedding of ecocritical methodologies within Irish cultural criticism. While 'land' and 'value' have always been related concepts, the ways in which land came to be valued and hungrily sought after in Irish society reflected a new configuration in the 'structures of feeling' that sustained the relations between Irish people and their surrounding environment. There is a seam of continuity here with Sheeran's assessment, but the Celtic Tiger was different in nature and degree to the Ireland of the previous decade. Unoccupied spaces; exposed rural fastnesses; unproductive farmland all became transvalued in an economy that became motored by the unreflective fetishisation of property. Landscape became commercialised at accelerated, and unsustainable, rates as the value-system of significant, and influential, sectors of Irish society changed, and only one measure of 'value' became dominant: market value. Any Irish ecocritical intervention must engage with the country's Celtic Tiger period, and focus on the idea of values and valuation, edging towards the reclamation of a sustainable ecological and cultural ethics of landscape valuation.

Writing almost forty years ago in *The Country and the City*, Raymond Williams captures the debilitating dynamic that was so recently in the ascendant in Ireland: 'We live in a world in which the dominant mode of production and social relationships reaches, impresses, offers to make

---

7   Graham Huggan and Helen Tiffin, 'Green Postcolonialism', *Interventions: International Journal of Postcolonial Studies* 9, no. 1 (2007), 10. See also, Graham Huggan and Helen Tiffin, *Postcolonial Ecocriticism: Literature, Animals, Environment* (London: Routledge, 2010).

normal and even rigid, modes of detached, separated, external perception and action: modes of using and consuming rather than accepting and enjoying people and things'.[8] Williams's critique of liberal capitalist sociality is a given, but what is of consequence to the current discussion is the idea that such a worldview 'detaches' people from their fellow humanity and the proximate domains of non-human ecology. In this vein, Irish society has seen a toxic surfeit of financial investment in land as property in recent times, and this has been matched by a deficient investment in the affective, historical values of the country's geographies. Contrary to a productive ethics of ecological dwelling, Irish property mania was conditioned by erotics of speculation and consumption, as land and property assumed totemic proportions.

Akin to any burgeoning field of inquiry and analysis, ecocriticism is assuredly not uniform in its politics or its methods. Quite clearly in broaching an aggregation of human and non-human ecologies, ecocriticism is a series of composite approaches that are not confined by disciplinary sensitivities, though as John Wilson Foster outlines in the Irish context, not all disciplines are equally represented within debates on environmentalism in Irish Studies. In Wilson Foster's view, 'only the economic and scientific have not been culturally celebrated by many literary critics, while science's productions – from nature-writing to scientific papers and monographs – are largely ignored by critics and anthologists, and by writers who are scientifically unsympathetic, indifferent or unconversant. Yet eco-criticism requires the scientific paradigm'.[9] Wilson Foster is well-placed to review the shortcomings of ecocritical inquiry in Ireland, having co-edited, with Helena C. G. Chesney, the monumental volume *Nature in Ireland: A Scientific and Cultural History*, in 1997.[10] This exemplary collection of essays touches upon topics as diverse as botany, fishing, geology, mammology, popular

8   Raymond Williams, *The Country and the City* (Oxford: Oxford University Press, 1973), 298.
9   John Wilson Foster, 'Challenges to an Irish Eco-criticism', *The Journal of Ecocriticism* 5, no. 2 (2013), available online: <http://ojs.unbc.ca/index.php/joe/article/view/515/452> [accessed 10 September 2020].
10 John Wilson Foster and Helena C. G. Chesney (eds), *Nature in Ireland: A Scientific and Cultural History* (Dublin: Lilliput Press, 1997).

science and Victorian naturalists. Thus, in hindsight the thirty two-essay edition is part of the genealogy of Irish ecocriticism, much as Sheeran's earlier essay articulates ecocritical concerns *avant la lettre*. As we shall see below, some of the aforementioned disciplinary exclusions are currently being addressed at institutional levels within Irish academia.

On foot of Gerry Smyth's hopeful prediction in 2001 that: 'It seems likely that Irish Studies and ecocriticism will have much to say to each other',[11] the field of Irish Studies has begun to exploit the critical and analytical resources of ecocriticism. The ecocritical terrain is, of course, far from homogenous, and these 'green' shoots have appeared within a diversity of literary and cultural studies in book-length publications and editions by Christine Cusick, Eamonn Wall, Maureen O'Connor, Kathryn Kirkpatrick, Donna Potts, Lucy Collins, Nicholas Allen, Robert Brazeau, Derek Gladwin and Tim Wenzell.[12] Indeed it might seem unnecessary, even invalid, to 'name' an Irish ecocriticism given the scale and nature of the issues that the field confronts and negotiates. But such a national nomination is not advocating for any form of Irish exceptionalism, rather it is an acknowledgement of the peculiar experiences of a variety of Irish contexts at a variety timepoints in Irish history. The critics cited above collate, critique and contest the activities and outputs of a range of Irish

---

11   Gerry Smyth, *Space and the Irish Cultural Imagination* (Basingstoke: Palgrave, 2001), 11.
12   See, Christine Cusick (ed.), *Out of the Earth: Ecocritical Readings of Irish Texts* (Cork: Cork University Press, 2010); Eamonn Wall, *Writing the Irish West: Ecologies and Traditions* (Notre Dame: University of Notre Dame Press, 2011); Donna Potts, *The Pastoral Tradition in Contemporary Irish Poetry* (Columbia: University of Missouri Press, 2011); Lucy Collins and Andrew Carpenter (eds), *The Irish Poet and the Natural World: An Anthology of Verse in English from the Tudors to the Romantics* (Cork: Cork University Press, 2014); Robert Brazeau and Derek Gladwin (eds), *Eco-Joyce: The Environmental Imagination of James Joyce* (Cork: Cork University Press, 2014); Maureen O'Connor, *The Female and the Species* (Oxford: Peter Lang, 2010); Kathryn Kirkpatrick and Borbala Forago (eds), *Animals in Irish Literature and Culture* (London: Palgrave, 2015); Nicholas Allen, Nick Groom and Jos Smith's edited volume, *Coastal Works: Cultures on the Atlantic Edge* (Oxford: Oxford University Press, 2017), and Tim Wenzell, *Emerald Green: An Ecocritical Study of Irish Literature* (Newcastle: Cambridge Scholars Press, 2009).

activists and writers. Just as postcolonial criticism embedded Irish history within the global machinations of imperial capitalist modernity, from a material perspective, Irish ecocritics underscore the exigency of linking the exploitation and destruction of localities and resources on the island to the broader urgencies of global environmentalism. In the literary sphere, ecocritics analyse the representational politics of literary engagements with non-human ecologies. While the latter might appear to be a reiteration of the toothless abstraction decried by Sheeran, in fact, such analyses are exemplary of the ways in which we must 'read' the world and the signifying systems around us if we are to make environmentally ethical and informed choices.

If we momentarily return to the shared features of postcolonial studies and ecocriticism, one of the primary faults identified by antagonists of international postcolonial studies was the field's apparent concentration upon the politics of representation. In other words, postcolonial studies was rejected because it seemed to retain a politically impotent culturalist bias; it was merely a word game produced and propagated by academics and theorists.[13] Of course, such sweeping dismissals never grasp the genuine differential complexities of any given field of study, but it is salutary to remain conscious of the ease with which a discipline could potentially lose sight of its principal goals and responsibilities. The development of ecocriticism has seen equivalent contestations regarding its intermittent priorities and trajectories. For instance, in its early incarnations in the United States, there was a concentration on the politics of the local and the signal importance of place as redemptive environmental agents. However, as the interconnections of global climate change became more evident, apparent retreat to local fastnesses seems less and less viable as effective critical and political strategies.

There are lessons here for Irish ecocritical scholars, particularly given the historical tendency of literary studies and historical studies to dominate

---

[13] For example, see Aijaz Ahmad, *In Theory: Classes, Nations, Literatures* (London and New York: Verso, 1992); Benita Parry, 'Directions and Dead Ends in Postcolonial Studies', in *Relocating Postcolonialism*, edited by David Theo Goldberg and Ato Quayson (Oxford: Blackwell, 2002), 66–81; and Epifanio San Juan Jr, *Beyond Postcolonial Theory* (Basingstoke: MacMillan, 1998).

and to set the agendas for the broader field of Irish Studies. Again, in this respect we only have to reflect upon the development of and conflicts within and without Irish postcolonial studies over the past three decades.[14] Notwithstanding the capaciousness of *Nature in Ireland*, the early endeavours of Irish ecocritics were dominated by literary analyses. This is readily apparent in Tim Wenzell's *Emerald Green: An Ecocritical Study of Irish Literature* (2009). Wenzell's book is the first ecocritical approach to Irish literature by a single author. The broad literary survey is useful in terms of its engagement with the politics of literature and landscape across Irish literary history. However, it is confined to a singular disciplinary methodology – literary criticism, and it rehearses many familiar ecological or topographical readings of canonical Irish authors such as WB Yeats, Patrick Kavanagh and Seamus Heaney.

Shortly after Wenzell's volume, Christine Cusick published an edited collection of essays, *Out of the Earth: Ecocritical Readings of Irish Texts* (2010). Cusick's volume of essays was accomplished intervention in the emerging field of Irish ecological criticism. The chapters in this volume take a long historical sweep in their discrete foci, including, for example, pieces on J. M. Synge, Edna O'Brien, Paula Meehan, George Moore and Michael Longley. Furthermore, the following year, Eamonn Wall published his wide-ranging study, *Writing the Irish West: Ecologies and Traditions* (2011). Wall's book provides detailed readings of a selection of Irish poets and prose writers, including, Sean Lysaght, Mary O'Malley, Richard Murphy, John McGahern and Tim Robinson. Wall's book is a powerful engagement with the idea of the Irish 'West', and how this has been culturally processed in contemporary writing. It is not a new idea in Irish cultural criticism – the centrality of the 'West' to the Irish national imagination is a commonplace notion – nevertheless Wall's readings in terms of the American West are insightful and provocative. What all three of these publications have in common is an almost exclusive focus on the literary and on representation. Likewise, they are progressively more engaged with the work of international and historical ecocriticism – Wall's integration

---

14 On these debates within Irish Studies, see my *Ireland and Postcolonial Studies: Theory, Discourse, Utopia* (Basingstoke: Palgrave, 2009).

of such theorisation into his readings of Irish primary texts is the most thorough in this regard.

On foot of these pioneering interventions, the majority of subsequent work in Irish ecocriticism has remained literary-critical and literary-historical in nature. However, the degree of theoretical sophistication and interdisciplinarity has increased appreciably. For instance, while a single author ecocritical study of a canonical author may seem likely to centralise the literary and the textual in its foci. However, in their co-edited volume, *Eco-Joyce: The Environmental Imagination of James Joyce* (2014), Robert Brazeau and Derek Gladwin convene a sequence of essays that significantly advance both Joyce studies and Irish ecocritical studies. The edition is powerfully enabling as it theorises and historicises Joyce's work drawing upon natural history, ecofeminism and ecophilosophy. Gladwin's contribution to Irish ecocriticism continues in a 2015 publication centred on the work of the artist, cartographer and author, Tim Robinson. The single author focus belies the diversity of critical responses to his oeuvre contained within the volume of essays. *Unfolding Irish Landscapes*, co-edited by Gladwin and Christine Cusick, grapples with Robinson's prolific output as a mapmaker, non-fiction writer, visual artist, linguist and environmentalist. The range of texts gestured to here and above are necessarily, and merely, representative, but what they indicate is that the field of Irish ecocriticism is dynamic and evolving. Yet, keeping Wilson Foster's comments in mind, there is a sense that despite evermore theoretical and philosophical sophistication – including an embrace of animal studies perspectives, ecofeminism, island studies and the Anthropocene, there remains a concentration on the politics of representation in the majority of publications within the field.[15]

15   For animal studies and ecofeminism, see Maureen O'Connor, *The Female and the Species* (Oxford: Peter Lang, 2010), and *Animals in Irish Literature and Culture*, edited by Kathryn Kirkpatrick and Borbala Forago (London: Palgrave, 2015) Focusing on archipelagic cultural histories and natural histories, see Nicholas Allen, Nick Groom and Jos Smith's edited volume, *Coastal Works: Cultures on the Atlantic Edge* (Oxford: Oxford University Press, 2017). For a survey of many of these areas including, ecopoetics, ecofeminism, the Anthropocene, environmental justice and the links between postcolonial studies and ecocriticism, see my *Ireland and Ecocriticism: Literature, History and Environmental Justice* (London: Routledge, 2016).

However, when we turn our attention to institutionally-sited projects within the field of ecocriticism, or more accurately in these cases, environmental studies, the material dimensions of Irish pasts and presents have gained more purchase. Incarnating Wilson Foster's call for an increase in cross-disciplinary transactions in the field, Trinity College Dublin houses the Trinity Centre for Environmental Humanities. Indeed, the term 'Environmental Humanities' now circulates as freely as, and even more often than, 'ecocriticism', as it appears to implicitly express the notion that the Humanities are just one strand in any concerted environmental or ecocritical project. The initiative at TCD is well-established and firmly interdisciplinary, showcasing empirical and theoretical research in the field, and researchers have undertaken projects including: *The Digital Literary Atlas of Ireland, 1922-1949*; *Climates of Conflict in Ancient Babylonia*; *Humanities for the Environment*; the Irish Environmental History Network; and *ClimConflict: Historical Dynamics of Violence, Conflict and Extreme Weather in Medieval Ireland*. The series of interdisciplinary and international projects ongoing at TCD are the largest in scale in the field, but collaborative projects and critical showcases have also been established at both UCD and UCC. Primarily hosted by School of English, Drama and Film, Sharae Deckard leads the Environmental Humanities research theme at UCD. While there is a clear concentration of humanities scholars involved in this research theme, on foot of Deckard's explicitly materialist ecocritical writing, the showcases convened by this project never remain confined to the narrowly representational. The research priorities of this research collective are informed by both the work of Jason Moore on the concept of 'world ecology', and as well as the materialist criticism of the Warwick Research Collective, of which Deckard is a member.[16]

Launched in 2016, and funded by the Irish Research Council, Deep Maps: West Cork Coastal Cultures harnesses the interdisciplinary expertise envisioned by Wilson Foster. The project was led by investigators, Professor Claire Connolly and Dr Rob McAllen, from the Schools of English and

---

16 See Jason W. Moore, *Capitalism in the Web of Life: Ecology and the Accumulation of Capital* (London: Verso, 2015), and by the Warwick Research Collective, the collaboratively authored, *Combined and Uneven Development: Towards a New Theory of World-Literature* (Liverpool: Liverpool University Press, 2015).

Biological, Earth and Environmental Science, respectively, and delved into the cultural and maritime history of Roaring Water Bay in County Cork. Akin to the approach taken at Trinity College Dublin, this project consisted of a number of strands or priorities, including Biodiversity and Conservation, Climate Change, Pollution and Community Perspective. The interdisciplinary possibilities are self-evident from this list, but what is also clear is that there are opportunities for the resolutely local to be placed within a broader range of global pasts, presents and futures. Indeed, the latter strand above is, perhaps, key to the prospects of any ecocritical project in Ireland; namely, divining impactful ways in which the theoretical and speculative can be translated into local engagement. And while the Deep Maps project is geographically and historically targeted the methodologies and the resources made accessible via workshops and a legacy website are available for equivalent future research elsewhere.[17] More recently, Connolly has also taken a lead role in a project entitled Ports, Past and Present in collaboration with Aberystwyth University, The University of Wales Trinity St David and Wexford County Council. Launched in March 2020 and funded by the European Regional Development Fund, this new venture segues from the consideration of the maritime histories of a single local area in *Deep Maps*, to an analysis of the human and cultural traffic across time at a variety of ports in Ireland and Wales. The project, then, engages with the interlocked histories of migration, economic decline and political conflict that pockmark that relationships across the Irish and British archipelago.

Ecocriticism and the wider field of the Environmental Humanities face significant challenges at present, not just in the Irish context. We are currently in the throes of a global pandemic that is directly linked to our exploitation of the non-human world, to which our very survival as a species is inextricably wedded. Moments of acute and widespread crisis can allow, and have allowed, individuals and communities to excel in terms of the alleviation of shared suffering. But given the simultaneous political crises in which we are also imbricated, there is not always an alignment

---

[17] The project website is accessible here: <http://www.deepmapscork.ie/> [accessed 23 September 2020].

between progressive environmental and social policies, and the brute cynicism of realpolitik. Future and ongoing interventions in ecocriticism and the Environmental Humanities will have to reckon with the legion injustices and inequalities that both predate and have been exacerbated by the pandemic, and scholars and activists in Ireland have a role to play in these inevitable debates. Thus, an area such as environmental justice is key for future Irish ecocritics, given that it encompasses our implication in climate change, pollution, resource extraction and land use. These issues pertain to our own society but also to the ways in which we benefit from the immiseration of others, through the destruction of their environments and the impoverishment of their landscapes.

As is so often the case, literature can provide us with an exemplary critical voice, though we must move beyond the lyricism to some form of practical response. The penultimate poem in Rita Ann Higgins's collection, *Ireland Is Changing Mother* (2011) reminds us that Ireland's 'boom' years were not just marked by relative experiences of material well-being and deprivation, but that the crises of the Celtic Tiger and its legacies are equally issues of environmental and social justice. Though it telescopes a particular location in Ireland, 'The Brent Geese Chorus', firstly, signals the relentlessness of global resource extraction and, secondly, resonates with a host of other embattled local communities elsewhere that see their landscapes sundered. The poem narrates the long-running tensions between a consortium of companies headed by Royal Dutch Shell and the activist-residents [and external supporters] in the north-west Mayo region of Erris. With a more protracted pre-history than the immediate Celtic Tiger period, the poem is consistent with many others in the collection that rail against the social injustices and the environmental wounds that the 'boom' occasioned. The battle, physical and legal, over access to and potential exploitation of the Corrib Gas Field is the most ecological contention in modern Irish history, and Higgins's work provides a poeticised 'brief history' of the corrupted procedures of those intent on securing a viable and profitable pipe-line. Her poem details a corporate campaign of 'soft' and then 'hard' persuasion by Shell, until the State is revealed as comfortably complicit in the coercion of its own resistant citizens. Higgins alerts us to the agency of the local community in cultivating an efficacious campaign of resistance, and this appears to be metaphorised as the durable, migratory Brent Geese:

> And there is a chorus of Brent Geese
> singing all over Erris
> Shell to hell, to hell with Shell,
> and that chorus ran in and out of the bog
> and it was everywhere in North Mayo.[18]

Higgins's localisation of the politics of ecological despoliation is suffused with ethical indignation, and these activist-residents thoroughly engage with the corporate transvaluation of their physical environment. To return to our point of departure, Higgins's work poeticises and documents the reality of the groundwork protest undertaken to preserve a locality. Campaigns and representations such as this one are, then, surely indicative of a nascent will and capacity for, as Sheeran would hope, a genuine Irish sense of place to emerge.

18 Rita Ann Higgins, 'The Brent Geese Chorus', in *Ireland Is Changing Mother* (Newcastle-upon-Tyne: Bloodaxe Books, 2011), 70.

GRACE NEVILLE

7 Poverty-Trapped: French Traveller Accounts of Poverty in Ireland over the Centuries

'O Wad some Pow'r the giftie gie us/ To see oursels as ithers see us!' wrote Scottish poet, Robert Burns (1759–1796) in 1786.[1] These lines have rippled far and wide, and are even reprised in *Ulysses* when Stephen sees himself in a mirror held up by Buck Mulligan.[2] For centuries, French traveller accounts of their visits to Ireland have allowed us to see ourselves as other see us, to perceive what may otherwise have escaped us as we lack the critical distance enjoyed by French onlookers. Organisations like the SOFEIR (Société Française d'Etudes Irlandaises), Irish Studies centres in French universities and French academics themselves have long played a pioneering role here. In this context, the *Reimagining Ireland* series, now publishing its 100th book since its inception barely a decade ago in 2009, has become a major international vehicle and impetus for much of this research. This chapter aims to add to this ongoing work by analysing one theme threaded through centuries of French writings on Ireland: the theme of poverty.

Spectacular scenery, spectacular hospitality, spectacular poverty: this could summarise five centuries of French travellers' representations of Ireland. Here, the intense poverty they witness seems to shock them most: there is poverty ... and then there is Irish poverty. Or, to quote

1 Robert Burns, *Poems Chiefly in the Scottish Dialect, by Robert Burns* (Kilmarnock: John Wilson, 1786), 192–194.
2 See Kimberley J. Devlin, 'See Ourselves as Others See Us: Joyce's Look at the Eye of the Other', *PMLA* 104, no. 5 (October 1989), 882–893; Cleo Hanaway-Oakley, 'See Ourselves as Others See Us: Cinematic Ways of Seeing and Being in Joyce's *Ulysses*', *Roll Away the Reel World: James Joyce and Cinema*, edited by John McCourt (Cork: Cork University Press, 2010).

combative ecclesiastical preacher and author of anti-Catholic tracts, Napoléon Roussel (1808–1878), who spent three months in Ireland in 1853 hoping to convert the French attending the Great Industrial Exhibition in Dublin:

> 'L'Irlande, se dit le Parisien, c'est un pays triste, sombre, sale et dégoûtant et surtout misérable; on n'y voit que des landes, on n'y rencontre que des guenilles, on n'y mange que des pommes de terre quand on n'y meurt pas de faim'
>
> ('Ireland, or so the Parisian tells himself, is a sad, dismal, dirty, disgusting and, especially, miserable country: all you see there are moors, all you come across are rags, all people eat are potatoes – that's when they are not dying of hunger').[3]

These French commentators, some with obvious agendas, others much less so, visit Ireland for numerous reasons. Most are men. They include social reformers, political analysts, lawyers, teachers and journalists. Most have been forgotten. Some, like Coquebert de Montbret (1753–1825), Gustave de Beaumont (1802–1866) and Alexis de Tocqueville (1808–1859), will live forever. Everywhere they go they encounter poverty, in towns and cities large and small and throughout the countryside. This chapter will analyse the depictions of poverty that fill their travelogues. It will focus mainly, but not exclusively, on eighteenth-, nineteenth- and early twentieth-century texts: earlier ones are scarcer, later ones are frequently unremarkable. They were published mainly in Paris, but also in provincial French cities as well as Ghent and Montreal.

Ireland and poverty have long been associated in Continental European minds. Alongside the classic study by Marx and Engels[4] are lesser-known ones, including a Hungarian investigation published on the eve of the Famine in 1840.[5] In France, an 1847 analysis, *Le Livre du Pauvre*, by publisher Adrien-César Egron (1773–1853), includes a case-study tellingly entitled 'Du paupérisme en Irlande'.[6] The Great Famine fills countless French

---

3 Napoléon Roussel, *Trois Mois en Irlande* (Paris: Grasset, 1853), 1.
4 Karl Marx and Friedrich Engels, *On Ireland* (London: Lawrence and Wishart, 1971).
5 Jozsef Eotvos, *Poverty in Ireland, 1837: A Hungarian View* (Dublin: Phaeton, republished in dual-language version, 2015).
6 Adrien-César Egron, *Le Livre du Pauvre* (Paris: Librairie des Livres Liturgiques Illustrés, 1847).

texts, many of them contemporaneous with that catastrophe. Indeed, during and after the Famine, poverty and hunger in Ireland were the focus of sermons preached in Paris churches, prompting massive fundraising drives throughout France.[7] But poverty in Ireland rose up not just from words spoken in churches or written on pages: Irish poverty could be witnessed at first-hand by French travellers even outside Ireland, spilling out in the form of Irish emigrants to London, Liverpool, Boston and Montréal. It was as if Irish poverty was so colossal that the island of Ireland could not contain it in its entirety. Director of *La Revue Britannique* and falconry expert, Pierre-Amédée Pichot (1795–1877), says as much: in London's East End in the 1840s, it was mainly the poverty and squalor of Irish emigrants that struck him.[8] Consequently, as they stepped onto Irish soil, French travellers came already primed, fully expecting to witness poverty.

They were not disappointed. However, the sheer scale of the poverty they encounter astounds them. They talk in shocked superlatives: 'on ne voit rien de semblable en France' ('you see nothing comparable in France').[9] The suffering of beggar women collecting seaweed near the Giant's Causeway so horrifies l'Abbé Charles-Benjamin Poisson (1809–1885) as to make him shiver.[10] Extreme comparisons are needed by prolific writer and publicist, Saint-Germain Leduc (1799–18?) to convey the awfulness of houses in Galway: 'Des étables à cochons sont des palais comparés à ces maisons'('Pig styes are palaces compared to these houses').[11] Poverty-related problems are legion: in 1820s Dublin, Edouard de Montulé, intrepid explorer, gifted

---

7 See Grace Neville, 'Remembering and Forgetting the Great Famine in France and Ireland', *New Hibernia Review* 16, no. 2 (Winter 2012), 80–96; Grace Neville, 'Il y a des larmes dans leurs chiffres: French Famine Relief for Ireland 1847-89', *Revue Française de Civilisation Britannique* 19, no. 2 (2014), 67–89.
8 Pierre-Amédée Pichot, *L'Irlande et le Pays de Galles* (Paris: Guillaumin et Cie, 1850), 271.
9 Charles-Benjamin Poisson, *Angleterre, Ecosse, Irlande, souvenirs et impressions de voyage* (Orléans: Herluison, 1895), 225. See, however, constant references to poverty in the classic study, Eugen Weber, *Peasants into Frenchmen: The Modernisation of Rural France, 1870-1914* (Stanford: Stanford University Press, 1976).
10 *Ibid.*, 225.
11 Saint-Germain Leduc, *L'Angleterre, l'Irlande et l'Ecosse, relation d'un voyage dans les trois royaumes* (Paris: Levrault, 1838), volume 4, 265.

illustrator and military man, witnessed prostitution, perhaps even child prostitution.[12]

So, what does Irish poverty look like? A more pertinent question would be: what do the Irish poor look like? The answer, overwhelmingly, is that they look like beggars. Accounts of beggars and begging in Ireland could fill a lengthy monograph. Roussel summarises: 'Mendier, toujours mendier, voilà la grande industrie de l'Irlande' ('begging, forever begging: that's the national industry in Ireland').[13] On a traveller's arrival in any Irish town:

> un groupe compact de pauvres des deux sexes, en haillons, couverts de plaies, attend l'arrivée de cette voiture qu'il enveloppe de toutes parts, tendant les mains, implorant la charité d'une manière si plaintive, que la compassion gagne les plus endurcis. C'est un spectacle étrangement affreux pour un Français, que cette multitude de mendiants aux inflexions de voix si diverses, si poignantes; elles étreignent le coeur et la pensée. Quel soulagement on éprouve quand, reprenant la marche, on échappe aux solicitations de telles misères!!!

> ('a solid group of impoverished men and women, ragged and covered in wounds, awaits the arrival of this carriage which it then surrounds from all sides, hands outstretched, pleading for charity so plaintively that even the most hardened are moved. To French eyes this sight is strangely awful – these beggars all sounding so different, so poignant; they break the heart and the spirit. What a relief to move on and to escape such imploring, such misery').[14]

Beggars come in all shapes, sizes and ages. Visiting Cork – ironically for the showcase Great International Exhibition in 1902 – military doctor, Charles Schindler, is followed for 200 metres by an intrepid barefoot infant beggar.[15]

These beggars do not simply ask for money: French visitors sketch their countless begging strategies. These include moral blackmail tinged

---

12 Edouard de Montulé, *Voyage en Angleterre et en Russie pendant les années 1821, 1822 et 1823* (Paris: Bertrand, 1825), 18.
13 Roussel, 138. See also Audrey Woods, *Dublin Outsiders: A History of the Mendacity Institution 1818-1998* (Dublin: A. and A. Farmer, 1998).
14 Edouard Déchy, *Voyage, Irlande en 1846 et 1847* (Paris: Comon, 1847), 91. In French, 'misère' can mean misery or extreme poverty. My translations in this article try to express this duality.
15 Charles Schindler, *En Irlande, de Londres à Dublin* (Paris: Félix Juven, 1903), 104.

with despair as when a mother, a child in her arms, challenges a French visitor: 'Will this gentleman let my child die of hunger?', before dissolving into tears.[16] Elsewhere, another beggar lies that her husband is incapacitated but, as architecture expert, Félix Narjoux (1836?–1891) quips, he is merely drunk. Even children have their tactics: two children pretend that their mother is dead and that they need money to bury her.[17] All the while, perceived physical intimidation can leave French visitors shaken and terrified.

What do the poor look like? Accounts of their clothing would again fill a whole study, with the terms 'haillons' and 'guenilles' (rags) everywhere: 'En parcourant les quartiers pauvres, nous vîmes une population nombreuse, hideuse par ses haillons, sa saleté et sa grossièreté' ('The crowds we saw in the poorer areas that we visited were ragged, dirty and coarse – hideous, in fact').[18] Clothes can be deconstructed as pitiful reminders of past glories: in 1730, on the streets of Cork, Lady Roche could be seen begging, wearing a ragged court dress.[19] Sometimes, rags are, in fact, cheap clothing imported from England, colonial castoffs, the detritus of Empire.[20] The dismal ugliness of emigrants' clothing in the 1920s puzzles the young Celtic scholar, Marie-Louise Sjoestedt (1900–1940): is this a disguise; have they forgotten what they could or should look like?[21]

Rags frequently hide the people wearing them, as if the viewers' gaze cannot penetrate the wrapping, the exterior, to see the person underneath. If Ireland is 'hideuse par ses haillons', 'un enfer déguenillé',[22] ('hideous in its rags', 'a raggedy hell'), where are the people themselves, the actual wearers of

---

16   Félix Narjoux, *En Angleterre, Ecosse, Irlande* (Paris: Plon, Nourrit et Cie, 1886), 290.
17   Ibid. See also the award-winning 2003 DEA thesis at l'Université de Caen by Mélanie Marchand, *La Prise en charge des enfants les plus démunis en Irlande 1850-1922*.
18   Poisson, 240.
19   Emmanuel Domenech, *Les Gorges du diable, voyage et aventures en Irlande, souvenirs d'un touriste* (Paris: E. Maillet, 1864), 255.
20   Jacques Boucher de Perthes, *Voyage en Angleterre, Ecosse et Irlande en 1860* (Paris: Jung-Treuttel, 1868), 225.
21   Marie-Louise Sjoestedt, 'L'Irlande d'aujourd'hui: Gens de la Terre et de la Côte', *Revue des Deux Mondes* (15 June 1930), 841.
22   Pichot, 228.

those rags? Ultimate irony, ultimate impoverishment: they are frequently written out of the picture.

Beyond rags is nakedness. While adults wear rags, we read again and again of children going naked. In Galway, as in Killarney and Foxford:

> 'des groupes nombreux d'enfants (car la fécondité des Irlandais paraît égale à leur misère), nus comme le bon Dieu les a faits, jouent dans les ruisseaux avec les canards'
>
> ('crowds of children [because the fertility of the Irish is equalled only by their destitution], naked as the good God made them, play in the streams with the ducks').[23]

What do the poor sound like? These commentaries allow us not just to see but also to hear them. All too often, they possess no words, no language. In the mid-1880s, the crowds of beggars greeting visitors to Belfast 'vous harcèlent, vous poursuivent de phrases difficiles à comprendre: plaintes, lamentations bruyantes, pleurs, sanglots, gestes exubérants, désespérés' ('harass you, follow you with unintelligible phrases: wailing, noisy laments, tears, sobs, wild despairing gestures').[24] This language (or metalanguage) rarely persuades or moves the listeners. Of starving beggars outside the presbytery in Rosmuc in 1880, lawyer Jean Canis (1840–19?) recounts: 'leurs plaintes ne se traduisent que par des cris rauques; arrivés à un tel état d'épuisement complet, ils se retirent et vont tout aussi vainement frapper à d'autres portes' ('their wailing takes the form of hoarse cries; having reached such a state of total exhaustion, they step back and go knocking equally unsuccessfully on other doors').[25] In Kenmare, Quebec traveller, Jules-Paul Tardivel (1851–1905) is saddened to witness a people who have lost their own language but not managed to master their conquerors' one.[26] Just as poverty deprives individuals of language, it can similarly shroud in silence the places they inhabit. For Roussel, Dingle is not just poor and miserable, but silent also.[27]

---

23   Leduc, 265.
24   Narjoux, 290.
25   Jean Canis, *Les Massacres en Irlande* (Paris: E. Dentu, 1881), 121–122.
26   Jules Tardivel, *Notes de Voyage* (Montréal: Eusèbe Sénécal et Fils, 1890), 33.
27   Roussel, 86.

Where do the poor live? These French travellers realise that not all of Ireland is poverty-stricken, that there is a geography of poverty. In Queenstown, 'cette partie de l'Irlande ne me paraît pas pauvre outre mesure. La misère noire est plus à l'ouest' ('this part of Ireland does not seem excessively poor to me. Intense poverty is more to the west').[28] Towns themselves are patchworks where wealth and poverty co-exist even on the same street: in Belfast, beggars lie drunk on the street while ladies dressed for tennis or stylishly attired in sailor suits amble past.[29] Even housing betrays religious differences, with fine Protestant houses contrasting with miserable Catholic ones nearby.

In this context, it is surely significant that, as they crisscross the country, French travellers often record the housing of the poor rather than the poor themselves. Just as we see rags rather than their wearers, we see houses rather than their inhabitants: Galway, according to journalist and Socialist politician, Philippe Daryl (1844–1909), possesses as many ruins as inhabited houses.[30] But where are the people? Whatever the reason (perhaps simply recording these houses from the outside was easier than meeting their inhabitants: French travellers often allude to the high status of the people they were planning to encounter in Ireland), this renders poverty and the poor more invisible still. Within the overall reality of poverty, there are, of course, degrees of impoverishment and of invisibility, with the poorest of the poor simply disappearing, swallowed up in unspeakable surroundings: in Waterford, a drunken mother and her baby vanish into a slum that opens onto a filthy backyard where the poorest of the poor live.[31]

If their clothes are in rags, then – in close symmetry – their towns are in similar disrepair. If French visitors came to Ireland on a typically nineteenth-century Romantic search for interesting ruins, they were to be disappointed: in 1872, Mitchelstown looks as if some recent invasion has flattened it.[32] Like their clothes, people's houses provide little or no

28 Tardivel, 23.
29 Narjoux, 292.
30 Philippe Daryl, *La Vie Partout* (Paris: 1888), 238.
31 Marie-Anne de Bovet, *Irlande 1889: Trois mois en Irlande* (Plougastel: An Here, republished 1997), 116–117.
32 *Suite du récit d'une petite fille de quatorze ans réfugiée française pendant la guerre* (Angers: E. Barasse, 1872), 93.

shelter. In Galway, the houses are in ruins, the people are gloomy, it rains often and it is cold.[33]

Squalor all too often goes hand in hand with poverty. Again and again, we read of the extreme squalor of Irish towns. The outskirts of Galway, like all the other villages Leduc passes through, are dirty beyond words.[34] Apart from the quays, the streets of Waterford are narrow, crooked, badly paved and exceedingly filthy, proclaims diplomat, Marc de Bombelles (1744–1822).[35] Cork is dirty, badly ventilated and squalid. Limerick streets are strewn with human excrement.[36] The weather doesn't help. If French travellers in nineteenth-century Ireland are to be believed, it never stops raining, even in summer.[37]

Poverty is dirty, unhygienic, wet … and it smells. In a one-roomed house in Bellaghy, lying on hay are three fever-struck people breathing in the stink of rubbish strewn outside. This is not unusual: there are similar scenes in every house.[38] It is not just their surroundings that smell, however: the poor seem to have merged with their environment since, up close, they too smell: mobbed by beggars in Dungarvan, Pichot cannot forget their horrible cries or their stinking breath.[39]

Time and again, we read that Irish towns are not just dirty, fetid and unhygienic but ugly – a further impoverishment that is not just material but aesthetic this time. They provide little or no food for the soul or for the eye: Kildare is just a small, ugly town;[40] in Limerick, there is a most ugly old town, the cathedral is old and horrid, its square tower crowned with ridiculous high towers;[41] Wexford is one of the ugliest and filthiest towns

---

33 Narjoux, 340.
34 Leduc, 265.
35 Marc de Bombelles, *Journal de voyage en Grande Bretagne et en Irlande, 1784* (Oxford: Voltaire Foundation, 1989), 264.
36 Pichot, 9–10.
37 Roussel, 69.
38 Canis, 133.
39 Pichot, 226.
40 Leduc, 262.
41 Poisson, 240.

in all of Ireland.[42] The sheer ugliness of working-class Belfast horrifies Paris journalist Simone Téry (1897–1967):

> quartiers sordides [...] les mares de boue et les pavés inégaux de la chaussée défoncée [...] nous nous engageons dans des ruelles noires; cinq semaines de pluie n'ont pas réussi à laver la suie des murs de briques sales: maisons ouvrières misérables ... longues façades plates, percées de fenêtres sans volets, béantes, comme des bouches édentées.
>
> ('sordid districts [...] mud puddles and uneven pavements in the sinking footpaths [...] off we head down dark alleyways; five weeks of rain have not managed to wash away the soot from the dirty brick walls: workers' miserable houses ... long flat facades pierced with windows without shutters, gaping like mouths with no teeth').[43]

The material and aesthetic impoverishment visited on the poor is intensified by intellectual and even spiritual deprivation. Galway, a town of 40,000 inhabitants, is without a single bookshop or reading space.[44] In Tralee, over a century later, little had changed: Sjoestedt notes the absence of monuments other than bland churches offering the soul no more than some lifeless refuge.[45]

Poverty does more than disgust or bore the passer-by, however: it redefines time. In fact, it can kill time stone dead:

> Morne apathie de ces petites villes irlandaises qui nourrirent pourtant tant d'âmes fortes. Villes non pas pauvres (voire des banques, des maisons d'apparence bourgeoise), mais dénuées: dénuées de beauté, de confort, d'activité. Hôtels maussades dont je connais à l'avance l'invariable et insipide menu. Cabarets, pubs à l'anglaise, où l'on consomme debout, appuyé au comptoir de bois, les pintes de porter noir.
>
> ('the dull lethargy of these little Irish towns that nonetheless produced so many strong souls. Not that these towns are poor [see all the banks and bourgeois-looking houses] but rather bereft: bereft of beauty, of comfort, of activity. Sulking hotels whose

---

42 Jacques-Louis de la Tocnaye, *A Frenchman's Walk through Ireland, 1796-7*, translated by John Stevenson (Dublin: Blackstaff Press, facsimile of 1917 edition, reprinted 1984), 53.
43 Simone Téry, *En Irlande, de la guerre d'indépendance à la guerre civile, 1914-23* (Paris: Ernest Flammarion, 1923), 108.
44 Leduc, 265.
45 Sjoestedt, 842.

invariable and insipid menus I already know. Bars, English-style pubs where people drink pints of black porter, standing up and leaning on the wooden counter').[46]

Poverty brings with it a listlessness, a deadness, reducing everything to black and white, levelling and narrowing time into just one dimension: an eternal present in which people are trapped like characters in some Beckett play where – as the joke goes – nothing happens, twice. Time stands still for the poor, it smooths away the contours of their days which now stand empty. Time is something to be overcome, to be killed. Corkonians spend their time yawning.[47] Young people in Tralee lean on walls for hours on end, not knowing what to do with themselves, their faces reflecting the hopelessness all around.[48] Further west, in Dingle, Poisson notes tumble-down houses, their roofs covered in long grass which is certain to trap rain and cause the roofs and houses to collapse. Their occupants, however, are 'devant la porte occupés à ne rien faire' ('outside their doors, busy doing nothing').[49] Poisson's annoyance is palpable: why don't these people just get up and tidy the place? An alternative interpretation could be that they are suffering some kind of psychic breakdown, frozen in a never-ending present, unable to imagine a better future into which they might haul themselves by taking even tiny steps out of their misery.

At an intimate level, poverty can even mark the body, erasing evidence of time passing from the faces of the poor and aging them prematurely. Of the beggar women on the Giant's Causeway, Poisson confesses that he cannot guess their age as they seem worn down equally by age and destitution.[50] The words chosen to describe the poor betray the travellers' mindsets. Poor children in Killarney *swarm*;[51] in Waterford, they go about in *herds*;[52] destitute Scots heading for Belfast in a surely doomed search for a better life reminds Swiss scientist, Marc-Auguste Pictet (1752–1825), of

---

46   Sjoestedt, 842.
47   De la Tocnaye, 73.
48   Sjoestedt, 842.
49   Poisson, 88.
50   *Ibid.*, 225.
51   Daryl, 98.
52   De Bovet, 117.

Poverty-Trapped

animals.⁵³ The poor build mud huts for themselves, often sharing them with their animals; they live in 'lairs' and forage for food,⁵⁴ drink water from streams running through Cork city⁵⁵ and go about naked. They have no intelligible language, no evidence of intellectual life. It would be pointless to talk to them or try to reason with them for they could not understand. Pichot uses a horsewhip to forge his way through a crowd of beggars, as if they were animals.⁵⁶ When alms are given to them – coins or handfuls of oats – these are often not handed to them but thrown at them, scattered on the ground in front of them.⁵⁷ The pigs wandering through the poorer areas of Limerick scavenging for food are graphically described by Pichot as 'des mendiants irlandais à quatre pattes' ('four-legged Irish beggars').⁵⁸ This image says it all.

There is more. Old beggar women on the Giant's Causeway have witch-like faces⁵⁹; an old man begging in Kenmare is a 'vieux sorcier'.⁶⁰ In Dungarvan, Pichot felt trapped by hoards of hideous, Hydra-like heads more awful than anything out of mythology, or anything in Dante's or Virgil's worst dreams.⁶¹ In other words, the poor are in no way 'normal' or 'civilised' but wild and possibly mad:

> De jeunes filles, sans coiffure, échevelées, parées de haillons couvrant une crinoline, les pieds nus dans la boue ou sur un pavé aigu et froid, riant presque comme des idiotes.
>
> ('young girls, dishevelled, decked out in rags covering a crinoline, their feet naked in the mud or on a rough, cold pathway, laughing almost like idiots').⁶²

Human or not, creatures not of nurture but of nature, the poor are not even always whole: frequently denied any bodily integrity, they are merely

---

53 Pictet, 111.
54 Poisson, 225.
55 De la Tocnaye, 74.
56 Pichot, 228.
57 De la Tocnaye, 75.
58 Pichon, 13.
59 Poisson, 225.
60 Pichot, 379.
61 *Ibid.*, 227–228.
62 Poisson, 240.

unattached, disjointed, begging hands, grimacing heads or piles of disembodied rags. A three-headed 'monster' spotted in Dungarvan during the Famine by Edouard Déchy (a self-described 'ancien militaire' 'former soldier') turns out to be a mother carrying two children on her shoulders. And so, there we have it: this centuries-long descriptive avalanche hints at a species not quite human, closer to animals or mythical creatures, to the nightmare worlds of Bosch or Brueghel than to anything resembling normality. Poverty has transmogrified the poor into something different, alien, out there.

Why are they poor? Is their poverty inevitable or not? These travellers try to understand why the Irish strike it rich everywhere except in Ireland.[63] External reasons are advanced by journalist Charles Legras (1872–1942): it is simply because Ireland is a colony, like India or Egypt.[64] There is thus nothing exceptional about poverty in Ireland: is poverty not the fate of all colonies? Then again, poverty can follow war[65] or flawed legislation.[66] Explanations are found closer to home: the economic stagnation and resulting poverty all too visible on the empty streets of Cork in 1881 are attributed by Canis to the Land League which scares the locals into staying at home.[67] A generation or so later, nothing has changed: this time, Cork's empty streets are ascribed to escalating violence which frightens people from venturing outdoors.[68]

Commentators sometimes seek explanations not in external factors like politics, but in the people themselves, for instance in their religion. One of many dichotomies running through these texts distinguishes the industrious (Protestant) North from the indolent (Catholic) South: Lisburn is thriving,[69] Belfast is booming.[70] For some French onlookers, the explanation

---

63   De Bovet, 79.
64   Charles Legras, *Terre d'Irlande* (Paris: Paul Ollendorff, 1898), 80.
65   Jordan, 130.
66   Prévost, 1846, 266.
67   Canis, 149.
68   *Rapport de la commission envoyée en Irlande par le parti travailliste anglais*, translated from English by J. Gros (Paris: La Délégation Irlandaise, 1921), 30.
69   Bombelle, 224.
70   Daryl, 292.

is clear: the North of Ireland is not Irish;[71] in fact, Belfast is Scottish.[72] Indeed, entering prosperous Derry is like stepping into another world.[73] Other explanations emerge: again and again, we are told that the Irish are poor because they drink too much. Some commentators wonder, however, whether alcoholism is a cause or a consequence of poverty. Explanations of a more personal and intimate nature are advanced by photographer and teacher, Marguérite Mespoulet (1880–1965), who quotes a Galway fringe-maker in 1913 explaining that if she had fewer children, she would have more time for remunerated work.[74] Perhaps such a rare confession for the period – a woman regretting having too many children – could have been made only to another woman, one of the rare women among these French travellers.

Essentialist 'explanations' are advanced: poverty results from something in the Irish DNA. The Irish prefer contemplation to action. To put it more brutally, the Irish are lazy. From the seventeenth century onwards, this trope is everywhere. Irish laziness 'explains' why commercial possibilities obvious to French commentators everywhere on the streets of the country, visible in Mitchelstown even to a French adolescent girl, a refugee from the Franco-Prussian War, remain untapped. Irish men, more than their womenfolk, are guilty here. In Killarney, men seem tired from doing nothing.[75] Male 'flâneurs' fill the streets of Limerick while their womenfolk are busy making lace.[76] Some commentators such as l'Abbé Domenach challenge this equation of Irishness with laziness,[77] but their voices are drowned out. For Daryl, as for prolific author and intrepid travel, Anne-Marie de Bovet (1855–1919), perceived Irish listlessness is some sort of 'aménie'.[78] With another telling medical image De Bovet lambastes the Irish: 'la mendicité, ils

71 Jean Gabriel Cappot de Feuillide, *L'Irlande* (Paris: Dufey, 1839), 259.
72 De la Tocnaye, 222.
73 Daryl, 279.
74 Marguérite Mespoulet, *Carnet d'Irlande* (Paris: Musée Albert Kahn, 2005), item number 15.
75 Daryl, 98.
76 Pichot, volume 2, 9.
77 Domenech, 116.
78 Daryl, 16 ; de Bovet, 140.

l'ont dans le sang' ('begging is in their blood').[79] The message is clear: the Irish are fated to be lazy: it is in their blood.

In this context, the anti-poverty measures witnessed often stem from outside the community in question. Protestant women in the poverty-stricken West enable local women to earn money through embroidery and textile work.[80] A Quaker presence is credited with the cleanliness of the village of Ballytore.[81] A Protestant presence 'explains' why Ventry, unlike neighbouring villages, is buzzing with life and learning.[82] Limerick owes its lace-making to Nottingham entrepreneurs.[83] Overseas (especially Scottish) merchants develop industry in Cork.[84] Schindler regrets the loss of French Huguenot business acumen to cities like Belfast.[85] The list is endless but the implication is clear: left to their own devices, the Irish poor are feckless, incapable of helping themselves.

This allegation is further intensified by constant depictions of the Irish as children. Even well-disposed travellers employ this infantilising, proto-colonial discourse: in a seemingly well-disposed passage, writer and journalist, Louis Enault (1824–1900), notes how quickly onlookers forget their recent trauma of witnessing throngs of emigrants leaving the port of Cork.[86] Like children, they live in the moment, with little or no sense of time, quickly forgetting recent sorrows, with eyes for no one but their new best friends.

Travellers' reactions are as numerous and diverse as the travellers themselves. They do not merely record what they witness: they let us in to their thoughts which then become part of their commentaries. At one extreme, they are without pity: the poor are undeserving – indeed, they are not poor, just pretending to be poor to trick innocent passers-by: Tardivel claims that child beggars in Queenstown are better dressed than himself.[87] The

79 De Bovet, 140.
80 Roussel, 133, 138.
81 Bombelle, 260.
82 Roussel, 86.
83 Pichot, 10.
84 De la Tocnaye, 74.
85 Schindler, 112.
86 Louis Enault, *Angleterre, Ecosse, Irlande. Voyage Pittoresque* (Paris: Morizot, 1859).
87 Tardivel, 23.

poor-but-happy trope surfaces: near Thurles, Enault encounters children who are stark naked but, he stresses, happy, well-fed and healthy-looking.[88] In fact, perversely, poverty can be the mark of the true aristocrat![89] Enault is adamant: the women of Limerick, though ragged, barefoot and dishevelled, look like Greek goddesses or queens disguised as beggars.[90] Much could be said about this fetishisation/ eroticisation of female poverty. However, the overall message is clear: although these women are poor, this is unimportant as they possess invisible riches. This absolves the observer's conscience: he need not help them as they are doing just fine.

Then there is the perverse and cruel logic of commentators like Pichot: being poor and handicapped is actually an advantage; indeed, poor families with members suffering from some physical or mental problem are particularly fortunate as this will generate generous alms, he claims.[91]

The poor are annoyingly intrusive: Poisson complains that his companions had to suffer the rough, insulting, mocking curiosity of a bedraggled people.[92] The sight of ragged, penniless crowds ruins the traveller's enjoyment of the riverbanks in Waterford.[93] Indeed, de la Tocnaye advises not that poverty should be tackled but that beggars and tramps should be removed from the streets.[94] In short, poverty should not be solved but hidden, Potemkin-style. Worse than annoying, however, the poor are terrifying, they strain the nerves.[95] The warning of poet-revolutionary, Lamartine (1790–1869), comes to mind: 'le pauvre a faim et la France a peur' ('when the poor are hungry, France gets worried').

No matter what the poor do, it is wrong. If they do nothing, they are lazy. If they imitate the young girls trying to sell trinkets to tourists in Killarney by running frantically after their carriages, they are slammed as prostitutes.[96] If they copy the seasonal beggars who erect miserable huts

88 Enault, 445.
89 Sjoestedt, 850.
90 Enault, 497.
91 Ibid., 229.
92 Poisson, 239.
93 Déchy, 197.
94 De la Tocnaye, 62.
95 Pichot, 228–229, 387.
96 Poisson, 245.

along the roads around Killarney to beg from passing tourists, they are annoying.[97] In any case, all beggars are guilty of the sin of theft, as a French Protestant helpfully explains to a beggar in Cork![98]

Can such poverty ever be eradicated? The poor themselves reject certain 'solutions': in famine-stricken Mayo, in 1835, Pichot records a man who would rather die than humiliate himself by begging; others refuse to enter the workhouse as this would mean leaving one's wife[99] or surrendering children possibly to be raised as Protestants or sent far away.[100] They refuse to migrate to the towns: albeit impoverished, they remain on ancestral lands where the halo effect of past glories and past status comforts them in their present destitution: 'là du moins ils étaient regardés jadis comme des rois et des reines' ('there at least, they were once seen as kings and queens').[101] They beg, entertain or harass passers-by for alms, they strike for a just wage, they help each other, they protest. This is a poignant scene is from Daniel O'Connell's hometown of Cahersiveen:

> 'accompagnés de leur curé qui s'était mis à leur tête, ces pâles affamés se promenèrent un jour dans les rues de leur ville, portant un drapeau noir, symbole poignant, sur lequel était écrit en gros caractères: Travail et pain'.
>
> ('accompanied by their priest who was at the front, these pale, starving creatures paraded through their town one day, carrying a black flag, a poignant symbol, on which was written in large letters: Work and bread').[102]

With their pittances, they finance O'Connell who is consequently scorned by a Protestant French visitor to Cork as the king of the beggars. Many vote with their feet: they emigrate. Cork is thronged with would-be emigrants, forever waiting as the departing boats are constantly

---

97   De la Tocnaye, 107.
98   Pichot, 377.
99   *Ibid.*
100   De la Tocnaye, 75.
101   Anne Keary, *L'Irlande il y a quarante ans*, translated from English by Madame de Witt (Paris: Hachette, 1889), 115.
102   Canis, 113.

full.¹⁰³ Ironically, these emigrants are, insists Legras, the very people most needed, the most energetic, the most intelligent.¹⁰⁴

These French travellers are, however, in the main, a resolutely positive bunch. They see solutions everywhere. They refuse to be beaten. Alongside discussions on macro solutions, travellers like the young de Tocqueville walk the streets of the country seeking local answers to poverty. To every problem he encounters he scatters pragmatic solutions. People in Cork are reduced to collecting rain water and to drinking from streams on the streets? Provide running water to the entire city. People want to work? Build workhouses, establish public works schemes. The poor seem content to live in squalor? Give them a decent standard of living and they will respect it. He even goes so far as to supply a recipe for baking bread!¹⁰⁵

Ireland's poor haven't gone away, nor have French commentators on this endemic problem. To this day, economic matters in Ireland – including poverty – are regularly scrutinised in France by voluntary organisations including ADT Quart Monde-France and SSVP-France (Société de Saint Vincent de Paul-France) and even by bloggers.¹⁰⁶ Our understanding of poverty in Ireland owes much to the insights of traveller-witnesses such as de Tocqueville, and of French academic studies ranging from the Great Famine to the Celtic Tiger and its aftermath, for instance, in rich collections such as the aforementioned *Reimagining Ireland* series at Peter Lang. Journalists in *Le Monde*, *Libération* and *La Croix* have tracked the emergence of Ireland from poverty from the 1950s onwards through the work of Sean Lemass (1899–1971) and T. K. Whitaker (1916–2017), the impact of foreign direct investment, the rise and demise of the Celtic Tiger, down to the possible emergence of new poor in Ireland following Brexit and Covid-19. At another level, issues like the exorbitant cost of student accommodation in Ireland also attract French attention, as did the heartwarming story of the millions of euro collected in Ireland in 2020 for the

103   *Ibid.*, 126.
104   Legras, 81.
105   De Tocqueville, 75.
106   My thanks to Oliver O'Hanlon for alerting me to Johanna Jacquot-Albrecht's blog. See, for instance, her blog on the plight of women immigrants to Ireland, in *L'Obs avec Rue89*, 25 January 2017.

Choctaw native American people now ravaged by Covid-19, as payback for the 170 dollars they sent to the starving Irish at the height of the Famine in 1847. As Pierre Bouvier remarks in *Le Monde* on 6 May 2020, the generosity in 1847 of a people themselves poor, a people expelled from their ancestral lands following the Indian Removal Act, found an echo in 2020 at the other side of the ocean in Ireland among people who have never forgotten what it felt like to be poor and starving. Perhaps here, somewhere, is a lesson in solidarity and a message of hope for these troubled times.

Pour Lynda O'Toole: hommage, amitiés

EAMONN WALL

8 Irish Studies in North America: Reflections

Academic Irish Studies in North America is framed inside a narrow timeline: the American Conference for Irish Studies (ACIS) was established in 1960 and the Canadian Association for Irish Studies/ *L'association canadienne d'études irlandaises* (CAIS/RCÉI) was founded in 1973. Both ACIS and CAIS have succeeded in attracting, developing and sustaining membership and scholarship through the past half-century. Before these organisations appeared, scholars whose work focused on Ireland and its Diaspora worked on the margins of other organisations such as the Modern Language Association and the American Historical Association, organisations that aligned themselves with more traditional embraces of British and American literature, history, culture, methodologies and so on. For the purposes of this chapter, my focus will be primarily of Irish Studies in the United States. Except for joint ACIS/CAIS conferences, I have not had the opportunity to attend CAIS conferences or Irish Studies events in Canada, so my firsthand knowledge is limited.

Though they dominate the field today, ACIS and CAIS have not completely absorbed all Irish-focused scholarship: for complex reasons, Ireland's history and literature continue to occupy space within the AHA and the MLA. What divides ACIS and CAIS from these older organisations is their wider critical lens focus, and their transgressive nature. Irish Studies is an interdisciplinary activity that allows one to cross boundaries and push down barriers. In separating itself from the MLA, while retaining a foothold there by hosting panels at annual conferences, ACIS was breaking with the older association's more monochrome ways of thinking in relation to scholarship. Irish Studies requires a greater space. In this chapter, in keeping with the spirit of Irish Studies scholarship and attitude, I will seek to align two narratives and two styles. I will recount some of the activities that I have found notable within Irish Studies while underlining this with details from my own experience as a member and past President of ACIS.

It is notable that ACIS began in 1960, the year that JFK was elected President. Kennedy's election and the *Zeitgeist* it set in motion, alongside the entry of under-represented communities into third-level education, push-started demands for the inclusion of Ethnic Studies in curricula. Ethnic Studies scholars aligned with new approaches to research such as critical theory in literary studies, these new emphases accommodating the work of scholars who sought to work across disciplines. Both ACIS and CAIS were fortunate to have these new methodologies available to their members at a time when they were forming themselves into professional associations and seeking ways to make their scholarship different in tone, outlook and manner from their antecedents. In addition to focusing on Ireland and its Diaspora separately, Irish Studies scholars, helped by how the UK, the US, Canada and Ireland have intersected through the centuries, have been able to revise and undermine received narratives of Ireland. In literary studies, for example, Irish Studies scholars may read *The Tempest* and *Beowulf* in more nuanced ways than others might. Perhaps at its core Irish Studies, following Friel's *Translations*, is the product of resistance to English, the primary language of its scholarship. In Canada, Irish Studies is both/ and the Canadian Association for Irish Studies/*L'association canadienne d'études irlandaises*: the Anglophone and Francophone being equal. This in itself is significant. Working across disciplines, scholars inhabit large interdisciplinary and self-reflexive spaces as they push to understand Ireland and its Diaspora. In literary studies, to give an example, the 'New Criticism' was ill-suited to revealing the totality of the Irish narrative swerve – other strategies such as New Historicism were required to complement it.

Ireland, a European country, occupies a unique, and not always readily understood, place in American Ethnic Studies. For the most part, Irish Studies scholars in the US are more interested in Ireland than they are in Irish America. At the same time, academic Irish Studies associations, both in North America and internationally, excepting the island of Ireland, are closely entwined with the Diaspora, whereas in Ireland scholars gather in themed conferences and colloquia. Scholars in Ireland belong to the everyday lived experience of Ireland: Irish Studies scholars in North America and elsewhere belong to the Diaspora. In addition to their academic components, CAIS and ACIS serve as homes away from home for scholars, and as ropes that link them as individuals to Ireland and to one another. This highly personal and deeply emotional aspect should not be underestimated. A great many members of both organisations can trace ancestry back to Ireland; however, many others have come to Irish Studies through an interest in a theme, book, song, a time period, or some other act of awakening that occurred on a college campus, at a theatre, in a book read in a library, or a song heard on the radio. It is as natural for an American or Canadian Irish Studies scholar to be interested in Ireland as it is for someone in Limerick or Belfast studying America to be interested in studying the Battle of Gettysburg, or the novels of Maya Angelou. We can become Canadian, American, Irish through embrace of place and culture.

Ireland is a small country so it is easy for scholars living there to connect and belong. The US is large and Canada is vast, with the result that ACIS and CAIS are not just convenient but also career- and life-sustaining. One might argue that an Irish Studies organisation in Ireland would seem redundant, though this is not a simple notion. North American national and regional conferences are also international affairs, as they attract scholars from Ireland, and elsewhere, who deliver plenaries and papers and this has been productive in terms of the sharing of research and expertise as well as creating opportunities for dialogue and collaboration. Though scholars in the many other American Ethnic Studies groups trace connections between the United States and countries and regions that immigrants have come to America from, their primary focus is on life in America. Irish Studies scholars prefer to look beyond the American neighbourhood, parish, village, factory and farm to Ireland, 'the land of the heart's desire'. Though many brilliant scholars of Irish America have presented papers at ACIS and written important books on the subject, Irish America has remained something of a minor interest to scholars. Recently, as Ireland has become more multicultural and multi-ethnic, it has appeared to be more closely aligned with multicultural America than with Irish America. In this respect, the work of such Irish American writers as James T. Farrell and

Mary Gordon has become more relevant to understanding the immigrant experience in Ireland.

The interdisciplinary nature of Irish Studies separates ACIS and CAIS from other academic associations that focus on Ireland. The International James Joyce Foundation, founded in Dublin in 1967 and located at the University of Tulsa today, has as its mission the study of Joyce's work and his milieu. The Harvard Celtic Colloquium focuses on the Celtic languages, including Irish. Harvard's Department of Celtic Languages and Literatures also sponsors an annual lecture in honour of John V. Kelleher. Kelleher, Harvard's first professor of Irish Studies, is considered by many to be the founding figure of Irish Studies in the US. Celtic Studies has had a presence at Harvard since 1896, an indication that the academic study of Ireland has always held a foothold in American universities. Footholds, in the form of individual historians, literary scholars, archaeologists and political scientists, have been a constant if invisible presence on university campuses for a long time, indeed, for as long as the Irish have featured in cultural life.

In addition to universities, cultural organisations have promoted Ireland through events such as lectures, exhibitions, readings and publications from the eighteenth century to the present. We should not assume that all serious inquiry and performance takes place on college campuses. Arguably the most famous of all of these artistic events was Oscar Wilde's 1882 American tour. As Peter Wyse Jackson has pointed out in reference to Wilde's St Louis visit:

> On a Saturday night in February 1882, Wilde spoke to the assembled crowd. Some 2,000 ticket buyers packed the largest hall in St. Louis, that of the Mercantile Library on the corner of Broadway and Locust. He lectured on 'The Decorative Arts'. Perhaps owing to the local preference for plain speech … this 'elocution on aesthetics' did not go down too well.[1]

Though Wilde was not always reverently received and often lampooned during his tour, he used the platforms provided to speak on the Irish issues of the day, even taking the opportunity to express his support for The Land

---

1 Peter Wyse Jackson, "Foreword," in *Oscar Wilde in St. Louis*, edited by John Wyse Jackson (St Louis: Missouri Botanical Garden and UMSL, 2012), 6.

League in his interview with *Globe-Democrat* in St Louis.[2] Wilde, Yeats, and the many other authors and public figures who embarked on speaking tours in America in the nineteenth and twentieth centuries played important roles in turning American heads towards Ireland and framing it as a unique and complex place capable of producing formidable literary figures. These events seeded Irish Studies. The speakers were eloquent, and eloquence has always been an admired element throughout the Irish Diaspora. Irish Americans flocked to literary events and performances and turned out in even greater numbers to hear political figures speak. These political figures were promotors of both Irish culture and political ideology.

We are inclined to think that the Catholic Church was the centrepiece of Irish American life and this is quite true; however, public lectures, societies and trade unions provided opportunities for Irish Americans to educate themselves before third-level education became an option for most people. Universities did not invent Irish Studies; rather, they brought it into the academy where it has been funded and rebranded. Of course, through literary festivals, lectures, film screenings and Irish film festivals, Canadian and Irish American associations continue to provide their audiences with major events that often include presentations from academics affiliated with ACIS and CAIS. The most popular traditional Irish art form in the US is music. Each year at its largest gathering, the Milwaukee Irish Festival, the programme includes, in addition to concerts and workshops, many lectures and readings. Academic organisations are important, but so are more community-based organisations, many of long-standing. Among well-known organisations in the US are IACI, the Irish American Cultural Institute, founded in 1962, and the American Irish Historical Society, founded in 1897, and an important presence in the cultural life of New York. Many North American cities have societies and centres – large and small – dedicated to the study of Ireland. Important Irish Studies literary/academic journals founded in North America and operating still include the *Canadian Journal of Irish Studies/Revue canadienne d'études irlandaises* (*CJIS/RCÉI*), the official scholarly publication of CAIS, begun in in 1974; *Eire-Ireland*, published by IACI since 1966; and *New Hibernia*

2   Ibid., 74.

Review, published by the Center for Irish Studies at the University of St Thomas since 1996. ACIS does not publish its own journal; however, *The Irish Literary Supplement*, a review of work in Irish Studies, is distributed to its members.

At one of the first ACIS conferences I attended, a Midwest regional meeting held at and co-sponsored by the Irish American Cultural Center in Chicago, I sat for an hour after lunch talking with Lawrence J. McCaffrey, an ACIS founder, past president and major figure in Irish Studies. Larry spoke to me about travelling to Ireland by boat as a young scholar after the Second World War, visiting his relatives in the border areas where he heard women keen at the wake of a relative, working in the National Library and wandering though the cafes and pubs in Dublin conversing with scholars, writers and ordinary people. Of a generation who had seen service in armed conflict overseas, Larry had no fear of joining into conversations with strangers. I asked him about Richard Ellmann and Larry said he was ubiquitous in the Dublin of that period when fewer American scholars than is the case today were present in Ireland. I asked him about Austin Clarke and quizzed him regarding the theatre of the time – his visits to the Abbey and Gate – which, among other cultural matters, I was curious about. Blanche Touhill, another ACIS founder, headed to Australia with her husband Joe for her research on the Young Irelanders, a voyage of some novelty at the time. At that time, I still thought of international travel as involving either emigration or vacation rather than scholarly activity. My own family background was in business: the old people I grew up around spoke of intellectuals and professors with suspicion.

Of course, waiting in O'Hare to get my flight home to Omaha the next day, I counted off the many questions I should have asked Professor McCaffrey. The conversation brought home to me the importance of having scholars born outside Ireland research and write about Ireland. Yes, they had the background and training but, more importantly, their experience growing up outside of Ireland allowed them to bring unique perspectives to the study of Ireland. From that day on while attending conferences, I have embraced the idea that, for example, a great way to understand the tight world of an Irish town as revealed in the work of an Irish novelist such as John McGahern is through the lens of a writer like Alice McDermott or

William Kennedy, Irish American masters of the grainy, urban, claustrophobic locale.

As a writer/scholar, Larry McCaffrey, like many Canadian and American scholars following in his wake, engaged with Irish people on the ground as he sought to absorb the *blas* of Ireland to add to the understanding he absorbed from books and documents. My favourite anecdote of that Chicago afternoon in 1993 was his description of a cold call he had made to Seán Ó Faoláin's home: Larry knocked on the door, announced who he was – a young, unknown scholar from Chicago – and was invited in to share a pot of tea and thus began a friendship. Professor McCaffrey asked me about my own scholarship, what books I would write and encouraged me to maintain my connections to my homeplace in Ireland while building a life in the US, and to work in the field of Irish America. Irish America is an important subject, he told me, but not popular among young scholars, who all look towards Ireland because they want to go there and engage with that world of fable and magic. These American and Canadian scholars reimagine Ireland. Perhaps, I might reimagine Irish America.[3]

I was flattered by Larry's confidence in me, though dismayed that he thought me capable of writing books at a time when the prospect of presenting a conference paper to a room of professors unnerved me no end. 'You', Larry went on, 'grew up in Ireland, you know it well, so I encourage you to explore what you do not yet fully understand: immigrant life in America. You are a scholar and an immigrant'. He ended the conversation by handing me additional drink tickets for the conference reception taking place that evening – to seal the deal! A couple of years later, Edna Longley provided a summary dismissal of Irish America, 'the politics of that East Coast construct "Irish America"', a reminder of the contested nature of all things Irish.[4] Of course, she was wrong. I was in Chicago, another Irish America that did not follow in anyone's footsteps, certainly not New York's or Boston's.

---

3   It is apposite that this chapter should appear in the 100th volume of the *Reimagining Ireland* series for that fact alone!
4   Edna Longley, 'Irish Bards and American Audiences', *The Southern Review* 31, no. 3 (Summer 1995), 757.

I took Professor McCaffrey's advice: I learned more about Irish America while maintaining old loyalties and ties in Ireland. Intuitively, I felt that Larry had been able to divine what I was thinking, to trace the outline of the road I might travel. In Eavan Boland's term, he had given me permission.[5] ACIS and CAIS have given scholars permission to think about Ireland as a subject and avenue and not just as an afterthought or alley way as had been the case in the past. A few years later, when mentoring became a much-used term in academia, I understood that it underlined Larry's purpose. Our impromptu dialogue represented not only a meeting of people who thought from the outset that they could talk to each other disarmingly, but it was also a warm gesture of welcome to a young scholar by a senior member of the clan. Years later, Charles Fanning told me that Professor McCaffrey greeted him at his first ACIS conference by telling him that he had read his (Fanning's) recently completed dissertation, something that amazed Fanning, at that time a young scholar setting out on his own career path. It is important that young scholars be welcomed, spoken to and encouraged, otherwise they may not come back a second time and those wonderful articles or monographs will dissipate like smoke rather than find their way into print. In hindsight, I realised that Larry had read the short article I had written on the Irish artistic activity in New York in the late 1980s and early 1990s.

Recently, guided by the conversations spawned by the *Me Too* movement, I have wondered if women scholars in Irish Studies in the United States at that time were afforded similar opportunities. I hope that this has been the case; certainly, at ACIS, many women have served as President of the organisation and on the executive committee as well as guiding our scholarship in new directions. I should add that women scholars in Irish Studies in the United States, going by what they have shared with me, often casually, have provided me with great encouragement and sustenance though the decades: Jeanne Flood, Patricia Boyle Haberstroh, Janet Nolan, Maureen Murphy, Nathalie F. Anderson, Donna Potts, Mary Pat Kelly, to mention just a few of many women whose interventions have helped me

---

5   Eavan Boland, *Object Lessons: The Life of the Woman and the Poet in Our Time* (New York; Norton, 1995), xii.

greatly in the professional sphere. Scholars are greatly aided by their spouses and partners at home, who rarely attend conferences but who must make sacrifices so that we can hear papers, greet colleagues and enjoy late nights.

Also, except for my recent monograph, all of my books have been acquired, edited and seen into print by women: Mary Elizabeth Braun at the University of Wisconsin Press, Barbara Hanrahan at the University of Notre Dame Press, and Jessie Lendennie and Siobhan Hutson at Salmon Poetry. At these presses that sustain scholarship and writing, almost all of the work in editing, indexing, design, production and marketing, is done by very highly skilled and brilliant women. My recent book is with Arlen House, a press with a long history of publishing the work of women across the spectrum of the arts.

After that Chicago meeting I knew that I would return to ACIS gatherings. In fact, through the decades ACIS has become a second home. Academics working in our field in North America are likely to be solo Irish Studies flyers at their colleges, so Irish Studies conferences are important venues for discussion and also, at a very basic level, opportunities to meet with people who speak our language. The immigrant's deficit is his/her homeplace; for me, ACIS has always been more than an association that I have belonged to – it's been a homeplace. The United States and Canada are enormous spaces where we can easily become lost, and our work colleagues are not always interested in, or even aware of, what we do; and this is why CAIS and ACIS are so important to our morale and our very survival as scholars/teachers.

Is Irish Studies in North America guided by a worldview? Have scholarly and pedagogical apparatuses being developed to underwrite our work? Where do we stand politically? At the outset of my involvement, this matter did not concern me, so nervous was I about whatever paper I had to deliver. In that same 1995 essay referenced earlier, Edna Longley noted:

> the mainly traditionalist critical approaches of the American Conference for Irish Studies (ACIS), a body that spans history and literature; and a new theorized and politicized phenomenon called Irish Cultural Studies. Irish Cultural Studies derive from an intersection between literary theory and Irish Republicanism, and tend to apply 'post-colonial' parameters in a historically dubious way.[6]

6   Longley, 'Irish Bards and American Audiences', 763.

By way of contrast, Longley praises the more highbrow American scholars of Yeats and Joyce, because 'these generally ignore contemporary Ireland', with the result that, in her view, critical standards have not been undermined by such issues such as ethnicity, gender, identity and class. In other words, these scholars have retained their new-critical might and insight.

Through the decades, ACIS scholars of literature have been guided by the work of theorists from Derrida, to Lacan, to Cixous, to Eagleton, to Bakhtin and so on. Literary scholarship for ACIS is, philosophically, a kind of portmanteau affair, and, as such, hardly traditional. In literary studies, Longley herself is a traditionalist so it is not easy to divine what she means when she decries ACIS scholars' 'traditionalist critical approaches'. I think that the current generation of scholars are more sophisticated than my generation has been in integrating text and theory in sophisticated ways. However, no house critical philosophy has emerged and this has been a strength. My sense is that Irish Studies in Europe is more deeply grounded in theory. But there are exceptions to this – the early driving force of ecocriticism, for example, has emerged through the work of American and Canadian scholars such as Christine Cusick, Derek Gladwin, Kathryn Kirkpatrick and others. North American scholarship works best when it moves in tandem with work carried out in Ireland and elsewhere, with the spread of ecocriticism through Irish scholarly communities worldwide being a good example of this.

Longley's contention that Irish Cultural Studies is somehow related to Irish Republicanism does not makes great sense, and assumes that Irish Studies in North America promotes, or used to promote, the agenda of the IRA. ACIS has been closely aligned with the Irish and British governments through their co-sponsorships of conferences, an indication of where both the organisations and governments see themselves ideologically. The British and Irish governments have worked closely with ACIS because they have viewed the work of the membership as a buffer against the message of violent republicanism. Absent from ACIS have been scholars who are avowedly republican, an indication that such scholars view ACIS as an unwelcome venue. At the 1995 ACIS symposium, hosted by Queen's University, Belfast, the conference banquet was hosted by the DUP mayor of the city. ACIS has never been a political organisation to the extent that its leadership promotes a political agenda though it has been sensitive to change as recently seen in its addition of a 'Women's, Gender, and Sexualities Studies Representative' to its board. Through the decades, I would have liked the organisation to have been more involved in activism on the part of Irish immigrants; however, many good reasons exist for a contrary view, so it is something I never pushed in public.

Looking towards the future of Irish Studies in North America, the prospects seem quite mixed. On the one hand, the strong, vibrant and well-funded programmes such as those at Concordia University in Montreal, University of Notre Dame, New York University and Boston College in the US are likely to maintain their strength and grow. All Irish Studies scholars depend on these programmes for the leadership they provide, for the light they shine on our activities and for the graduate students they train. Other universities in the US and Canada are more focused on undergraduate education, providing their students with detailed introductions to Irish material as well as study-abroad opportunities in Ireland. These programmes are important in many respects, not least because they reach many people, and these include many long-standing mainstays of Irish Studies such as Villanova University and the University of St Thomas in St Paul, among others. Also, the Irish holdings at American libraries, such as those at Emory University, the University of Texas, and elsewhere, will continue to draw scholars from all over the world to the US. Even smaller and less well-known institutions such as Southern Illinois University-Carbondale with its extensive Brian O'Nolan archives, among other holdings, is important in this respect. Around the same time that SIU-Carbondale was collecting Irish material, the University of Victoria in British Columbia was assembling its holdings of the work of contemporary Irish writers. North America will remain central to Irish Studies scholarship, because the great libraries are well-funded and will continue to collect Irish material. Delegates will continue to travel to the US and Canada for conferences and to submit their work for publication in the excellent journals published in North America. When I co-chaired the committee that brought the 1994 ACIS to Creighton University, we were thrilled to welcome 200 delegates. Numbers attending are habitually more than double that today.

For all the great growth in numbers and the rising quality of presentations, serious storm clouds have gathered. One wonders how sustainable Irish Studies will be in the academia of the future given the dearth of funding available to universities and the belief on the part of university leaders that education can be run on American business models. In other words, how many of the great graduate students we hear presenting their work at conferences will be able to find employment in universities? If these women and men do not secure academic appointments, will they continue with their writing and research, or will they give up? Of course, Americans and Canadians will still travel to Ireland, literally and imaginatively, but these efforts will not be enough to sustain the scholarly footprint.

When I was a student in New York in the 1980s and working as a part-timer at Borough of Manhattan Community College in New York, I would often stop into Keshcarrigan Bookshop to chat with its owner Angela Carter, the bookshop getting its name from her home place in Co. Leitrim. This tiny bookstore in the heart of the financial district was carefully curated, so there was always something of interest to find there. Angela was a fountain of knowledge and opinion. Even though she promoted everything Irish, her great love and passion was for the Irish language. Angela believed that Irish Americans should donate less to the Catholic Church and more to Irish cultural institutions. I think that she was right. Now that funding for cultural initiatives and university programmes has been curtailed, for ideological and other reasons, it is time for these organisations and institutions to seek private sector partners. In the past, private donors have provided the funding that has made the great programmes at Notre Dame, NYU, Boston College possible and this model should be replicated elsewhere. We should seek support for initiatives such as scholarships, programmes, salaries, fellowships, endowments, bursaries for travel and research and conference registration and expenses, etc. Though Irish Americans are generally viewed as being conservative, they are not a monolith. Many have been to Ireland and, if asked, will support such endeavours.

It is my belief that academic organisations should work more closely with their non-academic counterparts to help promote and sustain one another. Working with both over the years, I am often surprised to discover how unaware they sometimes are of each other. Attending the Chicago Irish festival at the Irish Heritage Center, run over three days and full of performances, readings, lectures and demonstrations, I have always been in awe of its energy and its sense of being a cultural street fair. When I leave,

I wonder how we can find ways to have organisations like ACIS work with the Chicago Irish Festival on initiatives. Though I am a die-hard fan of live concerts and lectures, digital media does provide us with opportunities to expand the audience for Irish Studies, both in terms of events and publications. Of course, we must remain relevant, and our complex history does not fit simply into any mould. But when we bring people from outside into our domain, we are often reminded of how central Ireland is to lived experience elsewhere. The University of Missouri-St Louis, where I work, is located across a highway from Ferguson, where Michael Brown was killed by a police officer, this tragedy playing a key role in the formation of the Black Lives Matter movement. When I have my students view, side by side, two Bloody Sunday films – Paul Greengrass's *Bloody Sunday* (2002) and Ava Du Vernay's *Selma* (2014) – the discussions that follow remind me of how important our Irish and American experiences are and what knowledge, comfort and experience can be absorbed from what we read and see, but also from one another in this diverse world. Of course, Irish Studies, first and foremost, is concerned with tracing the breadth of Ireland and its diaspora through the centuries but our work also belongs to a global discourse that informs it and is informed by it in turn. We must continue to offer a welcome to new scholars and to remain open, thinking across frontiers, to new thoughts and methodologies.

MAUREEN O'CONNOR

9 Irish Women's Writing

On the face of it the idea of doing any justice to the topic of 'Irish Women Writers' in a few thousand words is absurd. Would anyone dare attempt sum up the history of 'Irish Men Writers' so succinctly? Of course, the reason such an approach, however inadequate, is necessary lies in the long history in the West of women's restricted social roles, limited access to education, and a general disbelief in their intellectual and artistic capabilities. While most of the writing done by Irish women up to the eighteenth century, and possibly much after, is lost to us, women had been writing religious tracts, cookery books, 'poetry, nuns' writing, petition-letters, depositions, biography, and autobiography' for generations.[1] Irish women who wrote in any genre at any time prior to the late nineteenth century had the rare privilege of literacy and access to books, if not formal education, which means that writing for women was even more closely linked to class – which in Ireland was almost always associated with confessional affiliation – than would have been true for their male peers. The literary canon has largely been determined by accidents of birth. Many of the Irish women whose writing has survived, even if no longer remembered in the twenty-first century, were the daughters or wives of established, successful men, often writers themselves.

However, some successful Irish writers were the mothers of famous men, such as Blanaid Salkeld (1880–1959), mother of artist Cecil; Jane Francesca Elgee Wilde (1821–1896), mother of Oscar; and Frances Sheridan

---

1   Marie-Louise Coolohan, *Women, Writing, and Language in Early Modern Ireland* (Oxford: Oxford University Press, 2010). See also *Women's Life Writing and Early Modern Ireland*, edited by Julie Eckerle and Naomi McAreavey (Lincoln: University of Nebraska Press, 2019).

(1724–1766), mother of Frances Brinsley; the success of the latter two men was secured via the London stage. Sheridan was also the great-grandmother of two other acclaimed and witty writers, both women admired by Oscar Wilde, the sisters Caroline Norton (1807–1877) and Lady Dufferin, born Helen Sheridan (1807–1867), best remembered for her ballad, '(Lament of) The Irish Emigrant', written in the 1840s. Irish women writers nurtured, inspired, parodied, collaborated and competed with men, as well as with each other. They were not just inheritors of a tradition but instrumental in establishing Ireland's international reputation for literary production.[2]

Jane Wilde, who became Lady Wilde when her husband William was knighted, and who used the penname 'Speranza', is an example of an Irish woman writer at once famous and obscure. Even in her own lifetime, her younger son was taken aback, during his lecture tour of the United States in 1882, when confronted with the esteem in which she was held by Irish Americans.[3] That same son's downfall contributed to the fading of Speranza's reputation, as she came to be blamed for his personal and artistic faults. She was certainly an important influence on her son's memorable wit and general tendency towards iconoclasm, as he heeded her advice to lift people 'out of old grooves by the intellectual dynamite', and to be an 'audacious thinker and talker'.[4] She was a writer who encouraged other writers, famous for her Dublin literary salon, attended by figures as eminent as Bernard Shaw and the young W. B. Yeats, and inspired by the Dublin gatherings of an earlier writer, Sydney Owenson, better known as Lady Morgan (c.1781–1859).[5] Both Wilde and Morgan were prolific writers of works on history, politics,

---

2   A number of twenty-first-century anthologies have attempted to do justice to this particular tradition, beginning with volumes 4 and 5 of the *Field Day Anthology of Irish Writing*, edited by Seamus Deane (Cork: Cork University Press, 2002–2003), to most recently, Clíona Ó Gallchoir and Heather Ingman (eds), *A History of Modern Irish Women's Literature* (Cambridge: Cambridge University Press, 2018).

3   Wilde's touring experiences are recounted by Davis Coakley, *Oscar Wilde: The Importance of Being Irish* (Dublin: Town House, 1994) and Richard Pine, *The Thief of Reason: Oscar Wilde and Modern Ireland* (New York: St. Martin's Press, 1995).

4   Jane Francesca Wilde, *Social Studies* [1893] (Cambridge: Cambridge University Press, 2010), 70.

5   On the parallels between the women's salons, see Joy Melville, *Mother of Oscar: The Life of Jane Francesca Wilde* (London: John Murray, 1994), 79, 115.

and feminist issues, such as Wilde's essay 'The Bondage of Women' (1893) and Morgan's *Woman and Master* (1840). They are best remembered for their critiques of empire. Wilde's anti-colonial writing appeared in essays and poetry, while Morgan expressed her positions more obliquely, through fiction, such as the novel that made her fame, *The Wild Irish Girl* (1806).[6]

Wilde adopted the penname 'Speranza' in her writing for *The Nation* (1842–1848), the newspaper of the Young Ireland movement. One of its editors in particular, Charles Gavan Duffy, welcomed contributions from women writers, including the young Jane Elgee. The mid-nineteenth-century Irish nationalist movement was, according to Marjorie Howes, 'aware of the potential intersections between feminine sentimentality and political reform'.[7] Other women who regularly wrote for *The Nation* include Eva O'Doherty (1825–1910), Ellen Downing (1828–1869), Elizabeth Treacy Varian (1821–1896) and Olivia Knight (1830–1908).[8] The newspaper was considered seditious by Dublin Castle authorities and was often suppressed. When Gavan Duffy was arrested in 1848, his sister-in-law Margaret Callan and Speranza took over editorial duties, with Speranza assuming credit for an especially incendiary, treasonous article, 'Jacta Alea Est', which effectively led to the British government shutting down the paper. Not all Irish women writers of the early nineteenth century were nationalist, of course. One of the most successful writers of the period was Charlotte Elizabeth Tonna (1790–1846), defender of working women and animals, evangelical Christian, anti-Catholic crusader, and author of numerous works, including

---

6   For details on Wilde's writing career, see Melville, Coakley, Pine, Richard Ellmann, *Oscar Wilde* (New York: Knopf, 1988), and Eibhear Walshe's recent *Jane Wilde* (Brighton: Edward Everett Root, 2020). On Morgan, see Mary Campbell, *Lady Morgan: The Life and Times of Sydney Owenson* (Surrey: Pandora Press, 1988); James Newcomer, *Lady Morgan the Novelist* (Lewisburg: Bucknell University Press, 1990); Lionel Stevenson, *The Wild Irish Girl: The Life of Sydney Owenson, Lady Morgan (1776-1859)* (New York: Russell & Russell, 1969); and Julie Donovan, *Sydney Owenson, Lady Morgan and the Politics of Style* (Bethesda: Academica Press, 2009).

7   Marjorie Howes, 'Tears and Blood: Lady Wilde and the Emergence of Irish Cultural Nationalism', in *Ideology and Ireland in the Nineteenth Century*, edited by Tadhg Foley and Seán Ryder (Dublin: Four Courts Press, 1998), 151–172, 161.

8   See Rose Novak, 'Reviving "Eva" of "The Nation?": Eva O'Doherty's Young Ireland Newspaper Poetry', *Victorian Periodicals Review* 45, no. 4 (Winter 2012), 436–465.

Siege of Derry, or, Sufferings of the Protestants (1844), *Letters from Ireland* (1837) and *The Rockite: An Irish Story* (1829), which in its opening paragraph observes that 'Ireland alone has been fated, from age to age, to furnish, from among children of her soil, those enemies who should drench it in kindred blood; and devastate their mother land more effectually, more hopelessly, than a host of stranger foes would have aimed to accomplish'.[9]

Tonna's writing on Ireland aimed to encourage the reform of uncivilised native habits and to inform an English audience about the exotic Irish who officially joined the United Kingdom in 1801. Other women's writing in this mode, popular after the Act of Union, include *Sketches of Irish Character* (1829), by Anna Maria Hall (1800–1881),[10] and *Cottage Dialogues Among the Irish Peasantry* (1822), by Mary Leadbeater (1728–1826), which features a preface and notes by the most famous Irish woman writer of the century, Maria Edgeworth (1768–1849). Edgeworth's best-known novel, *Castle Rackrent* (1800), fulfils a similar anthropological remit to Hall and Leadbetter's non-fiction books, but, as in her other Irish novels, the humour and complexity of the writing makes her political and national sympathies undecidable at times. *Castle Rackrent* is often credited with establishing the Irish genre of 'Big House' writing, to which numerous other Irish women writers have contributed: the co-authors Edith Somerville (1858–1949) and Martin Ross (penname of Violet Martin, 1862–1915), in *The Real Charlotte* (1894) and *The Big House of Inver* (1925); Elizabeth Bowen (1899–1973), especially *The Last September* (1929) and *A World of Love* (1954); Molly Keane (1904–1996), in *Good Behaviour* (1981), *Time after Time* (1983), and *Loving and Giving* (1988); Jennifer Johnston (b.1930), in books like *The Captains and the Kings* (1972), *The Gates* (1973), and *Fool's Sanctuary* (1987); Iris Murdoch (1919–1999), in *Unicorn* (1963); and Edna O'Brien (b.1930), especially *The House of Splendid Isolation* (1994).[11] Traditionally a conservative Anglo-Irish genre, it is often read as expressing anxiety about

---

9   Charlotte Elizabeth Tonna, *The Rockite* (London: Dennet, 1829), 1.
10 Hall was also co-proprietor of *St James Magazine* with another woman, perhaps the most prolific, popular Irish writer of the century, Charlotte Riddell (1832–1906).
11 For more on the Big House novel, see Claire Norris, 'The Big House: Space, Place and Identity in Irish Fiction', *New Hibernia Review* 8, no. 1 (Spring 2004), 107–121; Jacqueline Genet (ed.), *The Big House in Ireland: Reality and Representation*

threats to British ownership of Irish land. However, a distinguishing feature characterising most of the texts by women writers listed here is the comic, from slapstick to subtle, sometimes melancholy, irony, a textual element that positions the authorial voice as one speaking to power, rather than unproblematically emanating from a secure place of privilege.

The alignment of Edgeworth's comic sensibilities with disempowered is most evident, in her ironically titled 'An Essay on the Noble Science of Self-Justification' (1795), in which the narrator recommends all kinds of 'feminine' imbecility to her female audience in order that they may frustrate, undermine and manipulate their men, or the 'common enemy', more effectively. The narrator's advice regarding the best methods of winning every argument with the 'enemy' includes the subversive suggestion that in the company of a man 'possessed of an opinion of his own eloquence [...] you will then, when he flatters himself that he has fixed your eye with his *very best* argument, suddenly grow absent'.[12] Following in the rich tradition of women's often bittersweet comic fiction in Ireland, in addition to Keane, Bowen, and Somerville and Ross (possibly best known today for their series of comic *Irish RM* stories), some standout examples include: short fiction by Maeve Brennan (1917–1993), but especially her 1960s *New Yorker* column, 'The Long-Winded Lady'; the short fiction and novels of Clare Boylan (1948–2006), including *Black Baby* (1988); the stories and novels of Anne Enright (b.1962), including *The Wig My Father Wore* (1995); *One Day as a Tiger* (1997), a dystopian sheep-cloning tale by Anne Haverty (b.1959); the Celtic Tiger satire, *The Devil I Know* (2012), by Claire Kilroy (b.1973); the Cork criminal underground series by Lisa McInerney (b.1981), beginning with *The Glorious Heresies* (2015); the recent comedy of twenty-first-century sexual manners, *Exciting Times* (2020), by Naoise Dolan (b.1992); the Booker-prize-winning *Milkman* (2018), by Anna Burns (b.1962), about sexual predation against the backdrop of the Northern Irish Troubles; and the story collections of Nicole Flattery (b.1991), *Show Them a Good Time* (2019), and June Caldwell,

---

(Dingle: Brandon, 1991); Vera Kreilkamp, *The Anglo-Irish Novel and the Big House* (Syracuse: Syracuse University Press, 1998).

12 Maria Edgeworth, 'An Essay on the Noble Science of Self-Justification', in *Letters for Literary Ladies* (London: J. Johnson, 1799), 195–240, 217. Emphasis in the original.

Room Little Darker (2017). Ireland's bestselling comic novelist is Marian Keyes (b.1963), whose international reputation led to her appointment to the board of the Edinburgh Fringe's 2018 Comedy Women in Print Award. Keyes could be seen as writing in the populist tradition of Maeve Binchy (1939–2012), one of Ireland's internationally bestselling writers, whose work, including a number of plays, is characterised by warm and gentle humour. Another internationally successful Irish writer, Edna O'Brien, like Binchy, a novelist and playwright, is also consistently humorous in her fiction, beginning with *The Country Girls* (1960), though her flair for the comic is only rarely acknowledged. The terror and mystery of the novels of another bestselling author, Tana French (b.1973), is often tinged with wry comedy.

Nancy Walker considers women's humour, like racial minority humour, to be 'a means of dealing with frustration or anger, rather than celebratory or fun'.[13] It is not only in fiction that Irish women's writing hits its comic mark, but also in poetry, from the popular satires of Henrietta Battier (c.1751–1813), encouraged by Samuel Johnson in her career, beginning with *The Mousiad: An Heroic Comic Poem* (1787), to 'March' (1890), a poem by Mary Elizabeth Blake (1840–1907), which artfully uses dialect to admit defeat before the weather, to the work of satirist Susan L. Mitchell (1866–1926), who never hesitated to take aim at her highly esteemed peers, as might be gleaned from the titles of her poems, 'The Ballad of Shawe-Taylor and Hugh Lane' (1905), and 'George Moore Eats a Grey Mullet', the latter included in *Aids to the Immortality of Certain Persons in Ireland, Charitably Administered* (1913). More contemporary poets known for their humour include Eithne Strong (1923–1999) and Rita Ann Higgins (b.1955), whose work ranges from farcical to mordant. The performance poets of Ireland also often have recourse to humour to make their political points, including work by Sarah Clancy (b.1973) and Elaine Feeney (b.1979). Performance poetry, especially when disseminated through social media, has emerged as an important outlet for young poets of colour, like Chiamaka Enyi-Amadi, born in Lagos, raised in Galway, writer of both poetry and prose. Irish women writers of colour often use humour to deal

---

13 Nancy Walker, *A Very Serious Thing: Women's Humor and American Culture* (Minneapolis: University of Minnesota Press, 1988), 106.

with what Walker refers to above as 'frustration and anger', like *Paddy Indian* (2001) and *The Uncoupling* (2003), by Cauvery Madhavan, which chart the immigrant experience, or *Pomegranate Soup* (2008), by Marsha Mehran (1977–2014) about three Iranian sisters opening a Persian café in a small Irish village. Emma Dabiri's 2019 memoir, *Don't Touch My Hair*, about growing up black in 1980s Ireland, often deploys irony in its stinging exposure of the long-disavowed reality of Irish racism.

One forgotten comic writer, Frances Sheridan, may have been more responsible than is widely known for one of her son's most famous comedies, *The Rivals* (1775). There is evidence that Richard Brinsley copied extensively from his mother's unpublished play, *A Trip to Bath* in writing his own work.[14] Collaboration supplying the opportunity for appropriation has been the fate of some other Irish women writers, like Frances Sara Hoey (1830–1908), whose novels, *Land at Last* (1866), *Black Sheep* (1867), *Forlorn Hope* (1867), *Rock Ahead* (1868), and *A Righted Wrong* (1870), were claimed by Edmund Yates,[15] or Lady Augusta Gregory (1852–1932), whose co-authorship with Yeats of the plays *Kathleen Ni Houlihan* (1902) and *The Countess Cathleen* (1892) was unacknowledged in her lifetime, as was her innovation in creating a unique Hiberno-English, hallmark of early Abbey Theatre productions.[16]

Examples of genuine, properly credited collaboration can also be found in the history of Irish women's letters, such as that between Anna Maria and Samuel Carter Hall (1800–1899), Anna (1829–1922) and Thomas Haslam (1825–1917),[17] and William Thompson (1775–1833) and Anna Doyle Wheeler (c.1780–1848). These last two writing collaborations produced

14   See Elizabeth Kuti, 'Rewriting Frances Sheridan', *Eighteenth-Century Ireland* 11 (1996), 120–128.
15   Gaye Tuchman and Nina E. Fortin, 'Fame and Misfortune: Edging Women Out of the Great American Tradition', *American Journal of Sociology* 90, no. 1 (July 1984), 72–96, 74.
16   See Anthony Roche, *The Irish Dramatic Revival 1899-1939* (London: Bloomsbury, 2015), and Robert Welch, *The Abbey Theatre 1899-1999: Form and Pressure* (Oxford: Oxford University Press, 1999).
17   For more on the Haslams, see Carmel Quinlan, *Genteel Revolutionaries: Anna and Thomas Haslam and the Irish Women's Movement* (Cork: Cork University Press, 2002).

feminist texts arguing for women's access to suffrage, education and the professions. Thompson and Wheeler produced a book that was over a century ahead of its time, *Appeal of One Half of the Human Race, Women, Against the Pretensions of the Other, Men* (1825). Thomson gave much of the credit for the book's insights to Wheeler, who would go onto publish *The Rights of Women* (1830).[18] A similar kind of partnership obtained between the married couples Francis (1878–1916) and Hanna Sheehy Skeffington (1877–1946) and Margaret (1878–1954) and James Cousins (1873–1956). The husbands in these unions co-edited the nationalist-feminist newspaper *The Irish Citizen* (1912–1920), connected to the Irish Women's Franchise League. Both women's journalism was published in this paper and elsewhere, with Cousins going on to publish numerous books on international women's issues, including *The Awakening of Asian Womanhood* (1922) and *Indian Womanhood Today* (1941). The Cousins also wrote a joint autobiography, *We Two Together: A Duography* (1950). The editorship of the newspaper was taken over in 1916 by another Irish writer and suffragist, Louie Bennett (1870–1956), who, in addition to her journalism, wrote the novels *The Proving of Priscilla* (1902) and *A Prisoner of His Word* (1908).

The theme of female friendship and solidarity is a common one in all women's writing. Irish examples range from 'To Laetitia Van Lewen, at a Country Assize' (1748), written by Constantia Grierson (1706–1733), friend to Jonathan Swift, to fellow poet, Laetitia Pilkington (1712–1750), asking that her friend forsake the dull company of 'beaux', whose only conversation is of hunting or writs, and, instead, 'bless the longing eyes / Of your Constantia,'[19] to 'Withered Flowers' (1881), by Helena Callanan (1864–1937), an ode on the decaying memento of a departed friend, concluding, 'how / Could I despise them in decay / She wore them on her bridal day',[20] to Eva Gore-Booth (1870–1926) describing her love for her

18 See Dolores Dooley, *Equality in Community: Sexual Equality in the Writing of William Thompson and Anna Doyle Wheeler* (Cork: Cork University Press, 1996).
19 Constantia Grierson, 'To Laetitia Van Lewen at a Country Assize', in *The Cabinet of Irish Literature: Selections of the Works of the Chief Poets, Orators, and Prose Writers of Ireland*, 4 volumes 1879–1880, edited by T. P. O'Connor, vol. 1 (Edinburgh: Blackie and Son, 1893), 148.
20 Helena Callanan, 'Withered Flowers', in *The Household Library of Ireland's Poets*, edited by Daniel Connolly (New York, 1887), 318.

sister as unaffected by distance in 'Comrades' (1929): 'We meet beyond earth's barrèd gate / Where all the world's wild Rebels are'.[21] The tradition of the literary salon was taken up by Irish women writers at the turn of the twentieth century, often with the specific purpose of creating support for fellow women professionals. Sometimes such affiliations grew out of political activism,[22] as in the case of the Ladies Land League, created in 1881, an auxiliary branch of Michael Davitt's Land League, devoted to the reduction of rents, the eventual seizure of land from landlords and achievement of land ownership to tenant farmers. The Ladies' Land League offered what was at the time a rare opportunity for women's collaborative political activity. The organisation provided inspiration for first-wave Irish feminism and has also been associated with emerging Irish women artists of the *fin de siècle*, especially those identified as 'New Women', that is, feminists and social reformers. Members of the League included the writers Katharine Tynan (1859–1931), the Parnell sisters, Fanny (1848–1942) and Anna (1852–1911), and Hannah Lynch (1859–1904), an internationally productive journalist and writer of fiction.[23] Fanny Parnell's poem 'Ireland, Mother!' and Tynan's 'Erin', like Gore-Booth's 'Lament of the Daughters of Ireland', express some disappointment at men's failure to make the sacrifices women are ready to endure for their country, if only they had the opportunity. These writers supported and championed each other as well as women around the world, with the result that a number of eminent 'New Women' were Irish, including the novelist who coined the phrase, Frances Bellenden Clarke (1854–1943), better known as 'Sarah Grand', the pen name she adopted with the publication of *The Heavenly Twins* (1893). Other

---

21   Eva Gore-Booth, *Poems of Eva Gore-Booth: Complete Edition*, edited by Esther Roper (London: Longmans, Green and Co., 1929), 511.
22   For more on the phenomenon of women's writing clubs and coteries, see Anne Mulhall, 'Women Poets and Irish Periodical Culture in the Mid-Twentieth-Century', *Irish University Review* 42, no. 1 (24 May 2012), 32–52. Deirdre Brady's forthcoming monograph, *Literary Coteries and the Irish Women Writers' Club (1933-1958)*, will provide further details of women's writing salons.
23   For a comprehensive account of the cultural and literary contexts for Irish women writing in this period, see Faith Binckes and Kathryn Laing, *Hannah Lynch: Irish Writer, Cosmopolitan, New Woman* (Cork: Cork University Press, 2019).

notorious Irish New Women, whose work was considered immoral and corrupting, include George Egerton (pen name of Mary Chavelita Dunne Bright; 1859–1945), whose stories, beginning with the collection *Keynotes* (1859), feature independent, unmarried women who are nevertheless unapologetically sexually active, and Katherine Cecil Thurston (1874–1911), whose novel *Max* (1910) depicts transsexuality.[24]

It has been necessary to omit the name and works of thousands of women, to all but ignore dozens of the themes and genres with which so many of them engaged. In addition to the poets identified here, other world-renowned, prize-winning figures include Rhoda Coghill (1903–2000), Eavan Boland (1944–2020), Medbh McGuckian (b.1950), two of the three women who have, with Ní Dhomhnaill, held the post of Ireland Chair of Poetry, Éiléan Ní Chuilleanáin (b.1942) and Paula Meehan (b.1955), Vona Groarke (b.1964), and Moya Canon (b.1956), a drastically truncated list. Irish women dramatists, such as Frances Sheridan, have enjoyed success for centuries, and, like Lady Gregory, were instrumental in creating a national theatre. There is no space left to do more than name a few: Susanna Centlivre (1667–1723), Mary Davys (1674–1732), Mary Devenport O'Neill (1879–1967), Leland Bardwell (1928–2016), Teresa Deevey (1994–1963) and Marina Carr (b.1964).

A number of the women already discussed have written for the stage as well as for children and young adults, another genre that has produced important writers, like Eliza Dorothea Cobbe (c.1764–1850), Alicia Catherine Mant (1788–1869), L. T. Meade (1844–1914) and Louise O'Neill (b.1985). In addition to her English-language novels and short stories, Éilís Ní Dhuibhne (b.1954) writes children's books in Irish, under the (ironically Anglicised) name, Elizabeth O'Hara. Eilís Dillon (1920–1994) also wrote in Irish for children. The best-known women writing in Irish, however, tends to be by poets, such as Máire Mhac an tSaoi (b.1922), Síle Ní Chéileachair (1924–1985), Biddy Jenkinson (b.1949), Nuala Ní Dhomhnaill (b.1952), Colette Nic Aodha (b.1967) and Doireann Ní Ghríofa (b.1981), who recently published her first prose work, in English, *A Ghost in the*

---

24 For a full account of this political and cultural phenomenon, see Tina O'Toole, *The Irish New Woman* (Basingstoke: Palgrave, 2013).

Throat (2020), a hybrid of fiction and memoir. Memoirs by Irish women writers have been hugely successful, from O'Brien's *Mother Ireland* (1976) and Nuala O'Faolain's (1940–2008) *Are You Somebody?* (1996), to the recent 2019 publications, *Constellations: Reflections on Life*, by Sinéad Gleeson and *Notes to Self*, by Emily Pine (b.1977). The confessional mode can be found in work focusing on conversion or other religious subjects by Margaret Anna Cusack (1829–1899; known as the Nun of Kenmare), Cecil Frances Alexander (1818–1895), Catherine Mary McSorley (1828–1929), Mother Mary Teresa Carroll (1835–1909) and Emily Henrietta Hickey (1845–1923). Writing in order to educate and persuade from the scientific side has also been well represented by Irish women who published in professional journals and produced popular books for a non-professional audience, especially in the nineteenth century, such as astronomer Agnes Mary Clerke, (1842–1907), naturalist Mary Ward (1827–1869), botanists Henriette Beaufort (1778–1865) and Evelyn Mary Booth (1897–1988) and archaeologist N. P. Figgis (1939–2014).

The wealth of texts produced by Irish women is impossible to capture in a few pages, but reminding readers of this trove of work is worth doing repeatedly. Recent years have seen the emergence of an impressive number of talented young Irish writers. A few names to be added to those identified so far would include Sally Rooney (b.1991), Eimear McBride (b.1976), Wendy Erskine, Sara Baume (b.1984); Maggie O'Farrell (b.1972); Caoilinn Hughes (b.1985); Sarah Davis-Goff, and Jan Carson. While these authors have reached wide and appreciative audiences, literary critics can throw up barriers to success. The novelist and journalist Kathleen McMahon, writing about her grandmother, the short story writer Mary Lavin (1912–1996), observes that 'The label "women's writing", with its implication of being of no interest to readers other than women, is an insult that has not gone away,'[25] while Dawn Miranda Sherratt-Bado notes that for generations, from O'Brien to Rooney – writers singled out by McMahon as well – 'Irish women writers [...] face blatant sexism from a phalanx of

---

25   Kathleen McMahon, 'Irish Women Writing Fiction Were Dismissed as 'Quiet'. Ireland Wasn't Listening', *The Guardian*, 30 July 2020, available online: <https://www.theguardian.com/books/2020/jul/30/irish-women-writers-described-as-quiet-ireland-sally-rooney-women-writers> [accessed 24 August 2020].

male critics who attempt to exclude them from cultural tradition'. In particular, writing about female desire inspires critical outrage, as illustrated by the loud minority protesting against the RTÉ television adaptation of Rooney's *Normal People* (2018) in early 2020. As Sherratt-Bado concludes, 'The pathologising of female sexuality due to a misogynistic false piety is nothing new, and it persists in the field of literary criticism'.[26] Even a few thousand words here and there can push against this regrettably robust tradition of silencing and suppression.

---

26 Dawn Miranda Sherratt-Bado, 'Likability', *Dublin Review of Books* 124 (July 2020), available online: <https://www.drb.ie/blog/writers-and-artists/2020/08/15/likability> [accessed 23 August 2020].

HARRY WHITE

10 'Monuments of Its Own Magnificence': Musicology within Irish Studies

I

In a 2017 post on the popular science website Edge.org, Steven Pinker provides an answer to the question, 'What scientific term or concept ought to be more widely known?' as follows:

> The Second Law of Thermodynamics states that in an isolated system (one that is not taking in energy), entropy never decreases ... Closed systems inexorably become less structured, less organized, less able to accomplish interesting and useful outcomes, until they slide into an equilibrium of gray, tepid, homogeneous monotony and stay there.[1]

Pinker's acknowledgement of this forbidding state of affairs (one which, on a bad day, might apply to any number of long-term scientific or scholarly enterprises, not excluding musicology in Ireland), is not, however, an end but a beginning, at least insofar as it leads him to a conclusion which is as transcendent and optimistic as it is far-reaching and (proverbially) universal:

> The Second Law of thermodynamics defines the ultimate purpose of life, mind, and human striving: to deploy energy and information to fight back the tide of entropy and carve out refuges of beneficial order.[2]

---

1   See Steven Pinker, 'The Second Law of Thermodynamics', *Edge* (2017), available online: <https://www.edge.org/response-detail/27023> [accessed 21 August 2020].
2   Pinker, 'The Second Law of Thermodynamics'.

Human life as a rearguard action against the otherwise overwhelming and inevitable disintegration of the universe may not be to everyone's taste as an implicit principle of behaviour, but the resilience of this principle has a long history, even if it is not often formulated with such lapidary (not to say optimistic) grace, and especially not at the present moment, when the rage for order in human affairs is so violently contested and endangered. Pinker's universe, governed by entropy and resisted by human striving, is in any case a scientific phenomenon which axiomatically excludes the ultimate and redemptive governance of God or Allah or any other such supreme intelligence. I dare say that it would not be offensive to moderate Christians or Muslims to define the quest for God as a quest for order, but if the universe is a long, slow drift into nothingness, the refuge of 'beneficial order' proposes a radically different mode of redemption. The quest for order nevertheless abides. It survives the void identified by human intelligence, by the discovery that the firmament is naturally (indeed inherently) indifferent to our very existence. Despite these grim tidings, we go on (and deprived of the consolations of religious belief, we go it alone). The quest for order is endemic to the human condition, and it preoccupies science and art almost by definition, whatever else such disciplines might seek to achieve.

It certainly preoccupies music, 'the supreme mystery in the science of mankind', to borrow the definition of one of Pinker's most distinguished forebears, Claude Lévi-Strauss,[3] and for those who apprehend that mystery, who aspire to a science of music which might engage its structural intelligence, its semantic prowess and its cultural meaning through history and society, this preoccupation is exemplary. One might even say that musicology exists as a means of perception, as a 'beneficial refuge' in relation to music itself. I freely admit that if asked why I am a musicologist, I would be unlikely to respond that my motivation is 'to deploy energy and information' or to 'fight back the tide of entropy', even if such terms actually seem attractive and germane in the context of a society which is often indifferent to music except as a diversionary enchantment or public commodity. But

---

3   See Claude Lévi-Strauss, *The Raw and the Cooked* (*Muthologiques, Vol. 1*) (New York: Harper and Row, 1969), 18.

the proposal which I would like to rehearse in this chapter nevertheless speaks directly to musicology as an ingathering or mode of perception in which intelligible order is paramount. The universals which animate scientific enquiry (as in Pinker's 'ultimate purpose of life, mind and human striving') are, I hope, no less applicable to the noisy island in which we find ourselves, even if the quest for entertainment looms much larger in our general perception of music in Ireland than the quest for order. One might justifiably argue that music often lies to one side of 'Irish Studies' as a cognitive mode or category, so that the high seriousness which elsewhere determines our reception of Irish history, literature and artistic engagement is notable by its absence when it comes to music. The plain corollary of this state of affairs is that music itself often remains beyond the pale of serious historical or critical inquiry.

Two recent publications (among many) exemplify this normative and long-standing exclusion. *The Cambridge History of Ireland* (edited by Thomas Bartlett in 2018) is a four-volume survey which includes 'essays that address the full range of social, economic, religious, linguistic, military, cultural, artistic and gender history'.[4] Despite this generosity of address, music is absent from all four volumes. This is likewise the case with *Modern Ireland in 100 Artworks*, edited by Fintan O'Toole and published by the Royal Irish Academy and The Irish Times in 2016, in which the same omission is even more egregious and indeed more immediately significant. The exclusion of musical works from the latter publication presupposes that music is admissible only as a mode of cultural practice: it doesn't seem to have occurred to anyone connected with this volume that the musical work might enjoy the same claim to the status of 'artwork' as that of any other medium. I think that this in turn betrays a characteristically Irish reluctance to conceive of music as anything other than a relief from the high seriousness and generic jurisdiction of literary forms in particular. Another

---

4   See Thomas Bartlett, et al. (eds), *The Cambridge History of Ireland* (Cambridge: Cambridge University Press, 2018) (from the publisher's blurb, available online: <https://www.amazon.co.uk/Cambridge-History-Ireland-HardbackSet/dp/1107167299> [accessed 21 August 2020]). See also Fintan O'Toole (ed.), *Modern Ireland in 100 Artworks* (Dublin: The Royal Irish Academy and The Irish Times, 2016).

way to frame this problem is to invoke Pinker's notion of 'closed systems', incapable of 'taking in energy' or speaking to each other. With such 'closed systems' in play, we would declare an incompatibility between 'musicology' and 'Irish Studies' as preoccupations which almost by definition exclude mutual enrichment. The purpose of my deliberations in this chapter, however, is to counter this doleful conclusion with a very different reading of musicology as a constituency of immediate interest to Irish Studies. To that end, I shall privilege a recent (but as yet unrealised) proposal at the leading edge of Irish musicology, which takes its cue directly from recent developments in the field itself.

II

Anyone with more than a passing interest in the development of musicology in Ireland over the past thirty years could scarcely mistake its formative impulses, its quest, if you will, for order: through the agency of individual research, new domains of enquiry and a seam of pioneering conferences, edited collections and monographs, our comprehension of 'music in Ireland' is incontestably richer than it was a generation ago. In this sense at least, the relationship between musicology and Irish Studies is much closer than it once was.[5] The maps of Irish musical experience have been entirely redrawn over the past generation, so that it is no longer possible to confine the perception of music in Ireland to those atavistic binaries (as between 'folk music' and 'art music', or the claims of ethnicity versus the recovery and restitution of colonial musical culture, to say little of the religious, social and political divides which underlay these binaries) which for so long curbed and delimited the discourse of music in Irish affairs. Even a random sampling of Irish musicology since the early 1990s would exhaust the space allocated to this chapter, but some indication of its astonishing plurality and pioneering engagement is necessary

---

5   For musicology of an earlier vintage, see Harry White, 'Musicology in Ireland', *Acta Musicologica* 60 (1988), Fasc. 3, 290–305.

nevertheless. Source studies, identity studies, new modes of ethnography and social anthropology, genre studies, repertorial investigations, popular music studies and biography have recently deepened the complexion of music in Ireland to an unprecedented degree.[6]

One notable result of this deepening is *The Encyclopaedia of Music in Ireland* [*EMIR*] (2013), a resource which drew richly upon the expertise accumulated in the years leading up to its publication in a collaborative engagement which represents (to date) the largest and most extensive musicological enterprise in the history of the state.[7] But much of the music surveyed in the course of this ten-year project still languishes in the archives of silence. Our vastly increased awareness of musical practices and compositional repertories, as these have manifested themselves throughout Irish history, deserves a correlative domain which would make this music audible, visible and available. The sounding forms of Irish music as an intelligible and meaningful phenomenon are (almost by definition) resistant to complete recension, but the palpable, if neglected existence of music as a definitive expression and conduit of public and private life in Ireland can hardly be suppressed on that account.

In an address to the annual conference of the Society for Musicology in Ireland in 2017, I proposed an ambitious solution to this impairment, a solution subsequently taken up by the Research Foundation for Music in Ireland.[8] In brief, I suggested a new research project entitled *Musica*

6   For an indication of the range and authorship of these studies, see the bibliography attached to Mark Fitzgerald and John O'Flynn (eds), *Music and Identity in Ireland and Beyond* (Farnham: Ashgate, 2014), 287–315. See also Axel Klein, *Ireland* (Oxford Bibliographies, 2018), available online: <https://www.oxfordbibliographies.com/view/document/obo-9780199757824/obo-9780199757824-0246.xml?rskey=eoRWIt&result=1&q=axel+klein#firstMatch> [accessed 21 August 2020].

7   See Harry White and Barra Boydell (general editors), *The Encyclopaedia of Music in Ireland* (Dublin: University College Dublin Press, 2013).

8   Harry White, '*Musica Hibernica:* A Proposal', unpublished address delivered at the 15th Annual Plenary Conference of the Society for Musicology in Ireland, Queen's University Belfast, June 2017. Current research undertaken under the auspices of the Research Foundation for Music in Ireland [RFMI] (located in the Conservatory of Music and Drama, TU Dublin) explores ways in which this proposal might be realised. For details of the RFMI see <www.musicresearch.ie> [accessed 21 August 2020].

Hibernica, intended to curate, preserve and record the gamut of Irish musical art as an online resource. *Musica Hibernica* denominates (and envisages) an editorial encounter with Irish music sufficiently pliant to respond to its protean complexion and sufficiently generous to respond to the topography of Irish musical experience over a very long period. (The Latin denomination of this proposal, I should add, is no more than a nod to the partial precedent of *Musica Britannica*, a monumental edition – of which more below – which curates and reanimates important traces of British musical life otherwise difficult of access.) As I envisage this project, *Musica Hibernica* would countenance the widest possible purview of music which is intelligibly understood as belonging to the matrix of Irish musical culture. It would comprehend, for example, the monastic repertory of medieval Irish plainchant as imperturbably as it would seek to recover (and represent) the theatre music of eighteenth-century Dublin or the Irish symphony of the later twentieth century. It would privilege not a once-off anthology but an incremental (and gradual) archive and repository of Irish musical culture. It would also editorially recognise the difference between music as art and music as practice in Ireland. I'm tempted to add that like Joyce's fiction, it would keep the professors busy for years.

Unlike Joyce's fiction, however, the terms of reference which would apply to *Musica Hibernica* are far from easy to define. Even if we leave to one side the vexed question (one might say the overwhelming question) of what constitutes 'Irish music', especially in relation to its conceptual sibling, 'Music in Ireland', the cultural and social inheritances addressed by this project remain formidably complex. The three domains of musical practice I nominated a moment ago from which *Musica Hibernica* would seek to represent the repertories of Irish plainchant, eighteenth-century theatre music in Dublin and the Irish symphony after 1945 – random and uncomplicated as these may seem – could be vitally and differently imagined, so that the last of them might, for example, dovetail into a distinct gathering of orchestral music by Irish women composers, especially given that the role of women in Irish music has in recent years become a prominent category of research in its own right.[9] Mere representation, editorial

9   As examples of such research see Ita Beausang and Séamas De Barra, *Ina Boyle (1889-1967): A Composer's Life* (Cork: Cork University Press, 2018) and the initiative

or otherwise, is rarely what it seems. If *Musica Hibernica* were to curate editions of early eighteenth-century composers such as Johann Sigismond Cousser and Matthew Dubourg (whose Irish work was almost wholly indentured to the Crown), for example, this would almost certainly entail a correlative acknowledgement (and contextual consideration) of music as an expression of vehement and often hostile political sentiment during the same period. Many such considerations would undoubtedly complicate the editorial choices underlying such a project. But such considerations can scarcely be allowed to supervene the virtues of musical retrieval and rehabilitation (in many cases, after centuries of silent neglect) which the project itself would represent. Even since the appearance of *EMIR* seven years ago, the kind of research undertaken by musicologists including Estelle Murphy, Ita Beausang, Jennifer O'Connor, Triona O'Hanlon, Una Hunt, Maria McHale and Catherine Ferris in Irish music between 1700 and 1950 (to look no further in either direction) handsomely promotes the case for scholarly editions and performances (available online as well as in hard copy) of the music which this research comprehends. In certain instances, moreover, the kind of precedent established by Una Hunt's work on Thomas Moore (as a performer as well as a scholar) likewise attests the general value of what is self-evidently – even at first glance – an exceptionally ambitious and long-term undertaking. Perhaps it is not too much to add that *Musica Hibernica*, like *EMIR* itself, also seems to me not only a national undertaking, but an island-wide one.

Like *EMIR*, too, the question of precedent looms large when we consider *Musica Hibernica* in relation to the preservation and reanimation of musical repertories in Europe. I have already mentioned *Musica Britannica*,

---

Sounding the Feminists, described on its website as ' an Irish-based, voluntary-led collective of composers, sound artists, performers, musicologists, critics, promoters, industry professionals, organisations, and individuals, committed to promoting and publicising the creative work of female musicians' (see <www.soundingthefeminists. com> [accessed 21 August 2020]). A forthcoming volume in the *Irish Musical Studies* series, edited by Ita Beausang, Jennifer O'Connor and Laura Watson, will draw on a series of conferences and research papers on the theme of 'Women and Music in Ireland'.

established in 1951, which took its cue from the great German, Austrian, Italian and French musical monuments of an earlier vintage, and indeed from earlier monuments yet within the boundaries of British musical scholarship.[10] This does not mean, of course, that such models entail an untroubled or uncomplicated adoption when they are employed elsewhere, or that one can afford to disregard differences in context, motivation and even social history as between an original research mechanism and its use in Ireland. In this regard, Julian Rushton's online introduction to *Musica Britannica* provides an instructive consideration in the present context:

Musica Britannica is indeed a monument to our musical culture. Its Latin title, rather than 'Music in Britain', is a sign not of modesty, but of pride in the rich heritage we owe to the superimposition of cultures on these islands. The subtitle is 'A National Collection of Music'. It is the collection which is national: the music is international, both in its quality (to borrow the vocabulary of research assessments) and in its scope.

It is piquant to recall how nearly the founders of the edition got one thing wrong. *Musica Britannica* was the product of the determination of the Royal Musical Association, expressed in its 1948 Memorandum of Association, to publish 'English Music derived from non-copyright sources earlier than the twentieth century which has not been made available to the public by commercial publishers'. Fortunately, 'English' was quickly corrected. Scottish composers appeared in an early volume; composers from Ireland reflect a past political reality, while those from Italy (in *Italian Madrigals Englished*) may anticipate a future one. Although we need not include Handel, British by residence, we publish the children of immigrants, such as Alfonso Ferrabosco and Stephen Storace; and we

---

10   It is perhaps worth remarking in this connection that it is a feature of collaborative editorial projects in Ireland that they often follow – at least in this empirical regard – precedents established elsewhere. Thus, *EMIR* was modelled on the *Encyclopedia of Music in Canada* (which was the first such reference work of its kind devoted to the music of a single country anywhere); the *Dictionary of Irish Biography* likewise followed the *Dictionary of National Biography* in the UK, and *The Field Day Anthology of Irish Writing* drew upon innumerable cabinets or anthologies of literature in Europe.

claim among 'our' composers Peter Philips and John Field, most of whose music was composed abroad.[11]

Both within and beyond the parameters of this proposal (i.e. *Musica Hibernica*), it might be time to reclaim the work of 'composers from Ireland' (John Field included), not as an act of counter-colonial repossession, but in order to reflect (to adapt Rushton's own words) 'a *present* political reality'. Few Irish composers attest so well as Field to the wisdom (and political *savoir faire*) of Rushton's distinction between a national collection and the international condition of music. I doubt that we would forego Field as a prospective presence in *Musica Hibernica*, not least because we still lack a complete edition of his works (notwithstanding two volumes of his music devoted to the nocturnes and the concertos in *Musica Britannica*). We might also with perfect fairness remark that James Joyce (since I've already mentioned him) published *all* his works abroad and has long since been reclaimed as an Irish writer *par excellence*. We now anthologise Joyce at will (at least since the expiry of his formidable copyright arrangements), but his global presence and his long exile from Ireland have never compromised his Irishness. It is legitimate to make a similar case for Field.

Nevertheless, this emphasis on the works of individual composers (complete or otherwise) is not necessarily a feature of *Musica Britannica* which one would want to replicate without considerable modification here (Most of the volumes in *Musica Britannica* are dedicated either to single works or to single composers, or both). I would be reluctant to privilege the 'complete works' or even the 'complete Irish works' of any given composer in *Musica Hibernica* as an exclusive consideration. This is for two reasons. The first is that generic and historical boundaries (as in the three I've indicated already) are more likely to soften the distinction between 'Irish music' and 'music in Ireland' than would an emphasis on composers per se, which in my view would exacerbate this difference; and the second reason is that 'genre' is itself a more pliant and historically responsive editorial point of departure, especially where 'composer' is either irrelevant

---

11   See Julian Rushton, '*Musica Britannica*. A National Collection of Music', available online: <https://www.musicabritannica.org.uk/index.html> [accessed 21 August 2020].

or much reduced in significance as a category. and even where composers loom large (as in the contribution of Irish composers to English opera or – conversely, I suppose – the music of English composers influenced by or written in Ireland), I remain unpersuaded that a composer's prominence (Irish or otherwise) would constitute the *decisive* reason for including his or her work in such a project, at least not independently of other considerations, including the consideration of genre itself.

And there are other considerations still: little of Arnold Bax's early orchestral music (his tone poems especially) has been given in Ireland to date, but most of it was profoundly influenced, indeed inspired by the literary revival (and by Yeats in particular); only part of Charles Villiers Stanford's vast musical estate addressed Ireland, but his presence in British anthologies is slender (to date but one volume of his music has appeared in *Musica Britannica*, e.g.). As with Field, Stanford composed most of his music elsewhere than here, but if we were to adopt the *Musica Britannica* precedent (a 'national collection of international music') we would take him whole and entire (if not in one gargantuan gulp) into *Musica Hibernica*. Or at least we would, if we were enterprising an editorial project more given to the 'Complete Works Edition' (which for many composers has become the very graveyard of reception history) than anything countenanced in this proposal. I trust it is not complacent to add that digital archives and online facsimile reproductions of scores and editions alike have recently thrown the long labours of the complete critical edition into question. I raise these problems not to disavow Stanford as a presence in *Musica Hibernica*, and I hope I do not underestimate the scholarly value of other projects such as the IMSLP (Petrucci) website (or the immensely valuable but now lapsed National Archive of Irish Composers, a project fostered under the stewardship of Una Hunt). Nevertheless, these projects do not answer the proposal I am outlining (or simply envisaging) here.[12]

12 There is no doubt that the increasing presence of archival materials online (and in this context, the digitisation of music manuscripts) represents a challenge to (and in some sense a relief from) the preparation of Complete Works editions, especially given the inordinate time which the latter require to produce. The International Music Score Library Project [IMSLP] (also known as the Petrucci Music Library) affords a degree of access to early editions and facsimile manuscripts of music

The prospect of getting such a project underway – however modestly it might begin in a series of well-defined generic clusters – is without doubt as daunting to me as it is exciting. To have had some part in the mapping of Irish musical experience across history in the ten years during which I was preoccupied by *EMIR* is an experience sufficient to warn me off anything similar (or of even greater magnitude) for the foreseeable future. These scruples aside, *Musica Hibernica* would recover the auditory experience and intellectual perception of music in this country to a degree of immediacy and felt life inaccessible to any work of reference, no matter how generous its purview. It would inevitably do so over a very long period of time, and would (I daresay) extend far beyond the working life of anyone likely to read this paper when it is first published. It would foster an institutional and personal intimacy between performance, musicology, publication and the internet, and it would – if achieved with sufficient expertise, care and scholarly verve – evolve into a permanent resource, and not simply a splendid record. It would – I have no doubt controversially – privilege the musical work (however completely contextualised, however variously understood) as something more than a record of cultural experience. It would consent to the musical work as a definitive trace and expression of the collective or individual imagination and not only as an historical document or source. It would not usurp the historian's narrative or the critic's analysis, but it would immeasurably endow both of these with a perspective otherwise (especially in Ireland) simply unavailable. In many cases, it would retrieve the sounding forms of music in Ireland and of Irish music against the indifference and inertia which has turned much music of even the past 100 years into an 'invisible art', to borrow a recently familiar

---

on a scale impossible to envisage prior to the internet. Among its collections are several editions of Stanford's music, so that this access is surely a consideration in proposing an editorial project of the scope of *Musica Hibernica*. For details of IMSLP, see <https://imslp.org/wiki/Main_Page> [accessed 21 August 2020]. The National Archive of Irish Composers, based in the National Library of Ireland, provides much more restricted (and much more expensive) access to a very limited number of works.

term.¹³ It would – to borrow another, older one – cleanse and throw open the doors of Irish musical perception.

III

In his great poem, 'Sailing to Byzantium', written when he was approaching 60, W. B. Yeats characteristically engaged music in two arresting couplets, first as a distraction from the exactitudes of science and the mind, and then as a metaphor of the imagination itself, triumphant in its contemplation of art as an emancipation from the decrepitude of old age. 'An aged man is but a paltry thing, a tattered coat upon a stick', Yeats declares, in terms which remind me of that 'equilibrium of gray, tepid, homogenous monotony' diagnosed by Steven Pinker as our universal or ultimate fate. Yeats first deplores the mortal sloth and decay of the human condition ('caught in that music all neglect/monuments of unageing intellect') but then repines in the second stanza, with its promise of art and the awareness of art, both of which outlast 'whatever is begotten, born and dies'. In the second music-couplet we find: 'Nor is there singing school, but studying/ Monuments of its own magnificence'.¹⁴ This, too, is an implacable answer to the second law of thermodynamics, an affirmation that art entails not only the creation of refuge from the long slide down to nothingness but an afterlife of contemplation sufficient to give it permanence, value and meaning. Almost self-evidently, Yeats is using music (as he often does) as a signature of art, and especially of poetry. But 'Monuments' is a noun

---

13 See Michael Dervan (ed.), *The Invisible Art. A Century of Music in Ireland, 1916-2016* (Dublin: New Island, 2016). In a review of this volume published in the Irish Times in December 2016, I remarked that 'much of the music in this book has not only remained invisible to cultural history, but inaudible to Irish audiences', available online: <https://www.irishtimes.com/culture/books/the-invisible-art-review-a-mosaic-of-music-brought-to-light-1.2887895> [accessed 21 August 2020].

14 'Sailing to Byzantium' was published in Yeats's collection, *The Tower*, in 1928. An online edition of the poem is available online: <https://www.poetryfoundation.org/poems/43291/sailing-to-byzantium> [accessed 22 August 2020].

that calls out irresistibly to the general heritage of preservation to which a project such as *Musica Hibernica* ultimately belongs, and although *actual* music is an illicit or ineligible candidate for art in Yeats's unmistakable view, this need not deter us from drawing his twofold 'Monuments' (in 'Sailing to Byzantium') into apposition with Pinker's 'refuges of beneficial order' expressly to meditate upon the meaning of such monuments in musicological terms.

More narrowly still, *Musica Hibernica* could be inclusive of those orders of musical experience which, in an Irish context, rival the artwork as points of access to the more general domain of Irish Studies. Popular music is an obvious site for this kind of anthologising impulse and accessibility alike; so too is 'Irish music in Britain' and indeed the contribution of Irish composers to British musical genres. The manifest dependency of traditional music in Ireland on American models of curatorship and rehabilitation is another. At the last, I would argue that such exemplars of musical art and practice can not only access Irish Studies (as in the often subdued but persistent role played by women composers in this country, a role which could and properly should connect music to women's studies in Ireland) but enlarge it. Nevertheless, it would be disingenuous to pretend that this kind of disciplinary enrichment will count for much unless it works both ways. Pinker's diagnosis of the inherent entropy of closed forms comes sharply to mind.

'Irish Studies' continues to resist music in Ireland as an agent of cultural discourse equal to history and literature, except where it acknowledges traditional music as a synonym for Irish music, to the practical exclusion of any other generic mode of musical behaviour. This is true even when studies in popular musical culture perforce intersect with Irish Studies as a general field of interest, but the converse is rarely (if ever) the case. Of course, there are occasional exceptions to this general aloofness, but for the most part serious musical scholarship lies at a distance from the general purview of Irish ideas. This is true even of the immensely distinguished series to which the present book belongs. It is frankly impossible to conceive a more generous, plural and intelligently engaged conception of Irish Studies than the one which prodigiously emerges from the hundred-fold volumes of *Reimagining Ireland*. Two reservations nevertheless occur to me, even if only one of these is relevant in the present context.[15] Put plainly, the presence of music in this series is comparatively muted, if not marginal. When music *does* feature, as in the collection of essays edited by Una Hunt and Mary Pierse entitled *France and Ireland: Notes and Narratives* (2015), the richness which accrues to this kind of interdisciplinary exchange between musicology and (in this case) Franco-Irish Studies throws the general absence into even sharper relief.[16]

Back in 1988 (which seems and is a very long time ago), I concluded my survey of musicology in Ireland by expressing the hope that it would develop 'as a discipline in its own right'. This optimistic avowal has been more generously and more imaginatively borne out than one could ever have imagined all those years ago. But for musicology to deepen and further flourish as an expression of Irish intellectual life, it requires not only a more available representation of its own retrievals in relation to music in Ireland, as in the model I have proposed in this chapter. It also needs the answering echo and collaboration of Irish Studies to 'fight back the tide of entropy'. I trust this is a soft imperative on which to end, but I do not shy away from adding that insofar as music in Ireland and its intellectual reception are concerned, indifference and complacency are justifiable synonyms for Pinker's more general term.

---

15   As a mild matter of record, the other reservation concerns the muted presence (if at all) of the visual arts in this series.

16   *France and Ireland: Notes and Narratives* is volume 66 in the series; *A History of Irish Ballet from 1927 to 1963* is volume 8 (2011).

ELKE D'HOKER

11 New Directions in Short Fiction

In 2019, Faber launched a series of beautifully illustrated standalone short stories, *Faber Stories*, to mark its ninetieth anniversary. Eight of the thirty stories are by Irish writers. Apart from canonical authors, like Joyce, Beckett, John McGahern and Edna O'Brien, the series also contains stories by Anna Burns, Julia O'Faolain, Claire Keegan and Sally Rooney. Since the *Faber Stories* showcase authors from all over the world, even in translation, the high incidence of Irish authors – almost one in three – is quite remarkable. It is a sign of the Irish short story's international standing, the widespread belief that the Irish are particularly good at the form. This reputation has been confirmed in recent years by the publication of many highly acclaimed short story collections, several of which have won major literary awards. To give just a few examples: Kevin Barry and Danielle McLaughlin received the Sunday Times Short Story Award in 2012 and 2019, respectively, while Edna O'Brien and Colin Barrett won the Frank O'Connor International Short Story Award in 2011 and 2014.[1] The many Irish titles on the five-title shortlist of the annual Edge Hill Short Story Prize, founded in 2007, are also a good reflection of the riches of the Irish short story in recent years: Wendy Erskine, *Sweet Home* (2019); Lucy Caldwell, *Multitudes* (2017); Thomas Morris, *We Don't Know What We're Doing* (2016); Bernie McGill, *Sleepwalkers* (2014); Kevin Barry, *Dark Lies the Island* (2013); Emma Donoghue, *Astray* (2013); Nuala Ní Chonchúir, *Nude* (2010); Gerard Donovan, *Country of the Grand* (2009); Anne

---

1 Since the Frank O'Connor International Short Story Award was able to direct considerable international attention to the short story, and the Irish short story in particular, it is a great pity that the prize was discontinued in 2016.

Enright, *Yesterday's Weather* (2009); and Colm Tóibín, *Mothers and Sons* (2007).

In addition, the popular Faber anthologies of new Irish short stories – most recently Kevin Barry's *Town and Country* (2013), Deirdre Madden's *All Over Ireland* (2015) and Lucy Caldwell's *Being Various* (2019) – have spotlighted established voices alongside new arrivals in the literary field, such as Eimear Ryan, Nicole Flattery, Andrew Fox and Melate Uche Okorie. Anthologies surveying the rich Irish short story tradition, on the other hand, have managed to raise public awareness of the genre in Ireland. Anne Enright's *The Granta Book of the Irish Short Story* (2010) and Sinéad Gleeson's prize-winning anthologies of women's short fiction, *The Long Gaze Back* (2015) and *The Glass Shore* (2016), certainly deserve credit in this respect. Finally, the extraordinary vibrancy of the Irish short story today is also in large part due to a flourishing magazine culture which has developed in Ireland since the early 2000s. By providing a forum for first-class short stories, literary magazines such as *The Stinging Fly*, *Winter Papers*, *Gorse* and *Tangerine* have raised the profile of the form as well as fostered the careers of many young writers.[2]

Irish literary criticism, however, scarcely reflects the high regard in which its tradition is held by international scholars and readers. Neither the history of the genre nor its most important practitioners get any attention in such recent literary histories as the two-volume *Cambridge History of Irish Literature*, the *Irish Literature in Transition* series or the multivolume *Oxford History of the Irish Book*.[3] Only *A History of Modern Irish Women's*

---

2   As Sarah Gilmartin puts it in the introduction to the anthology that marks *The Stinging Fly*'s twentieth anniversary: 'A story in *The Stinging Fly* is a proud moment for any new writer. It is also a calling card that gets the attention of busy agents and publishers. Many authors who appeared in *The Fly* early in their careers – Sara Baume, Kevin Barry, Colin Barrett to name a few – are now internationally acclaimed'. Sarah Gilmartin, 'Introduction', in *Stinging Fly Stories* (Dublin: Stinging Fly Press, 2018), x.

3   Margaret Kelleher and Philip O'Leary (eds), *The Cambridge History of Irish Literature*, 2 vols (Cambridge: Cambridge University Press, 2006); *Irish Literature in Transition*, 6 vols (Cambridge: Cambridge University Press, 2020); Clare Hutton and Patrick Walsh (eds), *The Oxford History of the Irish Book, Volume V, The Irish Book in English, 1891-2000* (Oxford: Oxford University Press, 2011).

Literature, edited by Heather Ingman and Clíona Ó Gallchoir, allocates a separate chapter to the short story.[4] In book series about Irish literature, similarly, critical studies about the short story or about major short story writers are few and far between. By comparison, the *Reimagining Ireland* series does quite well in this area, with one collection explicitly devoted to the form and several other studies of authors or themes that include chapters on Irish short fiction.[5]

Still, judging by the annual IASIL bibliographies of Irish literature, less than a dozen articles or book chapters about the genre of the short story are published every year. Most of these publications deal with contemporary writers and stories. This is also the focus of the only two special journal issues on Irish short fiction to have been published since 2000: in 2014, the Angers-based *Journal of the Short Story in English* devoted a special issue to 'The 21st-Century Irish Short Story' (2014), and in 2019, the *Canadian Journal of Irish Studies* followed suit with an issue on 'Contemporary Irish Short Stories'. This marked attention to the contemporary short story reflects the current vibrancy of the form, as well as its aptitude to respond quickly to new debates and trends.[6] Yet it is probably also the result of

---

4   Heather Ingman, 'The Short Story', in *A History of Modern Irish Women's Literature*, edited by Heather Ingman and Clíona Ó Gallchoir (Cambridge: Cambridge University Press, 2018), 277–293.

5   *Reimagining Ireland* has two volumes devoted to the short story: *The Irish Short Story: Traditions and Trends*, edited by Elke D'hoker and Stephanie Eggermont (Oxford: Peter Lang, 2014) and *Giving Shape to the Moment: The Art of Mary O'Donnell: Poet, Novelist and Short Story Writer*, edited by Maria Elena Jaime de Pablos (Oxford: Peter Lang, 2018).

6   The short story's topicality, a consequence of its relative brevity, explains its discussion in the context of studies about immigration, ageing, ecology, and multiculturalism in Irish literature. See for instance such recent publications as Paul Delaney, '"I wanted them not to be lost": Immigration and Irish Short Fiction', *Canadian Journal of Irish Studies* 42 (2019), 74–99; Teresa Caneda, 'Women on the Move: Mobility in Evelyn Conlon's Fiction', *Estudios Irlandeses* 12 (2017), 26–38; Sara Martín-Ruiz, 'Literature and Dissidence under Direct Provision: Melatu Okorie and Ifedinma Dimbo', in *Irishness on the Margins: Minority and Dissident Identities*, edited by Pilar Villar-Argáiz (Cham: Palgrave, 2018), 163–183; Elke D'hoker, 'Experiences of Ageing in Short Stories by Irish Women Writers', *Nordic Irish Studies* 17, no. 1 (2018), 145–160; Derek Gladwin, 'Ecological and Social Awareness in Place-Based Stories',

the virtual disappearance from the critical radar of such previous masters of form as Séan O'Faoláin, Frank O'Connor, James Plunkett, Michael McLaverty, Bryan MacMahon, Daniel Corkery and Liam O'Flaherty. With very few exceptions, all of their short stories are out of print, and most critical studies of their work date from the 1970s and 1980s.

This leaves us with the curious paradox that while the Irish short story is held in high regard internationally, and is often hailed as the national prose form in Ireland, there is a dearth of critical studies about the genre, its tradition, its formal characteristics and its major representatives. One reason for this paradox is no doubt the lower status of the short story in the critical hierarchy of genres: the taint of the classroom and the creative writing seminar that mark it as an apprentice form which critics can easily dismiss in favour of a given author's 'major' works. As a scholarly discipline, moreover, Irish literary studies has always focused more on themes, history and ideology, than on issues of form, genre or technique which explains its divergence from the international discipline of short fiction studies, which has primarily concerned itself with distinguishing the short story from neighbouring genres, particularly the novel. In most thematic studies about Irish literature, by contrast, short stories are discussed next to longer prose texts without any attention to the specificities of genre, while Irish literary histories are usually content with presenting an author or literary movement through reference to novels. What is needed, therefore, is a greater critical attention to the distinct form and tradition of the short story in Ireland. Only a clearer conception of its generic specificity, and a fuller understanding of its rich tradition, will guarantee the short story its rightful place in literary history and ensure its survival and continuing vibrancy in the future. Happily, several lines of research have emerged in recent years which can be drawn on to further develop Irish short fiction studies for the twenty-first century.

First, the recovery work of (mostly feminist) literary critics has rescued several forgotten short story writers from oblivion. Their stories have been

---

Canadian Journal of Irish Studies 42 (2019), 138–157; and Anne Fogarty, 'A World of Strangers? Cosmopolitanism in the Contemporary Short Story', in *The Irish Short Story. Traditions and Trends*, edited by D'hoker and Eggermont, 297–314.

revalorised and, in many cases, reissued so as to enable further critical study. This is the case for the experimental short fiction of New Woman writers like George Egerton, Sarah Grand and L. T. Meade, but also the tales of nineteenth-century local colour writers have received renewed attention.[7] Writers such as William Carleton, Anna Hall (Mrs S. C. Hall), Emily Lawless and Jane Barlow have thus come to be recognised as important predecessors of the modern short story.[8] Maeve Brennan's fascinating Dublin stories have entered the literary canon in the wake of Angela Bourke's biography, and the new editions of all her work.[9] It is to be hoped that the same critical reclamation will befall Norah Hoult, whose story collections *Poor Women!* and *Cocktail Bar* have recently been reissued.[10] Another forgotten Irish short story writer who deserves critical recognition is Ethel Colburn Mayne. A very prolific writer, who moved to London from Cork in her early 1940s, she published novels, biographies, translations as well as five collections of stories, which were routinely put on a par with the short fiction of Henry James and Katherine Mansfield.[11] Not all recovered writers are women, however. In 2018, James McKillop edited a collection of the short stories of Richard Power and also the new edition of Dermot Healy's short fiction should draw new readers and critics to his work.[12] In

---

7   See Tina O'Toole, *The Irish New Woman* (Basingstoke: Palgrave, 2013) and Elke D'hoker, *Irish Women Writers and the Modern Short Story* (Basingstoke: Palgrave, 2016).

8   See Heidi Hansson, 'Emily Lawless and History as Story', in *The Irish Short Story*, 61–82; Marguérite Corporaal, 'Relocating Regionalism: The Fin-de-Siècle Irish Local Colour Tale in Transnational Contexts', *Irish Studies Review* 28, no. 2 (2020), 155–170; and Heather Ingman, *A History of the Irish Short Story* (Cambridge: Cambridge University Press, 2009), 15–48.

9   Angela Bourke, *Maeve Brennan: Homesick at the 'New Yorker'* (London: Jonathan Cape, 2004).

10 Norah Hoult, *Poor Women!: A Critical Edition*, edited by Kathleen P. Costello-Sullivan (Dublin: Anthem Press, 2016); Norah Hoult, *Cocktail Bar* (Dublin: New Island Books, 2018).

11 *Ethel Colburn Mayne: Selected Stories*, edited by Elke D'hoker (Brighton: Edward Everett Root, forthcoming).

12 Richard Power, *The Rebels and Other Short Fiction*, edited by James J. MacKillop (Syracuse: Syracuse University Press, 2018); Dermot Healy, *The Collected Short*

spite of these advances, many of the nineteenth- and twentieth-century writers mentioned in Ingman's excellent *A History of the Irish Short Story* await further study, and several more want their work actually rediscovered, reissued and placed within the tradition of the Irish short story.

The same holds true for the more popular forms of short fiction which have traditionally been excluded from the dominant tradition and have therefore escaped scholarly attention. Research about the British and American short story has shown that the emergence of the modern short story at the end of the nineteenth century was strongly connected with the enormous popularity of the fiction magazines, or story papers, which entertained an expanding lower- and middle-class readership with adventure, ghost and school stories as well as romances, detectives and science fiction.[13] While British magazines were also read in Ireland, Stephanie Rains and Michael Flanagan have shown how Irish publishers also developed an array of titles for their readers.[14] They were promoted as more wholesome and patriotic than the 'debauchery' imported from abroad, even though they tended to print the same popular, often sensationalist, stories as their British counterparts. While these popular magazines have been studied – if at all – within the context of media or cultural studies, their short fiction output also deserves attention from literary scholars. In their reliance on stereotypes, fixed plot patterns and generic conventions, these stories reflect dominant ideologies, and also provide insight into readers' tastes, as well as into the development of genres. In addition, many so-called literary authors also draw upon these plots in their own stories, either more or less

---

Stories, edited by Keith Hopper and Neil Murphy (Dublin: Dalkey Archive Press, 2015).

13   Mike Ashley, *The Age of the Storytellers: British Popular Fiction Magazines, 1880–1950* (London: British Library and Oak Knoll Press, 2006); Dean Baldwin, *Art and Commerce in the British Short Story: 1880–1950* (London: Pickering & Chatto, 2013).

14   Stephanie Rains, ' "Nauseous Tides of Seductive Debauchery": Irish Story Papers and the Anti-Vice Campaigns of the Early Twentieth Century', *Irish University Review* 45, no. 2 (2015), 263–280; Michael Flanagan, 'To Enlighten and Entertain: Adventure Narrative in the Our Boys Paper', *Irish Communication Review* 12, no. 1 (2010), available online: <https://arrow.tudublin.ie/icr/vol12/iss1/7> [accessed 20 July 2020].

unconsciously or with metafictional, experimental or ironic intent. Think of the adventure stories from '*The Union Jack, Pluck* and *The Halfpenny Marvel*' referred to in Joyce's 'An Encounter'; of the twisted murder plots in some of Mary Lavin's stories; or of Bowen's highly self-conscious ghost stories.[15] As these crossovers already indicate, the demarcations between popular and literary fiction, or between high-, middle- and lowbrow forms were often less clear than literary histories have retrospectively suggested. A highbrow, modernist writer like Bowen also published stories in popular story magazines, while the popular storyteller Bryan MacMahon published all of his early work in the literary magazine *The Bell*.

The interaction between short story writers and the periodical market forms a third line of research that awaits further exploration in an Irish context. From its emergence in the late nineteenth century to the present resurgence of the form, the fate of the modern short story has always been linked to the publication opportunities provided by the periodical press, from the popular story papers over mainstream monthlies to *avant-garde* little magazines. The impact of the *New Yorker* on the careers of Maeve Brennan, Mary Lavin and Brian Friel has recently been documented, as have Elizabeth Bowen's multifarious interactions with the periodical press.[16] Additional research is needed to map the negotiations with the periodical market in Ireland, Britain and the US of such internationally celebrated writers as O'Connor, O'Faoláin and O'Flaherty, as well as John McGahern, Edna O'Brien and William Trevor. Individual periodicals too need further scrutiny in terms of the short story poetics they propagated, and of the authors and stories they published. Literary magazines like the *Irish Statesman*, the *Dublin Magazine*, *The Bell* and *Irish Writing* clearly had a large impact on the development of the short story in Ireland, yet they have so far been studied primarily for their political allegiance or ideological

15 James Joyce, *Dubliners* (London: Penguin, 1992), 11.
16 Bourke, *Maeve Brennan*; Gráinne Hurley, 'Trying to Get the Words Right: Mary Lavin and the *New Yorker*', in *Mary Lavin*, edited by Elke D'hoker (Dublin: Irish Academic Press, 2013), 81–99; Scott Boltwood, '"Mildly Eccentric": Brian Friel's Writings for the *Irish Times* and the *New Yorker*', *Irish University Review* 44, no. 2 (2014), 305–322; Allan Hepburn, 'Introduction', in *The Bazaar and Other Stories*, edited by Elizabeth Bowen (Edinburgh: Edinburgh University Press, 2008), 1–27.

content.[17] Investigating the fiction output of these magazines, which typically took the form of the short story, requires short fiction criticism to draw on the insights and methods of periodical studies, which was first developed for the study of Victorian periodicals but has since branched out into the twentieth century.[18] In fact, Irish short story studies in general would be enriched by a greater engagement with the material turn in literary studies, which has called for more attention to the material objects and different publication contexts of literary texts. For a genre that is literally small, like the short story, these contexts are even more influential, as well as more diverse, than for novels. A short story is, as a rule, published together with other texts: in newspapers and magazines, collections and story cycles, anthologies or websites. Some of these publication formats have received critical attention in recent years,[19] but further research is needed to assess the impact of these publishing contexts on the production, reception and canonisation of the short story in Ireland.

As Ingman has argued, one strand of short fiction that has long been side-lined in histories or anthologies of the Irish short story is that of fantastic, metafictional or experimental writing.[20] It is a strand that runs from the stories of Sheridan Le Fanu to W. B. Yeats, James Stephens and Flann

17   For ideological discussions of Irish literary periodicals, see Frank Shovlin, *The Irish Literary Periodical 1923-1958* (Oxford: Clarendon Press, 2003) and Bryan Fanning, *The Quest for Modern Ireland: The Battle for Ideas, 1912-1986* (Dublin: Irish Academic Press, 2008). For the influence of *The Bell* on Irish short fiction, see Elke D'hoker and Phyllis Boumans, 'Moulding the Twentieth-Century Irish Short Story: Séan O'Faoláin and *The Bell*', *Irish Studies Review* 28, no. 3 (2020), 287–304.
18   See for instance, the three-volume *Oxford Critical and Cultural History of Modernist Magazines*. Its first volume addresses Britain and Ireland, but contains only two chapters on Irish literary magazines: Alex Davis, 'Yeats and the Celtic Revival' and Frank Shovlin, 'From Revolution to Republic: Magazines, Modernism, and Modernity in Ireland', in *The Oxford Critical and Cultural History of Modernist Magazines, Vol. I, Britain and Ireland 1880-1955*, edited by Peter Brooker and Andrew Thacker (Oxford: Oxford University Press, 2009), 152–175, 734–758.
19   The new *Edinburgh Companion to the Short Story in English*, edited by Adrian Hunter and Paul Delaney, devotes attention to these publication formats (Edinburgh: Edinburgh University Press, 2019), with chapters on short story cycles and collections, magazines and the short story anthology.
20   Ingman, *A History*, 12–13.

O'Brien to Keith Ridgway, Anne Enright and David Hayden.[21] Although several of these authors have received ample scholarly attention in other contexts, their short fiction was not studied as part of the tradition of the Irish short story, which has long been considered an exclusively realist tradition. Recent studies have successfully challenged this all too narrow image, and have integrated these writers into the short story canon.[22] This renewed attention to formal experiment in short fiction has also highlighted the short story's characteristic generic hybridity, as it easily moves between prose and poetry, fiction and non-fiction, or incorporates elements from earlier tale and sketch traditions. While these and other formal characteristics of the genre have often been commented on in international short fiction studies, a formalist approach has largely been lacking in Irish short fiction studies.[23] Nevertheless, a consideration of the distinctive generic characteristics of the short story; of the specific effects it can generate; and of the plot patterns and formal conventions it typically draws upon, would usefully complement the dominant thematic approach. It would perhaps also prevent writers' achievements in the form from being dismissed in favour of their novels in author studies and literary histories alike.

For all of these lines of research, short fiction studies needs to strike up an allegiance with other disciplines, whether these be feminist theory and gender studies, media history and cultural studies, periodical studies and book history, or narrative and genre theory. Such collaborations and

---

21 Rob Doyle has recently put the spotlight on this tradition with his anthology *The Other Irish Tradition* (Dublin: Dalkey Archive Press, 2018).

22 See Ingman, *A History*; the chapters on LeFanu, Beckett and Flann O'Brien in D'hoker and Eggermont, *The Irish Short Story*; and a recent article like Alessandra Boller, '"A Most Violent Encounter": Disruption, Transgression and Intertextuality in David Hayden's "Darker with the Lights on"', *Interférences littéraires/Literaire interferenties* 24 (May 2020), 62–76, available online: <http://www.interferenceslitteraires.be/index.php/illi/article/view/1068/927> [accessed 20 July 2020].

23 See for instance Charles May, *The New Short Story Theories* (Athens: Ohio University Press, 1994); Susan Lohafer and Jo Ellyn Clarey (eds), *Short Story Theory at a Crossroads* (Baton Rouge: Louisiana State University Press, 1989); and Dominic Head, *The Modernist Short Story: A Study in Theory and Practice* (Cambridge: Cambridge University Press, 1992).

crossovers are necessary in order to achieve a better and more inclusive understanding of the very rich tradition of the Irish short story. In light of these new insights – some of them already achieved, many more hopefully to come – it is also high time for a reconsideration of the traditional canon of the Irish short story: Moore and Corkery, O'Faoláin, O'Connor and O'Flaherty. Most of their work is out of print and only a handful of anthologised stories are still read and responded to. Yet their short fiction certainly deserves a renewed critical examination, informed by the new theories, expanded canon and more fully mapped material and cultural contexts that have been developed for the Irish short story in recent years. Even if we no longer agree with the rather narrow, essentialist view of the short story developed by O'Faoláin and O'Connor, we can learn from their untiring promotion of the form to provide the short story with the critical background it needs to match and sustain its status as the Irish national prose form well into the twenty-first century.

SYLVIE MIKOWSKI

12 No Country for Young Girls?: Representations of Gender-Based Violence in Some Recent Fiction by Irish Women Writers

The representation of domestic violence and of sexual abuse is nothing new in Irish fiction. One only has to remember the harrowing, sadistic scene at the opening John McGahern's second novel *The Dark*, published in 1965; Edna O'Brien's description of the horrendous treatment of a young victim of incestuous rape, charged with attempted abortion in *Down the River* (1997); or some of the grotesque but still horrifying episodes of Patrick McCabe's *The Butcher Boy* (1992); or Roddy Doyle's heartbreaking portrayal of a battered female protagonist in *The Woman Who Walked into Doors* (1996). Those novels, apart from their striking literary qualities, have very often been read as denunciations of the patriarchal, conservative, oppressive, hypocritical society that emerged in the years following Irish independence and the long period when Fianna Fáil (under the leadership of Eamon de Valera) dominated Irish political and social life.

It has, however, become a cliché to claim that Irish society was revolutionised at the turn of the twenty-first century by the Celtic Tiger economy, which ushered in a new era of prosperity and opened up the country to new waves of changes and modernisation, aligning it with the moral standards of other Western societies, even though it was followed by the utter collapse of the banking system, accompanied by severe recession and dire austerity. The Celtic Tiger era was based on what is commonly referred to as neo-liberalism, which was not confined to an ever-increasing degree of globalisation of the economy, but also a complete reshuffling of individual moral values and behaviours, especially regarding sexuality. The Catholic

Church lost its ascendancy over society in the wake of a string of appalling revelations about the conduct of some of its clergy in the past, enabling, together with other factors, the approval by referendums of same-sex marriage (2015) and abortion (2018), turning Ireland into one of the most progressive societies in the world.

One can therefore imagine how moral and sexual oppression domestic abuse, and violence more generally such as described by the aforementioned Irish novelists, would no longer be a topical subject for contemporary, emerging Irish fiction writers. That supposition, however, is contradicted by the flow of recent high-quality Irish novels actually dealing with areas such as gender-based violence, murder, assault, rape, drug addiction, human trafficking, or prostitution, many of which are written by women writers. Apart from Tana French's novels, which belong to the distinctive genre of crime fiction, we can list Lisa McInerney's *The Glorious Heresies* (2016) and its sequel *The Blood Miracles* (2017); Louise O'Neill's *Asking for It* (2015); Eimear McBride's *A Girl Is a Half-Formed Thing* (2013); Lisa Harding's *Harvesting* (2017); and Mia Gallagher's *Hellfire* (2006). To that list we could add Anna Burns' *No Bones* (2002) and *Milkman* (2018), which, while situated in the period of the Northern Ireland Troubles, nevertheless lay emphasis on the exploitation and abuse of women's bodies. Even the much-celebrated *Normal People* by Sally Rooney (2018) alludes to a large extent to a sense of physical and psychological abuse inflicted on the female protagonist. Apart from this thematic focus among emerging women novelists on the representation of violence, generally directed at women, many of these narratives fit the comment made by a *Guardian* journalist in relation to Louise O'Neill's novel *Asking for It*, that, 'it's not the kind of the book you enjoy, it is a book you endure'.[1] Indeed, the extent of the physical and moral suffering evoked in the novels just listed, the graphic descriptions of horrible pain inflicted on the characters' bodies and souls, are not the only sources of the frequent uncomfortable reading experience provided by these works: the very language, the stylistic devices the writers have recourse to often present a challenge. The most extreme

---

1   Available online: <https://www.theguardian.com/childrens-books-site/2016/apr/10/asking-for-it-louise-oneill-review> [accessed 2 September 2020].

example of such stylistic audacity and experimentation is undoubtedly Eimear McBride's *A Girl is a Half-Formed Thing*, a story of rape, incest and death, accompanied by bodily decay and psychic self-destruction written in a disjunctive, a-grammatical, incoherent style which at times denies the reader what Roland Barthes called the pleasure of the text.[2]

Apart from this search for unsettling forms of expression, many common points can be found among that string of novels published since the 2000s by some Irish women writers: foremost among them is the choice of one or several teenage female protagonists, as in Lisa Harding's *Harvesting*, McBride's *A Girl Is a Half-Formed Thing*, Burns' *No Bones* and *Milkman*, O'Neill's *Asking for It*, or again Mia Gallagher's *Hellfire*. We can also mention the role of the parents, and most of all of the mother, as being generally deficient, absent or overbearing, addicted to religious devotion or to alcohol. Another, newer feature of this literature is a deep awareness of the divide between rich and poor and of social determinism, which for instance lies at the core of Rooney's *Normal People* and to a large extent explains the fate of Gallagher's protagonist in *Hellfire*.

The coincidence of the publication of these works undoubtedly suggests that the progressive evolution of Irish society in the wake of the Celtic Tiger has not eclipsed the growing problems of class divisions and social inequalities. But most of all, it signals that the role and image of woman in Irish society, what Claire Bracken calls 'the fixity of women's position in the Irish imaginary since the foundation of the state',[3] have become more and more openly questioned and are now the object of vivid, if not strident, denunciation requiring innovative modes of representation, as pointed out by the various kinds of experimentations with language, narrative technique and style displayed by the aforementioned novels. Two different critical approaches may therefore prove relevant here: a socio-ideological reading which would account for the feminist activism at play in these novels, and also an aesthetic one, which would analyse the strategies employed to represent violence, especially sexual abuse, including rape or prostitution, and

---

2   Roland Barthes, *The Pleasure of the Text*, translated by Richard Miller (New York: Hill and Wang, 1975).
3   Claire Bracken, *Irish Feminist Futures* (London and New York: Routledge, 2016), 3.

the artistic as well as ethical issues they involve, particularly as far as the role of the reader is concerned.

In either case, one may wonder whether the authors have served their purpose, in the sense that most of the novels of female education, far from staging their protagonists' progress from oppression to empowerment and liberation, leave them damaged, destroyed, institutionalised, or dead, trapping them in seemingly inevitable victimhood. That pattern can be set in parallel with what Conor Carville has called the 'pathography' which he considers to be underlying Irish culture, which he also defines as a 'trauma culture'.[4] To what extent indeed do *A Girl Is a Half-Formed Thing*, *Hellfire*, *Harvesting*, *Asking for It*, or even Anna Burns' *Milkman*, break away from the traditional tropes and themes of trauma narratives? Does their search for a specific way of expressing women's physical and psychic pain limit itself to a portrayal and denunciation of gender-based violence, or does it offer the reader, especially young female readers, inspirational images of resistance and empowerment? How is it that self-destructive, masochistic conduct looms so large in all those girlhood narratives, ending up for most of them in utter destruction and defeat? I shall try to investigate these questions with reference mainly to McBride's, Harding's and Gallagher's stories.

Stories of Violence

In Gallagher's *Hellfire*, young Lucy Dolan's fate of drug addiction, crime, psychiatric confinement and imprisonment seems sealed from the start, as noticed by critic Niall Griffiths in his review for *The Guardian*: 'Her downward spiral begins when she's still in the womb, and is black and steep and extreme'.[5] The daughter of a convict, Lucy becomes dependent from a

---

4   Conor Carville, 'Keeping that Wound Green: Irish Studies and Trauma Culture', in *What Rough Beasts? Irish and Scottish Studies in the New Millennium*, edited by Shane Alcobia-Murphy (Newcastle: Cambridge Scholars Publishing, 2008), 45–72.
5   Niall Griffiths, *The Guardian*, Sat, 21 October 2006, available online: <https://www.theguardian.com/books/2006/oct/21/featuresreviews.guardianreview22> [accessed 2 September 2020].

very early age on a perverse and violent boy named Nayler, to whom her first-person narrative is addressed in an apparent effort to settle accounts with him. After he initiates Lucy to shop-lifting, and then to drugs, he subsequently uses her as a courier and gets her involved in the dangerous rivalries between dealers. Gallagher's novel is scattered with scenes describing the most horrendous violence. Right through the 658 pages of this bulky novel, the reader attends Lucy's descent into hell, as well as that of some other female characters, not to mention the peak of horror reached when the body of Lucy's 12-year-old sister Samantha is found, having been tortured and killed in the most atrocious circumstances.

Harvesting also does little to spare the reader's sensitivity, as noted by journalist Deirdre Conroy, who declared: 'This is one of the most gut-wrenching, shiver-inducing pieces of fiction I have ever read'.[6] The novel alternates between Sammy's narrative and that of Nico, both girls turned into sex slaves, locked up in a suburban house from where they are whisked away every night to various hotels or private homes so as to serve the 'clients'' sexual needs. McBride's *A Girl Is a Half-Formed Thing*, described by Fintan O'Toole as an 'emotionally ferocious first novel',[7] spares none of the gory details either with regard to the female protagonist's dire experience of rape. For much of the story, she lets herself be treated so brutally that the reader is under the impression that 'the girl' is raped several times, not only by her uncle but by other men she meets by accident or to whom she offers herself in her ongoing self-destructive drive.

The theme of debasement, defilement and soiling is prominent in these narratives, foregrounding the process of abjection undergone by the female protagonists, in which the mothers play a central role, in accordance with the definition of the term by Julia Kristeva. In McBride's *A Girl*, images of dirt, vomit, mud and uncleanliness are scattered all along the narrative, either as a warning on the part of the mother at an early age,[8] or later when the girl is more or less assaulted by various men, generally in disgusting places: 'On the bar in my slip shoes. Pool and cake of it. Puddles and fag ash stink of sweat. This place smells like shite'.[9] The girl is repeatedly drawn to

---

6   Deirdre Conroy, *Independent.ie*, 15 May, 2017.
7   Fintan O'Toole, *The Irish Times*, 2 September 2016.
8   Eimear McBride, *A Girl Is a Half-Formed Thing* (London: Faber & Faber, 2014), 9.
9   *Ibid.*, 115.

water, at first perhaps in an effort to purify herself but then in an impulse to drown herself, driven by a death wish, the urge to dissolve her body and to return to her initial state of non-being by which the novel opens: 'Mammy me? Yes you.'[10] The lack of reference for the pronouns 'me, you' points to the lack of difference between the mother's and child's bodies, the idealised primary union which according to Kristeva, following Lacan, precedes the entrance into the symbolic order and the advent of the speaking subject. As Winfried Menninghaus summarises it, 'The act of repulsion of the maternal is the core of Kristeva's theory of abjection … all signification requires the repudiation of the undivided maternal being'.[11] However, everything happens as if 'the girl' was unable all along to establish a clear boundary between her body and that of her own mother, preventing her from rising to the status of subject, remaining only 'a half-formed thing', as evidenced by her inability to accede to grammatical language, and becoming herself an object of disgust and repulsion. In all the novels mentioned, the fathers are conspicuously absent from their daughters' lives–having deserted home and family in *A Girl*, or completely given up on their paternal duties in *Harvesting*, being locked up in jail in *Hellfire*, or dead in *Normal People*. The mothers are clearly held responsible for their daughters' predicament, often suffering themselves from some sort of psychic disorder leading to toxic dependence on an unreliable man, or some surrogate habit or creed. In *A Girl*, the mother is dependent on her own father, who has rejected her, and is obsessed by religion.

In *Hellfire* Gallagher recounts her protagonist's family story starting with the grandmother, as if the cause of Lucy's fate was to be found in the story of her foremothers. In *Harvesting* the mother is a depressive, suicidal alcoholic. These unloving, rejecting mothers deprive their daughters of the unconditional love they lacked themselves and tend to reproduce the gender bias they suffered from in favour of their male children. Lucy in *Hellfire* blatantly blames her mother, whose favourite child is her older brother: 'Because if she hadn'a blamed us, she'da ta take a good look at who or what had turned us bad–and for once I'm not talking about you here,

---

10   *Ibid.*, 3.
11   Winfied Menninghaus, *Disgust: Theory and History of a Strong Sensation*, translated by Howard Eiland and Joel Golb (New York: SUNY Press, 2003).

Nayler'.[12] Sammy in *Harvesting* is also convinced that her mother hates her: 'She wishes she'd pushed me back inside her the minute I slithered out, and demanded I be turned into a boy who would grow into a big strong man to worship the ground she walks on. Instead, she got this awful girl'.[13] In *Normal People* the mother takes sides with the bullying brother against her daughter. Far from nurturing self-confidence and moral strength in their daughters, the neurotic mothers expose them to the dangers that eventually damage them. For example, the mother introduces the rapist uncle to her home in *A Girl*; Lucy's mother sleeps with her daughter's persecutor; Sammy's mother is so indifferent that she doesn't wonder where her 15-year-old daughter is spending the night.

The Search for a Proper Language

Most of the novels under study flaunt daring, experimental literary techniques, in keeping with the violence they are trying to represent. They combine the difficulty, if not near-impossibility, of putting physical pain and trauma into words. As Elaine Scarry puts it: 'Physical pain does not simply resist language but actively destroys it, bringing about an immediate reversion to a state anterior to language, to the sounds and cries a human makes before language is learned'.[14] As to trauma, according to Cathy Caruth and other trauma studies scholars, it is an event that fragments consciousness and prevents direct linguistic representation. Caruth also argues that the language of trauma is literary because it, 'defies, even as it claims, our understanding'. It is 'the story of a wound that cries out, that addresses us in the attempt to tell us of a reality or truth that is not otherwise available'.[15] Trauma is an unassimilated event

12 Mia Gallagher, *Hellfire* (London: Penguin Books, 2007), 395.
13 Lisa Harding, *Harvesting* (Dublin: New Island Books, 2017), 9.
14 Elaine Scarry, *The Body in Pain: The Making and Unmaking of the World* (Oxford: Oxford University Press, 1985), 4.
15 Cathy Caruth, 'Introduction', in *Trauma, Explorations in Memory*, edited by Cathy Caruth (Baltimore: Johns Hopkins University Press, 1995).

that shatters identity and remains outside normal memory and narrative representation.

Several of the novels we are dealing with have a first-person narrator, allowing us direct access to what Aran Ward Sell in his study of McBride's *A Girl* calls 'a damaged consciousness', 'characters whose minds do not work according to normative social grammars'.[16] In *Harvesting* Harding uses the first-person point of view to render the horrific violence of Nico's passage from innocence to knowledge, from the children's games she plays with her brother and the trust she places in her parents when she still lives at home, to her gradual discovery of what awaits her in Ireland and her first rape by a 'client', experienced as a kind of death: 'My body has taken a different shape and form and I am not sure I will ever live in it fully again'.[17] Nico's innocent, childish narrative voice – she still calls out to her Papa and Maman – is juxtaposed against that of Sammy, a sassy, street-wise, rebellious runaway girl.

Gallagher for her part has borrowed from the gothic, a mode which has often been associated with *écriture féminine*, in the sense that it was frequently used by women writers to convey specifically female anxieties, regarding their position in society, but also towards sexuality. Monstrous mothers and pervert fathers or uncles are thus staple ingredients of many a gothic tale. *Hellfire* accordingly contains numerous allusions to the supernatural, or to the return of the past, not to mention the nightmarish atmosphere the author often creates, or the ghoulish nature of some of the characters. *Écriture féminine* can also characterise McBride's dislocated, pre-linguistic language, closer to what Kristeva calls 'the semiotic', which demonstrates the heterogeneity of meaning and represents that which precedes the formation of the subject. As to Anna Burns, she plays in *Milkman* with the heterogeneity of meaning, subverting the domination of mainstream, mostly male, discourse, but not by employing the same incoherent, fragmented mode as McBride. Her strategy is to systematically distort the

---

16 Aran Ward Sell, 'Half-formed Modernism: Eimear McBride's *A Girl Is a Half-Formed Thing*', *Hungarian Journal of English and American Studies* 25, no. 2 (2019): 393.
17 Harding, *Harvesting*, 233.

relation between the signifier and the signified, through recourse to euphemisms, understatements, or circumlocution, which also constantly reminds the reader of the near-impossibility of, 'telling us of a reality or truth that is not otherwise available', as is the case in trauma according to Caruth. As Dawn Miranda Sherratt-Bado puts it: 'The surrealist mode allows (Burns) to represent the psychological effects of trauma – registering what she calls "the feeling of reality, rather than necessarily what happened"'.[18]

Several commentators have recently emphasised the role of affect and of the manipulation of the reader's response engendered by the peculiar kind of experimental writing devised by Eimear McBride, which could also be applied to Gallagher, Harding or Burns. Derek Attridge argues for instance that 'McBride's fractured language invites an emotional response on every page of *A Girl is a Half-Formed Thing*'.[19] For Billy Clark, 'the linguistic style of the novel is highly marked and arguably not realistic, but this encourages an immersive response where readers feel they are experiencing events from a perspective similar to that of the main character'.[20]

By calling upon the reader's empathy, the authors do not aim only at making him/her respond emotionally to the pain, abuse and violence suffered by the female protagonists, but also to enrol him/her in a protest against gender-based violence in all its various forms. At least two of the novels examined here were the result of their authors' commitment to a political or social cause: Lisa Harding confided having written *Harvesting* as a result of her involvement in the Children's Rights Alliance campaign (Stop Sex Trafficking of Children and Young People) launched in 2010. She reported that she 'was deeply shocked reading about the minors that were trafficked to Ireland (…) it was anger that motivated me to write about

---

[18] Dawn Miranda Sherratt-Bado, 'Gender in Conflict', *Dublin Review of Books*, no. 104 (October 2018), available online: <https://www.drb.ie/essays/gender-in-conflict> [accessed 2 September 2020].

[19] Derek Attridge, 'Modernism, Formal Innovation and Affect', in *Affect and Literature*, edited by Alex Houen (Cambridge: Cambridge University Press, 2020), 249–266.

[20] Billy Clark, 'Manipulating Inferences: Interpretative Problems and Their Effects on Readers', in *Stylistic Manipulation of the Reader in Contemporary Fiction*, edited by Sandrine Sorlin (London and New York: Bloomsbury Academic, 2020), 118.

these stories in the first instance'.[21] Mia Gallagher's first novel *Hellfire* grew from her experience working in prisons, at a time – the late 1990s – when several Irish cities were increasingly the sites of organised crime, gang wars, drug abuse and general economic and social deprivation. Several characters in *Hellfire* may owe their inspiration to the Crumlin-Drimnagh feud between rival criminal gangs in south inner-city Dublin. The feud began in 2000 when a drugs' seizure led to a split in a gang of young criminals in their late teens and early twenties, most of whom had grown up together and went to the same school: 'The resulting violence has led to 16 murders and scores of beatings, stabbings, shootings and pipe bomb attacks', according to Wikipedia.

Apart from crime and sex trafficking, most of the authors also emphasise social inequalities. The protagonist of *Hellfire* is deeply aware of social discrimination: 'I seen the looks on the faces a people when they walk past', Lucy says. 'Like we're dogs or rats or worse, livin' in filth, with the graffiti and the smell a piss on the stairway landin's'.[22] In *Normal People* Sally Rooney takes issue with the rising social inequalities which define Ireland in the twenty-first century. The very style she uses, close to what Roland Barthes called 'écriture blanche', or 'zero degree writing' makes the reader keenly aware of class nuances through the experiences of self-doubt, estrangement and social exclusion encountered by her two protagonists. In *Harvesting*, Harding also alludes to class division and the domination of the rich in the new, globalised, neo-liberal Ireland, first by choosing a migrant from Moldavia as a victim of sex trafficking and then by showing how the girls' 'clients' are rich, upper-class, arrogant white men, one of them the father of Sammy's best friend, a doctor. Aran Ward Sell places McBride's novel in the precise socio-economic context of the 2008 economic crisis: 'In many respects, *Girl* was ahead of its time; its brutal depiction of sexual trauma, and its Joycean, pre-linguistic prose, clearly needed to wait until the Tiger's collapse to find a sympathetic publisher'.[23]

---

21 'Lisa Harding on *Harvesting*, One Year on', *The Irish Times*, Tue, 6 November 2018, available online: <https://www.irishtimes.com/culture/books/lisa-harding-on-harvesting-one-year-on-1.3688310> [accessed 2 September 2020].
22 Gallagher, *Hellfire*, 56.
23 Sell, 'Half-formed Modernism', 7.

Female Empowerment?

The main cause endorsed by the writers we are discussing remains the struggle against gender-based violence, the exploitation of women's bodies, male domination, gender stereotypes and gender inequalities in contemporary Ireland, before, during and after the Celtic Tiger. Susan Cahill thus reads *A Girl* and Louise O'Neill's *Asking for It* as being feminist texts: 'These texts demand us to inhabit the consciousness of the teenage girl and to experience the effects of her damage in immediate and affective ways. This is often also coupled with an explicit feminist consciousness and critique, particularly in texts aimed at teenage girls themselves'.[24] However, beyond the mere denunciation of gender-based violence and exploitation, we may wonder whether the model proposed to the teenage girls in question by the narratives at hand might help them in any way to overcome gender stereotypes, especially that of the woman as helpless victim. In their introduction to the collection of essays *Feminism, Literature and Rape Narratives*,[25] Zoe Brigley Thompson and Sorcha Gunne warn about the pitfalls of certain rape narratives which reinforce gender roles by perpetuating the roles of 'victims' and perpetrators. Some feminists have indeed argued against the 'rape script', 'that presupposes masculine power and feminine powerlessness and that society more or less successfully inscribes on men's and women's psyches'.[26]

On the one hand, the stories mentioned here do make up for what Jane Elizabeth Dougherty has called 'the unwritten Irish girlhood',[27] as

---

24 Susan Cahill, '*A Girl Is a Half-Formed Thing?*: Girlhood, Trauma, and Resistance in Post-Tiger Irish Literature', *Lit: Literature Interpretation Theory* 28, no. 2 (2017), 153–171.

25 Sorcha Gunne and Zoe Brigley Thompson, *Feminism, Literature and Rape Narratives: Violence and Violation* (London & New York: Routledge, 2010), 11.

26 See for instance Sharon Marcus, 'Fighting Bodies, Fighting Words: A Theory and Politics of Rape Prevention', in *Feminists Theorize the Political*, edited by Judith Butler and Joan Scott (New York: Routledge, 1992), 390–391.

27 Jane Elizabeth Dougherty, 'Nuala O'Faolain and the Unwritten Irish Girlhood', *New Hibernia Review / Iris Éireannach Nua* 11, no. 2 (Summer, 2007), 50–65, available online: <http://www.jstor.org/stable/20558161> [accessed 2 September 2020].

opposed to a tradition of the Irish novel of education essentially centred around boys or young men, the arch-example being Joyce's *A Portrait of the Artist as a Young Man*. The terrible hardships and suffering described in the novels at hand are experienced by extremely young girls: Lucy Dolan starts stealing at the age of nine and has grown to be a heroin-addict by the age of 15, while her sister is killed at the age of 12; Nico and Sammy are caught up in the nets of prostitution at about the same age; in *A Girl*, the female protagonist is raped by her uncle at the age of 13. In Burns' *No Bones*, a novel which Fiona McCann describes as 'essentially a tale of death, destruction and limited recovery',[28] Amelia Lovett is molested by her brother when she is 17. On the other hand, none of the feminist texts treated here can be said to offer women, and young girls in particular, a model of a recuperative, healing narrative. Equally, none one of them presents the traditional pattern of personal and social development proper to the Bildungsroman, but each in its own way conforms to Shadia Abdel-Rahman Telliez's description of *A Girl*, 'a story of un-becoming'.[29] Contrary to what Kathleen Costello-Sullivan argues about how twenty-first-century Irish narratives 'increasingly turn from just recognizing traumatic experiences toward also exploring and representing the process of healing and recovery',[30] all the novels alluded to in this chapter conclude with the impossibility for their young protagonists to overcome their wounds and find a place in society, supporting Susan Cahill's fear that, 'what we see in the post-Tiger literary landscape is a marked increase in registering trauma and vulnerability within the contemporary moment'.[31]

---

28 Fiona McCann, 'The Good Terrorist(s)'? Interrogating Gender and Violence in Ann Devlin's 'Naming the Names" and Anna Burns' *No Bones*', *Estudios Irlandeses* no. 7 (2012), 69–78.
29 Shadia Abdel-Rahman Telliez, 'The Embodied Subjectivity of a Half-Formed Narrator: Sexual Abuse, Language (Un)formation and Melancholic Girlhood in Eimear McBride's *A Girl Is a Half-Formed Thing*', *Estudios Irlandeses* no. 13 (March 2018–February 2019), 1–13.
30 Kathleen Costello-Sullivan, *Trauma and Recovery in the Twenty-First Century Irish Novel* (Syracuse: Syracuse University Press, 2018).
31 Cahill, *A Girl Is a Half-Formed Thing*, 7.

Those young female protagonists are never allowed to develop and become fully-blown subjects: McBride's girl returns to a state of non-existence by dissolving her identity into water, remaining a 'half-formed thing'; what's more, the generic 'a' in the title of the novel seems to imply that the essential, unchanging nature of women is to remain 'half-formed things': a thing, not a person. If the protagonist's brother dies too, at least he dies of a *brain* (my emphasis) tumour, whereas the girl exists and suffers only through her sex, recreating the dichotomy between mind and body that underpins gender stereotypes. Lucy Dolan in *Hellfire* is chemically dependent on her persecutor who plans to make her a sacrificial victim in some weird black magic scenario. Even though her long narrative may be said to have a recuperative power, at the end of her long story she is left to process her various traumatic experiences – of drug addiction, violence and horrendous murder – in a psychiatric hospital, then in jail.

The loss of subjectivity and agency naturally reaches its apex in the case of *Harvesting*, a novel in which the girls are treated worse than animals, as can be seen in this remark by one of the traffickers: 'Her father sold her like a dog. She is worth nothing to nobody'.[32] The clients, including the rich, educated ones, ignore them, until the point where they use them as sex objects. Sammy ends up drowned, while Nico suffers a psychic death when she is institutionalised in a psychiatric hospital. In *Normal People*, Marianne is unable to determine what she wants and lets herself be used by men, including her brother. At the end of the story, her boyfriend Connell embarks on a career as a writer and is accepted on a Master of Arts program in a prestigious American university, but Marianne is left with no precise prospect except that of becoming 'normal' at last. Indeed, we may wonder whether her progress from girlhood to adulthood does not amount to a process of normalisation, that is to say an acceptance of prevailing gender norms. Her relationship with Connell takes on a decisive shape towards the end of the novel when she calls him her knight in shining armour, the one who rescued her from the clutches of her abusive brother, a conclusion which hardly offers a good advertisement for women's self-reliance and autonomy.

32   Harding, *Harvesting*, 138.

The position of 'deject'[33] in which most authors place their protagonists, also tends to perpetuate the subjection of women to male domination. In an article about Angela Carter, feminism and the abject, Richard Pedot argues that, 'the theory of the abject can both sustain and complicate feminism. Studies of the abject can bring to light a given group's or society's symbolic and semiotic scaffoldings and thus contribute to define which position those ascribe to the feminine. Yet they cannot suggest definite outlines for a feminist agenda since the abject is that which has no contours, not even being an object'.[34] For Kristeva abjection is the basis of masochism: 'The question remains as to the ordeal, a secular one this time, that abjection can constitute for someone who, in what is termed knowledge of castration, turning away from perverse dodges, presents himself with his own body and ego as the most precious non-objects; they are no longer seen in their own right but forfeited, abject. The termination of analysis can lead us there, as we shall see. Such are the pangs and delights of masochism'.[35]

In the singular Irish context this figuration of the young woman as helpless masochistic victim resonates with what Conor Carville calls 'a wound culture' or a 'trauma culture', a 'pathography phenomenon' which he sees in 'a number of novels which draw parallels between personal histories bedeviled by the secrets and violence of childhood and the history of the nation as a whole'.[36] But Carville connects this pervasive use of 'the language of abuse' both by writers and critics to 'a psychologizing of the relation between the present and the past',[37] whereas the stories we are studying here belong to the contemporary moment, except perhaps Burns'

---

33 'The one by whom the abject exists is thus a deject who places (himself), separates (himself), situates (himself), and therefore strays instead of getting his bearings, desiring, belonging, or refusing'. Julia Kristeva, *Powers of Horror: An Essay on Abjection*, translated by Leon S. Roudiez (New York: Columbia University Press, 1982), 8.

34 Richard Pedot, '"He Was a Shit, to Boot": Abjection, Subjection and Feminism in "Black Venus"', *Journal of the Short Story in English* [Online], 60 (Spring 2013). Online since 01 June 2015, available online: <http://journals.openedition.org/jsse/1366> [accessed 8 July 2020].

35 Kristeva, *Powers of Horror*, 5.

36 Conor Carville, 'Keeping that Wound Green', 47.

37 Carville, 'Keeping that Wound Green', 49.

Milkman, which revisits the Troubles from the angle of the oppression of women. Several feminist critics have insisted on the symbolic role attributed to women in Irish history, that of embodying the nation, as Gerardine Meaney reminds us: 'If the nation is experienced as "a body", then the body in Western culture is primarily figured as and through the female body … The psychodynamic of colonial and postcolonial identity often produces in the formerly colonised a desire to assert a rigid and confined masculine identity, against the colonisers stereotype of their subjects as feminine, wild, ungovernable. This masculine identity then emerges at state level as a regulation of "our" women, an imposition of a very definite feminine identity as guarantor to the precarious masculinity of the new state'.[38] And Claire Bracken recounts in her introduction to the edited book, *Irish Feminist Futures*, that throughout Irish history, 'The symbolic rendering of the feminine as icon of worship functions to strip women of their actuality, of their "realness". She is always object, never subject, in the varying political, religious, popular and literary discourses of Irish nationalism.'[39]

In post-nationalist, decolonised Ireland, women seem to have been returned to the 'realness' of their bodies which were for a long time strictly controlled, and altogether ignored; but the violence of the repression of women's bodies in the past seems to have paved the way for the violence of the return of the repressed in the present. This, together with the commodification of bodies which accompanies the turn in the twenty-first century to a neo-liberal, hyper-capitalist economy, makes for the devastating accounts of rape, sexual exploitation and psychological torture which have emerged in the recent period in writings by women. That is why, while undeniably conveying a feminist message, denouncing in the most harrowing manner the place of women, particularly young women, in today's Irish society, these narratives prolong and repeat the tradition of Irish trauma fiction already illustrated by the likes of John McGahern, Edna O'Brien, Patrick McCabe and others. They too were caught up in the circle of repetition proper to trauma, as Anne Whitehead explains in

---

38 Gerardine Meaney, 'Race, Sex and Nation', *The Irish Review*, no. 35 (Summer, 2007), 46–63, available online: <http://www.jstor.com/stable/29736319> [accessed 10 November 2020].
39 Bracken, *Irish Feminist Futures*, 7.

her introduction to *Trauma Fiction*: 'Trauma acts as a haunting or possessive influence which not only insistently and intrusively returns but is moreover experienced for the first time only in its belated repetition.'[40] It might still be some time before Irish women writers escape the repetitive pattern of trauma fiction, and create visions of a future for girls and young women which will not be stamped by the horrors of sexual violence, abuse, psychic disintegration and devastation.

---

40 Anne Whitehead, *Trauma Fiction* (Edinburgh: Edinburgh University Press, 2004), 5.

COLIN COULTER AND PETER SHIRLOW

13 Northern Ireland's Future(s)

That Northern Ireland ever came into existence in the first place was, of course, a matter of historical happenstance. Partition was the desired outcome of none but the most marginal players in the dramas of the Home Rule era. It would, nonetheless, become the imperial expedient deployed in an ill-starred attempt to square the circle of competing ethnonational projects. As with most unwanted children, the precise details of Northern Ireland's conception and birth remain somewhat opaque. As the centenary of the region has come into view, commentators have suggested several moments that might be adopted when marking the event. These have ranged from the advent of the Government of Ireland Act in late 1920 to the calamitous decision of the Boundary Commission in 1925 to leave the frontiers of the new political entity at the traditional borders of the six counties. In the end, it was determined that the centenary of Northern Ireland would be commemorated in May 2021 to coincide with the moment when the Government of Ireland Act came into force.[1] Writing just six months in advance of the festivities, it is hard to discern any real momentum behind – or indeed enthusiasm around – the plans to herald the region's second century. The distinctly muted tone of the commemoration project owes something, needless to say, to its coincidence with a global pandemic that has claimed many more lives than even the bloodiest year of the Troubles. It might also be attributed to the fact that as we approach the centenary of Northern Ireland, its existence is perhaps in greater peril than at any stage since the region's violent and chaotic birth.

1 Diarmaid Ferriter, 'Marking Centenary of "Bloody Awful Country" a Tall Order', *Irish Times*, 21 August 2020.

The Numbers Game

Over the last few years, those voices calling for a constitutional referendum on the future of Northern Ireland have become rather more numerous and insistent. In part, the growing demand for a 'border poll' has been encouraged by what appears to be an imminent, and historically significant, demographic transition in the six counties. Although commentators still occasionally refer to Northern Irish Protestants as the 'majority' community, the reality is that they have not merited that status for several decades. In the most recent census, held in 2011, it was revealed that over the previous decade the Protestant community had declined by around 5,000 and at the time represented only 42 percent of the population. Over the same period, the Catholic community, in contrast, had grown by about 60,000 and now constituted 41 percent of people living in Northern Ireland.[2] Around half of that sharp increase may be attributed to the arrival of migrants from the Baltic states after the expansion of the EU in 2004. While members of these new communities are overwhelmingly Catholic, it cannot – or, at least, should not – be presumed that their disposition towards – or indeed interest in – the 'constitutional question' will mimic that of their co-religionists whose family ties in the six counties go back rather further. When a supplementary census question on the faith in which they were raised was put to those respondents claiming to have no religious affiliation, the numerical supremacy of the Protestant community grew but remained marginal nonetheless. In 2011, some 48 percent of the population claimed that they were socialised in the myriad churches that comprise Protestantism, while 45 percent disclosed that they had been raised Catholic.[3] The widespread assumption is that the demographic advantage that Protestants have enjoyed since the foundation of Northern Ireland will finally be overturned in the census scheduled for 2021. Over the period of the Peace Process, the Protestant

---

2   *Northern Ireland Census of Population, 2011*, Table KS211NI (Belfast: Northern Ireland Statistics and Research Agency, 2011).
3   *Ibid.*, Table KS212NI.

community has continued to grow older and dwindle in numbers. In large measure, this demographic decline stems from a crucial socio-cultural trend that dates back several decades but typically draws little public commentary, namely the relatively high propensity of younger Protestants to move 'across the water' to study and work. In stark contrast, the Catholic community is both younger in composition and growing in size. The burgeoning demographic advantage of Northern Irish Catholics is most dramatically apparent in the region's education system. At present, there are around 60,000 more Catholics than Protestants in Northern Irish schools.[4]

It seems entirely likely, therefore, that when the results of the 2021 census of population are published, they will reveal that Catholics represent the larger of the 'two communities' in Northern Ireland. Recent historical experience would suggest that such a dramatic demographic reversal would inevitably be greeted by widespread calls for the UK Secretary of State to use the powers furnished under the Good Friday Agreement to call a 'border poll' on the future of the six counties. When the data from the 2011 census were released, for instance, then Sinn Féin President Gerry Adams proclaimed that a constitutional referendum was warranted on the grounds that almost half – 46 percent to be precise – of respondents had ticked one of the boxes that acknowledged some version of Irish identity.[5] What the veteran republican failed to appreciate – or, perhaps, simply chose to ignore – was the significance of the fact that about half of the people on whose behalf he was claiming to speak identified themselves not as 'Irish' but rather as 'Northern Irish'. For many of those respondents, the first of those two adjectives would not be negotiable and the prospect of a border poll would not be palatable.

While the republican response to the last census of population seemed to involve clutching at straws, the outcome of the next one is likely to provide rather more grist to their mill. If the data released in 2022 were to disclose that Catholics were the largest community in Northern Ireland, Sinn

---

4   Simon Doyle, 'Number of Catholic Children in Schools at All-Time High', *Irish News*, 30 April 2019.
5   Gerry Adams, 'Demographics and Attitudes Are Crying Out for a Border Poll', *Irish Times*, 16 January 2013.

Féin would claim that there was now sufficient support for Irish unity and that a constitutional referendum was needed to facilitate such an eventuality. The republican movement should, however, be careful what it wishes for. The balance of probability is that – in the near future and under current circumstances at least – those campaigning for a united Ireland in a border poll would end up on the losing side. There are two principal reasons that this is likely to prove the case. First, should the demand for a border poll that will come on the heels on the census results actually be granted by the British Secretary of State, it will almost certainly prove to have been premature. Although Catholics might well outnumber Protestants in the general population, this will not necessarily prove to be the case among the population entitled to vote. In other words, the marked demographic advantage that the Catholic community now has among those of school age and younger will take a decade or longer to become apparent among the electorate. Until that process works its way out, it remains likely that the sectarian headcount of any future constitutional referendum would merely serve to maintain the status quo.

Those who will insist that the forthcoming census results mean there now exists a majority in the six counties willing to vote for a united Ireland are likely to be disappointed for a second, altogether more critical, reason. In public commentary on Northern Ireland, it has long since become commonplace to assume the region to be divided between a Protestant community that wishes to remain within the United Kingdom and a Catholic equivalent that aspires towards a united Ireland. The connections between ethnonational affiliation and political aspiration in Northern Ireland are, however, rather more complex than this familiar 'two communities' model tends to allow.[6] While Northern Irish Protestants often appear politically divided and culturally inarticulate, when asked what future they wish for the region they are absolutely unequivocal in their support for the Union. In the 2019 version of the Northern Ireland Life and Times Survey (NILTS),[7]

---

6   Colin Coulter, Niall Gilmartin, Katy Hayward and Peter Shirlow, *Northern Ireland a Generation after Good Friday: Lost Futures and New Horizons in the 'Long Peace'* (Manchester University Press, 2021), chapter five.
7   Northern Ireland Life and Times Survey, Various Years, Belfast: ARK. Available at: <https://www.ark.ac.uk/nilt/> [accessed 18 November 2020].

for instance, some 87 percent of Protestants chose the constitutional status quo. A rather different picture emerges when we come to consider Catholic respondents. Although the Catholic community frequently seems to have more political purpose and cultural confidence, these qualities are not reflected in the opinion poll data. In every version of the NILTS conducted since the Good Friday Agreement was signed, only a minority of Catholics polled have expressed a desire to live in a united Ireland. In the 2019 instalment, for example, Catholic support for Irish unity stood at just 47 percent. It would seem then that while the Protestant community is (uncharacteristically) united in its commitment to remaining citizens of the United Kingdom, the Catholic community is (uncharacteristically) equivocal in its desire to become citizens of a united Ireland. Indeed, if the NILTS data are to be believed, it would seem that at least half of those we routinely describe as Irish 'nationalists' living in the six counties are in fact anything but.

It might, of course, be countered that Catholic respondents are reticent about expressing what might be taken to be 'radical' views to opinion pollsters and that surveys such as the NILTS tend, therefore, to understate the true level of support for a united Ireland. There might well be some truth in this. The research conducted in the University of Liverpool during the 2019 UK General Election, for instance, provides a rather different snapshot of political opinion in Northern Ireland. In that poll, some 72 percent of Catholics said they wished to 'reunify with the rest of Ireland'. While the 2019 General Election survey[8] found greater evidence of Irish nationalism in the six counties, it also uncovered an even more heightened British nationalism in the region. Among those who identified as Protestants, a remarkable 95 percent disclosed that they wanted Northern Ireland 'to remain part of the UK'. It would appear that the heightened speculation over the future of the region over recent years has sharpened even further the commitment of the Protestant community to the Union.

---

8   Peter Shirlow and Jon Tonge, *Northern Ireland General Election Survey 2019* (University of Liverpool, 2020). Available at: <https://www.liverpool.ac.uk/media/livacuk/research/heroimages/The-University-of-Liverpool-NI-General-Election-Survey-2019-March-20.pdf>.

Although the findings of opinion polls often diverge substantially, none could be said to offer much comfort to those who anticipate a border poll paving the way to a united Ireland in the next few years. Surveys conducted in Northern Ireland suggest that the desire for constitutional change trails some way behind support for the status quo. Some even appear to indicate that a majority of Catholics in the six counties are either content with, or resigned to, the prospect of remaining British citizens for the foreseeable future. That such a degree of pragmatic – perhaps even grudging – acceptance of the prevailing order of things exists within the Catholic community owes a great deal of course to the existence and operation of the British welfare state. In particular, the vast sums that Westminster has channelled into Northern Ireland have created a Catholic middle-class comprising individuals who have often worked in the government sector and who have been able historically to access both excellent public healthcare and some of the best schools on 'these islands' free of charge.[9] The affluent lifestyles enjoyed by upwardly mobile Catholics have tended to suppress any real appetite for radical political change. For that to alter, the material circumstances that have encouraged the constitutional agnosticism of the Catholic middle classes would have to be deteriorate appreciably. And that, as we shall see later, is what might well be in the process of happening.

Mainstream commentary on Northern Ireland has habitually assumed a convenient intimacy between ethnoreligious origin and political orientation in the six counties. It is routinely held that there are two, and only two, communities in the region: one comprised Protestants of various stripes who are devoted to the Union, the other made up of Catholics who have their hearts set on a united Ireland. If opinion polls conducted over the course of the peace process are to believed, however, the patterns of political aspiration that exist in Northern Ireland are rather more complicated than commentators have tended to allow. While Protestant respondents emphatically reveal themselves as unionists, their Catholic counterparts appear deeply reticent about disclosing themselves as nationalists. And that

---

[9] Colin Coulter, 'Under Which Constitutional Arrangement Would You Still Prefer to Be Unemployed? Neoliberalism, the Peace Process, and the Politics of Class in Northern Ireland', *Studies in Conflict & Terrorism* 37, no. 9 (2014), 763–776.

reticence suggests that any border poll conducted in the near future would leave the constitutional status of Northern Ireland unchanged. There is, however, at least one further – and, perhaps, even more crucial – sense in which the long-presumed association between communal affiliation and political aspiration in the six counties might be deemed problematic. In recent years, it has become ever more apparent that there exists in Northern Ireland a large swathe of people who eschew the binaries of 'Protestant'/ 'Catholic' and 'unionist'/'nationalist' as well as the often taken-for-granted symmetries between them. It is towards those who consider themselves to be 'neither' that we turn our attention next.

The 'Neithers'

During the peace process, the long-established 'two communities' model has appeared ever more ill-suited to the increasingly complex realities of contemporary Northern Ireland. A society that appeared profoundly religious only a generation ago has undergone an accelerated process of secularisation in the period since. There has been a decline in church attendance among both principal ethnoreligious traditions but this has been rather more dramatic in the case of the Catholic community.[10] Over the last two decades, the proportion of Catholics who report high rates of religious observance has halved, with only two out of five now claiming they go to Mass at least twice a month. The secularisation of Northern Irish society finds a reflection – albeit, arguably, an understated one – in the most recent census of population. The aspect of the 2011 census that drew most public attention was, predictably, the marked rise in the size of the Catholic community. Perhaps the rather more significant trend revealed in the survey was, however, that the number of people in Northern Ireland who did not disclose church membership had risen once more, on

---

10   Coulter et al., *Northern Ireland a Generation after Good Friday*, chapter five.

this occasion by 72,000.[11] In 2011, one in six of those living in the region either stated they had no religion or declined to disclose that information. While a growing section of the population in Northern Ireland appears to have dispensed with the distinction between 'Protestant' and 'Catholic', a rather greater number of people would seem to have turned their backs on the political identities traditionally assumed to be their proxies. Since the advent of the Good Friday Agreement, the proportion of Northern Irish people who do not recognise themselves in the designations 'unionist' and 'nationalist' has grown apace and in the 2018 edition of the NILTS some 50 percent of respondents claimed to be 'neither'. That percentage would fall back to 38 the following year, a shift that issues a timely reminder to exercise caution when examining opinion poll data on Northern Ireland.

In the absence of more authoritative information, it might be reasonable, however, to assume that there is at the very least a substantial minority of people in Northern Ireland – perhaps around a third – who no longer feel that the traditional tags of 'unionist' and 'nationalist' capture their outlook on the world. As one might anticipate, this propensity to reject the ethnopolitical identities that have long since dominated public life in the region proves especially pronounced among those who came of age after the Troubles drew, finally, to a close. As the 2019 edition of the NILTS reveals, the number of respondents aged 25–44 selecting 'neither' exceeds the total choosing either 'unionist' or 'nationalist'. It would seem then that there might exist in Northern Ireland a 'peace generation' that has largely chosen to leave behind the forms of ethnonational affiliation and prejudice that so often appeared to animate their predecessors. That comforting narrative is disrupted somewhat, however, when we consider some of the responses in the 2019 edition of the NILTS of those who most recently left school. Among those aged 18–24, almost twice as many respondents disclosed themselves to be 'unionist' or 'nationalist' as claimed to be neither. This unanticipated exception to the broader trend lends weight to the suspicion that many of the more insidious cultural and political sentiments

11   Northern Ireland Statistics and Research Agency, *Religion in Northern Ireland* (Belfast: NISRA, no date). Available at: <http://www.ninis2.nisra.gov.uk/public/census2011analysis/religion/religioncommentary.pdf> [accessed 18 November 2020].

that sustained the Troubles have persisted into what is, in principle, the 'post-conflict' era.

While keeping that crucial qualification in mind, it remains possible perhaps to suggest that there has emerged in Northern Ireland a 'peace generation' that has come to question, and in many cases reject, the ethnonational identities so cherished by their predecessors. The political outlook of those predominantly younger people who see themselves as neither 'unionist' nor 'nationalist' seems, broadly speaking, to be liberal, secular and cosmopolitan. Those who reached adulthood after the end of the Troubles appear, like their counterparts elsewhere, to be motivated by issues such as the global environmental crisis and a range of personal freedoms centred especially on issues of gender and sexuality. Successive instalments of the UK General Election Survey, for instance, have revealed that younger age cohorts in Northern Ireland are strongly supportive of both gay marriage and a woman's right to choose.

The emergence of a generation of younger people who often cannot recognise themselves in the ethnonational identities and issues that have long dominated Northern Irish public life has begun to find some expression in mainstream electoral politics. Over the last decade, the proportion of voters supporting parties other than those in the unionist and nationalist traditions has doubled and currently stands at around one in five. The principal beneficiary of this shift in electoral allegiance has of course been a party that was widely expected to face extinction during the peace process. Tapping into widespread public disaffection in the period between 2017 and 2020 when the Stormont institutions remained in cold storage, the Alliance Party would see a surge in its popularity, reaching a high water mark in the 2019 European election when Naomi Long secured 19 percent of first preferences and claimed a seat.[12] While the growing willingness of Northern Irish voters to cast a ballot for candidates that are neither unionist nor nationalist has primarily assisted a party that has been around for half a century, there are also signs of the emergence of more authentically 'new' forms of politics in the six counties. Recent elections have seen

---

12   Sean Haughey and James Pow, 'Remain Reaffirmed: The 2019 European Election in Northern Ireland', *Irish Political Studies* 35, no. 1 (2020), 29–45.

the emergence of younger voices more concerned with environmental and economic issues than with the 'constitutional question'. Most significantly, the 2019 local government elections would see seven Greens and Socialists elected onto Belfast City Council, bringing radical younger voices into a civic forum that has often provided a stage for the most anachronistic and visceral forms of sectarian enmity.[13]

While the emergence of a 'peace generation' who see themselves as neither unionist nor nationalist has certainly found expression in the way in which some people have voted over recent years, it has also been illustrated rather more palpably in the way in which many people have chosen not to vote at all that stretches back rather farther. The era of the Peace Process has witnessed a marked decline in voter turnout. While the first election to the Northern Ireland Assembly held in 1998 saw 70 percent of those entitled to vote do so, by the time of the 2016 poll, that figure had fallen to a mere 55 percent. The charged political atmosphere that followed the suspension of the Stormont institutions in early 2017 would revive turnout in subsequent elections but that is likely to prove an aberration in a more established trend of escalating voter apathy. The growing disenchantment of the Northern Irish electorate derives in part from the consociational parliamentary protocols that flowed from Good Friday Agreement. When politicians are returned to serve in the Stormont Assembly they are required to identify themselves as 'unionist', 'nationalist' or 'other'.[14] While all three designations have, in principle, equal status, in practice only the first two carry any weight in the calculations as to whether certain critical forms of legislation have cross-community support. In effect, therefore, the operation of these parliamentary conventions serves to disenfranchise those who do not see themselves as 'unionists' or 'nationalists'. While around a third, possibly even more, of the electorate in Northern Ireland consider themselves to be 'neither', these people often have little incentive to vote as any candidate they might return would have little real influence in a Stormont Assembly that operates on the assumption that everyone

---

13   Lisa Claire Whitten (2020), '#LE19 – A Turning of the Tide? Report of Local Elections in Northern Ireland', *Irish Political Studies* 35, no. 1 (2020), 61–79.
14   Coulter et al., *Northern Ireland a Generation after Good Friday*, Introduction.

belongs to one of the two traditional ethnopolitical camps. It should come as little surprise then that the 2019 General Election Survey revealed that while more than 80 percent of those who self-identified as 'unionists' or 'nationalists' had voted, only 50 percent who consider themselves to be 'neither' had done likewise.

Many of those who eschew the twin ethnonational affiliations long presumed to exhaust the field of political identity in Northern Ireland have, then, chosen to withdraw from elections over which they feel they have no influence and that inevitably result in the eternal recurrence of the same sectarian squabbles. Those who consider themselves to be 'neither' might well, however, be persuaded to vote in rather larger numbers in a future border poll which would be a unique and critical moment and one with real potential to alter the existing order of things. What might act as a further incentive is that those who reject the conventional ethnonational binary may prove to be the constituency that decides Northern Ireland's constitutional future. Given that those who deem themselves 'neither' represent around a third – maybe even rather more – of the electorate, it is entirely possible that the outcome of the ancient quarrel between unionists and nationalists might be decided by a younger generation of people who have dispensed with those categories altogether. When we consider how this body of people is likely to vote in a border poll, the evidence is, once again, less than heartening for those who aspire towards a united Ireland. As Hayward and McManus illustrate,[15] those who fall into the 'neither' category are two-and-a-half times more likely to vote for the status quo than for constitutional change in a future border poll. That said, an unusually high proportion of this group – around two in five – say that they either would not vote or do not know how they would cast their ballot. There is, then, a significant swathe of this significant constituency who might, in principle at least, be open to persuasion by *both* the competing sides in any prospective referendum on Northern Ireland's future.

Surveying the balance of political forces in the six counties, it becomes increasingly apparent that the confidence that republicans, in particular,

15   Katy Hayward and Cathal McManus, 'Neither/Nor: The Rejection of Unionist and Nationalist Identities in Post-Agreement Northern Ireland', *Capital & Class* 43, no. 1 (2019), 139–155.

have placed in the outcome of the border poll they covet will prove to have been misplaced. While the evidence before us certainly remains imperfect, it does suggest with no little consistency that there are three things that we might presume to be true. First, those who call themselves 'unionists' appear unequivocally committed to the Union and can be expected to vote overwhelmingly in favour of the constitutional status quo. Second, those who self-identify as 'nationalists' are much more reticent on the issue of Irish unification than is often assumed and seem unlikely, perhaps, to cast their ballots *en masse* in the cause of constitutional change. Third, those who deem themselves to be 'neither' will in all probability vote in favour of remaining within the UK, although a large minority of them may never darken the door of a polling station. In sum, the prospects are that, under current circumstances at least, republicans would lose any referendum called on Northern Ireland's future. But what if those circumstances were to change? There exist perhaps a couple of discrete social and political processes that have *the potential* to shift significantly the balance of forces in any border poll called in the next few years. We will turn our attention now to the more obvious of the two.

The Brexit Conjuncture

If there was a single moment this century that might be said to have transformed the political landscape of Northern Ireland it was, needless to say, the decision on 23 June 2016 of a slim majority of the UK electorate to leave the European Union. While Northern Irish affairs had barely featured in the fevered public debates that preceded the Brexit referendum – and most (56 percent) of those who cast a ballot in the region voted 'remain' – its repercussions would prove especially dramatic in the six counties.[16] The historic decision of the UK to terminate its membership of the EU raised for a time the possibility that there would once

---

16   Feargal Cochrane, *Breaking Peace: Brexit and Northern Ireland* (Manchester: Manchester University Press, 2020).

again be a 'hard' border on the island of Ireland. That calamity appeared to have been avoided once and for all in October 2019 when London and Brussels agreed the Northern Ireland Protocol. This accord would see the six counties remain a de facto part of the EU's single market and customs union, creating the prospect of what would in effect be a trade frontier running not along the Irish border but rather through the Irish Sea.

Although the deal struck between the EU and UK negotiators in October 2019 was widely cast as the final resolution of the Brexit saga, we should perhaps have anticipated that there would be at least one further twist in this most convoluted of plots. In September 2020, the British government announced the introduction of an Internal Market Bill that would potentially give Westminster the power to override the Northern Ireland Protocol that had, finally, allowed the Withdrawal Agreement to be signed. According to seasoned Brexit observer Chris Grey,[17] were the proposal to become law it would mean that 'the UK government could unilaterally change or do away with customs formalities on goods travelling from Northern Ireland to Great Britain, and unilaterally remove the role of EU law and regulation in state aid policy in Northern Ireland'. That the introduction of the Internal Market Bill represented a deliberate attempt to breach international law was acknowledged quite explicitly in the quixotic statement of Northern Ireland Secretary Brandon Lewis to the House of Commons that the prospective legislation would infringe the Withdrawal Agreement, but only 'in a very specific and limited way'.[18] The most common reading of this dramatic turn of events depicts the apparent *volte-face* of the Johnson administration as simply a calculated gamble to strengthen London's hand in the negotiations with Brussels that began in early September 2020 and mark the end of the post-Brexit 'transitional period'. Another school of thought suggests that the appearance of the

---

17 Chris Grey, 'The Descent into Political Insanity', Brexit blog, 11 September 2020. Available at: <https://chrisgreybrexitblog.blogspot.com/> [accessed 3 November 2020].

18 Denis Staunton, 'Westminster Sketch: Commons Bewildered as Brandon Lewis Drops Bombshell', *Irish Times*, 8 September 2020. Available at: <https://www.irishtimes.com/news/world/uk/westminster-sketch-commons-bewildered-as-brandon-lewis-drops-bombshell-1.4350081> [accessed 5 November 2020].

Internal Market Bill signals the moment when British Prime Minister Boris Johnson has acceded finally to those ideological zealots within and without his party who wish the UK to leave the EU without an agreement on future trading relations. The advent of a 'no deal' Brexit would, of course, raise the prospect once again of a 'hard border' that has the potential to place even greater pressure on Northern Ireland's already troubled peace settlement.

While the balance of probability suggests that the Conservative administration at Westminster will in the end strike a deal that respects the terms of the Northern Ireland Protocol, the Brexit saga has already had a profound impact on the political topography of the region. The prospect that there would once more be a hard border demarcating the six counties has inevitably inflamed nationalist opinion across the island of Ireland. In the period since the fateful June 2016 referendum, the possibility that Northern Ireland might, at some point in the near future, no longer exist has often seemed more real than at any point since its inception. Although republicans had not even bothered to register to campaign during the Brexit poll,[19] they were, predictably, quick to realise its historic significance. The morning after the referendum result was called, Sinn Féin announced that the time was now right, once more, for a vote on Northern Ireland's future.

While the enthusiasm of republicans for a border poll was, and remains, entirely understandable, their optimism about its likely outcome continues to be misplaced, as we have seen above. The data garnered by the NILTS suggest that since the 1998 Good Friday Agreement the proportion of Northern Irish Catholics who aspire towards a united Ireland has been in gradual, ongoing decline. That long-running trend would, however, be arrested by the decision of the UK to rescind its membership of the EU. In the period since the Brexit referendum, the body of Catholic respondents identifying a united Ireland as their optimal political outcome has grown by 12 percent. This represents a substantial shift in political aspiration and may well of course understate the proportion of Catholics living north of the border who wish to see it erased altogether. Nevertheless, it could hardly be mistaken for the seismic change in Catholic political opinion that would be required for a border poll to signal the end of Northern Ireland.

19 Haughey and Pow, 'Remain Reaffirmed', 6.

It should be remembered, however, that the impact of the Brexit referendum has been felt well beyond the confines of the Catholic community in Northern Ireland. That the principal representatives of political unionism, the Democratic Unionist Party, have been such zealous advocates of the UK leaving the EU has often invited the inference that the strategy enjoys universal popularity across the Protestant community. In reality, however, two out of every five Protestant voters opted to 'remain' in the June 2016 referendum. This position would seem to have been especially prevalent among middle-class unionists who are more likely to have lived and studied abroad and to travel regularly to other European states for work. The class profile of unionists who wish to retain their EU citizenship was reflected in the 2016 referendum when the only two constituencies with sitting Unionist MPs to vote 'remain' were South Belfast and North Down, the most affluent constituencies in all of Northern Ireland. This pattern was repeated in the 2019 General Election when candidates opposed to Brexit were returned in both areas. In affluent South Belfast, other 'remain' candidates stood aside to allow Claire Hanna of the SDLP take the seat from the DUP, while in even more prosperous North Down Stephen Farry astonished most political commentators by registering Alliance's sole victory of the campaign.[20] The latter result should not, however, have come as that much of a surprise. North Down had, after all, been represented previously by Lady Sylvia Hermon, the only Unionist at Westminster opposed to the Brexit project. That particular political succession in what is often referred to as Northern Ireland's 'gold coast' makes perfect sense then, illustrating that there are many among the more affluent sections of the unionist community who are deeply troubled by the prospect of leaving the EU. That sense of loss is even more keenly felt, perhaps, by that large minority of the Northern Irish population who feel themselves to belong to neither of the 'two communities'. In the Ipsos/Mori poll conducted during the Brexit referendum, for instance, some 70 percent of those who did not identify as either 'unionist' or 'nationalist' disclosed they were in favour of the UK

20   'North Down: Alliance "Elated" with Stephen Farry's Shock Victory', *Belfast Telegraph*. Available online at: <https://www.belfasttelegraph.co.uk/news/politics/general-election-2019/north-down-alliance-elated-with-stephen-farrys-shock-victory-38781817.html> [accessed 18 November 2020].

remaining in the EU.[21] While that figure fell some way short of the proportion of 'nationalists' who voted 'remain' – 88 percent – it underlines once more that those who are 'neither' tend to be broadly liberal in their political disposition.

It seems reasonable, therefore, to suggest that the decision of the UK to leave the EU has been alienating for a swathe of Northern Irish society that is rather broader than usually assumed. The impact of Brexit on the nationalist community in the six counties has been widely acknowledged and documented. What is perhaps less well appreciated is that the prospect of leaving the EU has proved deeply troubling for those who consider themselves members of neither of the 'two communities', as well as the more affluent and educated sections of the unionist tradition. While that diverse body of people – nationalists, unionists and neither – who are alienated by the prospect of no longer living in the EU is certainly substantial, it has yet to tilt opinion polls in favour of the demand for constitutional change. It needs to be remembered, however, that Brexit is not an event, but rather a process. And that process is about the begin in earnest. It remains to be seen how precisely the decision to leave the EU will pan out in practice and how people will respond to eventualities that even now remain difficult to foresee. There is, of course, at the very least the prospect that those who have counselled that Brexit will damage the social and economic fabric of Northern Ireland will be proved right. Indeed, we have already had a serious premonition of the chaos that might ensue when the Withdrawal Agreement finally comes into full effect in 2021. The Northern Ireland Protocol that finally allowed London and Brussels to strike a deal means that goods coming to the region from other parts of the UK will need to adhere to EU regulatory standards and procedures, which will inevitably produce delays and increase costs. This has prompted serious fears that, in general, supply lines might be affected and that in particular some British supermarket chains might withdraw from Northern Ireland, resulting in

---

21   John Garry, 'The EU Referendum Vote in Northern Ireland: Implications for Our Understanding of Citizens' Political Views and Behaviour', *Northern Ireland Assembly: Knowledge Exchange Seminar Series*, 2016. Available at: <http://www.niassembly.gov.uk/globalassets/documents/raise/knowledge_exchange/presentations/series6/garry121016ppt.pdf> [accessed 18 November 2020].

food shortages. In November 2020, these concerns prompted Arlene Foster and Michelle O'Neill to pen a joint letter to the head of the European Commission, Michel Barnier, looking for assurances that the imminent transition to the new arrangements would work smoothly.[22] While the pleas issued by the First and Deputy First Ministers might be seen as a strategically astute attempt to secure an advantage as the negotiations between London and Brussels approach endgame, they might also disclose the genuine misgivings of those in the best position to anticipate the chaos that might ensue when Brexit finally becomes a reality at the start of 2021.

If some of the more lurid tales of those opposed to the UK leaving the EU were to come to pass, the impact on public opinion in Northern Ireland is likely to be profound. If there were long queues at the ports and empty bread shelves in the supermarkets, the desire of nationalists, and perhaps even of 'neithers', for Irish unity might well sharpen dramatically. It is even possible that those middle-class unionists who voted 'remain' would be prepared to throw in their lot with a united Ireland in which they would, once again, be EU citizens. As so often in contemporary debates about Northern Ireland, we are operating here in the realm of pure speculation. It remains possible that growing alienation at the chaos that might come on foot of Brexit would create the tide that would sweep the region out of the UK. But it is entirely feasible that the fate of Northern Ireland will be sealed, one way or the other, by a process that is perhaps even more crucial and yet features much less often in debates on its constitutional future.

The Unionist Trump Card

In his account of what he sees as the masochistic forms of English nationalism that drove the Brexit enterprise, Fintan O'Toole makes a telling observation on what it was that lured previous generations of his family to relocate to Britain. In *Heroic Failure*, the cultural commentator suggests

22 Lisa O'Carroll, 'No Need for Border Checks on Northern Ireland Supermarket Food, Foster Tells EU', *The Guardian*, 10 November 2020.

that his relatives who moved 'across the water' had emigrated 'not so much to England as to the welfare state'.[23] While the Unionist politicians who governed Northern Ireland at the time were deeply reticent about the new welfare measures introduced by the Labour government after the Second World War, these would in time prove to be perhaps the most persuasive case for maintaining the Union. The National Health Service is the only British state institution that enjoys the widespread affection of people across the ethnonational divide in the six counties. Its cultural significance was underlined at the onset of the coronavirus pandemic in the spring of 2020 when a simple wall mural in republican west Belfast declared: 'St James supports our brave NHS'.

While the institutions of the British welfare state exert an appeal for all communities in Northern Ireland, they have of course been under attack for several decades. The advent of the 2012 Welfare Reform Act – extended to the six counties four years later – has seen many of the most vulnerable within Northern Irish society deprived of essential forms of social security.[24] These changes have led to a steep rise in the number of food banks operating across the UK, and in the twelve months to the end of March 2020 more than 45,000 emergency three-day food parcels were distributed in Northern Ireland alone.[25] The dismantling of the British welfare state under Conservative and Labour administrations alike has been further apparent in the systematic underfunding of the NHS and in the parallel proliferation of private health care. In a Northern Irish context, the mounting pressure on socialised health provision would be heightened further by the suspension of the Stormont institutions for three years until their restoration in January 2020. In that period, waiting lists for even the most elementary procedures would grow to unprecedented lengths and nurses would go on strike for pay parity with other UK regions, an industrial dispute that drew enormous public support and in effect shamed local politicians back into talks. Starved of resources while the representatives of unionism and

---

23 Fintan O'Toole, *Heroic Failure: Brexit and the Politics of Pain* (London: Head of Zeus Press, 2018), 10.
24 Colin Coulter, 'Northern Ireland's Elusive Peace Dividend: Neoliberalism, Austerity and the Politics of Class', *Capital & Class* 43, no. 1 (2019), 123–138.
25 Trussell Trust, End of Year Stats (Trussell Trust, 2020). Available at: <https://www.trusselltrust.org/news-and-blog/latest-stats/end-year-stats/> [accessed 19 November 2020].

nationalism squabbled over less critical matters, the Northern Irish health system was ill-prepared for the onset of a global pandemic that has merely served to illuminate its current weakened state.

The erosion of the once cherished welfare state might yet prove to be critical in the debates about the future of Northern Ireland. There was a time when the relatively generous levels of social security and access to first rate public health care free of charge made a lucid case for the Union even among those with an emotional attachment to a united Ireland. Those days seem to be receding into the distance. The decline of the NHS especially has the potential to alter the balance of political forces within Northern Ireland. In particular, those middle-class Catholics who often seem so agnostic on the matter of a united Ireland might well become rather less averse to joining a society where they will have to pay for their operations now that the patient waiting lists have already persuaded them to take out private health insurance. It might well prove, then, that the leaders of political unionism have been the architects of their own downfall in at least two different ways. First, the most popular figures within unionism cheered on a Brexit project that has politicised once again a border on the island of Ireland that had, quite literally, become invisible. Second, the unionist political class has colluded in the dismantling of the British welfare state, acting as willing advocates of the erosion of social security and championing the privatisation of what were once respected public institutions. While most commentators have assumed it is the former that poses a real and present danger to the Union, it might, in the end, prove to be the latter that represents the most serious threat to the constitutional status of Northern Ireland.

The Inbetweeners

While republicans proclaim that we are living in the last days of the Union, and unionists that Northern Ireland will live well into its second century, the truth is that no one can make such claims with any genuine conviction. The uncertainty that surrounds the future of Northern

Ireland is reflected in the often wildly different outcomes of opinion polls on the matter. One survey published in February 2020 suggested that the majority who would vote for the region to remain within the UK was less than 2 percent.[26] Another that appeared in the same month indicated that the gap between the two sides stands at 23 percent.[27] While the outcome of a prospective border poll will remain difficult to call, the balance of evidence suggests that the constitutional status of Northern Ireland will remain unchanged, in the immediate future at least. For all the increasingly febrile speculation about its political destiny, the most likely prospect facing the region is that it will continue for some time yet to exist in its seemingly eternal state of 'inbetweeness'. Northern Ireland will, in other words, remain both on the window ledge of the British state and on the very edge of the field of vision of the Irish state; an economy that remains subject to the same regulatory protocols as the state to the south to which it does not belong, rather than the one to the east to which, in principle at least, it does; a society that in so many ways has moved beyond the sectarian enmities that sustained its recent violent past and yet, at the same time, remains prone to their gravitational pull. While that condition of interregnum may well cast up fresh political possibilities, it is also likely, as Antonio Gramsci reminded us, to produce monsters.[28]

---

26   Eimear McGovern, 'Northern Ireland Poll Shows 45.4% Back Irish Unity and 46.8% Support Union with UK', *Belfast Telegraph*, 25 February 2020.
27   Suzanne Breen, 'Just 29% in Northern Ireland Would Vote for Unity, Major Study Reveals', *Belfast Telegraph*, 18 February 2020.
28   Antonio Gramsci, *Selections from the Prison Notebooks* (London: Lawrence and Wishart, 1971), 556.

JOHN WALSH

14 'Real' Language Policy in a Time of Crisis: Covid-19, the State and the Irish Language

Introduction

In this chapter I intend to explain the current relationship of the Irish state to the Irish language, whose constitutional status as 'first official' and 'national' language stands in contrast to its minoritised position in society. I begin by reviewing data about knowledge and use of Irish both in the Gaeltacht and elsewhere before outlining relevant theoretical underpinnings to the concepts of language policy and ideology in sociolinguistics. This conceptual framework guides the analysis which follows the historical trajectory of language policy since 1922. A case-study of the implementation of the Official Languages Act 2003 in the era since Covid-19 is also presented. I conclude with a consideration of the future prospects for Irish in a vastly changed context to that understood by the founders of the state 100 years ago.

This chapter relates to the Irish language as a plank of public policy, a statement that requires some clarification at the outset. The Irish language has become increasingly marginalised as a public policy concern, a reflection of the language's status in Irish society. It has enjoyed not insignificant institutional support since the foundation of the state, for instance in the education system, media, public signage and as a language used sparingly in ceremonial or formal occasions, but a majority of the population claims no knowledge of it and it is used regularly by only a small minority. This social twilight zone is mirrored in the language's status within academia and its capacity to influence fields other than its own. While the discipline of Irish Language Studies (Léann na Gaeilge) is long-established and continues to broaden its focus from literature to include newer sub-fields such as sociolinguistics and media, scholars such as Máirín Nic Eoin have argued that the Irish language and its literature remain marginal within Irish Studies because of that field's Anglophone focus. However, she also contends that the decision of Irish-language critics to write predominantly in Irish – although politically and linguistically defensible – may have reduced their capacity to influence Irish Studies or other related fields.[1] Social science conducted in Irish – for instance, in sociolinguistics and language policy – can suffer the same fate and remain at the margins of sociology or political science.

Sociolinguistic Context

The status of Irish is noteworthy because of the difference between the use of the language by the population and its elevated legal position. Simultaneously the 'national' and 'first official' language according to the Constitution of 1937,[2] it is also minoritised within its own nation-state. It retains a foothold as vernacular language in parts of the Gaeltacht, scattered pockets of territory spread mostly along the western seaboard, although a process of language shift to English has been continuing there for generations.[3] While the Gaeltacht continues to contract, prompting concern about the demise of Irish as a community language,[4] the number

---

[1] Máirín Nic Eoin, 'Margins or Thresholds? Directions in Twentieth-Century Irish-Language Literary Criticism'. Keynote lecture at International Association for the Study of Irish Literatures conference, Trinity College Dublin, 23 July 2019.

[2] 'Constitution of Ireland', *Irish Statute Book*, available online: <http://www.irishstatutebook.ie/eli/cons/en/html> [accessed 25 September 2020].

[3] Tadhg Ó hIfearnáin, 'Family Language Policy, First Language Irish Speaker Attitudes and Community-Based Response to Language Shift', *Journal of Multilingual and Multicultural Development* 34, no. 4 (2013), 348–365.

[4] Conchúr Ó Giollagáin, Seosamh Mac Donnacha, Fiona Ní Chualáin, Aoife Ní Shéaghdha and Mary O'Brien, *Comprehensive Linguistic Study of the Use of Irish in*

and percentage of Irish speakers have increased in almost every census taken since the foundation of the state. This is a direct result of the language-in-education policy pursued since 1922, when Irish became a core subject along with English and Mathematics, a position it maintains to the current day.[5] The status of Irish in the education system is arguably its most important policy plank because without it, the vast majority of people living in Ireland would have little or no exposure to the language. Despite occasional controversies about 'compulsory Irish' in the media, over 80 percent of people in the Republic favour its core status and its place in education has contributed significantly to the headline census figure of knowledge of Irish.[6]

In the Republic of Ireland in 2016 (Census 2020 was postponed due to Covid-19), a significant minority (39.8 percent or 1,761,420) said that they could speak Irish. The Census provides does not enquire about level of competence, however, and instead questions are asked about frequency of use. It is possible to interpret self-reported daily speakers outside the education system as a core Irish-speaking group, even though that assumption is fraught with difficulties. Be that as it may, only 73,803 (1.7 percent) of the population reported using Irish daily outside education, a slight drop on the percentage recorded in 2011. Two-thirds of this group are located in the Gaeltacht, where a majority of the population (63,664 or 66.3 percent) claim competence in Irish. This majority is not overwhelming, however, and has been declining with each census. Only 20,586 (21.4 percent) of the Gaeltacht population report using Irish daily outside education, a decline of 11 percent since 2011. This reflects the fact that although a number of core Gaeltacht areas remain strongly Irish-speaking, the majority of the areas

---

the Gaeltacht: Principal Findings and Recommendations (Dublin: Department of Community, Rural and Gaeltacht Affairs), 2007.

5   Gearóid Ó Tuathaigh, 'The State and the Irish Language', in *A New View of the Irish Language*, edited by Caoilfhionn Nic Pháidín and Seán Ó Cearnaigh (Dublin: Cois Life, 2008), 26–43.

6   Merike Darmody and Tania Daly, *Attitudes towards the Irish Language on the Island of Ireland* (Dublin: Foras na Gaeilge & ESRI, 2015), 81.

officially designated Gaeltacht are not substantially different linguistically to the rest of the country.[7]

While this chapter focuses on the language policy of the Irish state, a contemporary account of Irish would be incomplete without considering its position north of the border. The status of Irish in Northern Ireland was enhanced initially by the 1998 Good Friday Agreement between the Irish and British governments. It got a further boost in 2020 with the publication of *New Decade, New Approach* (NDNA), which ended three years of political stalemate and re-established Stormont. Following years of campaigning for an Irish Language Act by Irish-language activists, NDNA committed to enacting legislation establishing an Irish-Language Commissioner. However, the legislative proposals stopped short of granting official status to Irish or rights to its speakers, as had been demanded by campaigners.[8] In the very different political context of Northern Ireland, knowledge and use of Irish is lower still and largely confined to the nationalist population. The Northern Ireland census enquires about the self-reported language skills of speaking, reading, writing and understanding, rather than frequency of use as in the Republic. It is not certain that even a person possessing all four skills would be a competent, regular speaker as levels of ability are not researched, but it is not unreasonable to assume a higher level of competence. In the 2011 census, 184,898 (10.6 percent) claimed some knowledge of Irish while 64,847 people (3.7 percent) reported possessing the four skills.[9]

---

7   Central Statistics Office, *Census of Population 2016 – Profile 10 – Education, Skills and the Irish Language* (Cork: Central Statistics Office, 2017), available online: <https://www.cso.ie/en/releasesandpublications/ep/p-cp10esil/p10esil/> [accessed 25 September 2020].

8   John Walsh, 'What's the Real Deal with Stormont's Irish Language Proposals?', *RTÉ Brainstorm*, 15 January 2020, available online: <https://www.rte.ie/brainstorm/2020/0115/1107583-whats-the-real-deal-with-stormonts-irish-language-proposals/> [accessed 25 September 2020].

9   Northern Ireland Statistics and Research Agency, *Census 2011: Key Statistics for Northern Ireland* (Belfast: Northern Ireland Statistics and Research Agency), 2012, available online: <https://www.nisra.gov.uk/sites/nisra.gov.uk/files/publications/2011-census-results-key-statistics-northern-ireland-report-11-december-2012.pdf> [accessed 12 August 2020].

Language Policy and Ideology

There is a considerable literature about language policy as a sub-field of sociolinguistics, where it is sometimes used interchangeably with the term 'language planning'. Language planning has been around since time immemorial and was used by kings and empires to suppress languages deemed inconducive to national unity or the public good. Sociolinguistics as a discrete discipline dates only from the 1960s, and the academic study of language planning as a sub-field is more recent again, gaining ground in tandem with the waves of decolonisation in the second half of the twentieth century, newly independent countries grappled with choices over which languages to prioritise in the new order. Seen as top-down and interventionist in approach, language planning has been described as a concept steeped in western ideologies about monolingualism which view language as 'a finite, standardized, rule-governed instrument for communication'.[10] With its apparent emphasis on solutions, language planning was taken up by academic and community proponents of minority languages in places as diverse as Wales, Canada and Finland, where it gained ground as a theoretical and practical approach for dealing with the minoritisation of local languages. The field of study was often engaged with 'a "language revitalization paradigm" which generally accepted the Fishmanian approach to "Reversing Language Shift",[11] a reference to the work of one of the founding fathers of sociolinguistics, Joshua Fishman, who mapped different levels of strategic interventions to strengthen minority languages. 'Language planning' is a common term

---

10   Thomas Ricento, 'Language Policy, Theory and Practice – An Introduction', in *An Introduction to Language Policy: Theory and Method*, edited by Thomas Ricento (Oxford: Blackwell, 2006), 15.
11   Bernadette O'Rourke, Joan Pujolar and Fernando Ramallo, 'New Speakers of Minority Languages: The Challenging Opportunity – Foreword', *International Journal of the Sociology of Language* 231, no. 1–20 (2015). Available online: <https://www.researchgate.net/publication/269699324_New_speakers_of_minority_languages_The_challenging_opportunity-Foreword/link/54930c190cf22d7925d71e5e/download> [accessed 17 October 2020].

in English-speaking countries and the Irish government launched a 'language planning process', aimed mostly at the Gaeltacht, in 2012.[12]

However, scholars influenced by the European school of critical sociolinguistics have argued that language policy has a different meaning to language planning and focuses more on language ideologies both among policymakers and in the community. The Israeli sociolinguist Elana Shohamy is among those who has developed our understanding of this theoretical position:

> [W]hile language planning refers to control, it does not leave anything to the individual to decide, as the governing body decides not just what the person will know but also how he or she will arrive there […] Language policy attempts to be less interventionist and to refer mostly to principles with regard to language use. […] With the increase of less interventionist approaches, the role of planning is subsiding and policy is becoming the bona fide.[13]

A rich contribution to the study of language policy comes from another Israeli, Bernard Spolsky, who has proposed a tripartite understanding of the concept encompassing language practice (the ecosystem or use of the language), language beliefs (the ideology around the use and form of the language) and language management (the agency behind the interventions aimed at modifying use or beliefs, similar to the original planning concept). This allows a far wider conceptualisation of language policy than formal, codified government strategies alone. It also facilitates a broader analysis of the influence of ideology on the speakers of the language, the non-speakers and the policymakers and allows us to study how language policy can be accepted or contested on the ground.[14] One element of the discussion on language policy deals with the distinction between explicit

---

12   John Walsh, 'Sainiú na Gaeltachta: Pobail, ceantair agus líonraí', in *An tSochtheangeolaíocht: Taighde agus Gníomh*, edited by Tadhg Ó hIfearnáin (Baile Átha Cliath: Cois Life, 2019), 185–210.
13   Elana Shohamy, *Language Policy: Hidden Agendas and New Approaches* (London: Routledge, 2006), 49.
14   Bernard Spolsky, *Language Policy* (Cambridge: Cambridge University Press, 2004). See also Bernard Spolsky, *The Cambridge Handbook of Language Policy* (Cambridge: Cambridge University Press, 2012).

and implicit language policy, sometimes referred to as overt/covert or de facto/de jure. Scholars such as Shohamy and Schiffman[15] distinguish between the 'overt' language policy – that which is declared and codified – and the 'covert' language policy – the real story behind the bluster and the rhetoric:

> Overt LPs refer to those language policies that are explicit, formalized, de jure, codified and manifest. Covert LPs, on the other hand, refer to language policies that are implicit, informal, unstated, de facto, grass-roots and latent.[16]

Research on this ideological distinction is ongoing among sociolinguists working on the Irish language.[17] Language policy in any jurisdiction operates at these two levels and in order to understand it fully we need to consider both. We can call the covert policy the 'real policy' because it is the one in which most people believe, even if they don't say so when asked. Ireland is an excellent example of this split: on the one hand we have a first official and national language, with albeit limited protection in terms of state services, but on the other it is difficult for someone to do their business in Irish with the state and Irish is used regularly as an everyday language by only a small minority of the population. Ó hIfearnáin refers to the policy on public signage as 'an aspect of the real language ideology in Ireland' ('Gné d'fhíor-idé-eolaíocht na teanga in Éirinn'). Referring to the rule mandating the placing of Irish in lower case and italics on traffic signs, in contrast to upper case and normal type for English, he writes:

> Nuair a bhíonn an leagan Gaeilge i litreacha beaga iodálacha – agus é go minic loite ag drochghramadach agus mílitriú – tuigtear ionad na teanga. Sa Bhéarla a bhíonn an t-eolas. Maisiúchán a bhíonn sa Ghaeilge.[18]

---

15 Harold Schiffman, 'Language Policy and Linguistic Culture', in *An Introduction to Language Policy: Theory and Method*, edited by Thomas Ricento (Malden: Blackwell, 2006), 111–126.
16 Shohamy, *Language Policy*, 50.
17 For a discussion in Irish, see Tadhg Ó hIfearnáin and John Walsh, *An Meon Folaithe: Idé-Eolaíochtaí agus Iompar Lucht Labhartha na Gaeilge in Éirinn agus in Albain* (Baile Átha Cliath: Cois Life, 2018).
18 Tadhg Ó hIfearnáin, *Beartas Teanga* (Baile Átha Cliath: Coiscéim, 2005), 16.

When the Irish version is in small, italic letters – and often ruined by bad grammar and mis-spelling – the place of the language is understood. Information is in English. Irish is a decoration (my translation).

This stands in stark contrast, of course, to the stated policy towards Irish since the foundation of the state and its constitutional status as first official language. While 'revival' dominated in the rhetoric for the first four decades after independence, Ó Riagáin has argued that the state never envisaged anything other than a bilingual approach.[19] In the 1960s, the formal policy shifted more explicitly to bilingualism while not abandoning the original aims entirely. The shift was described by a former civil servant charged with co-ordinating the change as 'a new realism'.[20] Since the 1980s, a discourse of minoritisation has been gaining ground, where the 'real' language policy sees Irish as a minority question rather than a matter of concern to the general population.[21] The language policy framework has been caught between these two poles since – on the one hand, the remnants of a formal megapolicy of revival/restoration and on the other, a more limited approach to bilingualism as a minority concern. In the background is a powerful ideology of English monolingualism (itself a major constraining factor on language policy in general, not only in relation to Irish) and widespread public support for a symbolic role for Irish and its limited institutional use, encapsulated in the familiar phrase 'the *cúpla focal*' (a few words of Irish).[22]

---

19   Pádraig Ó Riagáin, 'Irish-Language Policy 1922-2007: Balancing Maintenance and Revival', *A New View of the Irish Language*, 55.
20   Séamus Ó Ciosáin, 'Language Planning and Irish', *Language, Culture and Curriculum* 1, no. 3 (1988), 266.
21   Diarmait Mac Giolla Chríost, *The Irish Language in Ireland: From Goídel to Globalisation* (London: Routledge, 2005), 176–177, 190–191.
22   Bernadette O'Rourke and John Walsh, *New Speakers of Irish in the Global Context: New Revival?* (London: Routledge, 2020), 149–168.

Official Languages Act 2003

The government's use of Irish since the eruption of the Covid-19 pandemic in March 2020 provides a revealing case-study of the 'real' language policy in practice and the dominant de facto policy of the state in relation to Irish. The Official Languages Act 2003 was the state's response to decades of campaigning by Irish-language activists for legislation to give meaning to the provisions of Article 8 of the 1937 Constitution which declared Irish the 'national' and 'first official' language. The gap between the desire expressed in Article 8 and the reality for Irish speakers had grown since the ending in 1975 of the requirement for all applicants to general grades in the civil service to pass an examination in Irish. Although there was never a programmatic approach to making Irish the default language of the state apparatus, the requirement – introduced first in 1923 – at least created a cadre of civil servants who had Irish-language skills. Far from bringing about widespread change in the linguistic make-up of the state's public bodies, the Official Languages Act was a mild attempt to redress the imbalance by providing for a limited number of core state services to be available in Irish. These are limited to three categories: (1) direct obligations covering certain core publications by and correspondence with state bodies; (2) obligations based on regulations, mostly in relation to recorded public announcements and signage and (3) obligations based on language schemes, internal language plans agreed between the Department of the Gaeltacht[23] and public bodies and monitored by the Irish-language commissioner, An Coimisinéir Teanga, an independent compliance and monitoring agency.[24] As yet, we have no rules about

---

23 The title of this department has changed many times over the years. At the time of writing it was known as the Department of Media, Tourism, Arts, Culture, Sport and the Gaeltacht. It is significant that 'Gaeltacht' comes at the end of that very long title.
24 Colin H. Williams and John Walsh, 'Minority Language Governance and Regulation', in The Handbook on Minority Languages and Communities, edited by Gabrielle Hogan-Brun and Bernadette O'Rourke (Basingstoke: Palgrave Macmillan, 2019), 115–117.

recruitment of bilinguals to the public service, an essential part of any bilingual public administration as illustrated by the experience of countries such as Wales, the Basque Country and Canada.

Language Legislation and Covid-19

One aspect of the regulations made under the Act, signage, is relevant to this discussion because it is a highly visible manifestation of a language policy that may be invisible to much of the public. The regulations require that all signage erected by public bodies should be bilingual, with equal space given to both languages or, if necessary due to the amount of information, two separate signs should be placed side by side. Because the provisions of the Act are weak by international standards, many of the duties imposed on public bodies are limited to that very visible realm which can be achieved by outsourcing limited text for translation. Therefore, as the most obvious manifestation of the Act, it is no surprise that signage regularly attracts the biggest number of complaints every year to An Coimisinéir Teanga.[25] Since the Covid-19 restrictions came into place, bright yellow signs have been erected by local authorities throughout the country advising the public about the dangers of the virus and advising people to practice social distancing. Restrictions of movement have prevented any widespread survey from taking place, but anecdotal evidence from around the country suggests that the vast majority of such signs are in English only, in breach of the Official Languages Act.

Since the restrictions were announced, Irish has also been marginalised in other areas, for instance online public health information. Websites of government departments or public bodies are not covered by any direct provision of the Act, despite their centrality to communication in the modern age. They fall under the provisions of language schemes which

25 An Coimisinéir Teanga, *Tuarascáil Bhliantúil/Annual Report 2019* (Galway: Oifig an Choimisinéara Teanga, 2020), 37, available online: <https:// coimisineir.ie/ userfiles /files/CT_TuarascailBhliantuil2019.pdf> [accessed 20 September 2020].

vary considerably from one public body to the next, with the result that few people could be expected to anticipate what level of Irish-language service would be available. The central information website <www.gov.ie> falls under the responsibility of the Department of Public Expenditure and Reform and was predominantly in English throughout the early stages of the pandemic in 2020. When the five stages to reopening the country were announced, there was no sign of them in Irish and in July 2020, almost two weeks after the introduction of Phase 3, the Irish version of <www.gov.ie> was still referring to Phase 2. In September 2020, when five new alert levels were introduced as part of the government's Living with Covid-19 plan, the website was still referring to Phase 3 of the reopening. The language scheme of the Department of Public Expenditure and Reform pledges to ensure that 'at least 25% of the static content on all new websites developed by it or on its behalf is made available bilingually',[26] but in the case of <www.gov.ie>, each government department or office is responsible for providing its own content, subject to whatever provision is contained in their language individual language scheme, if any. It is clear that this is not an adequate approach to ensure the ongoing availability of up-to-date information in Irish in a rapidly changing context. Therefore, the Act is not fit for purpose when it comes to providing basic public health information in Irish at the same time as information in English.

The website of the Health Service Executive (HSE; <www.hse.ie>) contains far fewer resources about Covid-19 in Irish, and they are scattered throughout the website rather than centralised. Despite ample options for accessing information in English – guides, videos, audio resources, banners and social media graphics – there is nothing comparable in Irish.[27] The HSE is one of many key public bodies which do not have a statutory language scheme at all, despite being requested to do so in 2007. Therefore, other than publication of core documents such as its annual report in Irish

26 Department of Public Expenditure and Reform, *Language Scheme 2015-2018 under Section 11 of the Official Languages Act 2003* (Dublin: DPER), 2015, 11, available online: <https://coimisineir.ie/userfiles/files/DepartmentofPublicExpenditureandReform2015.pdf> [accessed 25 September 2020].
27 'Coróinvíreas', accessed 20 September 2020, available online: <https://www2.hse.ie/gaeilge/coroinvireas/> [accessed 25 September 2020].

mandated by the direct provisions of the Act, the HSE has no statutory Irish-language obligations whatsoever in relation to its website, despite its central role as the country's public health provider. Incidentally, at the time of writing the information published by the HSE in twenty three immigrant languages ranging from Albanian to Yoruba appeared more organised and accessible than that in Irish.[28] The HSE has no statutory obligation to publish anything in such languages but would appear to have done so in response to the increasingly diversity of Irish society. However, two immigrant rights organisations, Together Ireland and the Migrant and Refugee Rights Centre, complained that the multilingual information was inadequate and published their own series of videos in thirty languages.[29] We can conclude that the HSE language policy appears deficient both in relation to Irish and other languages and that no linguistic minority is being served well by it.

In March 2020 the Irish government issued an information booklet about Covid-19 to every household in English only to every household in the country. A month later, the Irish version arrived, a breach of the Official Languages Act which requires all such mail shots to be bilingual (Section 9 (3)). There was some negative media commentary about the delayed Irish-language version, with one national newspaper, *The Irish Examiner*, opining that the booklet was proof that Ireland needed a dose of 'common sense' instead of 'idealism', an editorial line very much in keeping with the ideology of English monolingualism.[30]

---

28   'Covid-19 Translated Resources', available online: <https://www.hse.ie/eng/services/news/newsfeatures/covid19-updates/partner-resources/covid-19-translated-resources/> [accessed 20 September 2020].

29   Sorcha Pollak, 'Multilingual Videos to Better Inform Ireland's Migrants on Covid-19', *The Irish Times*, 19 May 2020, available online: <https://www.irishtimes.com/news/social-affairs/multilingual-videos-to-better-inform-ireland-s-migrants-on-covid-19-1.4256404> [accessed 20 September 2020].

30   Irish Examiner, 'Irish Examiner View: Do We Need Covid-19 Booklets in Both English and Irish?' *The Irish Examiner*, 1 May 2020, available online: <https://www.irishexaminer.com/breakingnews/views/irish-examiner-view-do-we-need-covid-19-booklets-in-both-english-and-irish-997200.html?> [accessed 15 September 2020].

The same problem applies to advertising, an important aspect of the information campaign about Covid-19. There have been regular full-page adverts in the national press about the latest health advice. All radio stations have broadcast public announcements, with the exception of the Irish-language RTÉ Raidió na Gaeltachta, which had to create its own in-house versions in the absence of any centralised supply. Government Covid-19 advice on the Irish-language television station TG4 has been in English for the most part. There is no statutory requirement for Irish-language versions because, despite its high visibility, advertising is not included in the regulations made under the Official Languages Act.

The daily press briefings by the National Public Health Emergency Team (NPHET) have been held in English only and with the exception of a few stock phrases in Irish in line with the *cúpla focal* ideology, addresses by both Leo Varadkar and Micheál Martin as Taoiseach have also been in English, although Martin in particular is a competent Irish speaker. In an indication of its exceptional nature, the former Minister for Health Simon Harris was praised in some quarters for issuing a rare tweet in Irish but a study found that less than 5 percent of his department's posts on Twitter were in Irish. As there is no mention of social media in the Department of Health's language scheme, it had no obligation to tweet anything at all in Irish.[31] However, the absence of the most powerful platform for political communication from the government's language policy is a serious problem for information flow in Irish. While a bilingual version of the government's Covid-19 contact tracing app was made available, another key interactive service announced during the early phase of the pandemic was firmly monolingual. In May 2020, An Coimisinéir Teanga began an investigation into the failure of the Department of Education to provide an Irish-language version of the Leaving Cert portal to calculate grades.[32]

31 Méabh Ní Thuathaláin, 'Níos lú ná 5% de phostálacha na Roinne Sláinte ar na meáin shóisialta i nGaeilge', *Tuairisc.ie*, 25 Meitheamh 2020, available online: <https://tuairisc.ie/nios-lu-na-5-de-phostalacha-na-roinne-slainte-ar-na-meain-shoisialta-i-ngaeilge/>[accessed 25 September 2020].

32 Tuairisc.ie, 'Teip na Roinne Oideachais maidir le Gaeilge ar shuíomh Ardteiste á scrúdú', *Tuairisc.ie*, 27 Bealtaine 2020, available online: <https://tuairisc.ie/teip-na-roinne-oideachais-maidir-le-gaeilge-ar-shuiomh-ardteiste-a-scrudu/> [accessed 25 August2020].

In an address to the Oireachtas Joint Committee on the Irish Language in autumn 2020, the commissioner highlighted the failings of the state as he saw it to provide an equal service in Irish at a time of crisis and said that the pandemic had been used as an excuse not to provide services.[33]

Monolingual public information in multilingual settings is not limited to Ireland. At the beginning the pandemic, the Council of Europe – responsible for the European Charter for Regional or Minority Languages – warned that public health information about coronavirus was not being disseminated systematically by the authorities in minority languages.[34] Similar trends were visible in relation to French in Canada[35] and Catalan in Spain.[36] In Ireland, the experience since the arrival of Covid-19 leads to the conclusion that there is no room in the de facto state language policy for up-to-date information in Irish during a public health emergency. Instead of planning systematically so that public health information is issued simultaneously in both languages, Irish is left out entirely or belatedly included when the information has moved on. Even at its most basic level – the provision of bilingual signage – the state has failed to deliver and the Act has proven itself unable to influence the rapid, online communication so characteristic of late modernity.

33 Rónán Ó Domhnaill, presentation to Oireachtas Joint Committee on the Irish Language, the Gaeltacht and the Irish-Speaking Community, Leinster House, 21 October 2020.

34 Council of Europe, 'Covid-19 Crisis: Vital that Authorities Also Communicate in Regional and Minority Languages', Council of Europe, 30 March 2020, available online: <https://www.coe.int/en/web/portal/-/covid-19-crisis-vital-that-authorities-also-communicate-in-regional-and-minority-languages> [accessed 25 September 2020].

35 Francois Larocque and Linda Cardinal, 'Coronavirus: Important Products without Bilingual Labels Endangers Francophones', *The Conversation*, 11 May 2020, available online: <https://theconversation.com/amp/coronavirus-importing-products-without-bilingual-labels-endangers-francophones-138198> [accessed 25 September 2020].

36 Bernat Surroca, 'Denuncien que el Consorci Sanitari del Maresme distribueix contingut sobre el coronavirus només en castellà', *Nació Digital*, 26 May 2020, available online: <https://www.naciodigital.cat/noticia/203074/denuncien/consorci/sanitari/maresme/distribueix/contingut/sobre/coronavirus/nomes/castella> [accessed 15 September 2020].

Conclusion

The Programme for Government between Fianna Fáil, Fine Gael and the Green Party agreed in 2020 contained a commitment to enact the revised Official Languages Bill by the end of the year, but the fact that the legislation has been under review for almost a decade did not inspire hope that the provisions could be strengthened meaningfully. With no sign of an end to the pandemic, it is clear that the issue of public health information in Irish needs to be addressed more comprehensively in the new legislation. Interactive online platforms, information in multimedia formats, public service advertisements and constantly changing social media accounts should all be included; arguably these are more important to Irish speakers than translations of annual reports or accounts. The question of public health information in Irish cannot be avoided in whatever legislative arrangement emerges from the NDNA agreement in Northern Ireland. There is also a strong case for enhanced information in immigrant languages, many of whose speakers may have limited English or, as is often the case in marginalised groups, poor literacy skills.

The elephant in the room is the ideology of monolingual public administration on both sides of the border and this entrenched culture poses a challenge to meaningful change without substantial political pressure. Whatever about the specific circumstances of Northern Ireland, the marginalisation of Irish by the state founded at least partly on the aim of restoring its minority language comes into sharp relief as that state approaches its centenary. The political importance of the Irish language has waned, with both Fianna Fáil and Fine Gael relegating it to the corner of an increasingly crowded ministry and appointing Ministers of State for the Gaeltacht without proficiency in Irish.[37] It is a far cry from the founding aims of

---

37 Christina Finn, '"Whatever You're Having Yourself": TD Questions New "Jumble Drawer" Ministry', *The Journal.ie*, 27 June 2020, available online: <https://www.thejournal.ie/catherine-martin-ministry-5135244-Jun2020/> [accessed 25 September 2020].

Fianna Fáil in 1926 where, second only to the reunification of Ireland was the restoration of the Irish language.[38]

Although Irish speakers continue to diminish as a percentage of the population of the Gaeltacht, the language persists in some communities in every one of the seven Gaeltacht counties. Despite an ongoing process of language shift, there are competent Irish speakers in all generations from throughout the Gaeltacht and some families retain Irish as their primary language.[39] Although severely under-funded, the Gaeltacht 'language planning process' has the potential to raise language awareness and support those who wish to learn Irish. Many 'new speakers' of Irish – people who speak the language fluently and regularly although they were not socialised in it in early childhood – are involved in language revitalisation initiatives throughout the country.[40] Recalling Spolsky's sophisticated language policy model, it is worth emphasising that despite the timid approach of government, imaginative and energetic Irish-language activism continues in the spaces not captured by a monolithic state-centred conceptualisation of 'language policy'. There are important creative initiatives in fields such as Irish-language literature, media and the arts, supported to a limited degree by the state and with the potential for much more growth. Rather than considering it a forgotten corner of Anglophone Irish literary studies, the international, multilingual context of Irish-language writing has been emphasised,[41] and there have been calls for the public to be made more aware of the cultural perspectives and creative potential offered by Irish language and culture.[42] Despite the challenges of the fragmentation of the media landscape and a lack of resources, TG4 manages to commission highly

---

38 Noel Whelan, *Fianna Fáil: A Biography of the Party* (Dublin: Gill & Macmillan, 2009), 19.
39 Ó hIfearnáin, 'Family Language Policy'.
40 O'Rourke and Walsh, *New Speakers of Irish in the Global Context*.
41 Nic Eoin, 'Margins or Thresholds?'
42 Angela Bourke with Diane Negra, Discussion Paper 3: *The Gaeltacht, the Irish Language, Folklore and Vernacular Creativity / An Ghaeltacht, an Ghaeilge, an Béaloideas agus Cruthaitheacht na nDaoine* (Dublin: Royal Irish Academy, 2018) , available online: <https://www.ria.ie/sites/default/files/creative-ireland-gaeilge-english-version.pdf> [accessed 25 September 2020].

original visual media content and the mostly voluntary community radio station Raidió na Life in Dublin broadcast some of its most innovative programming yet during the national lockdown in spring 2020.[43] Voluntary cultural, political or sporting projects – sometimes emerging from sites of resistance in urban centres – add to the mix of Irish-language activism, sometimes eschewing state funding in order to maintain their edge. These include the Gaelic football and hurling teams in Dublin and Galway, informal Irish-language conversation circles throughout the country, the Liú Lúnasa festival in Belfast and online bloggers, multimedia content creators and activists, some from outside Ireland.[44] Not all of these groups share the same ideology but they are working generally towards the same goal: the realisation of a life lived through Irish, at least to some extent, and the consolidation of attractive social spaces towards which future speakers of the language can orient themselves.

The fortunes of the Irish language have been transformed in the past century and despite its fragile demographic base, the language has cast off the undeserved association that grew between it and rigid social conservatism in the early decades of the state. Irish is now at the centre of creative endeavour and its activists generally promote discourses of inclusivity and openness in an increasingly diverse Ireland. Although still associated with nationalism in the North, its ideological base is more civic in the Republic. Those committed to it need not to lose sight of the pitfalls of becoming too reliant on public funding and there remains a need for a more radical ideological strand to remind the state of its failings, as outlined in this chapter. The key challenge facing the core activist group is to be sophisticated enough to convince enough people, in ways that are appropriate for the noisy and crowded cultural stage of late modernity, of the need for a

---

43 European Centre for Minority Issues, 'Minority Language Media and the Covid-19 Pandemic – The Case of Irish. An Interview with Dr John Walsh', 30 July 2020, available online: <https://www.ecmi.de/infochannel/detail/minority-language-media-and-the-covid-19-pandemic-the-case-of-irish-an-interview-with-dr-john-walsh> [accessed 25 September 2020].

44 Stiofán Seoighe, '"Is libhse an chathair" – Pop Up Gaeltacht agus nuachainteoirí na Gaeilge', COMHAR*Taighde* 4 (2018), available online: <https://comhartaighde.ie/eagrain/4/seoighe/> [accessed 25 September 2020].

more robust policy framework. There were some hopeful signs at the end of 2020 when the most expansionary budget in the history of the state increased Irish-language expenditure by 23 percent, although by comparison the Arts Council budget grew by 62.5 percent.[45] Despite overseeing a crowded department, the new Green Minister Catherine Martin appeared more engaged with Irish than her predecessors and showed signs of pursuing a more thoughtful approach to language policy, linking it specifically to a sustainability discourse.[46] Modulating the 'real' language policy of neglect and apathy will not be easy but as the state approaches its centenary, it owes the Irish language far more meaningful and co-ordinated support than has been offered in previous decades.

45 Tuairisc.ie, 'Céim mhór chun cinn do phobal na Gaeilge – fáilte curtha roimh ardú ar bhuiséad na teanga agus na Gaeltachta', 13 October 2020, available online: https://tuairisc.ie/ceim-mhor-chun-cinn-do-phobal-na-gaeilge-failte-curtha-roimh-ardu-ar-bhuisead-na-teanga-agus-na-gaeltachta/> [accessed 25 September 2020].

46 Catherine Martin, 'Tá an Ghaeilge i measc na n-acmhainní is tábhachtaí againn', 5 October 2020, available online: <https://tuairisc.ie/ta-an-ghaeilge-i-measc-na-n-acmhainni-is-tabhachtai-againn-catherine-martin/> [accessed 25 September 2020].

RUTH BARTON

15   Reimagining Irish Film Studies for the Twenty-First Century

Irish film studies stands at an interesting moment in its history. What was not so very long ago a brash new discipline that gate-crashed the more established subjects in Arts-Humanities, is now undergoing its own challenges and identity concerns. In this country, as in others, questions are being raised as to its validity in the digital era, particularly now with the rising popularity of viewing platforms (Netflix, Amazon, Hulu and many more), and the turn towards long-form television. This was nowhere more evident than in the lockdown phenomenon that was *Normal People*.[1] Of the twelve episodes of the series, the first six were directed by Lenny Abrahamson, previously better known for his work in cinema (*Adam and Paul*; *Garage*; *What Richard Did*; *Frank*; *Room*; *The Little Stranger*).[2] Although Abrahamson, in collaboration with Mark O'Halloran, writer on *Adam and Paul* and *Garage*, had made a three-part television series, *Prosperity*, for RTÉ in the past, his reputation was founded on his minutely observed arthouse feature films.[3] From *Garage* onwards, these were produced by Ed Guiney and Andrew Lowe's Element Pictures. By the time of the release of *Normal People*, Element had become established as a leading European production company,

---

1   *Normal People*. 2020. BBC/ RTÉ. Produced by Element Pictures. Ireland.
2   *Adam & Paul*. 2004. Directed by Lenny Abrahamson. Produced by Johnny Speers. Ireland; *Frank*. 2014. Directed by Lenny Abrahamson. Element Pictures. Ireland; *Garage*. 2007. Directed by Lenny Abrahamson. Element Pictures. Ireland; *Room*. 2015. Directed by Lenny Abrahamson. Element Pictures. Ireland; *The Little Stranger*. 2018. Directed by Lenny Abrahamson. Element Pictures. Ireland; *What Richard Did*. 2012. Directed by Lenny Abrahamson. Element Pictures. Ireland.
3   *Prosperity*. 2007. RTÉ. Produced by Element Pictures. Ireland.

and home not just to Abrahamson, but also Yorgos Lanthimos, whose most recent films – *The Lobster* and *The Favourite* – they have also produced.[4] Although Element had been involved in some television work, with the acquisition of Sally Rooney's *Zeitgeist* novel, and Abrahamson's interest in directing it for television, suddenly the company had the opportunity to make an arthouse production that ran for approximately five and a half hours (running times of episodes varied) and allowed its story to unfold gradually, rather than in the compressed timeframe of a feature film. More than that, it attracted audiences in multiples of the normal Irish cinema release – in the first week of its release on BBC Three alone, it received, in a record for the platform, over 16.2 million viewing requests.[5] Just two years before the release of *Normal People*, in recognition of the variety of screen content emerging from Ireland, the Irish Film Board changed its name to Screen Ireland.

For the purposes of this chapter, I will trace the evolution of the discipline from its founding fathers (gender designation intended), to the plurality of writers on film today. The question of whether there is a place for Film Studies in contemporary screen culture is not unique to the Irish situation, but is interesting to consider in the local context. The particular geo-political history to the discipline, which I discuss below, gave rise to an often-polemical set of interventions that were in turn related to the evolution of Irish cinema as a set of production practices. In the career of Liam O'Leary (1910–1992), we can see how this tradition started. O'Leary was a filmmaker, archivist and author: his working life included jobs with the civil service, the Abbey Theatre, the British Film Institute and RTÉ. Although not an academic, he wrote frequently on film, advocating for state-funded local production and the development of film education for children. His major publications were his biography, *Rex Ingram: Master of the Silent Cinema* (1980) and the pamphlet, *Cinema Ireland 1896-1950*

---

4   *The Lobster*. 2015. Directed by Yorgos Lanthimos. Element Pictures et al. Ireland; *The Favourite*. 2018. Directed by Yorgos Lanthimos. Element Pictures et al. Ireland.
5   BBC. 'Normal People Drives BBC Three to Its Best Week Ever', news release, 5 May 2020, available online: <https://www.bbc.co.uk/mediacentre/latestnews /2020/ normal-people-viewing-figures> [accessed 25 September 2020].

(1990), written to accompany his exhibition of the same title.⁶ O'Leary is significant not only for his creation of a personal archive of Irish cinema, and his campaigning work in support of the establishment of a local industry, but also for insisting on the importance of the Irish diaspora to the evolution of Irish cinema.

This same impetus informs the canonical early textbook on Irish cinema, *Cinema and Ireland*, co-authored by Kevin Rockett, Luke Gibbons and John Hill.⁷ By now, a small-scale, largely avant-garde filmmaking culture (though hardly what could be understood as an industry), had come into being and all shared a sense that because indigenous Irish cinema was in its infancy, it was open to being shaped by intellectual discourse. Rockett, who subsequently compiled the then comprehensive *The Irish Filmography: Fiction Films, 1896-1996* covered the history of Irish film production, while championing the work of the first wave of Irish filmmakers, since that time often considered the golden era of Irish filmmaking.⁸ Gibbons placed *The Quiet Man* at the centre of his analysis of how Ireland had been shaped on film by a tradition of romanticism that lingered on the country's visual beauty, and was invested in an image of the Irish as pre-modern, charming rogues.⁹ Yet Gibbons, in an argument subsequently developed by Martin McLoone in his *Irish Film: The Emergence of a Contemporary Cinema*, also questioned to what extent the viewer was meant to take Ford's film at face value, or whether it intentionally subverted

---

6   Liam O'Leary, *Rex Ingram: Master of the Silent Cinema* (Dublin: Academy Press, 1980); Liam O'Leary, *Cinema Ireland 1896-1950* (Dublin: National Library of Ireland, 1990).

7   Kevin Rockett, Luke Gibbons, and John Hill, *Cinema and Ireland* (London: Croom Helm, 1987).

8   Kevin Rockett, *The Irish Filmography: Fiction Films, 1896-1996* (Dublin: Red Mountain Press, 1996). This database is now available online on the TCD library website: <https://www.tcd.ie/irishfilm/index.php> [accessed 28 August 2020]. See also: Maeve Connolly, 'Irish Cinema's First Wave: Histories and Legacies', in *A Companion to British and Irish Cinema*, edited by John Hill (Hoboken: John Wiley & Sons, 2019).

9   *The Quiet Man*. Directed by John Ford. Republic Pictures. Los Angeles.

its own aesthetic by drawing attention to its fictional devices.[10] Hill too was to develop his writings on Northern Ireland on film, first published in *Cinema and Ireland*, in his later *Cinema and Northern Ireland: Film, Culture and Politics*.[11] In both publications, Hill drew attention to the construction of Ireland by British filmmakers as a country defined by irrational and atavistic forces that were inevitably drawn to violence, thus obscuring the socio-political reasons for the Troubles.

As well as looking back to the colonised history of Irish filmmaking, so too the favouring of non-mainstream modes of production reflected a position common amongst the generation of academics writing in the 1980s and 1990s. To simplify a complex network of arguments, a national film industry could only critically address the national culture if it were to free itself from the escapist model of Hollywood filmmaking and adopt alternatives such as the Third Cinema movement that had emerged out of Latin America in the late 1960s.[12]

The debates around how a national cinema should look, and about its mode of address, spoke to the central societal concern of the day – the national question. With the Troubles dominating news headlines, so the part cultural production should play in the politics of the conflict weighed heavily on film academics as much as on other critics in Irish Studies. Written from the perspective of a Northern Irish Protestant, Brian McIlroy's analysis of how the North was represented on film, notably in his first edition of *Shooting to Kill: Filmmaking and the "Troubles" in Northern Ireland*, was received with some controversy.[13] McIlroy's attempt to recover a Protestant voice, and a Protestant spectator, in what he perceived as a monolithic pro-Nationalist cinematic canon, was received with little sympathy from the existing body of Irish film scholars. McIlroy proceeded to

10   Martin McLoone, *Irish Film: The Emergence of a Contemporary Cinema* (London: British Film Institute, 2000).
11   John Hill, *Cinema and Northern Ireland: Film, Culture and Politics* (London: British Film Institute, 2006).
12   McLoone, *Irish Film*; Jim Pines and Paul Willemen (eds), *Questions of Third Cinema* (London: British Film Institute, 1989).
13   Brian McIlroy, *Shooting to Kill: Filmmaking and the 'Troubles' in Northern Ireland* (Trowbridge: Flicks Books, 1998).

respond to these critics and defend his position in an updated and revised edition of his monograph.[14] Alongside that of the national question, the other issue which weighed on the minds of the first generation of academic writers on Irish cinema was that of societal inequality, exacerbated by the recession of the 1980s, and this is a concern that still echoes through critical analyses of Irish cinema.

By the turn of the century, Irish film studies had established itself as a distinct category of Irish Studies, with a particular emphasis on how film reflected (on) the national culture. By this stage too, its object of study, Irish cinema, had moved on from its roots in avant-garde/Third Cinema to embrace a more mainstream production model. Neil Jordan and Jim Sheridan had established themselves as the two leading auteurs of their generation, both winning Academy awards, international recognition and global audiences for their works. While many of the older trends noted by those writing on film in the twentieth century remained in place, the new century brought with it a distinctive new Irish cinema, one that now included at its centre, for instance, animation and documentary. It was also identifiably transnational, insofar as most of its productions, beyond the very low-budget, were co-financed with other territories. Where previously such a strategy had been viewed as a debasement of the national project, now critics both within Irish film studies and in the wider international academic circuit began to reappraise what transnationalism really meant for local industries. Many of the contributors to Brian McIlroy's edited collection, *Genre and Cinema: Ireland and Transnationalism*, saw the widening out of the production base of Irish cinema as an opportunity not just to break down the limits of the national but to inflect global filmmaking with Irish narratives; in other words, transnationalism was not just a two-way street, but a network of practices in which Irish cinema was able to occupy an influential place.[15]

14   Brian McIlroy, *Shooting to Kill: Filmmaking and the 'Troubles' in Northern Ireland* revised and updated edition (Richmond: Steveston Press, 2001).
15   Brian McIlroy (ed.), *Genre and Cinema: Ireland and Transnationalism* (London: Routledge, 2007). See also: Ruth Barton, *Irish Cinema in the Twenty-First Century* (New York and Manchester: Manchester University Press, 2019); Roddy Flynn and Tony Tracy, 'Contemporary Irish Film: From the National to the

In my own contributions to Irish Film Studies, I have always been interested in the intersection between popular culture and Irish identity construction. As the twenty-first century came more into focus, I revisited my earlier monograph, *Irish National Cinema*, and concluded that so much had changed since I had written it that a second edition would not do justice to the new landscape of Irish film production.[16] Instead, then, I published *Irish Cinema in the Twenty-First Century*.[17] I had never been alone in my interest in questions of gender representation, particularly the representation of women, but now I was able to consult a stimulating range of writings, notably Debbie Ging's *Men and Masculinities in Irish Cinema* and, more recently, Susan Liddy's *Women in the Irish Film Industry*.[18] Echoing the campaigning voices of the earlier writers on Irish film, Liddy in particular has used her platform as an academic to advocate for industry change around gendered hiring practices.

Where Irish film studies was somewhat out of step with the wider (largely Anglophone) world of film, film studies generally was actively engaged in the application of current trends in critical theory to the body of work. Film Studies has traditionally been a highly theorised subject, with journals such as *Screen* and *The Journal of Cinema and Media Studies* (previously *Cinema Journal*) embracing emerging and established critical discourses, often adapted from other disciplines, as vital methodological approaches to film analysis. Increasingly in the 2000s, new scholars have emerged to take on contemporary Irish cinema representations via the kind of methodologies that, say, Irish literary theorists have applied to the written canon. In gender studies, in particular, writers such as Anne Mulhall, Emma Radley, Jessica Scarlata, and Fintan Walsh have revisited older and contemporary works to offer new readings of the films in question

---

Transnational', *Éire-Ireland* 52, no. 1 (2017), available online: <https://doi.org/> [accessed 25 September 2020].

16   Ruth Barton, *Irish National Cinema* (London and New York: Routledge, 2004).
17   Ruth Barton, *Irish Cinema in the Twenty-First Century* (New York and Manchester: Manchester University Press, 2019).
18   Debbie Ging, *Men and Masculinities in Irish Cinema* (Basingstoke: Palgrave Macmillan, 2013). Susan Liddy (ed.), *Women in the Irish Film Industry* (Cork: Cork University Press, 2020).

informed by feminist theories, queer theories and theories of corporeality.[19] Another productive approach to film analysis has been the adaptation of theories of spatiality (borrowed from the discipline of geography) to the wider corpus of global cinema. Conn Holohan in particular has deployed the theories of de Certeau, Tuan and others to analyse issues of belonging (to the city space, to the home) and exclusion as reflected in contemporary Irish filmmaking.[20]

If these critical approaches link Irish film studies in to the flow of academic writing globally on film, another strand within the discipline has taken the foundational contributions of McLoone, O'Leary and Rockett et al. to develop the idea of Irish cinema as a diasporic cinema.[21] My own research has covered the careers of Irish actors in Hollywood, *Acting Irish in Hollywood* and a new biography of Rex Ingram.[22] My edited collection,

19 Anne Mulhall, 'A Cure for Melancholia? Queer Sons, Dead Mothers, and the Fantasy of Multiculturalism in McCabe's and Jordan's *Breakfast on Pluto*(s)', in *Theory on the Edge: Irish Studies and the Politics of Sexual Difference*, edited by Noreen Giffney and Margrit Shildrick (New York: Palgrave Macmillan, 2013); Emma Radley, 'Violent Transpositions: The Disturbing "Appearance" of the Irish Horror Film', in *Viewpoints, Theoretical Perspectives on Irish Visual Texts*, edited by Claire Bracken and Emma Radley (Cork: Cork University Press, 2013); Jessica Scarlata, *Rethinking Occupied Ireland: Gender and Incarceration in Contemporary Irish Film* (Syracuse: Syracuse University Press, 2014); Fintan Walsh, 'Mourning Sex: The Aesthetics of Queer Relationality in Contemporary Film', in *Viewpoints: Theoretical Perspectives on Irish Visual Texts*, edited by Claire Bracken and Emma Radley (Cork: Cork University Press, 2013).

20 Conn Holohan, *Cinema on the Periphery: Contemporary Irish and Spanish Film* (Dublin: Irish Academic Press, 2010); Conn Holohan, ' "Nothin But a Wee Humble Cottage": At home in Irish Cinema', in *Ireland and Cinema, Culture and Contexts*, edited by Barry Monahan (New York and Basingstoke: Palgrave Macmillan, 2015); Conn Holohan, 'Space and Place in Irish Cinema', in *A Companion to British and Irish Cinema*, edited by John Hill (Hoboken: John Wiley & Sons, Inc., 2019); Michel de Certeau, *The Practice of Everyday Life* (Berkeley: University of California Press, 1984); Yi-Fu Tuan, *Space and Place: The Perspective of Experience* (London, Minneapolis: University of Minnesota Press, 1977).

21 McLoone, *Irish Film*; O'Leary, *Rex Ingram*; Rockett et al., *Cinema and Ireland*.

22 Ruth Barton, *Rex Ingram: Visionary Director of the Silent Screen* (Lexington: University of Kentucky Press, 2014); Ruth Barton, *Acting Irish in Hollywood: from Fitzgerald to Farrell* (Dublin and Portland: Irish Academic Press, 2006).

Screening Irish-America, included scholars from both sides of the Atlantic, and from a number of different disciplines, in what was the first dedicated compilation of essays on representations of Irish America on film.[23] A contributor to that book, Diane Negra has been responsible, along with others such as Stephanie Rains, for bringing together cultural studies and film studies to understand how the evolving figure of the stereotype and discourses on gender, culture, and popular entertainment have produced a range of character types and narratives that have criss-crossed between Ireland and the United States in a dynamic set of fictional constructions.[24]

If the above conveys some idea of the rich panoply of work that continues to emerge in Irish film studies, then it might seem that the opening question as to the discipline's future has to be redundant. As I hope to have demonstrated, film studies thrives on its encounters with other disciplines, rummaging amongst them and ransacking them for new ideas and critical approaches. As far back as 2000, Lance Pettitt combined film and television studies in his *Screening Ireland: Film and Television Representation*.[25] Irish television production has not to date matched cinema in its imaginative approach to creating work in a small, relatively under-funded media environment. Once it does, and one hopes that the success of *Normal People* will tempt more Irish talent to engage with the medium, then inevitably the critical writing will follow. The big and small screens may indeed continue to merge in the areas of TV drama and streaming content, but it would be a mistake to lose in that process that argumentative, politically engaged tradition of Irish Film Studies.

---

23 Ruth Barton (ed.), *Screening Irish-America* (Dublin and Portland: Irish Academic Press, 2009).

24 Diane Negra, *Off-white Hollywood: American Culture and Ethnic Female Stardom* (London and New York: Routledge, 2001); Diane Negra (ed.), *The Irish in Us: Irishness, Performativity, and Popular Culture* (Durham and London: Duke University Press, 2006); Stephanie Rains, *The Irish-American in Popular Culture, 1945-2000* (Dublin and Portland: Irish Academic Press, 2007).

25 Lance Pettitt, *Screening Ireland: Film and Television Representation* (Manchester: Manchester University Press, 2000).

CATHERINE MAIGNANT

16 Religion in Irish Studies

Studying religion as a specialist of Irish Studies is a methodological challenge, or even, in the eyes of some, a total epistemological aberration. In an article entitled 'Death by Area Studies',[1] Aaron Hughes and Randi Warne warn that no serious academic work in the field of religious studies can be done by 'a generalist' who has had 'very little if no [sic] exposure to the critical theories and methods associated with the academic study of religion'. Clearly, the very notion of area studies and its legitimacy as an academic research area are problematic, on account of their necessary interdisciplinarity and their assumption that local and contextual knowledge is key to analysing an area's culture and history.

Yet if, as noted above, accusations by single disciplinary-oriented scholars that area experts – often based in modern languages departments – lack methodological and theoretical skills, still occasionally surface, hostilities between disciplines and area studies have eased. This is not to say that all difficulties have been resolved. Area studies were historically based in Europe, but concerned regions outside Western Europe. Initially, 'results arrived at during fieldwork *outside* Europe were recognised if they matched the theoretical assumptions developed *in* Europe'.[2] The basic postulate of researchers was often also that they (and their country of origin), were intellectually or societally superior to the society under examination, which limited the reliability of their findings. In any case, they had an agenda of

---

[1] Aaron W. Hughes and Randi R. Warne, 'Death by Area Studies', *Bulletin for the Study of Religion*, 26 November 2014, available online: <https://bulletin.equinoxpub.com/2014/11/death-by-area-studies/> [accessed 14 April 2020].

[2] Claudia Derichs, 'Shifting Epistemologies in Area Studies: From Space to Scale', *Area Studies* 4 (2015), 31, available online: <https://meta-journal.net/articleview/2981> [accessed 14 April 2020].

their own and were consequently viewed as being somehow biased. Area studies have now been extended to Europe but are still to a large extent conducted by foreign-based practitioners and the risk of biased perspective is still there. Awareness of the problem has led to new approaches but in addition they necessitate a delicate decentring of perspective and much humility on the part of the researcher.[3]

Irish Studies were born outside Ireland and developed in the main by members of the diaspora. They may therefore have originally been undermined by the above-mentioned attitudes, summarised by Linda Connolly as paternalism, culturalism and postcolonialism, sometimes leading to dissent with Irish experts' views.[4] Yet Irish Studies has more recently become established in Ireland itself and all Irish universities now offer interdisciplinary programmes in what is presented as a new discipline in its own right. Nowadays foreign experts have the privilege to test their views against those of Irish scholars, generally specialists in traditional disciplines. This no doubt contributes to an extraordinary diversification of approaches and to a redefinition of Irish Studies in keeping with current developments in area studies, whose strength today is held to rest on its 'capacity to enable dialogue between widely diverging views – if only between natives and outsiders – which gives it great originality, but also an acute sense of variation, tensions and interactions of all kinds'.[5] Area studies can now be combined with disciplinary approaches for the mutual benefit of all.[6]

---

3 Mickael Lucken and Karoline Postel Vinay, 'Déplacer les disciplines: le nouveau rôle des aires', *Espaces Temps.net* [online], Laboratoire (2020), available online: <https://www.espacestemps.net/articles/deplacer-les-disciplines-le-nouveau-role-des-aires/> [accessed 13 April 2020].

4 Linda Connolly, 'The Limits of "Irish Studies": Historicism, Culturalism, Paternalism', *Irish Studies Review* 12, no. 2 (2004), 139–162.

5 « La force des études aréales tient à sa capacité de faire dialoguer des points de vue extrêmement éloignés – ne serait-ce que ceux d'ici et de là-bas –, ce qui lui confère une grande originalité, mais aussi un sens aigu de la variation, des tensions et des interactions de tout ordre ». Translation from Lucken and Vinay, 'Déplacer les disciplines' is mine.

6 *Ibid.*

This is particularly true in the religious field. Yet as early as 1967, Lyman Legters commented that the place of religion in foreign area studies was a delicate one:

> It does seem clear that religion as an academic subject is caught between a prevailing secularism in most phases of university life and a powerful strain of sentimentality in the religious life of our society. Scholarship in religion that seeks to maintain thoroughgoing intellectual standards is in danger of isolation from its social constituency. Sentimentalized religious education or writing, on the other hand, risks losing whatever place it may still have in the university. To compound the difficulty, teachers and scholars in the field are presumably torn between the demands of the professional training of some of their students and the commitment to the place of religion in general education.[7]

Talking about the American context, he further suggested that this might partly account for the fact that 'scholarship in religion has played almost no part in the burgeoning of foreign area studies programs'.[8] In secularised France, the study of religious subjects was historically (and often still is) held in great suspicion and most certainly not encouraged in universities. Whether or not the same is true of other countries where Irish Studies have developed since the late 1960s, it is a fact that very few research students or academic researchers have dared move into that area, least of all those who were religious in their personal lives.

In Catholic Ireland, the problem was different but produced the same effects. Little critical academic discourse on religion was possible before the Church lost its moral authority and its vice-grip control over the general population and the elites. Outsiders' comments also tended to be dismissed on the grounds that only insiders could perceive and understand Irish realities.[9] As a result, the first notable academic works on religious issues,

---

7   Lyman H. Legters, 'The Place of Religion in Foreign Area Studies', *Journal of the American Academy of Religion* 35, no. 2 (June 1967), 163.
8   Ibid.
9   As late as 2007, a book about Irish Studies entitled *Ireland beyond Boundaries – Mapping Irish Studies in the Twenty-First Century*, edited by Liam Harte and Yvonne Whelan (London and Dublin: Pluto Press), was conceived, in the words of Danish Irish Studies scholar Michael Böss, as 'obviously written by and for insiders' (Book Review, *Nordic Irish Studies*, Vol. 8, 2008, 148). It would be tempting to say that the reverse is true of the chapter on religion authored by Tom Inglis

published in the 1970s and 1980s, were all works by notable Irish historians, political scientists or sociologists anchored in their disciplines. Let us mention among others John Whyte's *Church and State in Ireland, 1923–1970* (1971), Emmet Larkin's *The Roman Catholic Church in Ireland and the Fall of Parnell 1888-1891* (1979), Desmond M. Clarke, *Church and State* (1985), John Cooney's *The Crozier and the Dáil* (1986), Dermot Keogh's *The Vatican, the Bishops and Irish Politics* (1986) and *Jews in Twentieth Century Ireland* (1988).

Throughout that period, outside Ireland, most Irish Studies experts concentrated their research on the much less controversial study of Irish literature. Thus, the *Canadian Journal of Irish Studies*, launched in 1975, exclusively published literary articles until 1980 and it released its first interdisciplinary special issue in 1987. In France, the large majority of Irish Studies researchers were specialists in literature, at least until the 1990s, and the first major publications in the field were literary, for instance, Patrick Rafroidi's *L'Irlande et le romantisme – La littérature irlandaise-anglaise de 1789 à 1850 et sa place dans le mouvement occidental* in 1972[10] and Jacqueline Genet's *William Butler Yeats: les fondements et l'évolution de la création poétique, essai de psychologie littéraire* in 1976.[11]

The authority crisis to which the Irish Catholic Church was confronted in the 1990s and the controversies linked to the first abuse scandals that were disclosed at the time led to the multiplication of publications. Some were issued by prominent academics: Tom Inglis's now classic *Moral Monopoly: The Rise and Fall of the Catholic Church in Modern Ireland*

---

in which, far from defining the place of religion in Irish Studies, he explains what religious identity means to Irish people. Cf. Inglis, 'The Religious Field in Contemporary Ireland: Identity, Being Religious and Symbolic Domination', *Journal of Contemporary Religion* 22 (2007), 111–134. The difficulty to come to terms with the insiders/outsiders' connection in Irish Studies is therefore perfectly illustrated in this book.

10   Patrick Rafroidi, *L'Irlande et le romantisme – La littérature irlandaise-anglaise de 1789 à 1850 et sa place dans le mouvement occidental* (Villeneuve d'Ascq: Presses universitaires du Septentrion, 1972).

11   Jacqueline Genet, *William Butler Yeats: les fondements et l'évolution de la création poétique, essai de psychologie littéraire* (Villeneuve d'Ascq: Presses universitaires du Septentrion, 1976).

(1998) was published in that context. Others were published by theologians or religious actors to feed the debates that were tearing the Catholic Church apart. Monographs include Terence McCaughey's *Memory and Redemption – Church Politics and Prophetic Theology in Ireland* (1992) and P. J. McGrath's *Believing in God* (1995), but also the first of a series of books by Mark Patrick Hederman, *Kissing the Dark* (1999), and Tony Flannery, *From the Inside* (1999). Several collections of articles, often based on conference proceedings, were also published to the same effect, for instance Eamonn Conway and Colm Kilcoyne's *Twin Pulpits – Church and Media in Modern Ireland* (1997) and *The Splintered Heart – Conversations with a Church in Crisis* (1998). Others sought to defend the under siege Church. A good example is Eamonn Conway, Eugene Duffy and Attracta Shields's *The Church and Child Sexual Abuse – Towards a Pastoral Response* (1999). It is also worth noting the publication of the first of John O'Donohue's works, *Anam Cara* (1998) that was to become an unexpected international bestseller and to give visibility to the emergent late modern Celtic Christianity in Ireland. This list is far from comprehensive but gives an idea of the surge of interest in religious questions that was prompted by the context.

This intense publishing activity was carried into the next two decades. Among the monographs, important publications of the period include Marianne Elliott's *The Catholics of Ulster: A History* (2000) and *When God Took Sides – Religion and Identity in Ireland: Unfinished History* (2009); Mary Kenny's *Goodbye to Catholic Ireland* (2000); Louise Fuller's *Irish Catholicism since 1950 – The Undoing of a Culture* (2002); Eamon Duffy's *Faith of Our Fathers* (2004); Malachi O'Doherty's *Empty Pulpits – Ireland's Retreat from Religion* (2008); Diarmaid Ferriter's *Occasions of Sin: Sex and Society in Modern Ireland* (2009) or Gladys Ganiel's *Transforming Post-Catholic Ireland: Religious Practice in Late Modernity* (2016). In the meantime, religious actors went on actively contributing to the debate. Apart from the previously mentioned Mark Patrick Hederman and Tony Flannery, a special mention must be made of Vincent Twomey SVD (*The End of Irish Catholicism?*) (2003), Donal Dorr (*Time for a Change – A Fresh Look at Spirituality, Sexuality, Globalisation and the Church*) (2004), Gerry O'Hanlon S. J. (*A New Vision for the Catholic Church: A View from Ireland*) (2011) and Oliver Rafferty S. J. (*Violence, Politics and Catholicism in Ireland*) (2016), but there were many others.

To these must be added works about religions other than Catholicism, such as Laurence Cox's *Buddhism and Ireland: From the Celts to the Counter-Culture and Beyond* (2013) or *Ireland's New Religious Movements*, edited by Olivia Cosgrove, Laurence Cox and Carmen Kuhling (2011). This list would not be complete without a brief reference to the dozens of controversial books by authors who left Catholicism behind, like Dara Molloy, a former Catholic priest, now 'Celtic monk and druid',[12] who published *The Globalisation of God: Celtic Christianity's Nemesis* in 2009.

From our perspective in this article, however, what is particularly interesting is that a few of the previously mentioned academics were at that time involved with Irish Studies. Dermot Keogh, Tom Inglis, John Cooney, Oliver Rafferty and Laurence Cox, among others, occasionally contributed articles to various Irish Studies journals. Marianne Elliott, a historian of the highest calibre, even became the director of the Institute of Irish Studies, University of Liverpool. Historian Louise Fuller, for her part, regularly contributed to the works of the emerging research cluster in Irish religion and Franco-Irish Studies led by Eamon Maher, who edited and co-authored an impressive number of collections over the period: these chronologically comprise *Irish and Catholic? – Towards an Understanding of Identity* (2006), edited by Louise Fuller, John Littleton and Eamon Maher; *Contemporary Catholicism in Ireland – A Critical Appraisal* (2008); *What Being Catholic Means to Me* (2009); *The Dublin/Murphy Report: A Watershed for Irish Catholicism?* (2010), *Catholicism and Me* (2012), all of which were edited by John Littleton and Eamon Maher, and finally *Tracing the Cultural Legacy of Irish Catholicism – From Galway to Cloyne and Beyond* (2017), edited by Eamon Maher and Eugene O'Brien.

Nevertheless, while many books on religious issues were published in Ireland, it remains hard to know which can be ascribed to the field of Irish Studies, as the boundaries between disciplines have been blurred, and as a number of non-academic books or books including non-academic contributors have contributed to the national debate over the reinvention of national identity in a post-Christian era. What's more, when one looks at

---

12   See Dara Molloy's website available online: <https://www. daramolloy.com/> [accessed 28 April 2020].

the great Irish Studies collections of the major publishers or the various journals of Irish Studies in Europe, America and beyond, one is struck by the surprisingly small number of articles or book chapters dealing with religious subjects, even in recent times.

If we go back in time and peruse the back issues of the first Irish Studies journals to have come into existence in the 1960s and 1970s, the observation is less clear-cut. In some cases, the topics chosen by the various contributors in fact echo the traditional perception of Irishness at a time when the three fundamental pillars of Irish identity were still perceived to be nationalism, attachment to Gaelic culture and Catholicism. It is particularly true of *Éire-Ireland*, the interdisciplinary journal of the Irish American Cultural Institute founded as early as 1966. Its index for the 1966–1985 period includes a list of no less than thirty eight entries directly or indirectly related to religion, corresponding to seventy-six articles, most of them historical. Early Christian Ireland and its saints feature prominently, as do the Penal era and O'Connell's action in favour of Catholic Emancipation. A few articles also deal with religion and politics, particularly in the context of the Northern Ireland conflict.

By contrast, the *Canadian Journal of Irish Studies* whose first issue was, as said above, released in 1975, and *Etudes irlandaises*, which rapidly followed in 1976, published strikingly few religion-related articles in the first fifteen years of their existence. The former only published 5 between 1975 and 1989, while the latter, an interdisciplinary journal from the outset, published only nine out of a total of nearly 250 articles. The topics chosen were also different. The Protestant heritage, Northern Protestantism and sectarianism appeared prominently in both publications, while the only references to Catholicism in the French periodical concerned the visit of John Paul II to the Republic of Ireland in 1979[13] and the place of the priest in James Plunkett's *Strumpet City*.[14] The obvious distaste for things religious in the French context of *laïcité* certainly accounts for the seemingly

---

13 Richard Deutsch, 'Le voyage de Jean-Paul II en Irlande', and 'The Impact of Jean-Paul II's Journey to Ireland by His Eminence Cardinal Tomas O'Fiaich, Archbishop of Armagh and Primate of All Ireland, an Interview by Richard Deutsch', *Etudes irlandaises* 5, no. 2 (1980), 183–205, 207–220.

14 John Newsinger, 'The Priest in the Irish Novel: James Plunkett's *Strumpet City*', *Etudes irlandaises* 14, no. 2 (1989), 65–76.

limited interest of researchers, some of whom were nevertheless known to be practising Catholics. *The Canadian Journal of Irish Studies* was, for its part, founded as the mouthpiece of the Canadian Association for Irish Studies, launched in 1973 in a Catholic institution, St Michael's College, University of Toronto, by Robert O'Driscoll, a Professor of English of Irish descent who wanted to promote the study of Irish writers. This he did with the full support of Reverend John Kelly, president of St Michael's from 1958 to 1978.[15] What is clear is that all things considered, the three publications shied away from critical comments about the Catholic Church in that period. In addition, none of them published any article about subjects that might appear controversial either.

Major changes appeared in the 1990s and Noughties, as Irish Studies developed, leading to the creation of new journals, including *The Irish Studies Review* (1992), *The New Hibernia Review* (1997), which included some members of the editorial staff originally associated with *Éire-Ireland*, *Radharc, a Journal of Irish and Irish American Studies* (2000),[16] *The Australian Journal of Irish Studies* (2001),[17] or the *Journal of Franco-Irish Studies* (2008).[18] The success of EFACIS (European Federation of Associations and Centres of Irish Studies), launched in 1997, led to the development of Irish Studies on the continent, which led in turn to the creation of several journals, *Nordic Irish Studies* (2002), *Estudios Irlandeses* (2005), *Irish Studies in Europe* (2007) and *Studi Irlandesi* (2010). More recently, EFACIS launched the *Review of Irish Studies in Europe* (RISE, 2017); four years earlier, *Breac*, a new digital journal of Irish Studies, had been launched in the United States. A new generation of scholars, coming from a more diversified disciplinary background, and confident in the relevance of interdisciplinarity, had also come of age.

In the meantime, the context regarding religion had changed in Ireland, following unpalatable revelations about the serious misbehaviour of some

---

15   Joseph Ronsley, 'The Canadian Association for Irish Studies, 1968-1990: A History', *Canadian Journal of Irish Studies* 25, no. 1–2 (1999), 1.
16   It changed its name to *The American Journal of Irish Studies* in 2011.
17   Now *Australasian Journal of Irish Studies*.
18   A journal established by the National Centre for Franco-Irish Studies in Tallaght (Dublin), to be edited in the main by graduate students for graduate students.

clerics and religious from 1992, the liberalisation of legislation regarding the family and sexual morality, the transformations linked to the Celtic Tiger, the first reports about child abuse,[19] but also the Peace Process and Anglo-Irish Agreement in the North (1998). This evolution was bound to attract the interest of Irish Studies scholars, and it did, but to a limited extent only.

If we except *Éire-Ireland*, which saw the number of religion-related articles drastically diminish (only 4.56 percent of those issued between 1990 and 1999), interest and freedom of tone became the norm in other publications. The example of *Etudes irlandaises* is particularly telling if we consider that 3.6 percent of the articles published from 1976 to 1990 concerned one or the other aspect of religion, while 8.3 percent of those published between 1990 and 1999 did. This tendency was confirmed in the following decades with 8.57 percent and 10.05 percent in the 2000–2010 and 2010–2019 periods respectively.[20] If we now take into account the fourteen previously mentioned journals of Irish Studies, the result is less spectacular, but it still shows an increase in the proportion of religious-related essays from 4.95 percent in the 1990–1999 period to 5.58 percent in the Noughties, and a stagnation in the following period, with 5.52 percent from 2010 to 2019.[21] Apart from *Etudes irlandaises*, the journals with consistent results above this average include *Éire-Ireland* (8 percent in 2000–2010; 6.49 percent in 2010–2019), *The American Journal of Irish Studies* and *The Australasian Journal of Irish Studies*. Those that systematically published fewer articles than the average were *New Hibernia Review*, *Estudios Irlandeses* and *The Canadian Journal of Irish Studies*. In the latter case, a surge of interest in the 1990s (5.97 percent in that decade) was followed by a considerable drop (3.28 percent in 2000–2009 and 2.46 percent in 2010–2019). It is therefore extremely difficult to establish an overall pattern that would be in any way meaningful. It is hard to say if the reason for such disparities has to do with a clear editorial line and/or other less easily identifiable causes,

19   *Ferns Report*, 2005; *Ryan Report* and *Murphy Report*, 2009.
20   This includes a special issue on the religions of Ireland, edited by Eamon Maher and Catherine Maignant in 2014.
21   1990–1999: 54 out of 1089 articles; 2000–2010: 70 out of 1254 articles; 2010–2019: 108 out of 1955 articles.

including the contribution of local researchers who do or do not have an interest in religious issues at a given period of time.

The examination of publishing houses' Irish Studies collections leads to equally puzzling conclusions. First of all, most publishers do not have specific series that go by that name. Irish publishers prefer to announce 'Books about Ireland' (Cork University Press) rather than 'Irish Studies'. Oxford University Press for its part classifies its collections according to traditional disciplines. As for Palgrave Macmillan, which has specific collections of Asian, African and Latin American studies, it includes books about Ireland in classic disciplinary series, an interesting reminder of the origins of area studies. A curious case is that of Cambridge University Press, which was a forerunner in the area of Irish Studies, but rapidly gave it up, even though it does still have a number of Irish titles. Indeed, as early as 1981, Patrick J. Drudy, an economist lecturing in Trinity College Dublin and Fellow of St Edmund's House, Oxford, launched an Irish Studies series that looked like a journal, a move he explained in the following manner in his Preface to volume 1:

> Ireland and the Irish are probably best known for their literature (…). Unfortunately, much important historical work on Ireland is less well known. Similarly, research in the economic, social, political and more general cultural spheres has tended to be published within Ireland, mainly for an Irish readership. This series will attempt to redress the balance, and by appealing to an international audience, to reduce those misunderstandings about Ireland that may still remain. It is my view that a deeper understanding can be best achieved in the context of a wide range of scholarship over a wide range of disciplines.[22]

The contributors to this volume were also international in the main and included scholars from Britain, the United States, Norway, and only two from Ireland. One essay, by David Ford, concerned religion, and was entitled 'Church, State and Irish Christianity'.[23] Drudy published six more thematic volumes, none of which treated the issue of religion in any obvious way. But the series stopped in 1987. Since then Cambridge

---

22 Patrick J. Drudy, *Irish Studies*, Vol. 1 (Cambridge: Cambridge University Press), 1981, vii.
23 David Ford, 'Church, State and Irish Christianity', *Ibid.*, 21–34.

University Press has classified books about Ireland according to disciplines, but has recently (2020) published a book entitled *The New Irish Studies* (edited by Paige Reynolds) focusing on contemporary literature, but taking into account changes in the social and political fields:

> This collection tracks how Irish writers have represented the peace and reconciliation process in Northern Ireland, the consequences of the Celtic Tiger economic boom in the Republic, the waning influence of Catholicism, the increased authority of diverse voices, and an altered relationship with Europe.[24]

Among other British publishers a special mention must be made of Manchester University Press, which has published a large number of books about Ireland in recent years, several of them about religious questions, but has no designated Irish Studies series, and favours a classification of books by disciplinary subjects. By contrast, no doubt on account of the university's very active Institute of Irish Studies, Liverpool University Press has a number of Irish Studies series, in particular the new 'Liverpool Studies in Literature', 'Reappraisals in Irish History' and 'the publications of the Society for the study of 19th century Ireland'. Only one book in the second series touches on a religious subject[25] while just one other is published as a 'Non series Irish Studies'.[26] The case of the Aberdeen University Press is comparable due to the importance of Irish Studies in this institution, but just as its Research Institute specialises in Irish and Scottish Studies, the press issues a journal of Irish and Scottish Studies, but its books are classified according to traditional disciplines.

Among the other publishing houses that do have Irish Studies series, special mention has to go to Syracuse University Press, which was the first to launch an Irish Studies collection in America in 1981, with a view to 'publishing groundbreaking work in areas as wide ranging as performing arts,

---

24 Paige Reynolds (ed.), *The New Irish Studies*, Cambridge University Press website, available online: <https://www.cambridge.org/au/academic/subjects/literature/irish-literature/new-irish-studies?format=HB> [accessed 20 April 2020].
25 Ciaran McCabe, *Begging, Charity and Religion in Pre-Famine Ireland* (Liverpool: Liverpool University Press, 2019).
26 John Belchem, *Irish Catholic and Scouse – The History of the Liverpool Irish, 1800-1939* (Liverpool: Liverpool University Press), 2007.

Irish America, religion, language, literary studies and women's studies'.[27] To date, seven books on religious topics have been published in this series: Peter Harbison's *Pilgrimage in Ireland: The Monuments and the People* (1995); John Cooney's *John Charles McQuaid Ruler of Catholic Ireland* (2003); Peggy O'Brien's *Writing Lough Derg from William Carleton to Seamus Heaney* (2006); Emer Nolan's *Catholic Emancipations – Irish Fiction from Tomas Moore to James Joyce* (2007); *A Chastened Communion: Modern Irish Poetry and Catholicism*, edited by Laura Pelaschiar (2013); Abby Bender's *Israelites in Erin – Exodus, Revolution and the Irish Revival* (2015) and *Irish Questions and Jewish Questions* (2018), edited by Adam Beatty and Dan O'Brien.

Edward Everett Root Publishers and Anthem Irish Studies are also committed to innovative scholarship in Irish Studies, but have so far published no book on religious issues. Finally, Caen University Press, Lille/Septentrion University Press and Rennes University Press in France have had Irish Studies collections from an early date, but if we except occasional articles published in conference proceedings, they have not released any major work in the religious field, save *Ecole et religion*, published by Karine Fischer in Caen in 2012.

In this overall context, Peter Lang has launched an Irish Studies collection entitled *Reimagining Ireland* and quite a ground-breaking *Studies in Franco-Irish Relations* series, both enthusiastically edited by Eamon Maher, who has published widely in the area of religion, but most often with other publishers. While the first of these series includes no monograph on religion, the second includes two: Déborah Vandewoude's *L'Église catholique face aux défis contemporains en République d'Irlande – Redéfinition d'une institution désacralisée* (2012) and Edwige Nault's *L'avortement en Irlande, 1983-2013: Dimensions religieuses, socioculturelles, politiques et européenne* (2015). Collective works in both series, however, do include chapters on religious subjects. All of them concern contemporary issues. Among these books are *'Kicking Bishop Brennan up the Arse' – Negotiating Texts and Contexts in Contemporary Irish Studies*, by Eugene O'Brien (2009); *Cultural*

---

27 Syracuse University Press Irish studies webpage, available online: <https://press.syr.edu/supressbook-series/irish-studies/> [accessed 20 April 2020].

Perspectives on Globalisation in Ireland, edited by Eamon Maher (2009); *Ireland: Revolution and Evolution*, edited by John Strachan and Alison O'Malley (2009), and *Breaking the Mould: Literary Representations of Irish Catholicism*, edited by Eamon Maher and Eugene O'Brien (2011), which were published in the *Reimagining Ireland* series. As for the *Studies in Franco-Irish Relations* series, it includes books such as *Issues of Globalisation and Secularisation*, edited by Yann Bevant and Eamon Maher (2009), and *Non-Violent Resistance – Counter Discourse in Irish Culture*, edited by Agnès Maillot (2018), which comprise chapters about religion.

Following this rapid survey, which is in no way comprehensive, but gives a good idea of the interdisciplinary[28] Irish Studies publication scene since the 1960s, we cannot avoid the conclusion that defining the place of religion in Irish Studies is no easy task, essentially because of the difficulty of defining the discipline referred to as Irish Studies. But defining 'religion' as a subject within that loosely defined research area as understood by publishers and journal editors is just as complex, as a careful examination of the areas covered by Irish Studies religion scholars will demonstrate.

The first impression one gets when carefully listing all Irish Studies publications in the area of religion is one of extreme eclecticism. Another is that few of their authors actually choose to specialise in that field, and only occasionally publish on issues related to religion. The third preliminary comment is that methodological heterogeneity is also the rule. A brief typology of essays will easily prove that point. This typology is based on a sample of 385 religion-related articles, book chapters, monographs and unpublished PhD theses identified for the purpose of this research. The published works were all released between 1966 and the present day in Irish Studies journals, books published in Irish Studies or Franco-Irish Studies series, or by Irish Studies scholars in non-Irish Studies journals and book collections. In conformity with the comments of Aaron Hughes

---

28   Specialised Irish Studies journals such as *Irish Studies in International Affairs*, Chris Arthur's *Irish Essays*, *Hypermedia Joyce Studies*, *James Joyce Quarterly*, *Irish Theatre Magazine* and *The Journal of Irish Studies* (formerly *The Harp*) have deliberately not been taken into account (even though Irish Studies scholars do publish articles in them) precisely on the grounds that they are not interdisciplinary, a fundamental aspect of what Irish Studies are meant to be.

and Randi Warne in their article on area studies and religious studies already cited, none of them may be said to fall into the category of religious studies. All actually belong to the fields of literary studies, cultural studies or traditional social sciences such as history, sociology, political science or anthropology. Another characteristic is that they span the centuries from Celtic and early Christian times to the present, with a special emphasis on the nineteenth- to twenty-first-century period, hence the immediate impression of eclecticism.

As stated above, whatever the research area, few authors place religion at the heart of their reflections. It is particularly true of literary studies which generally focus on religious issues as but one aspect of a writer's work or personality. Other authors prefer a sociological approach of literature and will concentrate on the place of religion or aspects of religious practice in Irish writing. In these cases, literature comes first and religion second. The academics who adopt the opposite approach are generally specialists of Catholic or (less frequently) Protestant literature or Catholic/Protestant writing in general. They can be counted on the fingers of one hand. As an expert in French and Irish Catholic writing, Eamon Maher comes in first on the list.[29] But the historian Ann Wilson who writes about arts, crafts and Irish writing from that perspective[30] and Conall Parr, who is a specialist in Protestant culture and literature, also deserve mention.[31]

The same holds true in the field of cultural studies and social sciences. Popular subjects tend to be religion and the arts, religion and politics, religion and society, the place of religion in Irish history and religious practice. In recent years, many articles about religion and the arts focused on the cinema and television series. In the political field, most articles concentrated on the relationships between Church and State, religion and Northern Ireland politics, and Ireland's relationship with Rome. The largest number of essays, however, dealt with religion and society in all its

---

29   See in particular Eamon Maher, *'The Church and its Spire': John McGahern and the Catholic Question* (Dublin: Columba Press, 2011).
30   For instance in 'Irish Catholic Fiction in the Early 20th Century: The Power of Images', *New Hibernia Review* 18, no. 1 (2014), 30–49.
31   See Conall Parr, *Inventing the Myth – Political Passions and the Ulster Protestant Imagination* (Oxford: Oxford University Press, 2017).

different aspects: religion and the hierarchy in society; sectarianism; temperance; sexual morality and recent controversies; education; religion and collective/individual identities North and South; Ireland and the diaspora; women and the Church; heterodox religions and the growth of secularism. The place of religion in Irish history still appealed to researchers, particularly the nineteenth and twentieth centuries, but not solely those areas. Finally, articles about pilgrimages, funeral practices, devotion at shrines and apparitions in Ireland itself and in the host countries of Irish emigrants, constituted the bulk of the pieces devoted to religious practice. Few essays or books, however, may, from a methodological point of view, be categorised as belonging to the strict field of history of religions or sociology of religions. What is clear in this area as in the literary field is that research is heterogeneous, because fundamentally individual rather than collective.

The only identifiable small research cluster focusing on religion proper is still that which is led by Eamon Maher from TU Dublin. Today, it loosely connects researchers and religious actors across Ireland and France on an interdisciplinary basis. Individual but complementary research is carried out on the question of recent developments within the Catholic Church and Catholic Ireland in a spirit of open-mindedness that has in the past caused controversy, notably over the presence of Tony Flannery[32] at a conference on Catholicism,[33] a sign that writing freely about certain questions may still sometimes be difficult, especially when research focuses on matters that have a strong emotional charge. The research also includes the study of new religious movements and new religions in Ireland (in partnership with sociologists working in that field), and the interesting phenomenon of the religions of the internet. The group works in close association with the French national research group GIS-EIRE – in the diaspora on this particular instance, which has become an interesting project dealing with the Irish missions in collaboration with major Irish historians. A stimulating perspective might be the formalisation of these links around a common

---

32 Tony Flannery was silenced by the Vatican in 2012, after the condemnation of some of his published writings by the Congregation for the Doctrine of the Faith.
33 The conference was 'Catholicism on Trial' (6–7 October, 2017) and was moved from The Priory Institute to the Tallaght Campus of TU Dublin after it was discovered that Flannery was one of the speakers.

research project that would attract PhD students and contribute to the development of this research field.

To conclude on this hopeful note, religion is a promising area in Irish Studies, especially in light of heightened secularisation, the authority crisis that affects the Catholic Church and new initiatives of great interest in the religious/spiritual field that recall André Malraux's comment in 1946: 'The crucial problem at the end of this [the 20th] century will be the religious problem – in a form as different from that we know as Christianity was from ancient religions.'[34] It is time Irish Studies scholars took up the baton in greater numbers and investigated what is essentially a new age.

---

34 « Le problème capital de la fin du siècle sera le problème religieux – sous une forme aussi différente de celle que nous connaissons, que le christianisme le fut des religions antiques ». Quoted by Frédéric Lenoir in 'Malraux et le religieux', *Le Monde des religions* (September–October 2005), available online: <https://www.fredericlenoir.com/editos-monde-des-religions/malraux-et-le-religieux/> [accessed 21 April 2020].

PAUL ROUSE

17 Sport and the Irish

The meaning of sport is to be found in its unrelenting capacity to colonise the mind as well as the body. This simple truth goes a long way towards explaining the centrality and the ubiquity of sport in modern Ireland. There are aspects of sport in Ireland that are uniquely Irish and are defined by the peculiarities of a small island on the edge of Europe, where life has long been lived in the shadow cast by the power and prestige of its nearest neighbour. What is equally apparent, however, is that the Irish sporting world is unique only in parts; there is much of the story of Irish sport that is shared with that of other societies, near and far. This is partly a reflection of the universal instincts that draw humans to the idea of play, partly a reflection of the history of Ireland within what was once the British Empire, and partly, also, a reflection of an international cultural exchange where political and geographic borders are permeable.

Modern sport is often big business and it often, too, has a political function. The manner in which sport is continuously repackaged – not least by modern media – creates the illusion of constant change, and yet, the story of Irish sport is, at least in part, the story of people finding new ways of doing the same thing. Networks of modern life run through and around sporting clubs and sporting events. At the heart of these networks, for most people, is the love of play. It is this love, more than anything else, which places the story of sport in Ireland in a universal context. For all that people or institutions may wish for sport to be more than just play, for it to carry a purpose that is political or social, for it to mean something in particular, or fulfil some broader function of policy, sport can also simply mean nothing more than the love of playing. Nobody has captured the simple joy of sport more brilliantly than Seamus Heaney, who once had a trial for the Derry minor Gaelic football team. In 'Markings', Heaney writes of four jackets laid on bumpy ground for goalposts, teams picked and then, a game underway:

> Youngsters shouting their heads off in a field
> As the light died and they kept on playing
> Because by then they were playing in their heads
> and the actual kicked ball came to them
> Like a dream heaviness, and their own hard
> Breathing in the dark and skids on grass
> Sounded like effort in another world …
> It was quick and constant, a game that never need
> Be played out. Some limit had been passed,
> There was fleetness, furtherance, untiredness
> In time that was extra, unforeseen and free.[1]

I

Recent writing on sport has deepened understanding of Ireland and its modern culture. Over the past two decades, in particular, work in universities undertaken by historians, sociologists, archaeologists, political scientists, geographers and economists, has explored aspects of Irish sport from class to gender, and from identity to commerce. Long-form explorations of sport have also been undertaken by traditional media and by new internet-based sites. All of this has been accompanied by publications from state and semi-state bodies, including the Economic and Social Research Institute, the Central Statistics Office and Sport Ireland.

The relationship between sport and national identity has been the focal point for much of what has been written, particularly by historians, sociologists and political scientists.[2] The sheer scale of sporting engagement

---

1 Seamus Heaney, *Seeing Things* (London: Faber and Faber, 1991), 8.
2 John Sugden and Alan Bairner, *Sport, Sectarianism and Society in a Divided Ireland* (Leicester: Leicester University Press, 1993); Mike Cronin, *Sport and Nationalism in Ireland: Gaelic Games, Soccer and Irish Identity Since 1884* (Dublin: Four Courts Press, 1999); H. F. Moorhouse, 'One State, Several Countries: Soccer and Nationality in a "United" Kingdom', in *Tribal Identities: Nationalism, Europe, Sport*, edited by

in Ireland facilitates an exploration of ideas of nationality on an island of contested identities. Sport allows for an examination of what is peculiar to Ireland, but also of what is an experience shared through an international cultural exchange where borders are permeable. Perhaps inevitably, the story of the Gaelic Athletic Association sits at the heart of such explorations and its history has been extensively examined.³ That the largest sporting organisation on the island is one which promotes the 'native' games of hurling and Gaelic football sets it out as a clear marker of Irish national identity. The political aspect to the history of the Association and the words in its *Official Guide*, where identification with Irish nationalism is avowed and its organisational purpose is declared as 'a means of consolidating our Irish identity', underlines this point.⁴ The tension between the GAA's rhetoric and the reality of its day-to-day operations are extensive, however; it is

---

J. A. Mangan (London: Routledge, 1996), 55–74; Alan Bairner (ed.), *Sport and the Irish: Histories, Identities, Issues* (Dublin: UCD Press, 2004); Neal Garnham, 'Rugby and Empire in Ireland: Irish Reactions to Colonial Rugby Tours Before 1914', *Sport in History* 23, no. 1 (2009), 107–114; Timothy Harding, ' "A Fenian Pastime"? Early Irish Board Games and Their Identification with Chess', in *Irish Historical Studies* xxxvii, no. 145 (May 2010), 1–22; Sean Reid, 'Identity and Cricket in Ireland in the Mid-Nineteenth Century', *Sport in Society: Cultures, Commerce, Media, Politics* 15, no. 2 (2012), 147–164; Cathal Billings, *Athbheochan na Gaeilge agus an Spórt in Éirinn, 1884-1934* (PhD thesis, UCD, 2015).

3 See, for example, David Hassan, 'Still Hibernia Irredenta? The Gaelic Athletic Association, Northern Nationalists and Modern Ireland', *Culture, Sport, Society: Cultures, Commerce, Media, Politics* 6, no. 1 (2003), 92–110; Mike Cronin, 'Fighting for Ireland, Playing for England? The Nationalist History of the Gaelic Athletic Association and the English Influence on Irish Sport', *The International Journal of the History of Sport* 15, no. 3 (1998), 36–56; Mike Cronin, Mark Duncan and Paul Rouse, *The GAA: A People's History* (Cork: Collins Press, 2009); Mike Cronin, William Murphy and Paul Rouse (eds), *The Gaelic Athletic Association, 1884-2009* (Dublin: Irish Academic Press, 2009); Ross O'Carroll, *The Gaelic Athletic Association 1914-1918* (MA Thesis, UCD, 2010); W. F. Mandle, *The Gaelic Athletic Association and Irish Nationalist Politics*, 1884–1924 (Dublin: Gill & Macmillan, 1987).

4 Gaelic Athletic Association Official Guide – Part 1. Containing the Constitution and Rules of the G.A.A., revised and corrected up-to-date, and published by authority of the Central Council, 4.

almost entirely consumed with the practical operation of a modern sporting organisation and for much of its history this has been true.[5] Studies of the GAA's identity do not often give adequate consideration to this factor.

Other major field sports have also been studied, but the studies are invariably delineated by time or by local geography. There is, for example, no full academic history of any Irish sporting organisation. What has emerged, instead, is a somewhat scattered, episodic recording of the origins, development and impact of sport in Ireland. That is not to say that this work is without merit or importance. There is an excellent history of rugby in Munster, and one is currently being written on rugby in Leinster.[6] Similarly, there are histories of the early years of soccer focusing on its development around Belfast and in parts of Munster.[7] There are further histories which examine aspects of tennis, athletics, motor racing, ice hockey, game shooting, cricket, hunting and horse racing.[8] There are studies of

---

5 See, for example, Paul Rouse, *The Hurlers: The First All-Ireland Championship and the Making of Modern Hurling* (Dublin: Penguin, 2018).
6 Liam O'Callaghan, *Rugby in Munster: A Social and Cultural History* (Cork: Cork University Press, 2011).
7 Neal Garnham, *Association Football and Society in Pre-partition Ireland* (Belfast: Ulster Historical Foundation, 2004); David Needham, *Ireland's First Real World Cup: The Story of the 1924 Ireland Olympic Football Team* (Dublin: The Manuscript Publisher, 2012); David Toms, *Soccer in Munster: A Social History, 1877-1937* (Cork: Cork University Press, 2015).
8 Tom Higgins, *A History of Irish Tennis, Volumes 1-3* (Sligo: Sligo Tennis Club, 2006); Brendan Lynch, *The Irish Gordon Bennett Cup Race: Triumph of the Red Devil* (Dublin: Portobello Publishing, 2002); David Hassan, 'From Kings to Giants: A History of Ice Hockey in Belfast, 1930-2002', *Sport in History* 24, no. 1 (2004), 77–93; Peter Bacon, *Land, Lust and Gun Smoke: A Social History of Game Shoots in Ireland* (Dublin: The History Press, 2012); Patrick Bracken, 'Foreign and Fantastic Field Sports'. *Cricket in County Tipperary* (Kilkenny: Kilkenny People, 2004); Tom Hunt, *The Little Book of Irish Athletics* (Dublin: The History Press, 2017); Fergus D'Arcy, *Horses, Lords and Racing Men* (Kildare: The Turf Club, 1991); William H. Gibson, *Early Irish Golf* (Kildare: Oakleaf Publications, 1988); Colin A. Lewis, *Hunting in Ireland: An Historical and Geographical Analysis* (London: J.A. Allen, 1973); Michael O'Dwyer, *The History of Cricket in County Kilkenny: The Forgotten Game* (Kilkenny: O'Dwyer Books, 2006).

unique aspects of the Irish sporting world, including road bowling.[9] There are studies, also, of Irish involvement in the Olympic Games and of Irish emigrant sporting activity.[10] The monumental *Dictionary of Irish Biography* contains portraits of hundreds of sports people, extending back across centuries. In some instances, these biographies show how sport played the central part in the public life of a particular individual; in others, it was just one aspect of many, even a sidebar to a life.[11] A further strain of research is devoted to sporting histories of Irish counties, notably Westmeath, Tipperary and Donegal.[12] These studies offer complicated, nuanced assessments of the origins and development of modern sport in the lives of generations of Irish people in a local context. Further, there are excellent studies of sporting associational culture and of the relationship between sport and leisure.[13]

Much of this research of the Irish sporting world was drawn together in James Kelly's *Sport in Ireland: 1600-1840* and in Paul Rouse's *Sport and Ireland: A History*.[14] The limitations of both these books were manifest in the great silences that run through them on whole aspects of the Irish sporting experience. These are silences that will be filled in the coming decades, as the work of new scholars adds layers of depth and sophistication to the study of sport on the island.

[9] Fintan Lane, *Long Bullets: A History of Road Bowling in Ireland* (Ireland: Galley Head Press, 2005).

[10] Kevin McCarthy, *Gold, Silver and Green: The Irish Olympic Journey 1896–1924* (Cork: Cork University Press, 2011) and Paul Darby, *Gaelic Games, Nationalism and the Irish Diaspora in the United States* (Dublin: UCD Press, 2009).

[11] See, for example, John Rouse, 'Tom Kiely', in *Dictionary of Irish Biography*, edited by James McGuire and James Quinn (2009) and Patrick Maume, 'J.J. Walsh', in *Dictionary of Irish Biography*, edited by James McGuire and James Quinn (2009).

[12] Tom Hunt, *Sport and Society in Victorian Ireland: The Case of Westmeath* (Cork: Cork University Press, 2007); Conor Curran, *Sport in Donegal: A History* (Dublin: The History Press, 2010); Pat Bracken, *The Growth and Development of Sport in County Tipperary, 1840-1880* (Cork: Cork University Press, 2018).

[13] Alicia St Leger, *A History of the Royal Cork Yacht Club* (Cork: Royal Cork Yacht Club, 2005); Brian Griffin, *Cycling in Victorian Ireland* (Nonsuch Publishing, 2006).

[14] James Kelly's *Sport in Ireland, 1600-1840* (Dublin: Four Courts Press, 2014) and Paul Rouse, *Sport and Ireland: A History* (Oxford: Oxford University Press, 2015).

II

For all that there has been significant progress made since the turn of the millennium, it must be remembered that writing on sport in Ireland remains in its infancy. Scholarly engagement with sport gathered significant momentum in America, France and Britain – in particular – from the 1960s onwards. From these countries a new historiography and sociology of sport was produced which brought the publication of landmark monographs and peer-reviewed journals. In Ireland, the study of sport emerged slowly in the late 1980s and 1990s, but even allowing for the significant increase in published material over the past two decades, there remain significant, fundamental gaps.

Explorations on a thematic basis have tended to focus on gender, though the place of women in Irish sport remains hugely understudied.[15] Indeed, there is no overarching study of the history of women in Irish sport. In terms of individual sports, detailed exploration of women's hockey, women's golf, women's athletics, camogie, the growth and development of women's Gaelic football – and much else – remains to be undertaken. In part, such explorations are hindered by the absence of adequate, accessible archives; but such absence need not be an unsurmountable obstacle. If the study of sport and gender in Ireland has been limited, the study of sport and class has been virtually non-existent.[16] There is no Irish equivalent of John Lowerson's *Sport and the English Middle Classes* (1993) or Richard Holt's edited collection, *Sport and the Working Class in Modern Britain* (1990), and yet in Ireland it is clear that sporting engagement was significantly shaped by class. In the modern sporting world, the alliance

---

15   See, for example, Regina Fitzpatrick, Dónal MacAnallen and Paul Rouse, 'Freedom of the Field: First Fifty Years of Camogie', in *The Evolution of the GAA. Ulaidh, Éire and Eile*, edited by Dónal McAnallen, David Hassan and Roddy Hegarty (Armagh: Comhairle Ulaidh CLG, 2009).

16   Tom Hunt, 'Classless Cricket in Westmeath', *History Ireland* 12, no. 2, 26–30; James Kelly, 'The Pastime of the Elite: Clubs and Societies and the Promotion of Horse Racing', in *Clubs and Societies in Eighteenth Century Ireland*, edited by James Kelly and Martyn J. Powell (Dublin: Four Courts Press, 2010), 409–424.

of blood, land and commerce was forged in rugby, tennis and golf clubs of the growing suburbs. Money found money as the middle classes bought into the legitimacy conferred by association with the old sporting gentry. Conspicuous displays of wealth have always been important to sport in Ireland. In general, no economic history of sport in the country has been written. There is no text to compare with, for example, Wray Vamplew's *Pay Up and Play the Game: Professional Sport in Britain, 1875-1914* (1988) or Neil Tranter's *Sport, Economy and Society in Britain 1750-1914* (1998).[17]

The relationship between sport and settlement, and sport and demography, in Ireland remains largely unwritten. Although there are histories written of sport in Irish counties, there needs to be much greater exploration of the role of sport in urban life. A start has been made on country towns and the *Irish Historic Towns Atlas* series offers a fine insight in a general way, while the place of sports grounds in the landscape has been examined in Mike Cronin and Roisin Higgins, *Places We Play: Ireland's Sporting Heritage* (Cork University Press, 2012).[18] But, even allowing for Julien Clenet's ongoing project on the history of sport in nineteenth-century Dublin, sport in Ireland's cities needs a thorough examination.

As well as an absence of thematic studies of Irish sport, there are only extremely limited accounts of sport in medieval Ireland – and huge gaps in our knowledge of Early Modern sport and, indeed of medieval sport.[19]

---

17   Wray Vamplew, *Pay Up and Play the Game: Professional Sport in Britain, 1875-1914* (Cambridge University Press, 1988); John Lowerson, *Sport and the English Middle Classes* (Manchester University Press, 1993); Richard Holt (ed.), *Sport and the Working Class in Modern Britain* (Manchester University Press, 1990), and Neil Tranter's *Sport, Economy and Society in Britain 1750-1914* (Cambridge University Press, 1998).

18   Paul Rouse, 'Empires of Sport: Enniscorthy, 1880-1920', in *Enniscorthy: A History*, edited by Colm Tóibín (Wexford: Wexford Library, 2010), 333–368; Mike Cronin and Roisín Higgins, *Places We Play: Ireland's Sporting Heritage* (Cork: Collins Press, 2012).

19   Maighréad Ní Mhurchadha, 'Two Hundred Men at Tennis: Sport in North Dublin 1600-1760', *Dublin Historical Record* 61, no. 1 (Spring 2008), 87–106, 100–101; David A. Fleming, 'Diversions of the People: Sociability among the Orders of Early Eighteenth-Century Ireland', *Eighteenth Century Ireland/Iris an Dá Chultúr* 17 (2002), 99–111.

If nothing else, extended study of the past will shatter the belief that the present sporting world cannot hold a candle to that which has passed. This nostalgia for a lost and lamented sporting nirvana is no new thing. In 1733 – with the modern sporting world in the very early thrusts of its conception – a huntsman wrote: 'Perhaps there is no greater demonstration of the degeneracy of the present age, than the neglect and contempt of this manly exercise. Those useful hours that our fathers employed on horseback in the fields, are lost on their posterity betwixt a stinking pair of sheets. Balls and opera's [sic], assemblies and masquerades, so exhaust the spirits of the puny creatures overnight, that yawning and chocolate are the main labours and entertainments of the morning.'[20] Ever since, the sporting world has filled with nostalgia, expressions of loss and longing for a past, a 'Golden Era' of greats involved in acts of heroism the likes of which will never, can never, be seen again. This tendency, in itself, is enough to warrant a deeper study of the past.

The ethical dimension to sport merits much more serious investigation. More precisely, the question must be asked as to whether sport has a moral function? Certain sections of Victorian society certainly believed it did. Nonetheless, their notions of integrity and fair play that were wrapped around 'amateurism' were too often frontage for thinly disguised snobbery and class control. More importantly, the values of amateurism have not usually survived engagement with competitive sport. This was the case because, as the novelist Wilkie Collins wrote, far from teaching a man virtuous behaviour, sport taught him how 'to take every advantage of another man that his superior strength and superior cunning can suggest'.[21] This has lent itself time and again to the use of sport as a glib metaphor (for life and for war, to give the two most prominent instances). It has also facilitated the construction of easy assumptions about the character of sport; the tendency to judge the civilisation of a people by virtue of the sports they play is, in this respect, a triumph of Puritanical thought. Indeed, it remains

20 'A Country Squire' wrote that passage in his 1733 book, *An Essay in Hunting*, quoted in David A. Fleming, 'Diversions of the People: Sociability among the Orders of Early Eighteenth-Century Ireland', *Eighteenth Century Ireland/Iris an Dá Chultúr* 17 (2002), 99–111, 101.
21 Wilkie Collins, *Man and Wife* (1870), 207.

the case that the sporting past is measured for its march from barbarism to civilisation. Perhaps this reflects the very perception of sport as a marker of apparent human progress: breaking records suggests ineluctable advancement and the understood corollary is that the very history of sport must itself be a story of progression. The shortcomings of that understanding are everywhere visible. The sordid underbelly of modern sport – the cheating, fixing, drug-taking, violence, greed, exploitation and narcissism – leave no room for naïve adulation.

The importance of sport in the modern world inevitably means that the state has become increasingly involved in its operation. The relationship between the state and sport in a new millennium remains an amalgam of achievement and failure, good intentions and rampant hypocrisy. There is much that is admirable in the attempts by states to use sport to improve the health of the people who live within their boundaries. This is manifest in the dispersal of funds to improve local facilities and in campaigns to encourage people to exercise. The state seeks to do more than this, of course. It seeks, also, to use sport to promote the nation. An independent study of the money spent to do this would be most welcome – but, equally, reckoning with the capacity of sport to deliver the outcomes that are hoped for, or expected, is to be similarly desired.

It is possible, of course, to live in modern Ireland and to ignore sport, but it is not easy to do so and it certainly requires a conscious effort. This is a singular statement of the importance, the vitality and the sheer scale of modern sport. It is also testimony to the communications revolution that has seen sport become a central feature of modern media. Newspapers for more than a century and a half relied on sport for increasing column inches of content. The same has proven true of radio and television. Where once sporting events on television were occasional treats sparsely sprinkled across the schedule, they are now central to mainstream programming, as well as having a growing number of channels dedicated to their coverage. Combined with the rapidly expanding sports applications available on various devices from computers to smartphones, as well as the increased coverage on radio and in newspapers, there is no gainsaying the omnipresence of sport in the media. This is the ultimate example of the triumph of sport: there is now no event, regardless of how small and insignificant it might appear to others, that cannot be made accessible across the world using the internet. The relationship of sport and the media is the key to understanding the monetisation of sport in all its aspects from merchandising to ticket sales.

Related to a study of sport and the media in Ireland, central to future investigations of Irish sport is the manner in which the ubiquity of the smartphone in everyday life is fundamentally shifting engagement with sport. Indeed, there is no aspect of the modern world that has not been reshaped – in whole or in part – by the revolution that is taking place all around us. Whether one laments the manner in which the smartphone has changed the way people relate to each other, or whether one – by contrast – celebrates the possibilities created by their apparently boundless capabilities, there can be no denying the transformation that is being wrought on social life. At the extremes of this phenomenon, online addiction does not wreak the immediate and apparent physical toll that, say, addiction to alcohol or drugs or food usually does. But there is nothing benign about its danger: at its worse, it colonises human interaction with a compulsion to sacrifice everything to immersion in online activity. The content that flows from such immersion can range from shopping to gaming to celebrity fixation and much else. It is partly the fact that there is at least the illusion of there being no end to the possibilities of things that can be found on the internet that makes it so attractive. The manner in which so much of modern society – both in terms of popular social communication and even economic affairs – now revolves around smartphones leaves it very difficult to live a life entirely offline. and whatever prospect for such a life there is for people who have experienced a world before smartphones, there is none for those who have been born into this digital revolution. No understanding of the place of sport in modern Irish life will be complete, or even meaningful, without considering its relationship with smartphones.

In conclusion, the great forces of history that have shaped life in Ireland have inevitably shaped its sports. The spread of Christianity, the colonisation of the island, the rise of nationalism and the unending battles over sovereignty, the triumph of capitalism, globalisation, the growth of villages, towns and cities, the new and enduringly potent changes in communication, and so much else, have influenced the development of sport in Ireland. This is a story which stretches out in front of us. Sport is an essential part of modern life, a vital presence. But its importance lies usually in the fact that it is something that is also inessential, something that people pursue out of love and as a leisure activity. A seismic shift in sporting culture has obviously occurred through the centuries and this reflects the changes from pre-industrial to post-modern society in Ireland. Nonetheless, the human emotions that continue to drive sport in this new millennium remain essentially the same. This love of sport is not, though, a simple matter of escapism, an attempt to beat down the walls of 'real life' and find joy in an experience that exists outside normality. Sport, instead, is utterly real, a normal part of everyday life for millions of Irish people. It is something they do and something they think about. What makes it all the more potent is that it is also something they can imagine. It is this capacity of sport to make people dream, even as they play, that allows sport to transcend the mundane.

EUGENE O'BRIEN

18 The Dawning of Difference: Literary and Cultural Theory in Irish Studies

> Perhaps, then, the day is not so far off when Irish structuralists will meet in Belfast to discuss the latest reading of Barbara Johnson's reading of Derrida's reading of Lacan's reading of *The Purloined Letter*.[1]

Thus spoke Tom Paulin about the dawning of theory in Irish Studies, in 1984, embodying as he did Paul de Man's notion of the 'resistance to theory'. For de Man, the resistance to theory 'is a resistance to the use of language about language',[2] and in this particular case, the resistance was about 'theory' taking precedence over the disciplinary specificities of literature and history. Going back to the time of Immanuel Kant, keeping faculties separate was central to much academic thinking:

> The higher faculties must, therefore, take great care not to enter into a misalliance with the lower faculty, but must keep it at a respectful distance, so that the dignity of their statutes will not be damaged by the free play of reason.[3]

Intellectually, Irish Studies has the imperative of allowing the 'free play of reason' to range across different texts, from various disciplines, that outlined the Irish experience. However, it also had a hard-headed economic dimension, as American, and later European students, looked to understand the Irish experience, fuelled by diasporic connections with

1 Tom Paulin, *Ireland and the English Crisis* (Newcastle-upon-Tyne: Bloodaxe, 1984), 15.
2 Paul De Man, *The Resistance to Theory* (Minneapolis: University of Minnesota Press, 1986), 12.
3 Immanuel Kant, *The Conflict of the Faculties – Der Streit der Fakultäten* (New York: Abaris Books, 1979), 35.

the country, and were seen as a lucrative market. So, in the beginning, Irish Studies comprised the literary canon – Yeats, Joyce, Beckett, Synge – and readings of these as great writers against a broadly monological historical background. The Irish story was seen as one of exceptionality, where a gradual rise of nationalism against the colonial power eventually led to the 1916 Rising, a civil war and freedom. It was a narrative of accretive republican and nationalist success across a range of revolt and revolutions against British rule, and some cultural study of Ireland as a rural idyll. Close reading would have been the norm, and the default position of writers and readers was largely deemed to be a white, Catholic, republican (probably of the Fianna Fáil variety), middle-class man. It was not that the other voices were disparaged; more that they were not even considered and not seen or heard as being relevant. Issues of class, race and gender in any form were occluded, and the materiality of production and consumption was not an issue – this was largely an empiricist and humanistic process.

What Pierre Bourdieu might term the *habitus* of Irish studies was initially constituted by professional associations, derived from different disciplines, combining their work under this new designation. It was seldom taught as a subject, so convocation became its mode of being. The American Conference for Irish Studies (ACIS) was founded in 1962; The British Association for Irish Studies (BAIS) in 1985; the Spanish Association for Irish Studies (AEDEI) in 2000; the European Federation of Associations and Centres of Irish Studies (EFACIS) in 2013; and, in Ireland itself, the International Association for the Study of Irish Literatures (IASIL) in 1969. Originally known as the International Association for the Study of Anglo-Irish Literature (IASAIL), the second title was viewed as being more inclusive when it was brought into being in 1998. Paulin's stricture came true in in 1985, when literary theory arrived centre stage in Irish Studies at a conference on 'Critical Approaches to Anglo-Irish Literature' held in Queen's University, Belfast. Theory, however, was already an issue in the previous IASAIL conference held at the University of Graz, which had demanded that the association become more alert to literary theory.[4]

---

4   Shaun Richards, 'Irish Studies and the Adequacy of Theory: The Case of Brian Friel', *The Yearbook of English Studies* 35, *Irish Writing since 1950* (2005): 264.

Epistemologically, it can be argued that Irish Studies, in its broadening of inquiry and flouting of disciplinary barriers, was always already theoretical in orientation. Irish Studies is perhaps best understood as a discipline that is preoccupied by 'questions of beginnings, intention and method',[5] and as a discipline that is always already involved in deconstruction. As Colin Graham has perceptively noted: 'Ireland is a deconstructing Ireland'.[6] Liam Harte is surely correct when he notes that Irish Studies, as an academic field, allows for 'a more inclusive cultural, historical and sociological praxis'.[7] I would contend that part of the theoretical thrust of the area has been to put into question notions of 'essential' Irishness, as this field has been created by Diasporic Irish academics as much as by those from the home country. Hence, it is acutely self-aware of how the Irish experience involves an often contradictory, even paradoxical combination of 'the backward look' and 'breakneck modernization'.[8]

In this sense, Irish Studies was theoretical *avant la lettre*, as it looked to diversify and pluralise notions of Irishness, thereby deconstructing any sense of a monological nationalist unity through those inclusive discursive practices. In this sense it could be seen to mirror Jacques Rancière's idea that 'culture is always a form of disidentification: the possibility of speaking something other than the tongue of one's ancestors or of one's group or interest-group', and that such cultural discourse, if theoretically informed, will 'turn one's self-identical voice into a voice of alterity'.[9] This means that the area would be constantly asking questions of itself, both ontologically and epistemologically. It was never a smooth process and it tended to move paradigm, less in Thomas Kuhn's oft-quoted major shifts, and more in a

---

5   Joe Cleary, 'Misplaced Ideas? Colonialism, Location and Dislocation in Irish Studies', in *Theorizing Ireland*, edited by Claire Connolly (Basingstoke: Palgrave, 2003), 94.
6   Colin Graham, *Deconstructing Ireland: Identity, Theory, Culture* (Edinburgh: Edinburgh University Press, 2001), x.
7   Liam Harte and Yvonne Whelan, *Ireland Beyond Boundaries: Mapping Irish Studies in the Twenty First Century* (London: Pluto Press, 2007), 2.
8   John Goodby, *Irish Studies: The Essential Glossary* (London: Arnold, 2003), vii.
9   Thomas Docherty, *For the University: Democracy and the Future of the Institution* (London: Bloomsbury Academic, 2011), 33.

series of fits and starts, and discussions and debates often became disputes, as the canon came under interrogation: whom one should study; whom one should not study; how to study them; how much theory to use; what theories should be used, and how could all of these be squared with the nature and definition of the proper adjective in '*Irish* Studies'.

Interestingly, the rise of Irish Studies as an academic area was very much connected with the rise of the study of literary and cultural theory across universities in Ireland. Beginning as a way of introducing foreign, and mostly American, students and academics to Ireland, it developed from the ground up as literary Summer Schools – Yeats (1960), Joyce (1988) – followed by schools on Synge, George Moore and John McGahern, would lead to more politically and socially based ones like the Merriman and the McGill Summer Schools. Visiting students often wanted more on the history of the country and tours, lectures and multidisciplinary lectures became part of the experience. However, there would be a strong element of the canonical in these early schools, and when postcolonial perspectives on Joyce were introduced at the Joyce Summer School, for example, they were not met with a positive response. Reading literature as anything but an autotelic exercise was not seen as being of value in this climate.

Clearly, this has changed. We now see the flourishing of new writers, and new topics; the broadening of the canon to include previously occluded and attenuated voices; the multiplicity of theoretical and reading approaches and the concentration on material modes of both production and reception in Irish Studies; the reimagining of canonical writers through feminist, new materialistic, postcolonial, queer, deconstructive, psychoanalytic, ecotheoretical and postmodernist perspectives (this is not an exhaustive list). Such a change has been transformative of the discipline which is now vibrant and flourishing, as this 100th volume in the *Reimagining Ireland* series confirms, and in this chapter, I will contend that the advent of literary and critical theory was the agent that presaged the dawning of difference in both the field and in its epistemological constitution.

The answers to these questions are to be found in the broadening of educational opportunity in Ireland, with specific reference to the numbers of students attending third level, and in the resultant gradual application of literary and critical theoretical interrogations to the body politic and the body clerical in Ireland. Up until then, the societal, cultural and religious 'givens' of society were passed on in a largely unquestioned and unquestioning manner, a paradigm which, as we have seen, applied to the Irish State as well. Much has been made of the influence of French intellectual writings on raising student consciousness in Paris in 1968. The student uprisings of May 1968 in Paris, and those in Prague and Los Angeles of the same year, were largely inspired by French intellectual thought. 1966 saw the publication of Jacques Lacan's *Écrits* and Michel Foucault's *The Order of Things: An Archaeology of the Human Sciences*;[10] Jacques Derrida's *Of Grammatology* was published the following year.[11] These three texts asked seminal questions about the nature of culture and human organisations, questions which would prove to have destabilising force on the discourses of the human sciences, and none more so than Irish Studies, both in terms of *what* was deemed important to be read, and also of *how* that process of reading would be theoretically informed.

In a chapter of this length, it is necessary to simplify and exemplify, so I am suggesting that at the epistemological core of literary theory is the question. This is its synecdochic trope: the question that asks the unaskable, that suggests the unsuggestable and that looks at an encompassing horizon, and asks, what is on the other side? I would see such a process as ongoing and essentially deconstructive, involving the dismantling of received structures; the replacement of stock answers with probing questions; the opening up of new fields of study driven by those questions and not by the existing disciplines of the academy, and finally, the giving of voice to alterity, to the 'other' in all of its forms. This 'other' had not really been recognised within the Irish academic sphere, and the dawning of a multidisciplinary and interdisciplinary area such as Irish Studies would prove to be a structure that would be positive in addressing all forms of alterity. As Jacques

---

10   Jacques Lacan and Alan Sheridan, *Écrits: A Selection* (London: Routledge, 1977); Michel Foucault, *The Order of Things. An Archaeology of the Human Sciences* (London: Tavistock Publications, 1970).
11   Jacques Derrida, *Of Grammatology*, edited by Gayatri Chakravorty Spivak (Baltimore: Johns Hopkins University Press, 1976).

Derrida has said in *Of Spirit*, the origin of language is responsibility,[12] in the sense that to speak is to speak to someone else, to speak to the other, indeed to apostrophise the other,[13] and this has become a motivating trope in Irish Studies in terms of what to read, and how to read.

In terms of the latter, in Ireland, theoretical reading came to the fore in the early 1980s. Terry Eagleton makes the point that children make the best theorists since they do not automatically accept our routine social practices, or in the context of this discussion, our seemingly normative standards of literary value, as 'natural', but persist in subjecting such 'practices' and 'standards' to the 'most embarrassingly general and fundamental questions'.[14] Among the earliest books available on theory in the Irish system were Rene Wellek and Austin Warren's *Theory of Literature*,[15] which was followed in the early 1980s by Terry Eagleton's *Literary Theory: An Introduction* (1982),[16] and Ann Jefferson and David Robey's *Modern Literary Theory: A Comparative Introduction* (1982).[17] The *New Accents* series from Methuen (Routledge), edited by Terence Hawkes and launched in 1977, encompassing some fifty-two titles (including second and enlarged and revised editions; the actual number of original texts is forty one),[18] was a seminal influence in translating and applying French theory to the canon of English writing, and it offered a *vade mecum* for academics in Irish Studies, one that would bear fruit in the *Field Day Anthology*, which will be looked at later in this chapter.

In terms of how to read, literary theory challenged many of the preconceptions of the previous ideological regime: where there was sameness,

12 Jacques Derrida, *Of Spirit: Heidegger and the Question* (Chicago: University of Chicago Press, 1989), 132.
13 Jacques Derrida, Thomas Dutoit and Outi Pasanen, *Sovereignties in Question: The Poetics of Paul Celan* (New York: Fordham University Press, 2005), 119.
14 Terry Eagleton, *The Significance of Theory* (Oxford: Basil Blackwell, 1990), 34.
15 René Wellek and Austin Warren, *Theory of Literature*, 1st edition (New York: Harcourt, Brace, 1949).
16 Terry Eagleton, *Literary Theory: An Introduction* (Oxford: Basil Blackwell, 1982).
17 Ann Jefferson, David Robey and David Forgacs, *Modern Literary Theory, a Comparative Introduction* (New York: Barnes & Noble Books, 1982).
18 The full catalogue of these books, which have been reissued by Routledge, is available online: <https://www.routledge.com/New-Accents/book-series/SE0682>.

it offered difference; where there was singularity, it offered plurality; where there was close reading and absence of context, it offered close readings of both texts and contexts. It also posed questions about the canon, asking why some works were valued over others, and then probing the criteria of those valuations. It challenged the notion that 'literature' was an ontological category and that works seemingly automatically came into this category. One thinks of F. R. Leavis's *The Great Tradition*,[19] which set out a line of orthodoxy across the range of the English novel, seeing Jane Austen, George Eliot, Henry James and Joseph Conrad as the central figures in that tradition. Contentiously, Leavis, and his followers, excluded major authors such as Charles Dickens, Laurence Sterne, James Joyce and Thomas Hardy from his canon, and perhaps more tellingly, offered no real reasons for this apart from the ill-defined and untheorised notion of sensibility (after a long time in the academy, I am still vague as to what this actually means). Similarly, in *New Bearings on English Poetry*,[20] Leavis championed the modernist work of Gerard Manley Hopkins, William Butler Yeats, T. S. Eliot and Ezra Pound.

Leavis saw the act of reading as inevitably intuitive, and when asked by René Wellek to defend the philosophical choices inherent in his position, he refused to be drawn into abstract debate on the basis of the radical distinction between literature and philosophy.[21] His attitude to theory, and it was an attitude shared by many contemporary critics, was that it is outside the brief of the critic. For Leavis, theory was for philosophers, and he professed that he was 'no philosopher' as he had 'pretensions – pretensions to being a literary critic'.[22] This differentiation between theory and criticism, valorised by the distinction between the language of theory as 'abstract' and that of poetry as 'concrete',[23] is disingenuous. It is useful to call to mind a wry assertion of Terry Eagleton's, namely that 'hostility to

---

19   F. R. Leavis, *The Great Tradition* (London: Chatto & Windus, 1948).
20   F. R. Leavis, *New Bearings on English Poetry* (London: Chatto and Windus, 1932).
21   Peter Widdowson, *Re-Reading English* (London: Methuen, 1982), 129.
22   Leavis, *The Great Tradition*, 211–212.
23   *Ibid.*, 212.

theory usually means an opposition to other people's theories and an oblivion of one's own.'[24]

In her discussion of the use of theory in *Critical Practice*,[25] Catherine Belsey argues that Leavisite common sense, which seems to be anti-theoretical, is in fact based on an unstated theoretical model. The 'assumptions' about which Leavis expressed himself so reluctant to theorise, have been summarised by Belsey as drawing on the theory of 'expressive realism'. This theory proposes 'a *humanism* based on an *empiricist-idealist* interpretation of the world.'[26] Belsey details the theoretical premises of this philosophy, noting the 'humanist assumption that subjectivity, the individual mind or inner being, is the source of meaning and of action.'[27] The power of this argument is that it draws attention to the theoretical basis of all forms of criticism; the only difference is that some theories are explicitly stated, while others remain a series of shared assumptions, ideas and impressions. In her view, 'common sense' itself is ideologically and culturally constructed; it is produced in specific societies by the discursive practices employed by that society.

The unstated, and possibly unconscious politics of such a position is interesting. Ireland, as a newly independent nation, set about creating a form of cultural identity, largely through ideological practices like literature. As a small country with few natural or human resources, and with a history of colonisation, Ireland could boast about little enough on the world stage, but in literature in all its forms – short stories, novels, poems and plays – it was a significant player, and the mode of close reading and non-contextual criticism that prevailed in the reading of this literature partook, in an unspoken manner, in the notion that academic practices would remain largely separate in terms of politics and popular culture. It allowed for repetition and security in defining a small, elite cultural canon,

---

24   Terry Eagleton, *Literary Theory: An Introduction*, 2nd edition (Oxford Blackwell, 1996), viii.
25   Catherine Belsey, *Critical Practice* (London: Methuen, 1980).
26   Belsey, *Critical Practice*, 7.
27   Ibid., 3.

what Martin Heidegger would term the 'ever-sought-after Sameness of the Same'.[28]

The modes of close reading that one offered to Yeats, Joyce, Jane Austen or T. S. Eliot had no real application outside of the discipline of literature or literary studies; the politics espoused by these writers and in which they lived, was not a factor. Instead, the reading of Irish writers is a way of insinuating a type of Irishness that is essentialist and beyond the differences that inhabit a first-world country with a third-world history, and one that was very centrally governed both overtly and covertly by the hegemonic structures of a conservative, Catholic, republican (in some form or other) state. Such separation of critical readings of linguistic practices from the domain of the political and cultural participated in a type of Heideggerian *Versammlung* (gathering).[29] Close reading, biographical criticism and a rigid separation of the aesthetic realm from other cultural practices allows for a privileging of sameness and an exclusion of difference: in this way, literary criticism allowed for the passage of the same type of humanistic values to pass from generation to generation; it allowed for the creation of quite a static and conservative ideology, where the canon was created by those who had cultural power, and where there was neither theoretical not philosophical rationale for this. It meant that the study of literature was the same literature for different generations, and the mode of study – close reading or empiricist humanism – was also the same, and crucially, to quote Heidegger, we 'interpret Sameness to mean a belonging together'.[30]

This gradual deconstruction of sameness by difference is developed in Jacques Derrida's critique of binary oppositions. Seeing all knowledge as codified through binary oppositions which themselves were not ideologically neutral, he proposed a mode of thinking that would destabilise these. So, in the binary coloniser/colonised, the full weight of the Foucauldian couplet of knowledge and power lined up behind the former term, with

28 Martin Heidegger and William McNeill, *Pathmarks* (Cambridge: Cambridge University Press, 1998), xiii.
29 Martin Heidegger, *Martin Heidegger: Basic Writings*, translated by William Lovitt, edited by David Farrell Krell (New York: Harper & Row, 1977), 355.
30 Martin Heidegger, *Identity and Difference*, 1st edition (New York: Harper & Row, 1969), 28.

the latter being seen as weaker, less cultured and very much disempowered. Deconstruction is often seen as reversing the binary, so a view of postcolonial thinking would be to empower the discourse of the colonised at the expense of the coloniser, and focus on indigenous writing as opposed to the writings of the occupying culture. However, such thinking would only 'reverse the binary opposition ... to keep in place the assumptions already constructed by the opposition'.[31] For Derrida, the 'phase of overturning' is just the first step:

> To deconstruct the opposition, first of all, is to overturn the hierarchy at a given moment. To overlook this phase of overturning is to forget the conflictual and subordinating structure of opposition. Therefore, one might proceed too quickly to a neutralization that in practice would leave the previous field untouched, leaving one no hold on the previous opposition, thereby preventing any means of intervening in the field effectively.[32]

For Derrida, this inversion is only the initial phase in the process: it is necessary but not sufficient:

> we must also mark the interval between inversion, which brings low what was high, and the irruptive emergence of a new 'concept', a concept that can no longer be, and never could be, included in the previous regime. If this interval, this biface or biphase, can be inscribed only in a bifurcated writing (and this holds first of all for a new concept of writing, that *simultaneously* provokes the overturning of the hierarchy speech/writing, and the entire system attached to it, *and* releases the dissonance of a writing within speech, thereby disorganizing the entire inherited order and invading the entire field).[33]

This new concept is something that it is in flux and is not fixed: it is process as opposed to product; it is thinking as opposed to teleology. This kind of theoretical thinking was initially operative through postcolonial theory where, instead of seeing Yeats, Joyce and Beckett as parts of the

---

31 John Storey, *Cultural Theory and Popular Culture: An Introduction*, 7th edition (London: Routledge, 2015), 133.
32 Jacques Derrida, Alan Bass and Henri Ronse, *Positions* (Chicago: University of Chicago Press, 1981), 41.
33 Derrida, Bass, and Ronse, *Positions*, 42. Italics in original.

English literary tradition, they were now starting to be read as autochthonous voices – for example, the reading by Edward Said of Yeats as a postcolonial poet in 'Yeats and Decolonization'.[34]

In terms of Irish Studies, Cairns and Richards' book, *Writing Ireland: Colonialism, Nationalism and Culture*, opened a lot of doors through its imbrication of literature, theory and notions of colonialism and Marxist readings, by offering a different perspective of Ireland's literary, and by extension, socio-political, landscape.[35] There were attempts to expand the canon, and one of the most significant of these was the Field Day project, and it is to this redefinition of the quiddity of Irish Studies, of what one should read, that our discussion now turns. In the 1990s, postcolonial theory had achieved something like hegemonic status in Irish Studies; texts like *Anomalous States* by David Lloyd,[36] Declan Kiberd's *Inventing Ireland*,[37] and work by Luke Gibbons,[38] as well as the *Critical Conditions* series, published by Field Day and UCC Press, set out the terrain of this area.[39]

The culmination of this process was the *Field Day Anthology*,[40] published in 1991, with a stellar editorial board consisting of Seamus Deane, Andrew Carpenter, David Berman, Terence Brown, Nicholas Canny, Bryan Coleborne, Charles Doherty, Terence Dolan, J. W. Foster, Luke Gibbons, Alan Harrison, Seamus Heaney, Declan Kiberd, Pronsias MacCana, W. J. McCormick, Augustine Martin, D. E. S. Maxwell, J. C. C. Mays,

---

34   Terry Eagleton et al., *Nationalism, Colonialism, and Literature* (Minneapolis: University of Minnesota Press, 1990).
35   David Cairns and Shaun Richards, *Writing Ireland: Colonialism, Nationalism and Culture* (Manchester: Manchester University Press, 1988).
36   David Lloyd, *Anomalous States: Irish Writing and the Post-Colonial Moment* (Dublin: Lilliput Press, 1993).
37   Declan Kiberd, *Inventing Ireland* (London: Jonathan Cape, 1995).
38   Luke Gibbons, *Transformations in Irish Culture* (Cork: Cork University Press, 1996).
39   The current catalogue of these books is available online: <https://www.corkuniversitypress.com/category-s/2076.htm?searching=Y&sort=7 &cat=2076& show=3&page=1>.
40   Seamus Deane et al. (eds), *Field Day Anthology of Irish Writing*, 5 vols (Derry: Field Day, 1991 and 2002).

Christopher Murray, Eoin Ó hAnluain, Tom Paulin, Ian Ross. For Deane, this broadening of the Irish canon by including a raft of previously occluded writing in Irish, Latin and English, right back to medieval times, was an emancipatory exercise which would broaden the whole notion of Irish writing and allow the voice of the colonised to be heard loud and clear across thousands of pages; as he put it, writing 'is a system that produces audiences as well as works of literature'.[41]

In a deconstructive irony, this postcolonial emancipation of the canon which brought to the centre voices hitherto marginalised resulted in a dispute with feminist academics who felt that women's voices had been silenced by this whole project. This resulted in volumes IV and V, with an all-female editorial board (Angela Bourke, Siobhán Kilfeather, Maria Luddy, Margaret Mac Curtain, Gerardine Meaney, Mairín Ní Dhonnchadha, Mary O'Dowd and Clair Wills). The irony here is that the absence of women's writing in scholarly circles would never have come to the fore of academic debate without the *Field Day Anthology*. In many ways, it is through the critiques of the first three volumes that the other two came into being, as a result of demands from the audience of these volumes, an audience created, in part, by those very volumes. The latter volumes can be seen as a supplement to the former, in a Derridean sense in that they are a 'surplus, a plenitude enriching another plenitude, the *fullest measure* of presence'.[42] Secondly, however, these volumes are also filling in a gap, '*in-the-place-of*; if it fills, it is as if one fills a void'.[43] Thus, once the latter volume was published, they both added to the original and altered the epistemological status of the original at the same time. By offering a plurality of linguistic aspects of Irish writing, in Irish, English and Latin, and from both the colonisers and the colonised, the anthology was attempting to follow the same course by providing a plenitude, a culmination of a process of cultural definition. However, by attenuating the role of women in this process, the anthology actually precipitated a moment of disruption, thus leading to

---

41   Deane, *Field Day Anthology of Irish Writing*, I, xxi.
42   Derrida, *Of Grammatology*, 144.
43   *Ibid.*, 145.

volumes four and five at a pragmatic level, and to a further pluralising of the enunciation of Irish writing at an epistemological one.

This process is paradigmatic of the theoretical mode of thinking: there are only practices and processes, never finitudes. The attempt to create a full, self-present canon of Irish writing could never succeed, and indeed, became mired in disputes between postcolonial and feminist theories. In the wake of this issue, Linda Connolly argues, 'The Irish postcolonial framework appears totalising and contextually insensitive due to its inability to recognize the full epistemological potential of Irish feminist scholarship'.[44] Here the theoretical impulse to question and expand the canon was itself deconstructed, and resulted in the creation of a new, more inclusive canon. The fact that this came about through a process of contestation, interrogation, dispute and an attempted resolution is something that is central to what we can call the theoretical imperative. To the reader of 2020 and beyond, the single-gendered lists of editors looks bizarre and anachronistic, but our more enlightened paradigm (though gender parity is not yet achieved and there are still sites of considerable gender-contestation in the academic field) has come about precisely through these contested and interrogated editorial practices and their ongoing theoretical questioning.

This dispute brought feminist theory to the fore, and while consequently, although Irish feminism cannot claim victory in the recent canon-wars of Irish Studies, 'It can at least point to its parallel growth and to its remarkable advances in theory'.[45] It also brought forward a desire to 'mobilise wider conceptual frameworks'[46] across the area as a whole, which in turn led to the current theoretically diverse situation:

> The reality that illustrious postcolonial critics have tended to amalgamate selected aspects of women's history in grand appraisals of Irish culture to the neglect of specialist research on gender, generated by critics (including senior colleagues) in their own primary field (criticism), is perplexing. The in-depth writings of Pat Coughlan, Margaret Kelleher, Moynagh O'Sullivan, Gerardine Meaney, Anne Fogarty, Siobhán

---

44 Linda Connolly, 'The Limits of "Irish Studies": Historicism, Culturalism, Paternalism', *Irish Studies Review* 12, no. 2 (2004), 150.
45 Connolly, 'Limits of "Irish Studies"', 155.
46 Claire Connolly, 'Theorising Ireland', *Irish Studies Review* 9, no. 3 (2001), 307.

Kilfeather, Claire Connolly and other emerging scholars have created a limited impact on what constitutes the prevailing canon and concerns of Irish criticism.[47]

Notions of difference now permeate Irish Studies across all epistemological levels. The voices of women, immigrants, people of colour, the disabled are all now heard and valued; issues of race, class, gender and provenance are out in the open and no longer elephants in the room. The category of 'literature' itself, having been deconstructed by the use of the term 'Irish Studies', is now subject to critique, debate and discussion, and the material and ideological aspects that have been central to the creation of this term are very much to the fore in terms of discussion and debate. The voice of alterity, of the other, a voice hitherto not really heard in the more rigid views of Irish Studies, now blend in a choir (some would say one that can descend into cacophony at times), where different perspectives interact, interchange and interfuse to create a vibrant new discourse. The critical nature of this discourse is gradually permeating Irish society, a society that now seems very far removed from the Ireland of fifty years ago, which was monotheistic, monocultural, monological in terms of religion, ideology and political perspective, and one where issues of social class were seldom discussed.

Contemporary Irish Studies can be seen as an ever-evolving theoretical discourse, open to a plurality of hermeneutic and theoretical approaches and enunciating a polyvocal range of different voices: it no longer looks to voice the other, it now voices a plurality of others. So we can have Tina O'Toole writing about queering the Irish Diaspora,[48] and we can find a book examining the status of Muslim-Irish identities as posing 'a particular challenge to Irish national identity as standing outside conventional definitions of Irishness because of their different race, culture and religion'.[49] Even the aforementioned backward look has now adopted theoretical binoculars, as

---

47   Connolly, 'Limits of "Irish Studies"', 150.
48   Tina O'Toole, 'Cé Leis Tú? Queering Irish Migrant Literature', *Irish University Review* 43, no. 1 (Spring/Summer 2013), Queering the Issue (2013).
49   Oliver Scharbrodt, 'Being Irish, Being Muslim', in *Muslims in Ireland*, edited by Tuula Sakaranaho Oliver Scharbrodt, Adil Hussain Khan, Yafa Shanneik and Vivian Ibrahim (Edinburgh: Edinburgh University Press, 2015), 224.

Nicholas Andrew Miller, writing about Ireland, modernism and memory notes that the 'erotics of memory' explores the theoretical dimensions of memory's cultural function in general by examining the processes of textualisation, narrative and otherwise, through which memory recovers the past.[50] Gerry Smyth moves towards the field of post-modern geography or spatial studies in order to explore how identity 'is never contained in essences; rather, it is maintained through practices'.[51]

Practically all books that explore interdisciplinary and multi-disciplinary areas do so through theoretically informed practices. In *Crossroads: Performance Studies and Irish Culture*,[52] for example, Emily Mark-Fitzgerald speaks of performance theory,[53] while J'aime Morrison uses movement theory as a mode of analysis.[54] E. Moore Quinn avails of liminal theory,[55] Mathew Causey uses cultural theory,[56] while David Cregan employs dance theory.[57] Similarly, in *The Body in Pain in Irish Literature*,[58] we see use made of shame theory,[59] and trauma theory,[60] while Ailbhe McDaid, in her study of the poetics of migration, speaks of Diaspora theory,[61] Diasporic memory theory,[62] and migration theory,[63] as well as making use of notions of posthumanism.[64] There has been a

---

50 Nicholas Andrew Miller, *Modernism, Ireland, and the Erotics of Memory* (Cambridge: Cambridge University Press, 2002), 13.
51 Smyth, *Space and the Irish Cultural Imagination*, 13.
52 Sara Brady and Fintan Walsh, *Crossroads: Performance Studies and Irish Culture* (Basingstoke: Palgrave, 2009).
53 Brady and Walsh, *Crossroads*, 97.
54 Ibid., 75.
55 Ibid., 214.
56 Ibid., 157.
57 Ibid., 122.
58 Fionnuala Dillane, *The Body in Pain in Irish Literature and Culture* (New York: Springer, 2016).
59 Dillane, *The Body in Pain in Irish Literature and Culture*, 152.
60 Ibid., 177.
61 Ailbhe McDaid, *The Poetics of Migration in Contemporary Irish Poetry* (New York: Springer, 2017), 197.
62 Ibid., 1.
63 Ibid., 148.
64 Ibid., 206.

significant seam of research devoted to trauma theory, as can be seen in the following titles *History, Memory, Trauma in Contemporary British and Irish Fiction*, by Beata Piate;⁶⁵ *Trauma and Recovery in the Twenty-First-Century Irish Novel*, by Kathleen Costello-Sullivan;⁶⁶ *The Memory Marketplace: Witnessing Pain in Contemporary Irish and International Theatre*, by Emilie Pine;⁶⁷ and *Trauma and Identity in Contemporary Irish Culture*, by Melania Terrazas Gallego.⁶⁸

Gender, having been marginalised and then brought to the centre in something of a feminist clump in volumes IV and V of the *Field Day Anthology*, now permeates so much of contemporary writing in Irish Studies: one thinks of Mária Kurdi's *Representations of Gender and Female Subjectivity in Contemporary Irish Drama by Women*,⁶⁹ Cathy Leeney's *Seen and Heard: Six New Plays by Irish Women*,⁷⁰ Melissa Sihra's *Women in Irish Drama: A Century of Authorship and Representation*⁷¹ and Mary Trotter's *Ireland's National Theaters: Political Performance and the Origins of the Irish Dramatic Movement*.⁷² Theories of class are also to be found in Paul Murphy's *Hegemony and Fantasy in Irish Drama, 1899-1949*⁷³ and in

---

65   Beata Piątek, *History, Memory, Trauma in Contemporary British and Irish Fiction* (Kraków: Jagiellonian University Press, 2014).
66   Kathleen Costello-Sullivan, *Trauma and Recovery in the Twenty-First-Century Irish Novel* (Syracuse: Syracuse University Press, 2018).
67   Emilie Pine, *The Memory Marketplace: Witnessing Pain in Contemporary Irish and International Theatre* (Bloomington: Indiana University Press, 2020).
68   Melania Terrazas Gallego, *Trauma and Identity in Contemporary Irish Culture* (Oxford: Peter Lang, 2020).
69   Mária Kurdi, *Representations of Gender and Female Subjectivity in Contemporary Irish Drama by Women* (Lewiston: Edwin Mellen Press, 2010).
70   Cathy Leeney et al., *Seen and Heard: Six New Plays by Irish Women* (Dublin: Carysfort Press, 2001).
71   Melissa Sihra, *Women in Irish Drama: A Century of Authorship and Representation* (Basingstoke: Palgrave, 2007).
72   Mary Trotter, *Ireland's National Theaters: Political Performance and the Origins of the Irish Dramatic Movement* (Syracuse: Syracuse University Press, 2001).
73   Paul Murphy, *Hegemony and Fantasy in Irish drama, 1899-1949* (Basingstoke: Palgrave, 2008).

Michael Pierse's *A History of Irish Working-Class Writing*.[74] Developing this theoretical theme, in her 2013 article, Margaret Kelleher speaks of finding new partners for Irish Studies, and seeks:

> a disciplinary diversity that actively seeks to support the continuance of local and sub- jugated knowledges; a reciprocity of shared inter-institutional and intra-institutional resources that pro- motes and rewards meaningful collaboration; and a multilateral complementarity of public and civic engagement that can newly interrogate the enduring question 'whose Irish studies?'[75]

Similarly, ecocriticism and ecotheory have developed in Irish Studies, with books such as Christine Cusick's *Out of the Earth: Ecocritical Readings of Irish Texts*,[76] Eóin Flannery's *Ireland and Ecocriticism: Literature, History and Environmental Justice*,[77] Gerry Smyth's *Space and the Irish Cultural Imagination*,[78] Samuel Solnick's *Poetry and the Anthropocene: Ecology, Biology and Technology in Contemporary British and Irish Poetry*[79] and Eamonn Wall's *Writing the Irish West: Ecologies and Traditions*.[80]

So, in the final analysis, theory and Irish Studies have been mutually imbricated since the beginning; at times, this imbrication has been sporadic and patchy, occasionally one element of theory has been hegemonic to the exclusion of all others, and then there has been debate, discussion and dispute. However, it is to the credit, and I believe to the ultimate benefit of the whole area, that theory has become theories, and that the new and developing theoretical areas of exploration of what it means to

74 Michael Pierse, *A History of Irish Working-Class Writing* (Cambridge: Cambridge University Press, 2017).
75 Margaret Kelleher, 'Finding New Partners: Irish Studies and Its International Futures', *The Irish Review* 46, *Criticism and the Crisis* (2013), 68.
76 Christine Cusick, *Out of the Earth: Ecocritical Readings of Irish Texts* (Cork: Cork University Press, 2010).
77 Eóin Flannery, *Ireland and Ecocriticism: Literature, History and Environmental Justice* (London: Routledge, 2015).
78 Smyth, *Space and the Irish Cultural Imagination*.
79 Sam Solnick, *Poetry and the Anthropocene: Ecology, Biology and Technology in Contemporary British and Irish Poetry* (London: Routledge, 2017).
80 Eamonn Wall, *Writing the Irish West: Ecologies and Traditions* (South Bend, Indiana: University of Notre Dame Press, 2011).

be human, have found a welcoming home in the area of Irish Studies. Questions keep being asked and people come up with new answers which themselves become interrogated by yet more questions: it is a healthy and vigorous process. As an exemplar of the rude health of this theoretically-driven area, one need only look at the catalogue of the series in which this book appears, *Reimagining Ireland*, edited by Eamon Maher, to see the sheer range and diversity of multitheoretical approaches that are now the norm in Irish Studies, spanning over 100 volumes dealing with:

> Irish writing in English and Irish, Nationalism, Unionism, the Northern Troubles, the Peace Process, economic development in Ireland, the impact and decline of the Celtic Tiger, Irish spirituality, the rise and fall of organised religion, the visual arts, popular cultures, sport, Irish music and dance, emigration and the Irish diaspora, immigration and multiculturalism, marginalisation, globalisation, modernity/postmodernity and postcolonialism.[81]

May those debates, discussions and disputes continue *ad infinitum*.

---

81   The full catalogue of these books (at present 100 volumes) is available online: <https://www.peterlang.com/view/serial/REIR>.

MARGUÉRITE CORPORAAL

19 'The Words Will Come': Today's Legacies of the Great Irish Famine[1]

'As we confront a pandemic today, let us recall that the Great Famine was a public health emergency in its own right'. Thus argued Ireland's Minister for Culture, Heritage and the Gaeltacht, Josepha Madigan, at the sober but impressive ceremony to commemorate Ireland's Great Famine, on 18 May 2020. Her words reveal the relevance of historical and cultural legacies of the Famine in our present time, as we face the global Covid-19 crisis. Indeed, the Minister's speech drew parallels between the heroic fortitude shown by 'the doctors and nurses of the fever hospitals, in and outside Ireland, who risked their own lives to care for others' and 'the same qualities of courage and commitment to others in our healthcare staff today'.[2] The high rate of mortality in Ireland as well as across the world, caused by Covid-19, evokes memories of the outbreak of typhus, dysentery and the dreaded famine fever in famine-stricken Ireland,[3] as well as recollections of the religious orders who

---

1   The research for this chapter was funded by the Dutch Research Council, NWO, as part of the NWA-ORC project, *Heritages of Hunger: Societal Reflections on Past European Famines in Education, Commemoration and Musealisation* (NWA.1160. 18.197).
2   Available online: <https://www.chg.gov.ie/speech/speech-by-minister-for-culture-heritage-and-the-gaeltacht-josepha-madigan-t-d-at-the-national-famine-commemoration-2020/> [accessed 23 July 2020].
3   See, for example, Cormac Ó Gráda, *Black '47 and Beyond: The Great Irish Famine in History, Economy, and Memory* (Princeton: Princeton University Press, 2000), 88, 94–95; and Andrés Eiríksson, 'Paupers and Beggars Brats: Parsonstown Workhouse and Union Policy during the Famine', in *The Great Irish Famine and Social Class: Conflicts, Responsibilities, Representations*, edited by Marguérite Corporaal and Peter Gray (Oxford & New York: Peter Lang, 2019), 173–203.

nursed the severely diseased, newly arrived emigrants in the quarantine stations in, for example, Montreal.[4] Current remediations of the Famine past in the public sphere therefore, testify to the inherent fluidity of performances of memory which, as Astrid Erll observes, can travel through time and space, 'across [...] and also beyond cultures'.[5]

In our introduction to *Global Legacies of the Great Irish Famine* (2014) in the *Reimagining Ireland* series, Christopher Cusack, Lindsay Janssen and I concluded that, 'The cultural legacies of the Great Irish Famine continue to play a fundamental role in public discourse well into the twenty-first century'.[6] Six years on, this observation appears to have been prophetic, for the official annual Famine commemorations in Ireland were by no means the only recent occasions during which recollections of the catastrophe exerted an influence on ongoing public debates. Three years ago, when hunger and destitution affected people in South Sudan, Yemen and Somalia, the media raised questions about the responsibility of the Irish in offering relief in light of the starvation and deprivation endured by their ancestors in the 1840s. Thus, Dominic MacSorley, chief executive of Concern Worldwide, argued in *The Irish Times* of 27 March 2017 that, 'Ireland with its own tragic experience of both conflict and hunger [...] has afforded us an authoritative humanitarian voice, but also a responsibility'.[7] The drowning of migrants in the Mediterranean also generated a sense of awareness that Ireland too had

---

4   For further reading on this, see Mark McGowan, *Death or Canada: The Great Famine Migration and Toronto, 1847* (Toronto: Novalis-Bayard, 2009); and Jason King, 'The Remembrance of Irish Famine Migrants in the Fever Sheds of Montreal', in *Global Legacies of the Irish Famine: Interdisciplinary and Transcultural Perspectives*, edited by Marguérite Corporaal, Christopher Cusack, Lindsay Janssen (Oxford & New York: Peter Lang, 2014), 245–266.

5   Astrid Erll, 'Travelling Memory', in *Transcultural Memory*, edited by Rick Crownshaw (London: Routledge, 2014), 20.

6   Marguérite Corporaal, Christopher Cusack and Lindsay Janssen, 'Introduction', in *Global Legacies of the Great Irish Famine: Transnational and Interdisciplinary Perspectives*, 14.

7   Dominic MacSorley, 'South Sudan Famine Results from Failure of Political Will', *The Irish Times*, 27 March 2017, available online: <https://www.irishtimes.com/opinion/south-sudan-famine-results-from-failure-of-political-will-1.3022458> [accessed 30 July 2020].

been a country of refugees that had found new homes across the world. In 2015 Rowan Gillespie's Famine monument at Dublin's Custom House Quay even became the site of pro-refugee demonstrations,[8] thereby revealing the significance of the historical Famine in relation to today's global problems and our sense of 'historical duty'.[9] Moreover, at the height of the Covid-19 pandemic, Irish communities donated generously to the afflicted Hopi and Navajo tribes, to honour the memory of the $170 gift the Choctaw nation collected for Famine-stricken Ireland in 1847.[10]

As these examples illustrate, Famine memory today is not only what M. Jacqui Alexander has called 'palimpsestic', in the sense that past and present times appear to coalesce, and present generations are often able to identify with the plights of their ancestors.[11] The Famine also constitutes what Michael Rothberg calls 'multidirectional memory',[12] a form of remembrance operating in interaction with the experiences and memories of other cultural communities, in different times. Recent heritage initiatives have, furthermore, emphasised the transnational nature of the Famine past, through transatlantic collaborations with museums and institutes or through a specific focus on Famine migration histories. Thus, the Great Famine Voices roadshow, a project organised by Strokestown Park Famine Museum, the Irish Heritage Trust and the Quinnipiac Great Hunger Institute, has hosted events at, amongst others, Ireland Park Foundation in Toronto and Parkway central Library in Philadelphia.[13]

8   See David Kearns, 'Thousands Turn Out in Dublin and across Europe for Refugee Support Rally', *The Irish Times*, 12 September 2015, available online: <https://www.independent.ie/irish-news/thousands-turn-out-in-dublin-and-across-europe-for-refugee-support-rally-31522118.html> [accessed 29 July 2020].

9   For this concept in relation to refugees in Ireland, see Charlotte McIvor, 'Historical Duty, Palimpsestic Time and Migration in the Decade of Centenaries', *Irish Studies Review* 24, no. 1 (2016), 49–66.

10 Ed O'Loughlin and Mihi Zaveri, 'Irish Return an Old Favor', *The New York Times*, 5 May 2020. Available online: <https://www.nytimes.com/2020/05/05/world/coronavirus-ireland-native-american-tribes.html> [accessed 18 June 2020].

11 M. Jacqui Alexander, *Pedagogies of Crossing: Meditations on Feminism, Sexual Politics, Memory and the Sacred* (Durham: Duke University Press, 2005).

12 Michael Rothberg, *Multidirectional Memory* (Stanford; Stanford University Press, 2009), 11.

13 Available online: <http://greatfaminevoices.ie/> [accessed 18 June 2020].

The unveiling of a monument in Ballina, in commemoration of orphan girls from the local workhouse shipped to Australia (2019), and the launch of the National Famine Way (2019), a heritage trail to commemorate the poignant walk made by 1,490 famine emigrants from Strokestown Park to emigrant ships in Dublin in 1847,[14] illustrate the centrality of migration narratives to contemporary heritage construction. The fact that today the Great Famine is not so much what French philosopher Pierre Nora would call 'history', but 'memory', a living past,[15] also becomes clear from the ongoing production of Famine literature and cinema. The boom in Famine memory has not reached its point of saturation yet; quite the contrary, in fact. Recently, for example, the Irish-language Famine film *Arracht*, which premiered at the Talinn Black Nights Film festival in November 2019, won the Audience Award at the Glasgow Film Festival.[16] This chapter will therefore investigate recent cultural expressions about the Famine, focusing on the question of which developments in Famine memory they bear witness to. How do these literary and cinematic mediations of the Famine past from the 2010s and 2020 for instance reflect upon earlier visual and textual repertoires related to this period of wide-scale starvation?

Looking for an answer to this question, this study examines three Famine novels by Colum McCann, Paul Lynch and Marita Conlon-McKenna, as well as Lance Daly's internationally successful film *Black '47* (2018). It will be argued that these texts and this feature film reflect very explicitly on processes of trauma and memorialisation, while also displaying consciousness of a vast array of historical Famine representations that can be recycled.

---

14 Available online: <http://www.nationalfamineway.ie/> [accessed 18 June 2020].
15 Pierre Nora, 'Between Memory and History: *Les Lieux de Mémoire*', *Representations* 26 (1989), 9.
16 Michael Rosser, '"Arracht" Wins Glasgow Audience Award; Festival Draws Record Admissions', *Screen Daily*, 9 March 2020, available online: <https://www.screendaily.com/news/arracht-wins-glasgow-audience-award-festival-draws-record-admissions/5 147927.article> [accessed 29 July 2020].

Today's Famine Legacies: Representing Trauma

The Famine has primarily been associated with 'cultural trauma', and, as Emily Mark-FitzGerald contends, this notion of Famine trauma that involves 'a pathway towards some form of cultural rehabilitation', has had a 'pervasive influence on commemorative discourse and public monuments'.[17] This traumatic paradigm that is rooted in the assumption of a long silence about the Famine has for some time blinded scholars to the existence of early Famine literature.[18] Nonetheless, the trauma that the Famine inevitably caused to those who had to live through it, is a subject specifically addressed in recent Famine novels. In Marita Conlon-McKenna's *The Hungry Road* (2020), which is set in Skibbereen, the Union physician's wife and mother of a large family, Henrietta Donovan, suffers aftershocks when she finds a starving mother holding her dead infant on the town's main street. Henrietta cannot forget the 'terrible fear' that 'gripped her' when she sees the famished child: 'The small face was waxy, the skin almost translucent, with a blue sheen around its delicate lips and closed eyes'.[19] Subsequently, Henrietta is haunted in her dreams by the figure of Catherine Driscoll and her baby, and succumbs to despondency and temporary feelings of depression.

The 14-year-old protagonist in Paul Lynch's *Grace* is also tormented by spectres; in fact, the novel almost reads like a handbook on the effects of trauma and the process towards healing. Scholars in trauma and memory studies have often viewed spectres as expressions of the procession of painful pasts. For example, Dylan Trigg states that in the interaction between remembrance and repression, painful pasts resurface suddenly like unwelcome ghosts that establish, 'a portal between the past and the present'.[20] As such, the spectre which vanishes and re-emerges at random

---

17 Emily Mark-FitzGerald, *Commemorating the Irish Famine: Memory and the Monument* (Liverpool: Liverpool University Press, 2013), 8.
18 See also Marguérite Corporaal, *Relocated Memories: The Great Famine in Irish and Diaspora Fiction, 1846-70* (Syracuse: Syracuse University Press, 2017), 6–9.
19 Marita Conlon-McKenna, *The Hungry Road* (Dublin: Transworld, 2020), 125.
20 Dylan Trigg, 'The Place of Trauma: Memory, Hauntings, and the Temporality of Ruins', *Memory Studies* 2 (2009), 99.

can symbolise traumatic memory which, Cathy Caruth argues, resurfaces in 'delayed, and uncontrolled, repetitive occurrence'.[21]

Lynch's novel explicitly comments on trauma through the theme of spectrality. Grace is dressed up as a boy by her mother, is told to be 'the strong one now' and to go out on the road to fend for herself.[22] Her mother Sarah can no longer feed her, but nevertheless tries to protect her eldest daughter against sexual assault by her abusive lover Boggs, who began to take an unhealthy interest in the teenage girl. Through the harrowing situations she faces, Grace is haunted, on several occasions; for example, by the ghost of a woman she calls Mary Breshner. This spectral presence is modelled on the young mother that McNutt shot dead when he, Grace and her friend Bart attempted to rob a coach. Grace's repressed feelings of shock and guilt about being implicated in the assassination of a young infant's mother, leaving the baby with no one to care for, manifests itself in her seeing the apparition of the woman several times. Towards the end of the novel Grace is also haunted by her mother: 'Then the sudden day when she hears her mother calling for her as if from afar. Hears her mother's voice in the woods. Hears her in the narrowed dark of the room.'[23] Grace thus has to struggle with her pain about her mother's abandonment of her so she had to brave the dire conditions of famine all by herself. The spectre most prominent in the novel is that of Grace's younger brother Colly, who decides to join Grace when she is sent away, but then drowns in the river as he attempts to drag out the carcass of a cow. After his death, Colly 'travels' along with Grace, as a voice in her head which continuously comments on the events that she goes through, which admonishes her to act, and even as a voice that distorts her own consciousness, saying things that are disturbing or improper. In a scene in which Grace has to rebury the corpse of an old woman she found in a cottage where she looked for shelter, we can see that Grace tries to dissociate herself from the horrors she faces, only to find that she is incapable of blocking certain distressing details from her mind. Grace 'does not remember how she spaded the corpse onto the jute sack. Her eyes

---

[21] Cathy Caruth, *Unclaimed Experience: Trauma, Narrative, and History* (Baltimore: Johns Hopkins University Press, 1996), 181.
[22] Paul Lynch, *Grace* (London: Oneworld Publications, 2017), 12.
[23] *Ibid.*, 281.

shut and watering to the smell, her coat knotted to her mouth', but at the same time, 'Her mind holds a perfect picture – that what lies on the sack is a very old woman, dead as dead is, her body shrivelled to just a coating of skin, her rags falling away from jut-ribs'.[24] Colly – as a split off entity from Grace– comments explicitly on the cruelty of the dogs that had dug up and gnawed at the woman's body: 'Colly says, that dog was getting its revenge, the woman tried to eat it, so she did, it is only natural for the dog to feed on her or the other creatures in the wood, for that's what they do, a dead person is all the same to them'.[25] Colly, as is clear, serves as a projection through which Grace can mediate her disturbing experiences.

When hunger eventually drives Grace frantic and she sees no other way but to eat the flesh of a dead body herself, Lynch's narrative renders an inner monologue by Grace which bears evidence of her self-alienation and trauma. The first-person narrator that is introduced, obviously Grace herself, states that, 'Grace is dead' while she hears a 'laughing' that 'sounds like Grace'. The train of thought is disrupted and fragmented, showing that the speaker is disgusted by the meat she will taste while also trying to convince herself she should eat it:

> Sicky feeling all over just the smell of it and – who is that – dog again – dog digger digging at the ground where did that other dog come from [...] don't sick all over yourself the smell – there it is now bring to mouth – chew it off the bone will you – it is meat is it not? [...] tell yourself I said – it is cow – yes it is cow – it is bull – yes it is bull – what else is it.[26]

The scene is followed by a number of pitch-black pages without text. The novel seems to suggest that either Grace has lapsed into unconsciousness, or that the horrors of cannibalism are too harrowing and have to be eradicated from her mind. In the subsequent chapter it appears that Grace has been taken in by a religious sect which has nursed her back to health, but Grace has lost her capacity for speech: 'She wonders [...] if God will loosen her tongue when the world starts to listen and when might this be

---

24 Ibid., 113.
25 Ibid., 119.
26 Ibid., 235.

so?'[27] It is only years later when Grace is happily married, has wrestled with her mother's ghost, and is pregnant with her first child, that she regains her voice, even though she will not speak about the traumatic Famine years: '[Y]es, I will speak, the words will come and I will speak of what is now, of only this'. In so doing, she can experience a spiritual rebirth herself and embrace a future existence of bliss and fortune: 'This life is light'.[28]

Enactments of Memory

The discourse of trauma clearly surrounds contemporary cultural expressions of the Famine past. In an interview with *The Journal* on 8 September 2018, director Lance Daly talks about what he called the 'Famine' curse that surrounded the making of his film *Black '47*. The process was not just problematic because of the intensive action done on horseback, working in two languages and the recourse to, 'gunpowder and loads of stunts', but also because the trauma of hunger is so challenging to convey: '[I]t's hard because of how terrible a story it was to start with'.[29] The difficulty that Daly describes of representing famine as a phenomenon was an issue that nineteenth-century writers and artists also faced but managed to overcome by adopting narrative and visual strategies

Interestingly, recent novels and cinema convey an explicit awareness of the fact that they are performances of memory, embedded in longstanding traditions of 'narrative templates' and visual imagery concerning the Great Famine that have framed and provided interpretation of the event.[30] Memory scholars have not only directed their attention to

27   *Ibid.*, 250.
28   *Ibid.*, 283.
29   '"I Felt Like There Was a Curse Over the Thing": What It Was Like Making Ireland's First Famine Feature Film', 8 September 2018. Available online: <https://www.thejournal.ie/interview-lance-daly-black-47-4221694-Sep2018/> [accessed 29 July 2020].
30   For the term 'narrative templates', see James V. Wertsch, *Voices of Collective Remembering* (New York: Cambridge University Press, 2002), 6.

transgenerational mediations of the past, but also to what Astrid Erll calls the 'plurimedial production of travelling schemata':[31] the transmission of images and narratives that shape the past across various media of remembrance. This perspective is relevant in examining recent Famine novels and film which borrow Famine images, tropes and templates from earlier times – from engravings to fiction and then into cinema, for example, across the boundaries of form and genre. *Black '47* taps into these registers, narrative plotlines and images from the past in representing the effects of starvation.

Figure 19.1. Still from Lance Daly, *Black '47* September 5, 2018 (Ireland); Director: Lance Daly; Screenplay: Lance Daly, Pierce Ryan, P.J. Dillon; Producers: Macdara Kelleher, Tim O'Hair, Jonathan Loughran, Arcadiy Golubovich.

---

31   Astrid Erll, available online: 'From 'District Six' to District 9 and Back: The Plurimedial Production of Travelling Schemata' https://warwick.ac.uk/fac/cross_fac/ehrc/events/memory/rigney_transnational_memory.pdf [accessed 29 July 2020], in *Transnational Memory: Circulation, Articulation, Scales*, edited by Chiara de Cesari and Ann Rigney (Berlin/New York: de Gruyter 2014), 29–50.

Figure 19.2. *Bridget O'Donnell and Children* (1849). *Illustrated London News*, 22 December 1849. Engraving. High resolution image of Ireland's Great Hunger Museum, Quinnipiac University, Hamden, Connecticut.

The opening scene expresses the idea of mass famine through a zoom shot of a skull lying in a puddle of water. The range of greys strongly remind one of the engravings made by Cork artist James Mahoney for *The Illustrated London News* – one of the earliest visual reports of the dire conditions in blight-stricken Ireland, though Mahoney himself would not depict famished corpses. Indeed, one of the iconic engravings attributed to Mahoney, *Bridget O'Donnell and her Children*, printed in *Illustrated London News* on 22 February 1849, depicts the emaciated figures of a mother and two children, and is often interpreted as symptomatic of what Margaret Kelleher calls the 'feminization of famine':[32] the tendency to focus on female characters – especially mothers – in early representations of the Famine. Furthermore, early Famine fiction often portrays mothers who have to brave the Famine single-handedly and fail to procure nourishment for their children. Thus, in Mrs Hoare's story, 'The Black Potatoes' (1851), Jude Mahoney sees her children starve to death one by one as they wander around. Eventually they come back to the ruins of what was once their cottage and it is there that her brother-in-law James finds the widow, overwhelmed by hunger and presenting an 'awful scene'.[33]

Daly's film reproduces this image when the main character, former Connaught ranger Martin Feeney, enters the ruin of a cottage, which appears to be the abode from which his sister Ellie and her family had previously been evicted. Inside, unprotected against frost and wind, he finds a mother and child there, starved and frozen to death, that seem to be Ellie and her young son. The camera shot, which zooms in on their still figures, clearly echoes early visual representations about the Famine, such as Mahoney's illustration and Mrs Hoare's tale.

That *Black '47* is strongly indebted to nineteenth-century cultural repertoires in its attempt to represent mass starvation, also becomes clear from another key scene, in which Martin and his sister Ellie approach a number of dwellings from which the inhabitants have clearly been evicted. The camera's perspective on the ruined cottages appears to replicate the illustration

---

32   Margaret Kelleher, *The Feminization of Famine* (Durham: Duke University Press, 1997), 6.
33   Mrs Hoare, 'The Black Potatoes', in *Shamrock Leaves; or Tales and Sketches from Ireland* (Dublin and London: J. M'Glashan, Patrick and Oakey, 1851), 49.

Village of Moveen from *The Illustrated London News* of 22 December 1849, which shows the remnants of a deserted community. Such depictions of ruins were all too common in those days: William Carleton's *The Squanders of Castle Squander* (1852) sketches the depopulated villages, 'where a few dying wretches … are crawling or lying beside the ruins' of their former homes,[34] thereby aligning the wrecked cottages with the devastations of a people ruined by the potato blight.

Figure 19.3. *Village of Moveen* from *The Illustrated London News* of 22 December 1849. High resolution image courtesy of Ireland's Great Hunger Museum, Hamden, Connecticut.

This specific scene from *Black '47* is even more interesting because Martin and Ellie speak Irish to each other while wandering around the bleak, depopulated landscape, a fact which underscores the loss of Irish traditions as the rural population dies or moves away. Indeed, it can be argued that *Black '47* situates this demise of rural communities in a context of language oppression, not just by the Famine itself, but by those associated with British rule. A man stealing food to prevent his family from dying, and only able to communicate in Irish when appearing before Judge Bolton,

---

34 William Carleton, *The Squanders of Castle Squander* (London: Office of the Illustrated London Library, 1852), vol. 2, 235.

is denied proper defence: 'English is the language of this court, Mr. O'Sé'. Feeney, who eventually kills the judge to avenge his brother's hanging, in turn refuses Bolton the opportunity to state his case, as the language in his court of revenge is Irish: 'Ach anois tá tú ag dul chun cabhrú liom a shábháil mo chara'.[35] Landlord Kilmartin even denounces Irish as 'aboriginal nonsense' he does not care to understand. That language issues are so central to the plot of Famine suffering in *Black '47* is even more intriguing in view of the conflict between the DUP and Sinn Féin about an Irish Language Act at the time the film was released. Thus, existing cultural templates about the Famine are reused to engage with contemporary political issues.

In recent Famine fiction, we also see several examples of explicit borrowings from nineteenth-century cultural repertoires. McKenna's *The Hungry Road* contains a scene in which Doctor Dan Donovan conducts a post-mortem on, 'the emaciated corpse of Denis McKennedy, a labourer on the relief roadworks', for the coroner's inquest.[36] The condition of the starved body is rendered in disturbing detail, as Donovan notes that 'the corpse was lacking any sign of muscle or fatty tissue [...] There was no trace of fat anywhere around the abdomen and scarcely a vestige of omentum. All the adipose matter had been absorbed by the body'.[37] The clinical analysis of the Famine victim provided in the narrative resonates with similar, equally explicit scenes in early Famine literature. For example, the novel *O'Ruark* (1852) by Henry Monahan minutely portrays the bodily features of a famine victim during a coroner's inquest: 'The shrivelled hands; the sharp-pointed face with the yellow skin tightly drawn over it; the fleshless, worn body; these, indeed, placed beyond all doubt what the poor wretch had died of'.[38]

Interestingly, in both novels this inquest scene is followed by critique on the inadequacies of local policies. In *O'Ruark* the narrative shows that the jurors are unaffected by the spectacle of depravity that lies before them: 'Annoyed at having been taken away from their business at the fair',

---

35   'But now you are going to help me to save my friend'.
36   McKenna, *The Hungry Road*, 95.
37   Ibid., 96.
38   Henry J. Monahan, *O'Ruark; or Chronicles of the Balliquin Family* (Dublin: James Duffy, 1852), 268.

they order 'spirits and water', which they 'all seemed to drink […] with as much pleasure as if a corpse did not lie on the table before them'.[39] Those invested with authority could not care less about the conditions that caused the man's death, as the omniscient narrator ironically comments. In *The Hungry Road* the inquest offers Dan Donovan a platform to express public critique on the mismanagement of the public works, which results in the labourers not receiving the promised payment in a timely fashion. Dan testifies that: 'It's appalling that another good man was forced to walk miles and do heavy laboring work for a pittance without any sustenance and nourishment. This travesty cannot continue!'[40]

McKenna's novel even more explicitly situates itself in a repertoire of cultural memory through its inclusion of artists and writers who lived during the Famine, but here figure as fictional characters. Father Fitzpatrick is visited by George Boyle and Lord Dufferin, two students who travelled from Oxford to Skibbereen, who are known as the authors of a widely read travel account.[41] A few weeks later, the priest receives, 'a published copy of their journey from Oxford to Skibbereen, with the young Frederick Blackwood promising him that all the proceeds from their work would be donated to Skibbereen'.[42] Through this intertextual reference, *The Hungry Road* connects itself to writings from the Famine era. Additionally, the illustrator James Mahoney features in the novel as a character who joins Dan and a colleague on their sick rounds, and who draws sketches of the suffering he witnesses in Skibbereen. McKenna lets her character Mahoney speak about a 'poor woman [who] was carrying the corpse of a fine child in her arms' whom he encounters in Clonakilty. This woman, Mahoney states, 'was begging alms of us passengers to purchase a coffin to bury her dear little baby', an awful sight he 'will never forget'.[43] *Woman Begging at Clonakilty* is one of the engravings that Mahoney made for *The Illustrated*

---

39   Ibid., 267–268.
40   McKenna, *The Hungry Road*, 96.
41   Lord Dufferin and G. G. Boyle, *Narrative of a Journey from Oxford to Skibbereen, in the Year of the Famine* (Oxford: John Henry Parker, 1847).
42   McKenna, *The Hungry Road*, 193.
43   Ibid., 175.

London News of 13 February 1847, and McKenna's novel recollects this image through this dialogue between Mahoney and Donovan.

Figure 19.4. James Mahoney, *Woman Begging at Clonakilty*. *Illustrated London News*, 13 February 1847. Engraving. High resolution image courtesy of Ireland's Great Hunger Museum, Quinnipiac University, Hamden, Connecticut.

This famous illustration by Mahoney is more implicitly referenced as remembered Famine repertoire in Colum McCann's novel *TransAtlantic* (2013). Part of the novel revolves around Frederick Douglass's visit to Ireland in late 1845, where he lectures, promotes his book and, as a runaway slave, seeks support for the US Abolitionist movement. Horrified by the depravity and hunger he witnesses among the Irish, Douglass at one point is confronted with the gruesome appearance of a woman who thrusts her dead infant forward, as if the child were still alive and could still be saved: 'She flopped the child's arm out again and massaged the dead baby's fingers. The insides of its wrists were already darkening'.[44] This scene is strongly reminiscent of Mahoney's illustration.

TransAtlantic not only evokes and remediates Famine images such as Mahoney's engraving, but also comments on memory as a multidirectional process which may create potential for what Rothberg sees as essential components of remembrance: 'affect' and 'solidarity'.[45] McCann's Douglass is strongly affected by the scenes of suffering he encounters, and in his mind draws analogies between the conditions of the Irish and the American plantation slaves. Douglass is strongly aware of the uniqueness of both contexts: the Irish are in his view poor but 'not enslaved', an 'ownership of man and woman' he considers 'beyond toleration'.[46] At the same time he feels immense sympathy and shock for the abject state of the Irish, and the crowds which he addresses intimate they share a common cause: 'What about England? Would he not denounce England? Wasn't England the slave master anyway?'[47] The Liberator even calls Douglass the 'black O'Connell' in front of his audience.[48] The novel thus expresses awareness of how memories of the Famine and US slavery may intersect, and interestingly, in so doing, the text builds forth upon a tradition of interacting memory cultures that already existed in the 1860s. For example, Reginald Tierney in *The Struggles of Dick Massey* (1860) explicitly addressed Harriet Beecher Stowe to inform her and his readers that, 'for the one slave that has been lashed to death by his master, there have been a hundred Irishmen drowned by their landlords',[49] when forced to look for new homes in the New World on coffin ships.

---

44 Colum McCann, *TransAtlantic* (New York: Random House, 2013), 37.
45 Michael Rothberg, *The Implicated Subject: Beyond Victims and Perpetrators* (Stanford: Stanford University Press, 2019), 125–126.
46 McCann, *TransAtlantic*, 81.
47 *Ibid.*, 60.
48 *Ibid.*, 29.
49 Reginald Tierney, *The Struggles of Dick Massey; Or, The Battles of a Boy* (Dublin: James Duffy, 1860), 376.

'There isn't a story in the world that isn't in part, at least, addressed to the past'.[50] This reflection from McCann's prize-winning *TransAtlantic* suggests that the narratives we tell about ourselves and our pasts always reach back into the recesses of history. Today, novelists and filmmakers are clearly inspired by these past repertoires, especially in representing starvation and depopulation. Even more specifically, however, the texts and film discussed in this chapter display an awareness of their own implication in acts of remembrance and a consciousness of the dynamics of trauma processing that have become well-engrained in academic and public debates. This fits in with a larger tendency in the public sphere to reflect upon museum and commemoration practices: Minister Madigan unveiled a plaque to mark the first Famine commemoration at Dublin Castle in May 2008, thereby placing the 2020 commemoration in a chain of memorialising acts. How we remember the Famine is consequently made visible, and this may create an incentive for researching heritage practices in Irish Famine studies. It is not unthinkable that present-day developments such as 'Black Lives Matter' and the aftermath of Covid-19 will further impact our understanding of processes of remembrance, as will the present turn in academia to look beyond victims and perpetrators in patterns of recollection.[51] Famine researchers may moreover investigate both older and new expressions of multidirectional memory concerning the Famine, as can be seen in the publication of *Famine Pots: The Choctaw–Irish Gift Exchange, 1847–Present* (2020), a collection of essays and poems that reflect on the significance of a donation of $170 made to the Irish population by the Choctaw nation in 1847, and that brings the Famine past back to life from two perspectives, through a veritable blend of cultures and languages across national borders.[52] That Famine memory is such a dynamic phenomenon that it may well encourage us to anticipate new frontiers in any subsequent developments associated with it.

50   McCann, *TransAtlantic*, 295.
51   See Michale Rothberg, *The Implicated Subject: Beyond Victims and Perpetrators* (Stanford: Stanford University Press, 2019).
52   LeAnn Howes and Padraig Kirwan, eds, *Famine Pots: The Choctaw–Irish Gift Exchange, 1847–Present* (Ann Arbor: Michigan State University Press, 2020).

MICHAEL CRONIN

20 Language, Time and the Improbable in Contemporary Ireland

Utopias are often not only situated on islands. They are frequently the preoccupation of islanders. Thomas More, an Englishman, will imagine his sixteenth-century utopia as an island society. When the Gaelic chieftain and writer Maghnus Ó Domhnaill (1490–1564) in the same period wants to conjure up a vision of beauty and plenty in his prose piece *Turas go O'Brazeel*, he seeks out the island of Hy-Brazil, reputed to be off the west coast of Ireland. One of the most influential accounts of utopia in the medieval period is attributed to the Irish monk, St Brendan, and his *Navigatio Sancti Brendani* seeks out the Isle of the Blessed as the utopian end stop for his tired comrades. Brendan has a guide in the form of the Procurator who ultimately leads the Munster saint to the promised island:

> At the end of forty days, towards evening, a dense cloud overshadowed them, so dark that they could scarce see one another. Then the procurator said to St Brendan: 'Do you know, father, what darkness is this?' And the saint replied that he knew not. 'This darkness', said he, 'surrounds the island you have sought for seven years; you will soon see that it is the entrance to it'; and after an hour had elapsed a great light shone around them, and the boat stood by the shore.[1]

I would like to suggest that a consideration of the public role of modern languages in contemporary Ireland is long overdue and the almost total absence of modern language scholars from public intellectual debate in Ireland means that we are neglecting important utopian dimensions to

1 P. F. Moran, *Navigatio sancti Brendani abbatis* (1893), translated by Denis O'Donoghue, available online: <https://markjberry.blogs.com/StBrendan.pdf > [accessed 25 January 2019].

the acquisition and practice of these languages. In doing this, I am bearing in mind what Theodor Adorno says at the end of his *Negative Dialectics*, namely, that nothing can be saved by leaping to its defence.[2] Only that can be changed can be saved. In other words, defending modern languages in Ireland by saying that it is good for Irish business, good for Irish tourism and good for civic tolerance (it is good for all of these things), may not be enough. It may be time to transform how we think about saving modern languages and a core element of that transformation is indeed the question of time itself. In examining time and modern languages in Ireland, I want to consider two regimes, the regime of time itself and the allied regime of attention.

Regime of Time

The German sociologist Hartmut Rosa[3] speaks of the fundamental social formation of modernity which is oriented towards an ever-accelerating culture of infinite growth. The increasingly rapid accumulation of resources is based on a basic reorientation in modernity away from a society where there were fixed or pre-ordained positions or ranks in life towards a society where there is basically a privatisation of what constitutes the good life. What Rosa means by this is that each individual must determine what the good life is and organise access to the resources – health, wealth, human connections – that will ensure that this life becomes a possibility. The difficulty for the modern self, however, is twofold.

Firstly, getting access to resources gets more and more fraught as the basic principle of competition in contemporary societies means that the individuals are constantly asked to reinvent themselves – to become smarter, fitter, healthier, more performative – in an increasingly accelerated cycle of

---

2   Theodore Adorno, *Negative Dialectics*, translated by E. B. Ashton (London: Routledge, 2004), 391.
3   Hartmut Rosa, *Resonanz: Eine Soziologie der Weltbeziehung* (Berlin: Suhrkamp, 2016).

entrepreneurial self-invention. It is no accident, in this respect, that three of the nominees for the Irish Presidential elections in 2018 – the highest office in the land – were veterans of *The Dragon's Den*, the Irish television programme modelled on *The Apprentice*. *The Dragon's Den* was throughout the quintessential expression of an unbridled social Darwinism (the weak go to the wall) and the celebration of a culture of accelerated performativity. Secondly, the fixation on resources becomes an end in itself so that what these resources might be for is lost sight of and the increasingly desperate effort to procure the resources means that the ends they serve – physical, mental and social well-being – are increasingly remote. The faster you go, in effect, the more instrumental your relationship to self and your environment. You have less time to attend to your inner self and to your external world. The social consequences are a triple form of dissonance, ecological, social and psychological. Ecological, because the kinetic inferno of material growth ignores the limits to the natural sustainability of the planet. Social, because the dehumanisation of technological and market instrumentalism mean that more and more citizens feel left behind in the backwaters of political exclusion. Psychological, because the explosion of mental health issues in contemporary societies and the anti-depressants epidemic in the developed world detailed by Mark Fisher in *Capitalist Realism* point to the heavy toll on individual well-being of the pumping iron productivism of the modern corporatised workplace.[4] The question that might asked then is where do we situate modern languages in contemporary Ireland? Should modern languages be considered a resource in a logic of accelerated accumulation that will you make you richer, smarter, faster? Should they be subsumed to the extractivist logic of a pragmatic instrument used to capture or exploit foreign resources?

There is, of course, an immediate difficulty with this approach. The basic problem with language learning is that it requires time. Lots of it. As many unthumbed later chapters of language manuals attest, language acquisition is not for the faint-hearted. Students of modern languages are constantly ambushed by the old dictum that the more you know, the more

---

4   Mark Fisher, *Capitalist Realism: Is There No Alternative?* (Washington: Zero Books, 2009).

you know you don't know. As the applied linguist David Little pointed out in a lecture on the 5 October 2018 in University College Dublin on the Common European Framework of Reference for Languages (CEFR), as you move from level A1 to A2 and from level A2 to B1 each step requires, not an arithmetical, but a geometrical progression in the amount of time necessary to master the different skills. There is then, I would argue, a fundamental tension between what I have called elsewhere the instantaneous time of digital modernity and durational time of second language acquisition.[5] Indeed, arguably one of the major problems we have as advocates of modern languages in Ireland is that what we are proposing is seriously out of synch with the temporal regime of late modernity. However, what would happen if this problem was to become part of the solution? If, instead of trying to pass off language learning as something it is not – a quick fix – we were to make a virtue of its irreducible difference? That is, if we accept as we must, that acquiring an effective degree of proficiency in a foreign language requires an inescapable commitment to the long term, what are the consequences?

The first consequence is for the language policy itself. *Languages Connect*, the official Irish government policy document on modern languages, published in 2017, contained much of value.[6] From a durational perspective, however, the need is to make *Languages Connect* reconnect. Language learning at second level needs to be linked to language learning at primary and tertiary level. There needs to be an immediate restoration and expansion of the Modern Languages in Primary Schools Initiative, abandoned during the austerity period and never reinstated. At tertiary level there needs to be the development of modern language policies that are similar to the institutional requirement for Irish-language policies under the 2003 Official Languages Act. There need to be third-level second

---

5   Michael Cronin, 'Translation and Globalization', in *The Routledge Handbook of Translation Studies*, edited by Carmen Millán and Francesca Bartrina (London and New York: Routledge, 2013), 491–502.

6   Department of Education and Skills (2017), *Languages Connect: Ireland's Strategy for Foreign languages in Education*, available online: <https://www.education.ie/en/Schools-Colleges/Information/Curriculum-and-Syllabus/Foreign-Languages-Strategy/fls_languages_connect_strategy.pdf> [accessed 10 January 2019].

language acquisition experts on the monitoring and evaluation committees of the Languages Connect policy. Why? Because it is only by recognising that language learning is a long-term, lifelong commitment that we are likely to achieve real proficiency in a language as opposed to a delusional short-termism that promises learners, citizens and employers a competence that cannot be delivered.

The second consequence is how thinking in what Stewart Brand calls 'the Long Now' (considering the present from a long-range perspective) means asking why policies on modern languages exclude modern languages.[7] Why are Irish and English ignored in *Languages Connect*? One of the major insights to have emerged in sociolinguistic debates around translanguaging or what Alistair Pennycook and Emma Otsuji have dubbed 'metrolingualism' is that language users tend not to have rigidly compartmentalised areas of language practice.[8] In effect, speakers have language repertoires that encompass all the languages they possess and depending on situations they will pick and mix elements on this language continuum. As societies and cities become increasingly the site of what Jan Blommaert and others have called 'linguistic superdiversity',[9] translanguaging practices are more in evidence, a fact acknowledged in the CEFR aspiration to the formation of the 'plurilingual social agent'. It can be argued, however, that considering language as a lifelong practice means that second language acquisition must be considered holistically from a translanguaging perspective – integrating the teaching of the language with all the other languages the user speaks or acquires – rather than serially as a kind of additional multilingualism that layers discrete competences. A great many speakers on the island of Ireland have both Irish and English (to varying degrees of

---

7   Stuart Brand, *The Clock of the Long Now: Time and Responsibility* (London: Phoenix, 2000). See also Laurent Vidal, *Les hommes lents: résister à la modernité* (Paris: Flammarion, 2020).
8   Alistair Pennycook and Emma Otsuji, *Metrolingualism: Language in the City* (London and New York: Routledge, 2015).
9   Jan Blommaert, *Ethnography, Superdiversity and Linguistic Landscapes: Chronicles of Complexity* (Bristol: Multilingual Matters, 2013). See also Mike Baynham and Tong King Lee, *Translation and Translanguaging* (London: Routledge, 2019).

competence), but both languages are ignored in a national policy document on language acquisition.

The third consequence of a durational stance on language is to undo some cherished binaries. One, in particular, is the notion of the 'specialist' and the 'non-specialist'. There is frequently a notion that doing 'just' language is an inherently risky enterprise. That learning a foreign language requires the necessary alibi of business or law or politics to be taken seriously as a credible vocational undertaking. The language specialist needs an instrumental specialism to make his or her way in life. But learning a modern language is not primarily horizontal travelling, as it is often taken to be – a brief trip to an exotic locale – but a form of vertical travelling – a prolonged dwelling in a language and a culture. The longer the dwelling, the more extensive the journey into the history, the music, the politics, the geography, the sports, the literature, the media of a particular place. The specialist over time turns into the multispecialist. The language specialism becomes a perpetual opening up not an unavoidable closing down. This opening up brings us from the regime of time in modern languages in Ireland to the regime of attention.

Regime of Attention

Relating to others, whether human or non-human, implies, first and foremost, paying attention to them. 'Are you all sitting still and paying attention?' The familiar injunction of the school teacher has become the watchword of the new economy. If the notion of economy is based on the management of scarce resources, attention in a media-saturated world has become the most precious resource of all. Already by the mid-1990s Michael Goldhaber was arguing that with the emergence of digital technologies, traditional factors of production would decline in importance relative to that of attention.[10] Thomas Davenport and John Beck in *The*

---

10   Michael Goldhaber, 'Principles of the New Economy' (1996), available online: <well.com> [accessed 9 December 2018]. See also Goldhaber, 'Attention

Attention Economy: Understanding the New Economy of Business (2001) predicted the monetisation of attention where the attention of consumers would be so sought after that they would be supplied with services free of charge in exchange for a few moments of their attention.[11] We would be paid to pay attention. Google is the result. Users can now use extremely powerful search engines and all (apparently) free of charge.

From the point of view of an economics of attention, two challenges immediately present themselves. The first is how to protect attention from information overload to ensure an optimal allocation of this scarce resource (the vogue for time management courses) and the second is how to extract the maximum amount of profit from the capture of this scarce resource.[12] It is in the second sense, of course, that search engines come at a price. For Google, the user is the product and her attention span has a lucrative exchange value. The more she pays attention, the more Google gets paid for her to pay attention. What these developments highlight is a fundamental shift in economic emphasis from production to promotion. In information-rich environments, a series of media gates exist to filter information to potential users or consumers. Not all of these media gates have the same power co-efficient. An ad in a local college newspaper will not reach the same audience as an ad on prime time television. If the absolute cost of diffusing information has fallen dramatically over the centuries – it is substantially cheaper to post a blog in the twenty-first century than to print a book in the sixteenth – the cost of getting past the filters of preselection has risen exponentially.[13] In other words, as societies are more and more heavily invested in various forms of mediation, from the rise of the audiovisual industries to the emergence of digital technologies, it is

---

Shoppers!', *Wired*, 12, 5 (1997), available online: <wired.com> [accessed 10 December 2018].

11   Thomas Davenport and John Beck, *The Attention Economy: Understanding the New Currency of Business* (Cambridge, MA: Harvard Business School, 2001).

12   See Kessous, Mellet and Zouinar, 'L'économie de l'attention. Entre protection des ressources cognitives et extraction de la valeur', *Sociologie du travail* 52, no. 3 (2010), 359–373, 366.

13   See J. Falkinger, 'Attention Economies', *Journal of Economic Theory* 133 (2007), 266–294, 267.

less the production of goods and services than the production of demand through the capture of attention that absorbs increasing amounts of resources. Getting people to take notice is the main income generator for what McKenzie Wark has famously dubbed the 'vectorialist class'.[14]

There is a sense, of course, in which gaining people's attention may be a central feature of the new economy but is not necessarily novel in human experience. People have been trying to get others to sit up and take notice for millennia. As Richard Lanham points out, the central thrust of the art and science of rhetoric for more than two millennia has been to find ways of soliciting the attention of audiences.[15] Lanham argues that much of what has been debated under the heading of 'style' in literary criticism, art history, aesthetics, has largely been a matter of how writers and artists have sought to corner the attention of their readers or viewers in a field of competing media or stimuli.

Focusing on the economics of attention inevitably implies a certain set of assumptions, notably the maximisation of profits through the minimisation of costs in the context (real or imagined) of market competition. In the standard neo-classical paradigm, the economy is primarily concerned with the optimal management of scarce resources. The ends to which these resources are employed are normally outside its area of competence. However, a notion of attention which is solely concerned with means and not ends is scarcely viable as a theory of attention because attention is invariably bound up with value.

William James in his *Principles of Psychology* (1890) pointed out how a notion of attention that was purely passive was unable to account for the ways in which humans pay attention. James is critical of the British school of Empiricism (Locke, Hume, Hartley, the Mills and Spencer) for not treating of the notion of 'selective attention'. He argues that because their main concern is showing that 'the higher faculties of the mind are pure products of "experience"', experience itself must be thought of as 'something simply *given*' (his emphasis). James goes on to claim:

14 See K. McKenzie Wark, *A Hacker Manifesto* (Cambridge, MA: Harvard University Press, 2004).
15 Richard Lanham, *The Economics of Attention: Style and Substance in the Age of Information* (Chicago: University of Chicago Press, 2006).

the moment one thinks of the matter, one sees how false a notion of experience is which would make it tantamount to the mere presence to the senses of an outward order. Millions of items of the outward order are present to my senses which never properly enter into my experience. Why? Because they have no interest for me. My experience is what I agree to attend to. Only those items which I notice shape my mind – without selective interest, experience is an utter chaos. Interest alone gives accent and emphasis, light and shade, background and foreground – intelligible perspective, in a word. It varies in every creature, but without it the consciousness of every creature would be a grey chaotic indiscriminateness, impossible for us even to conceive.[16]

Out of the '[m]illions of items of the outward order' we choose to pay attention to certain items and not to others. Attention inescapably involves value as attention itself implies a choice determined by particular ends (safety, sanity, satisfaction) that are believed to be important. In the circular relationship of attention and value, subjects value that to which they pay attention and pay attention to that which they value. Ends cannot, therefore, be discounted in any credible attentionscape. The purely economistic representation of attention prevents us from asking the most basic question, to what ends are directed the attention that will decide our future? Or put another way, if our future is strongly determined by those things to which we might pay attention to in the present (e.g. public transportation in our cities), then must not the underlying value systems of our 'selective attention' be a matter of explicit and sustained public debate?

One of the immediate effects of engaging with another language is that you begin to pay attention to things that you previously ignored – news reports on the country where the language is spoken, songs on YouTube in that language, speakers of the language that you overhear on the Luas or the Dart or the bus. In 2013 Ethan Zuckerman, the Director of MIT's Media Lab, announced to the world an unsettling paradox.[17] The Internet Age which had promised a boundless utopia of global connectivity was delivering not openness, but closure. His extensive research on web and

16   William James, *The Principles of Psychology* (New York: Henry Holt, 1890), 402–403.
17   Etham Zuckerman, *Digital Cosmopolitans: Why We Think the Internet Connects Us, Why It Doesn't, and How to Rewire It* (New York: Norton, 2013).

social media usage showed that users overwhelmingly accessed content in their own language, about their own culture and in their own geographical area. The electronic frontier was fast turning into the digital backyard. The political consequences of this cyber narcissism soon became all too evident in the silo hatreds of the alt-right social media, rejecting the foreign, the migrant, the impure. Not learning foreign languages meant not paying attention. Or rather it meant only paying attention to what reinforced monocultural and monolingual supremacism.

Learning a modern language fundamentally alters an individual's regime of attention but could equally argue that this utopian promise extends to a whole society. Let us take one issue which has become the single most pressing social concern in Ireland today, the housing crisis. Why have we read no article on the Fondation Abbé Pierre publication *15 idées centre la crise du logement* (2017)? Why has there been no opinion piece on Marianne Leblanc Laugier's *La crise du logement: un jeu de dupes?* (2017). Both of these publications offer perspectives and solutions to the housing crisis that go beyond French borders. The most obvious answer to my question lies in my failure to translate the titles. They are in French. A similar point might be made about publications in German, Italian, Polish or Korean. Our regimes of attention in Ireland are hopelessly compromised by our failure to engage more fully with modern languages. The solutions, the perspectives, the insights to contend with major social problems available in other languages are simply ignored. This is why learning modern languages is not some decorative afterthought of the finishing school, but is at the heart of contemporary debates on political democracy in Ireland. A healthy pluralism in the public sphere is vitally dependent on expanding the range of policy and societal options on offer. And for this, more than ever, we need modern languages.

The Great Derangement

In *The Great Derangement: Climate Change and the Unthinkable* (2016), the Indian author and essayist Amitav Ghosh wonders why the subject of climate change has been largely absent from mainstream narrative fiction.

His basic contention is that the forms of bourgeois realism with their emphasis on the regular, the everyday and the predictable leave it poorly equipped to deal with improbability. The improbable, having been banished from realist narrative, languishes in the critical backwaters of fantasy, horror and science fiction. Of course, as we now know in ever more detail with the publication of reports by the Intergovernmental Panel on Climate Change and the experience of the pandemic the improbable will become even more probable. Michael, Calum, Sandy, Ophelia, Aidan, the guests from climate hell are there to remind us that change is already with us. Ghosh asks the metaphorical question, 'Are the currents of global warming too wild to be navigated in the accustomed barques of narration? But the truth, as is now widely acknowledged, is that we have entered a time when the wild has become the norm.'[18]

This brings us back in the short term to the long term. The core logic of language acquisition involves, as we have argued, a critical investment in the long term. Only a commitment over an extended period of time yields appreciable results. Modern language learning runs directly counter to the short term logic of extractivism that for Hartmut Rosa has produced chronic ecological dissonance. In celebrating the durational eco-logic of second language acquisition it might be objected that what is the achievement of the happy few should not be the concern of the indifferent many. The engagement in the long term is a utopian aspiration that ignores the harsh economic realities of just-in-time, 24/7 cycles of production and consumption. Dietmar Sternad is Professor of International Management in Carnithia University (Austria), James Kennelly is Professor of International Business at Skidmore College, New York and Dr Finbarr Bradley teaches at the Michael Smurfit Graduate Business School, UCD. Together they authored, *Digging Deeper: How Purpose-Driven Enterprises Create Real Value* (2016) where they argue that the most realistic and practical way to economic resilience in Ireland lay in putting down what they dub 'roots' or the 6Ls: '*Long-term orientation*, building and maintaining *lasting relationships*, *limits recognition*, having *local roots*, developing *learning communities*

---

18   Amitav Ghosh, *The Great Derangement: Climate Change and the Unthinkable* (Chicago: University of Chicago Press, 2016), 10.

and having *leadership responsibility* to create real value'.[19] These all clearly resonate with the experience and outcomes of modern language learning. The utopians in the short term turn out to be the realists in the long term. We need, in short, not so much to dig as to delve deeper into what we do in modern languages to show the democratic, ecological and participative promise of language acquisition on the island.

In the fourteenth century the Venetians decided they wanted a translation of the Brendan Voyage. *La Navigazione di Sancta Brendani*, the translation into Venetian dialect, contained two important changes. Instead of sailing west, the Venetians had Brendan sailing east. For the Most Serene Republic, the promised land of silks and spices lay to the east, not to the west. They were also disappointed in the Irish utopia which they found far too lacklustre ('When they had disembarked, they saw a land, extensive and thickly set with trees, laden with fruits, as in the autumn season'), a poor recompense for all that hard travelling. So, they upped the ante:

> Then we came closer to the wood, and there we found trees laden with precious stones, with leaves of silver and gold, and with gemstones on their branches. The other side of the trees seemed to be burning, and there came to our nostrils a fragrance so sweet we almost fainted; it was like incense, aloes, musk, balsam, rosemary, savin and roses, and like the scent of jasmine. But for all the fires we could not see any smoke.[20]

We may content ourselves with the austere grace of the Irish utopia or the lush plenty of the Venetian rewriting, but it is our voyaging through languages that will bring us to the only utopia worthwhile – the utopia of human possibility.

---

19   Sternad, Kennelly and Bradley, *Digging Deeper: How Purpose-Driven Enterprises Create Real Value* (London: Routledge, 2017), 21.

20   M. Davie, 'The Venetian Version', in *The Voyage of St Brendan: Representative Versions of the Legend in English Translation*, edited by W. J. S. Barron and G. S. Burgess (Exeter: University of Exeter Press, 2005), 155–230.

DEREK HAND

21 'What Would I Say, if I Had a Voice?': The Irish Novel and the Articulation of Modernity[1]

A cursory survey of the theories and definitions of the novel suggests that there is little agreement as to what precisely the novel is. In 'An Unread Book', Randall Jarrell offers the opinion that 'a novel is a prose narrative of some length that has something wrong with it'.[2] This provocatively playful remark perfectly encapsulates something fundamental about the novel form, that rather than being fixed and stable, it is perhaps awash with inherent contradictions. As Terry Eagleton argues, 'the novel is a genre which resists exact definition',[3] suggesting that if it cannot be reduced to merely one thing, then the novel is many things and many things simultaneously. Moreover, this sense of plurality is reflected and accentuated when Franco Moretti declares: 'Countless are the novels of the world'.[4] In doing so, Moretti points to the sheer number of novels that have existed in modern times and his critical method of 'distant reading' is an effort to make sense of that volume, discerning trends and contours that might illuminate the form, its themes and concerns, at any given historical moment. Nevertheless, even as he heralds the

---

1   Samuel Beckett, 'Texts for Nothing 4', in *Stories and Texts for Nothing* (New York: Grove Press, 1967), 91.
2   Randall Jarrell, 'An Unread Book', in *The Third Book of Criticism* (New York: Farrar, Straus and Giroux, 1969), 50.
3   Terry Eagleton, *The English Novel: An Introduction* (Oxford: Blackwell Publishing, 2005), 1.
4   Franco Moretti, 'On the Novel', in *The Novel: Volume I: History, Geography, and Culture*, edited by Franco Moretti (Princeton: Princeton University Press, 2006), ix.

loss of interest in the quirks of any one particular novel, he also signals that there are as many novels as there are readers of the novel. In other words, despite the desire to come to some collective and shared understanding of the form, the foibles of the individual reader will always have her ideas as to what the novel is, was and might be.

The novel form, characterised by contradictions and tensions, is not a problem: it is, rather, an asset. On the one hand, the novel is the great chronicler of the modern liberal subject,[5] and its pages are witness to the self-recognition of individuality and individual agency.[6] On the other hand, though, it is also the form which best portrays a society, acknowledging its various layers and machinations, offering readers 'imaginary modes of collective life'.[7] The novel, particularly in its links with realism, reflects the world as it is: in Stendhal's famous image, it is 'a mirror walking down the road'[8] – and for many critics, therefore, it a form that reflects the ideological power structures of society. And yet, the novel even as it shapes the world, 'resists its demands',[9] often becoming the location where rules and codes are deconstructed, where ideologies are challenged/critiqued and eventually unravelled.

Moretti's pluralist dictum and the acknowledgement of the intrinsic tensions within the novel form are also crucial from the perspective of the Irish literary critic. Quite simply, the template of the novel cannot be associated with any one location or with any one period. Therefore, the novel no longer needs to be thought of as exclusively attached to modern metropolitan life,[10] or as achieving its aesthetic apotheosis with the realist

---

5   D. A. Miller, 'The Novel and the Police', in *The Novel: An Anthology of Criticism and Theory 1900-2000*, edited by Dorothy J. Hale (Oxford: Blackwell, 2006), 543.
6   See Dorothy Hale, 'Marxist Approaches', in *The Novel: An Anthology of Criticism and Theory 1900-2000*, 349.
7   Peter Boxall, *The Value of the Novel* (Cambridge: Cambridge University Press, 2015), 10.
8   Stendhal, *Le rouge et le noir* (Paris: Editions Gallimard, 1972), 414.
9   Peter Boxall, *The Value of the Novel* (Cambridge: Cambridge University Press, 2015), 12.
10 For example, see Ian Watt, *The Rise of the Novel: Studies in Defoe, Richardson and Fielding* (London: The Hogarth Press, 1957/1987).

novel of the nineteenth century.[11] Instead, the novel becomes the perfect vehicle for scrutinising the periphery. Alternating, as it does, between the potential chaos inherent in its ability to plunder all other forms and genres,[12] it being, as Henry James said, 'a loose baggy monster',[13] and given its rage for order and narrative coherence, the novel form seems best suited to capturing the energies of an Irish historical experience that has moved between the poles of stability and social coherence, and the ever-present realities of division and conflict. The Irish novel, in its ability to register all of these competing conceptions and positions, these numerous stories, actually narrates the complexities of modernity and the movement into modernity and in doing so gives expression to the 'deep contradictions that define modern society'.[14]

I would argue that how the novel tells that story, the story of modernisation and particularly the individual's emergence into modernity, is what is particularly relevant to the novel's position in Irish literary discourse. Repeatedly in the Irish novel, we witness the struggle for articulation, at the level of both character and indeed artist, as both creator and created, strive to give voice to their reality and experience. Samuel Beckett in 'Texts for Nothing 4' offers an image of the troubled relationship between the artist and her material:

> Where would I go, if I could go, who would I be, if I could be, what would I say, if I had a voice, who says this, saying it's me? Answer simply, someone answer simply … There has to be one, it seems, once there is speech, no need of a story, a story is not compulsory, just a life, that's the mistake I made, one of the mistakes, to have wanted a story for myself, whereas life alone is enough.[15]

The tension described here is a recognition of the delicate balance between the demands of silence as a kind of refuge from the claims of the world, and the realities that the frailties of human desire and imagination

---

11 D. A. Miller, 'The Novel and the Police', 544.
12 Terry Eagleton, *The English Novel*, 1.
13 See Gowan Dawson, 'Literary Megatheriums and Loose Baggy Monsters: Paleontology and the Victorian Novel', *Victorian Studies* 53, no. 2 (2011), 203–230.
14 See Dorothy J. Hale, 'Marxist Approaches', 357.
15 Samuel Beckett, 'Texts for Nothing 4', 91.

mean that utterance is never too far away. It is, too, an acknowledgement of the power struggle inherent in speech and in telling stories, of the interplay of control for those who might tell a tale and, indeed, for those who might be spoken of in that narrative. Beckett's meditation gets to the heart of the novel's awkward position in Ireland's literary landscape: at once indicating the centrality of narrative, of story, to the pressures of lived experience, but also the persistent anxiety about speech and storytelling, of its value and worth concerning that lived experience. And, of course, in this piece, as in so much of Beckett's prose writing particularly, the uncertainty surrounding identity, of what it is to be, is made central. Here, the boundaries between the creator and the created are blurred and intermingle, becoming interchangeable. This ambiguity, in turn, intensifies the contradiction expressed that seems to suggest the necessity of story, and at the same time, the need to contest its control.

This Beckettian oscillation between the urgencies of expression and a resignation borne out of the knowledge that, perhaps, in the end there is nothing to be said can be read into the Irish engagement with the novel form from its inception to the present moment. In one of the earliest Irish novels, *The Irish Princess* (1693), the main character of the Prince happens upon his beloved Marinda being set upon by a band of Irish rapparees:

> The Prince rode up, and commanded them to desist, and let him know what was the cause of their Quarrel; one of them gave him a short Answer in Irish, and at the same time made a thrust at him with his Pitch-fork … the Prince drawing out a Pistol, returned the Irishman's complement with a shot, and laid him dead at his Horse's feet.[16]

Characters within the novel hear the word, but the reader is sheltered from it as the Irish-language words are only reported, but not written. The act of writing and the novel as a written form legitimises the English language and those who speak it, over the Irish language at this moment. The Irish language is both there, and not there, the world and experiences, and the unique complexities, that it might articulate tantalisingly close but never made fully visible. However, even in their absence, the Irish words' ghostly presence haunts the text, their silence a troubling counterpoint to

---

16   Anonymous, *Virtue Rewarded; or The Irish Princess*, a new novel edited and introduced by Hubert McDermott (Gerrards Cross: Colin Smythe, 1992), 82.

the act of violence surrounding them. The conundrum for the Irish novel and the Irish novelist, then, is to bring that silenced language – and all that it might speak of – into the text.

The voice of Thady Quirke, from Maria Edgeworth's *Castle Rackrent* (1801), exploded onto the pages of the nineteenth-century novel, offering a glimpse of alternative realties to the dominance of British imperial culture. His loquacious Hiberno-English lilt is ultimately a form of amusement for the metropolitan reader, an excellent example of the ways in which the sound of Irish speech has remained humorously fascinating to the international ear. Still, all Thady's talk only serves to deflect attention away from his son Jason who represents the new middle-class man, self-made and single-minded, who relies on his endeavour to gain wealth and position. Indeed, an account of Jason's life ought to be central to the novel, so focused is the form on the emergence of precisely this type of individual. Despite this, though, Jason escapes scrutiny and remains unknown, his story merely a shadowy presence lurking silently, and threateningly, in the background. Again and again in the Irish novel throughout the nineteenth century, Irish character is linked to voice and the difficulty of its being both heard and authentically articulated. Melancholia imbues each effort at expression, for both the creator and the created. The deployment of the Irish idiom is interesting this respect,[17] at once signalling the actuality of a native culture while also neutering any sense of it possessing real power in the real world. The same could be said for the fate of the Irish novel, which becomes marginalised during the literary revival of the late nineteenth and early twentieth centuries, as creative energy focuses on theatre and poetry as the locus of potential and possibility.

James Joyce rediscovered the promise of the novel, but also tellingly remains troubled and anxious about its merits in an Irish context. His famous declaration that in order to become the artist he wants to be, he will employ 'Silence, exile and cunning'[18] is decidedly curious. Curious because for a

---

17 For a discussion of the use of dialect in nineteenth-century Irish fiction see Seamus Deane, *Strange Country: Modernity and Nationhood in Irish Writing since 1790* (Oxford: Oxford University Press, 1997), 59ff.
18 James Joyce, *A Portrait of the Artist as a Young Man*, edited with and introduction and notes by Seamus Deane (Harmondsworth: Penguin Books, 1992), 268–269.

literary artist, the ultimate ambition ought not to be 'silence', or certainly not at this high modernist moment. It is notable, too, that this assertion comes just before the narrative breaks into the diary format, a form indicating private musings rather than public pronouncement. The seemingly confident assertions made in this section are, thus, undermined. When Dedalus ambitiously says he is going to 'create the uncreated consciousness of my race',[19] there is no one to hear him. He is only talking or writing to himself. It suggests a certain ambivalence about the nature of his chosen literary art, acknowledging the tightrope that must be negotiated between full-blown expression and the desire to keep something essential withheld from public judgement. Joyce is highly conscious of the power of speech:

> The language in which we are speaking is his before it is mine. How different are the words home, Christ, ale, master, on his lips and on mine![20]

Difference does not have to reside in meaning, but also in sound and particularly accent. Joyce flirts with the demarcation between speech and writing here, as he does throughout *Portrait* and *Ulysses*, considering the ideological power struggle between the two. Indeed, *Ulysses* brilliantly captures both the energies of the quintessential novel – its extemporisations, self-consciousness and playfulness – while also being the supreme anti-novel, superbly exploding the polite form as it stood in the late nineteenth and early twentieth centuries. In the 'Oxen of the Sun' episode, Joyce offers his readers a complex journey of developing prose styles, tracing the development of prose from antiquity to the present, imitating gestation toward birth. As it concludes, these overt literary allusions move toward speech, to a 'shout in the street':[21]

> and sky in one vast slumber, impending above parched field and drowsy oxen and blighted growth of shrub and verdure till in an instant a flash rives their centres and with the reverberation of the thunder the cloudburst pours its torrent, so and not

---

19 James Joyce, *A Portrait of the Artist as a Young Man*, 276.
20 James Joyce, *A Portrait of the Artist as a Young Man*, 205.
21 James Joyce, *Ulysses*, with an introduction and notes by Declan Kiberd (Harmondsworth: Penguin Books, 1992), 42.

otherwise was the transformation, violent and instantaneous, upon the utterance of the Word.

Burke's![22]

And then, appropriately enough, as Burke's is a pubic house, the literary parodies and imitations are abandoned as the speech patterns of the street, of jargon and slang come to the fore. His multifaceted creation interrogates both story and form, both language and writing, and in the process deliberately carving out a space that might allow for the complexities, and contradictions, of the Irish individual to be played out.

Elizabeth Bowen, too, flirts with the delicate balance between communication and silence. The IRA men in her 1929 novel *The Last September* are mainly silent, busily going about their business in ways that only accentuate the powerlessness and isolation of the Anglo-Irish inhabitants of the Big House of Danielstown. Lois Farquar, the focus of the novel, is all too aware of the debilitating potential of narrative. At one stage, she overhears a guest, Francie Montmorency, about to say who and what she thinks Lois is: She didn't want to know what she was, she couldn't bear to: knowledge of this would stop, seal, finish one.[23]
Lois desires the freedom not to have her story told, not to be fated or fixed. Formally this position is registered at the close of the novel as Lois's departure from Danielstown is merely told to the reader and not actually dramatised in the text itself. It has been argued that, like Stephen Dedalus, she escapes into art.[24] However, I would suggest that this ending is another articulation of the anxieties surrounding the novel form: the main character escapes into silence, outside the text and story, beyond its power and control.

Elizabeth Bowen offered advice to young writers in 'Notes on Writing a Novel', covering topics such as character and plot, and saying about the

---

22   *Ulysses*, 553–554.
23   Elizabeth Bowen, *The Last September* (London: Penguin, 1987), 60.
24   Cf. Robert Tracy, *The Unappeasable Host: Studies in Irish Identities* (Dublin: University College Dublin Press, 1998), 217ff. Tracy stresses the importance of Lois 'escaping' rather than merely departing the scene.

importance of place that 'Nothing can happen nowhere'.[25] The double negative here brilliantly describing the kind of haunted quality of Bowen's locations, their fragility bordering on collapse, and the existence of the people in those places itself potentially ghost-like. She goes on to expand on the idea of relevancy and while her comments revolve round issues of character and plot: 'Relevance – the question of it – is the headache of novel-writing'.[26]

It might be said that Bowen's discussion has a deeper resonance about the relevance, generally, of the novel form in the modern world. Indeed, the present moment sees the form under pressure with the catch-cry of its 'death' a common one.[27] As ever, though, the Irish experience of these global trends is somewhat different. The recent past gifted us the economic phenomenon of the Celtic Tiger, which gave its name to only one literary medium: the novel.[28] Since its emergence in the seventeenth and eighteenth centuries the novel, more so than poetry or drama, has been linked to the marketplace and the bourgeoisie – the middle-class liberal individuals – who discover themselves there. Nevertheless, an unease still lingers concerning the form, even in the midst of its celebrated status. Two acclaimed novels of the contemporary moment offer telling examples of this.

Formally, Mike McCormack's *Solar Bones* (2016) is simply one long sentence, a deceptively simple challenge to traditional structure. Marcus Conway's narrative told with the rhythm of a heartbeat narrates a story about his various roles as husband, son, father and lover, as well as his relationship to the Celtic Tiger Boom in his profession as an engineer. Its

25 See Elizabeth Bowen, 'Notes on Writing a Novel', available online: <https://www.narrativemagazine.com/issues/fall-2006/classics/notes-writing-ovel-elizabeth-bowen> [accessed 10 October 2020].
26 See Elizabeth Bowen, 'Notes on Writing a Novel', available online: <https://www.narrativemagazine.com/issues/fall-2006/classics/notes-writing-novel-elizabeth-bowen> [accessed 10 October 2020].
27 See Peter Boxall, *The Value of the Novel* (Cambridge: Cambridge University Press, 2015), 138–140. See also D. A. Miller, 'The Novel and the Police', in *The Novel: An Anthology of Criticism and Theory 1900-2000*, 543. 'The 'death of the novel' … has really meant the explosion everywhere of the novelistic'.
28 See Derek Hand, 'Novels of the Celtic Tiger' in *Recalling the Celtic Tiger*, edited by Eamon Maher, Eugene O'Brien and Brian Lucey (London: Peter Lang, 2019), 227.

relevancy speaks to the Celtic Tiger moment and the gains and losses that wealth produced and the consequent cultural shifts that it brought about. His daughter, Agnes, is a visual artist and her exhibition, a focal point in the novel, consists of transcribed newspaper articles from local Galway newspapers written in her blood:

> the red script which covered the entire gallery from ceiling to floor along its length, handwriting in various types and sizes, a continuous swathe of text … all dealing with court cases which covered the full gamut from theft and domestic violence to child abuse, public order offences, illegal grazing on protected lands, petty theft, false number plates, public affray, burglary, assault and drink-driving offences … rising and falling in swells and eddies through various sizes and spacings, congested in the tight rhythms of certain examples only to swell out in crashing typographical waves in others, a maelstrom of voices and colour.[29]

This art is a commentary on the novel's aesthetic at a remove. The novel, as its name would suggest, has always been linked, if not confused, with news, news as something immediate and utterly relevant. What is critical in Agnes' art is how her work combines the public and the private spheres, the stories of the crimes and misdemeanours of a community made personal in her rendering of them. She is both an artistic witness to these acts and a conduit to their expression, her art forcing her audience to 'see' these acts and 'see' too her act of communicating them. As her brother wryly remarks of her emails to him telling of the opening night of her exhibition: 'Her account was very vivid, a great colour piece – if the visual arts thing doesn't work out she has a bright future as a writer' (*SB*, 74).

Her struggle to make art, to give the world expression and to make that expression pertinent is what any good novelist ought to strive towards. Moreover, as a self-reflexive critique of his writerly efforts, McCormack indicates perhaps the ambitious scope of his work that plays out against the backdrop of the Celtic Tiger boom and the subsequent financial crash. That Marcus is a ghost telling his story to no one but himself, and perhaps (though it is not made clear), telling it from a purgatorial state and therefore

---

29 Mike McCormack, *Solar Bones* (Dublin: The Tramp Press, 2016), 42–43. Henceforth, will be designated as *SB* for in-text citations.

condemned to tell it over again and again, might suggest once more how silence is something not merely accepted but actively longed for.

In *Solar Bones*, as if to foreground the anxieties surrounding the tensions between an older world and the brash modern one, there are references to social media such as Facebook and the communications app Skype as well as references to the more traditional newspaper and local radio. McCormack is fully cognisant of how the contemporary novel must navigate between these media, making itself heard and of value amid the general noise. It can be argued that there seems little left for the novel to explore with the private sphere now the domain of reality television and social websites on the internet. Nevertheless, McCormack's novel does indicate that the form can meet the challenges of the current moment, that it can tell the story of the present and do so successfully in illuminating ways. The formal experimentation recaptures the vitality of the form in an Irish contest, at one level shocking the reader out of her comfort zone, challenging her to see what is familiar and known as something strangely new. For even if silence is being flirted with, the lack of punctuation also gives a sense of breathless urgency to the telling, implying that it is a story that must be told.

The world of modern communication, the realities of the internet and texts, is precisely the context of Sally Rooney's *Normal People* (2018). Up-to-date and thoroughly engaged with the here and now, Rooney's novel is regarded as the best of contemporary Irish fiction and has been celebrated as the 'Salinger for the Snapchat generation'.[30] Rather like the novels of Jane Austen, where the medieval world of physical combat and swordplay is transformed into verbal jousting, Rooney's characters exist, at one level, in the realm of conversation. Ease of access to a variety of modes of communication: mobile phone, texts, and emails does not lessen the degree of anxiety for the characters concerning meaning and interpretation. Words, as always, are never a clear lens, their openness to misinterpretation the basis for the tensions in Connell and Marianne's relationship. They are

---

30   See Sian Cain, 'Sally Rooney Teaches Us Millennials Should Be Written about, not Ridiculed', *The Guardian*, 5 September, 2018, available online: <https://www.theguardian.com/commentisfree/2018/sep/05/sally-rooney-millennials-normal-people#> [accessed 23 September 2020].

of a generation that can say whatever they want and yet, certain words cannot, or will not, be spoken. Words such as 'boyfriend', 'girlfriend' and 'love' carry weight and significance and their being said, or rather there not being said, have far-reaching consequences.

Interestingly Connell writes short stories, itself perhaps a comment on the state of the novel in the contemporary moment. He publishes a story in the college magazine, anonymously. In a world lived in the public sphere, where masks and pose are so important, this concealment suggests a desire to keep a part of himself private and unknown to his peers: 'Because no one knew he had written the story he could not canvass anyone's reaction, and he never heard from a single soul whether it was considered good or bad'.[31] In a way, it is as if he has written or said nothing. Still, this reticence does not last long, and the novel ends with Connell deciding to take up the offer of a place on a Creative Writing course in New York. Therefore, even in this most recent of works, the reader observes this wavering between speech and silence. Here we see Connell acknowledging the fraught nature of any artistic statement but also, at the close, ambitiously prepared to embrace the hope that something can be said after all. This too has been the chief characteristic of the Irish novel from its beginnings.

The novel writers of the present moment have been labelled 'the golden generation',[32] signifying clearly how they have taken on the challenges of telling relevant stories. This tag, though, might be something of a burden as I would argue that each generation actually sees itself as utterly unique and that the kind of things said about Irish writers now could be said about any Irish writer from any time in the past.[33] Even if, amid all this change, things remain the same, there can be no doubt but that the contemporary Irish novel is held in very high regard. The range and variety of the Irish form in the recent past, as well as its standing in popular discourse, is worthy of mention. Writers such as Deirdre Madden, John Banville, Claire

---

31   Sally Rooney, *Normal People* (London: Faber and Faber, 2018), 246.
32   See <https://www.irishtimes.com/culture/gynocrats-pimm-s-war-and-pj-harvey-he-borris-house-festival-of-writing-and-ideas-1.1423549> 11 June 2013. [accessed 11 October 2020].
33   See <https://www.thejournal.ie/how-a-new-generation-of-writers-are-changing-Irish-literature-3954282-Apr2018/> [accessed 12 October 2020].

Gilroy, Anna Burns, Kevin Power, Eimear McBride, Colum McCann, Kevin Barry, Sarah Baum, Emma Donoghue, Colm Tóibín, Anne Enright, Lisa McInerney, Dermot Bolger, Joseph O'Connor, Roddy Doyle, Donal Ryan and Eílís Ní Dhuibhne give us novels about the past and the future, telling us stories of the local and global world, confirming both what we know, while also offering us accounts of experiences which have been hidden and suppressed.[34] Each new novel, then, is a testament to the continuing effort to speak and to make a voice or voices heard.

The story of the novel's place in Irish literary discourse is a story of precariousness. Often side-lined and under-theorised in comparison to both poetry and drama, the novel has been misunderstood as a pallid imitation of a form that flourishes elsewhere, usually in metropolitan centres. I have argued that Ireland's marginal position brings the inherent contradictions of the novel form to the fore and that those contradictions capture the realities of the Irish experience of the move into modernity profoundly. To return to Samuel Beckett:

> You must say words, as long as there are any – until they find me, until they say me, strange pain, strange sin, you must go on, perhaps it's done already, perhaps they have said me already, perhaps they have carried me to the threshold of my story, before the door that opens on my story, that would surprise me, if it opens, it will be I, it will be the silence, where I am, I don't know, I'll never know, in the silence you don't know, you must go on, I can't go on, I'll go on.[35]

The Irish novel, as it is being written and read, brings its anxieties about itself to the surface, striving to create unity, and acknowledging its limits. And that is why, perhaps, the novel continues to be written and read, because that struggle is always apparent to the alert reader, energising the form and forcing us to engage with it, even with all its faults.

---

34   I am acutely aware of leaving authors out of this list, which is far from exhaustive, so apologies in advance for that.
35   Samuel Beckett, *The Beckett Trilogy: Molloy, Malone Dies, The Unnameable* (London: Picador, 1959/1979), 381–382.

Notes on Contributors

RUTH BARTON is Head of the School of Creative Arts and Associate Professor in Film Studies at Trinity College Dublin. She has published widely on Irish cinema and her works include *Irish National Cinema* (Routledge, 2004) and *Acting Irish in Hollywood* (Irish Academic Press, 2006). She has also written critical biographies of the Hollywood star, Hedy Lamarr: *Hedy Lamarr, The Most Beautiful Woman in Film* (University Press of Kentucky, 2010) and the Irish silent era director, Rex Ingram: *Rex Ingram, Visionary Director of the Silent Screen* (University Press of Kentucky, 2014). She is Principal Investigator for a Creative Ireland project, 'Ecologies of Cultural Production', an investigation into career construction in the creative industries. Her new monograph, *Irish Cinema in the Twenty-First Century*, was published in 2019 by Manchester University Press.

PROFESSOR COLIN COULTER teaches in the Department of Sociology, the National University of Ireland, Maynooth. He is the editor of *Working for the Clampdown: The Clash, the Dawn of Neoliberalism and the Political Promise of Punk* (Manchester University Press, 2019) as well as the co-author of *Northern Ireland a Generation after Good Friday: Lost Futures and New Horizons in the 'Long Peace'* (Manchester University Press, 2021).

MARGUÉRITE CORPORAAL is Full Professor in Irish Literature in Transnational Contexts at Radboud University. She was the principal investigator of the research project *Relocated Remembrance: The Great Famine in Irish (Diaspora) Fiction, 1847–1921*, for which she obtained a Starting Grant for Consolidators from the European Research Council (2010–2015). Furthermore, Corporaal was the director of the interdisciplinary *International Network of Irish Famine Studies*, funded by the Dutch research council NWO (2014–2017). She was recently awarded a VICI grant by NWO, for her project *Redefining the Region: The*

Transnational Dimensions of Local Colour (2019–2024). Furthermore, Corporaal is PI of *Heritages of Hunger: Societal Reflections on Past European Famines in Education, Commemoration and Musealisation*, which is funded as part of the NWA programme launched by NWO and the Dutch government. Among Corporaal's recent international publications are *Relocated Memories of the Great Famine in Irish and Diaspora Fiction, 1847–70* (Syracuse University Press, 2017); *The Great Irish Famine and Social Class* (co-edited, Peter Lang, 2019); *The Great Irish Famine: Visual and Material Culture* (co-edited, Liverpool UP, 2018); *Irish Studies and the Dynamics of Memory* (co-edited, Peter Lang, 2017).

MICHAEL CRONIN is 1776 Professor of French and Director of the Centre for Literary and Cultural Translation in Trinity College Dublin. Among his published titles are *Translating Ireland: Translation, Languages and Identity* (1996); *Across the Lines: Travel, Language, Translation* (2000); *Translation and Globalization* (2003); *Irish in the New Century/An Ghaeilge san Aois Nua*; *Translation and Identity* (2006); *Translation Goes to the Movies* (2009); *Translation in the Digital Age* (2013); *Eco-Translation: Translation and Ecology in the Age of the Anthropocene* (2017) and *Irish and Ecology: An Ghaeilge agus an Éiceolaíocht* (2019). He is an elected Member of the Royal Irish Academy and the Academia Europaea, an Officier in the Ordre des Palmes Académiques and a Fellow of Trinity College Dublin.

ELKE D'HOKER is professor of English literature at the University of Leuven, where she is also co-director of the Leuven Centre for Irish Studies and of the modern literature research group, MDRN. She has published widely in the field of modern and contemporary British and Irish fiction, with special emphasis on the short story, women's writing and narrative theory. She is the author of a critical study on John Banville (Rodopi, 2004) and of *Irish Women Writers and the Modern Short Story* (Palgrave, 2016). She has also (co-)edited several essay collections, including *Unreliable Narration* (De Gruyter, 2008); *Irish Women Writers* (Lang, 2011); *Mary Lavin* (Irish Academic Press, 2013); *The Irish Short Story* (Lang, 2015) and *The Modern Short Story and Magazine Culture*

(EUP, 2021). She is vice-president of EFACIS and a member of the editorial board of *RISE (Review of Irish Studies in Europe)*.

EÓIN FLANNERY lectures in the Department of English Language and Literature at Mary Immaculate College, University of Limerick. He has published over 60 scholarly articles and book chapters, and is the author of 4 books: *Ireland and Ecocriticism: Literature, History, and Environmental Justice* (2016); *Colum McCann and the Aesthetics of Redemption* (2011); *Ireland and Postcolonial Studies: Theory, Discourse, Utopia* (2009); *Versions of Ireland: Empire, Modernity and Resistance in Irish Culture* (2006). His next book, *Form, Affect and Debt in post-Celtic Tiger Fiction* will be published in 2021 by Bloomsbury. He has edited volumes on a variety of topics including Irish visual cultures, postcolonial studies, contemporary Irish fiction and ecocriticism. He is also currently working on an Irish Research Council-funded project on *Irish Studies and the Economic Humanities*.

DEREK HAND is Professor and Head of the School of English in Dublin City University. The Liffey Press published his book *John Banville: Exploring Fictions* in 2002. He edited a special edition of the *Irish University Review* on John Banville in 2006. His *A History of the Irish Novel: 1665 to the Present* was published by Cambridge University Press in 2011. He is also the co-editor of a collection of essays on John McGahern entitled, *Essays on John McGahern: Assessing a Literary Legacy*, published by Cork University Press in 2019.

KATY HAYWARD is Professor of Political Sociology at Queen's University Belfast (QUB) and Senior Fellow in the UK in a Changing Europe think-tank. A former Government of Ireland research fellow in University College Dublin and Irish Studies Research Fellow in QUB, Professor Hayward is an internationally-recognised expert on Brexit. The author of over 300 publications, she has (co)authored/edited several books, including *The Political Dynamics of Change on the Island of Ireland* (2017) and *The Border Into Brexit* (2019). In 2020, she received a special Ewart-Biggs Memorial Award for her work on the implications of Brexit for the island of Ireland and British-Irish relations.

BARRY HOULIHAN is an Archivist at NUI Galway and teaches Theatre History and Archives, Digital Cultures as well as working on various archive and digitisation projects. His recent books include the monograph *Theatre and Archival Memory: Politics, Social Change and Modernising Ireland* (Palgrave MacMillan, 2021) and the edited collection of essays, *Navigating Ireland's Theatre Archive: Theory, Practice, Performance* (Peter Lang, 2019). He has co-curated recent touring exhibitions such as *Judging Shaw* with the Royal Irish Academy (2019), *Yeats and the West* (2015) and *A University in Wartime and Revolution: The Galway Experience* (2016). Barry is the co-editor of the SHAW journal issue *Shaw and Legacy, the Journal of Bernard Shaw Studies* (2020).

DECLAN KIBERD is Professor Emeritus of Irish Studies at the University of Notre Dame. Among his books are *Inventing Ireland*, *Irish Classics*, *After Ireland*, as well as *Synge and the Irish Language* and *Ulysses and Us*. He co-edited *The Handbook of the Irish Revival* with P. J. Mathews and has been a director of the Abbey Theatre. He was elected in 2019 a member of the American Academy of Arts and Sciences.

MÁIRTÍN MAC CON IOMAIRE is a senior lecturer in the School of Culinary Arts and Food Technology at Technological University Dublin. He is the co-founder and chair of the biennial Dublin Gastronomy Symposium and is a trustee of the Oxford Symposium on Food and Cookery. He is chair of the Masters in Gastronomy and Food Studies in TU Dublin, the first such programme in Ireland. He is co-editor with Eamon Maher of *'Tickling the Palate': Gastronomy in Irish Literature and Culture* (Peter Lang, 2014), and with Rhona Richman Kenneally on 'The Food Issue' of *The Canadian Journal of Irish Studies* (2018). He has published widely in peer-reviewed journals and is a regular contributor on food in the media. In 2018, he presented an eight-part television series for TG4 called *Blasta* celebrating Ireland's food heritage. Along with Michelle Share and Dorothy Cashman, he is co-editor of the new *European Journal of Food, Drink and Society*.

EAMON MAHER is Director of the National Centre for Franco-Irish Studies in TU Dublin. He is currently General Editor of two academic book series with Peter Lang, Oxford: *Reimagining Ireland* and *Studies in Franco-Irish Studies*. In addition to publishing two monographs on John McGahern, he also wrote the definitive study of the French priest-writer, Jean Sulivan. He has edited and co-edited 24 books, three of which were published in 2019; with Derek Hand, *Essays on John McGahern: Assessing a Literary Legacy* (Cork University Press); with Eugene O'Brien, *Patrimoine/Cultural Heritage in France and Ireland* (Peter Lang); with Brian Lucey and Eugene O'Brien, *Recalling the Celtic Tiger* (Peter Lang). He is currently co-editing, with Sarah Balen, a book of essays entitled: *Voicing the Margins: Literary Examples from France and Ireland*, which will be published in early 2021. He is an Officier dans l'Ordre des Palmes Académiques and is currently writing a monograph on fictional representations of Catholicism in twentieth-century fiction.

CATHERINE MAIGNANT is Professor of Irish Studies at the University of Lille (France) where she was the head of a research group in Irish Studies for over twenty years. She was President of the French Association of Irish Studies (SOFEIR) and of the European Federation of Associations and Centres of Irish Studies (EFACIS) for a number of years. After writing a PhD on early medieval Irish Christianity, she now specialises in contemporary Irish religious history. Her research interests include the New Religious Movement, the response of the Catholic Church to secularisation, interreligious dialogue, Celtic Christianity and the religious aspects of globalisation. She has widely published in all these areas.

SYLVIE MIKOWSKI is Professor of Irish and English Studies at the University of Reims-Champagne-Ardenne (France). Her main interests are the contemporary Irish novel and popular culture. She completed her PhD on the novels of John McGahern in 1995, and defended her *habilitation* dissertation in 2003 on 'The Invention of a Tradition in the Irish contemporary Novel'. Her main publications include *Le Roman irlandais Contemporain*; *The Book in Ireland*; *Memory and History in France and Ireland*; *Irish Women Writers*; *Ireland and Popular Culture*; *Popular Culture Today* and *The Circulation of Popular Culture between Ireland and the USA*. She has also published numerous book chapters and articles on various contemporary Irish writers, such as John McGahern, William Trevor, Colum McCann, Patrick McCabe, Roddy Doyle, Deirdre Madden, Sebastian Barry. She served as literary editor of the French journal of Irish Studies, *Etudes irlandaises*, and is currently President of the SOFEIR, the French Society of Irish Studies, as well as President of the steering committee of GIS EIRE, a scientific grouping of universities. She is also review editor for *RISE (Review of Irish Studies in Europe)*.

BRIAN MURPHY is a Senior Lecturer in the School of Culinary Arts and Food Technology at the Technological University Dublin (TU Dublin) where he lectures on food and drink studies. He has a particular interest in gastronomic research and is keen to explore the role that place and story play in perceptions of food and drink. He has published a number of articles in this and related areas. A co-founder of the Dublin Gastronomy Symposium, he is also an active member of the National Centre for Franco-Irish Studies, which is also based in TU Dublin. In recent years, he has sought to expand the Centre's research remit to include strong elements of gastronomic culture.

GRACE NEVILLE is a graduate of University College Cork, (BA double first in French and Irish), Caen (maîtrise) and Lille (DEA/ Diplôme d'Etudes Approfondies and Doctorate). She is an emeritus Professor of French at UCC where she was also Vice-President for Teaching and Learning (2008–2012). Since retiring from UCC in 2012, she has been a member of numerous committees on aspects of French higher education reform at the ANR/Agence National de la Recherche, the French Ministry of Education, the Sorbonne, the HCERES and the CRI in Paris, as well as in the universities of Aix-Marseille, Rennes, Cergy-Pontoise, Ljubljana and the European Commission. Her research focuses especially on Franco-Irish links from medieval to modern times. She holds the Palmes Académiques and the Légion d'honneur.

EUGENE O'BRIEN is senior lecturer and Head of the Department of English Language and Literature in Mary Immaculate College,

University of Limerick, and is also the Director of the Mary Immaculate Institute for Irish Studies. He is the editor for the *Oxford University Press Online Bibliography* project in literary theory, and of the *Routledge Studies in Irish Literature* series. His more recent books include *Seamus Heaney as Aesthetic Thinker* (Syracuse University Press); *The Soul Exceeds Its Circumstances: The Later Poetry of Seamus Heaney* (Notre Dame University Press); *Recalling the Celtic Tiger*, with Eamon Maher and Brian Lucey (Peter Lang) and *Representations of Loss in Irish Literature*, with Deirdre Flynn (Palgrave). He is currently working on a monograph on the writing of Paul Howard (Routledge) and a co-edited book on Irish poetry and climate change with Andrew Auge (Routledge).

MAUREEN O'CONNOR lectures in the School of English in University College Cork. She publishes widely in the area of Irish women's writing. She is the author of *The Female and the Species: The Animal in Irish Women's Writing* (2010), and has co-edited, with Derek Gladwin, a special issue of the *Canadian Journal of Irish Studies*, on the topic of 'Irish Studies and the Environmental Humanities' (2018); with Kathryn Laing and Sinéad Mooney, *Edna O'Brien: New Critical Perspectives* (2006); with Lisa Colletta, *Wild Colonial Girl: Essays on Edna O'Brien* (2006); and, with Tadhg Foley, *Ireland and India: Colonies, Culture, and Empire* (2006). Her most recent book, *Edna O'Brien and the Art of Fiction*, is forthcoming from Bucknell University Press in 2021.

MARY S. PIERSE has taught a range of English literature modules at University College, Cork where she also gave courses on Irish feminisms for the MA programme in Women's studies. Instigator of the George Moore international conference series, she has edited and co-edited several volumes on Moore's works, including *George Moore: Artistic Visions and Literary Worlds* (2006). She has published on the writings of Kate Chopin, Antonio Fogazzaro, Katherine Cecil Thurston, and of contemporary Irish poets Dennis O'Driscoll and Cathal Ó Searcaigh. She edited and compiled the five-volume collection, *Irish Feminisms 1810-1930* (Routledge, 2010). Her ongoing research focuses on the often-intersecting topics of Moore's writings, on Franco-Irish artistic connections in visual art and music, and on Irish women writers at the *fin-de-siècle* period. A board member at the National Centre for Franco-Irish Studies, she also serves on editorial boards/scientific committees for publications in France and Spain.

PAUL ROUSE is Professor of history at University College Dublin. He has written extensively on the history of sport and popular culture in Ireland, including *Sport and Ireland: A History* (Oxford University Press, 2015) and *The Hurlers: The First All-Ireland Championship and the Making of Modern Hurling* (Penguin, 2018).

PROFESSOR PETER SHIRLOW is the Director of the Institute of Irish Studies in the University of Liverpool. He is the author of *The End of Ulster Loyalism?* (Manchester University Press, 2012) as well as the co-author of *Northern Ireland a Generation after Good Friday: Lost Futures and New Horizons in the 'Long Peace'* (Manchester University Press, 2021).

EAMONN WALL is a professor of Global Studies and English at the University of Missouri-St Louis. A past president of the American Conference for Irish Studies, he is also the author of *From Oven Lane to Sun Prairie: In Search of Irish America* (Arlen House, 2019); *Writing the Irish West: Ecologies and Traditions* (Notre Dame, 2011) and *From the Sine Cafe to the Black Hills: Notes on the New Irish* (Wisconsin, 2000), as well as many essays, articles and reviews. His most recent collection of poetry is *Junction City: New and Selected Poems 1990-2015* (Salmon Poetry, 2015). A native of Co. Wexford, he has lived in the US since 1982.

JOHN WALSH is a Senior Lecturer in Irish in the School of Languages, Literatures and Culture at the National University of Ireland, Galway where he teaches modules on sociolinguistics and media studies. John holds a BA (Irish and Welsh) from University College Dublin and an MA (International Relations) and PhD from Dublin City University. Previously he worked as a lecturer in Irish at Dublin City University, with the European Bureau for Lesser-Used Languages in Brussels and as a journalist with RTÉ, TG4 and independent radio. His research interests include language policy, language legislation, language and socio-economic development, minority language media, Irish-language archival collections and sound archives. John has published extensively in both Irish and English about various aspects of these topics. His recent monograph (co-authored with Bernadette O'Rourke), *New Speakers of Irish in the Global Context: New Revival?*, was published by Routledge in 2020.

HARRY WHITE is Professor of Music at University College Dublin and a Fellow of the Royal Irish Academy of Music. His recent publications include *Music, Migration and European Culture*, co-edited with Ivano Cavallini and Jolanta Guzy-Pasiak (Zagreb: Croatian Musicological Society, 2020) and *The Musical Discourse of Servitude* (New York: Oxford University Press, 2020). His current research is concerned with the conceptual prowess of the musical work in Irish cultural history, and with representations of privacy in early eighteenth-century music. He was elected to the Royal Irish Academy in 2006 and to the Croatian Academy of Sciences and Arts in 2018.

Reimagining Ireland

Series Editor: Dr Eamon Maher, Technological University Dublin

The concepts of Ireland and 'Irishness' are in constant flux in the wake of an ever-increasing reappraisal of the notion of cultural and national specificity in a world assailed from all angles by the forces of globalisation and uniformity. Reimagining Ireland interrogates Ireland's past and present and suggests possibilities for the future by looking at Ireland's literature, culture and history and subjecting them to the most up-to-date critical appraisals associated with sociology, literary theory, historiography, political science and theology.

Some of the pertinent issues include, but are not confined to, Irish writing in English and Irish, Nationalism, Unionism, the Northern 'Troubles', the Peace Process, economic development in Ireland, the impact and decline of the Celtic Tiger, Irish spirituality, the rise and fall of organised religion, the visual arts, popular cultures, sport, Irish music and dance, emigration and the Irish diaspora, immigration and multiculturalism, marginalisation, globalisation, modernity/postmodernity and postcolonialism. The series publishes monographs, comparative studies, interdisciplinary projects, conference proceedings and edited books. Proposals should be sent either to Dr Eamon Maher at eamon.maher@ittdublin.ie or to ireland@peterlang.com.

Vol. 1   Eugene O'Brien: 'Kicking Bishop Brennan up the Arse': Negotiating Texts and Contexts in Contemporary Irish Studies
ISBN 978-3-03911-539-6. 219 pages. 2009.

Vol. 2   James P.Byrne, Padraig Kirwan and Michael O'Sullivan (eds): Affecting Irishness: Negotiating Cultural Identity Within and Beyond the Nation
ISBN 978-3-03911-830-4. 334 pages. 2009.

Vol. 3   Irene Lucchitti: The Islandman: The Hidden Life of Tomás O'Crohan
ISBN 978-3-03911-837-3. 232 pages. 2009.

Vol. 4   Paddy Lyons and Alison O'Malley-Younger (eds): No Country for Old Men: Fresh Perspectives on Irish Literature
ISBN 978-3-03911-841-0. 289 pages. 2009.

Vol. 5	Eamon Maher (ed.): Cultural Perspectives on Globalisation and Ireland ISBN 978-3-03911-851-9. 256 pages. 2009.
Vol. 6	Lynn Brunet: 'A Course of Severe and Arduous Trials': Bacon, Beckett and Spurious Freemasonry in Early Twentieth-Century Ireland ISBN 978-3-03911-854-0. 218 pages. 2009.
Vol. 7	Claire Lynch: Irish Autobiography: Stories of Self in the Narrative of a Nation ISBN 978-3-03911-856-4. 234 pages. 2009.
Vol. 8	Victoria O'Brien: A History of Irish Ballet from 1927 to 1963 ISBN 978-3-03911-873-1. 208 pages. 2011.
Vol. 9	Irene Gilsenan Nordin and Elin Holmsten (eds): Liminal Borderlands in Irish Literature and Culture ISBN 978-3-03911-859-5. 208 pages. 2009.
Vol. 10	Claire Nally: Envisioning Ireland: W. B. Yeats's Occult Nationalism ISBN 978-3-03911-882-3. 320 pages. 2010.
Vol. 11	Raita Merivirta: The Gun and Irish Politics: Examining National History in Neil Jordan's *Michael Collins* ISBN 978-3-03911-888-5. 202 pages. 2009.
Vol. 12	John Strachan and Alison O'Malley-Younger (eds): Ireland: Revolution and Evolution ISBN 978-3-03911-881-6. 248 pages. 2010.
Vol. 13	Barbara Hughes: Between Literature and History: The Diaries and Memoirs of Mary Leadbeater and Dorothea Herbert ISBN 978-3-03911-889-2. 255 pages. 2010.
Vol. 14	Edwina Keown and Carol Taaffe (eds): Irish Modernism: Origins, Contexts, Publics ISBN 978-3-03911-894-6. 256 pages. 2010.
Vol. 15	John Walsh: Contests and Contexts: The Irish Language and Ireland's Socio-Economic Development ISBN 978-3-03911-914-1. 492 pages. 2011.

Vol. 16   Zélie Asava: The Black Irish Onscreen: Representing Black and
           Mixed-Race Identities on Irish Film and Television
           ISBN 978-3-0343-0839-7. 213 pages. 2013.

Vol. 17   Susan Cahill and Eóin Flannery (eds): This Side of Brightness: Essays
           on the Fiction of Colum McCann
           ISBN 978-3-03911-935-6. 189 pages. 2012.

Vol. 18   Brian Arkins: The Thought of W. B. Yeats
           ISBN 978-3-03911-939-4. 204 pages. 2010.

Vol. 19   Maureen O'Connor: The Female and the Species: The Animal in Irish
           Women's Writing
           ISBN 978-3-03911-959-2. 203 pages. 2010.

Vol. 20   Rhona Trench: Bloody Living: The Loss of Selfhood in the Plays of
           Marina Carr
           ISBN 978-3-03911-964-6. 327 pages. 2010.

Vol. 21   Jeannine Woods: Visions of Empire and Other Imaginings: Cinema,
           Ireland and India, 1910–1962
           ISBN 978-3-03911-974-5. 230 pages. 2011.

Vol. 22   Neil O'Boyle: New Vocabularies, Old Ideas: Culture, Irishness and the
           Advertising Industry
           ISBN 978-3-03911-978-3. 233 pages. 2011.

Vol. 23   Dermot McCarthy: John McGahern and the Art of Memory
           ISBN 978-3-0343-0100-8. 344 pages. 2010.

Vol. 24   Francesca Benatti, Sean Ryder and Justin Tonra (eds): Thomas
           Moore: Texts, Contexts, Hypertexts
           ISBN 978-3-0343-0900-4. 220 pages. 2013.

Vol. 25   Sarah O'Connor: No Man's Land: Irish Women and the Cultural
           Present
           ISBN 978-3-0343-0111-4. 230 pages. 2011.

Vol. 26   Caroline Magennis: Sons of Ulster: Masculinities in the Contemporary Northern Irish Novel
           ISBN 978-3-0343-0110-7. 192 pages. 2010.

Vol. 27	Dawn Duncan: Irish Myth, Lore and Legend on Film ISBN 978-3-0343-0140-4. 181 pages. 2013.
Vol. 28	Eamon Maher and Catherine Maignant (eds): Franco-Irish Connections in Space and Time: Peregrinations and Ruminations ISBN 978-3-0343-0870-0. 295 pages. 2012.
Vol. 29	Holly Maples: Culture War: Conflict, Commemoration and the Contemporary Abbey Theatre ISBN 978-3-0343-0137-4. 294 pages. 2011.
Vol. 30	Maureen O'Connor (ed.): Back to the Future of Irish Studies: Festschrift for Tadhg Foley ISBN 978-3-0343-0141-1. 359 pages. 2010.
Vol. 31	Eva Urban: Community Politics and the Peace Process in Contemporary Northern Irish Drama ISBN 978-3-0343-0143-5. 303 pages. 2011.
Vol. 32	Mairéad Conneely: Between Two Shores/*Idir Dhá Chladach*: Writing the Aran Islands, 1890–1980 ISBN 978-3-0343-0144-2. 299 pages. 2011.
Vol. 33	Gerald Morgan and Gavin Hughes (eds): Southern Ireland and the Liberation of France: New Perspectives ISBN 978-3-0343-0190-9. 250 pages. 2011.
Vol. 34	Anne MacCarthy: Definitions of Irishness in the 'Library of Ireland' Literary Anthologies ISBN 978-3-0343-0194-7. 271 pages. 2012.
Vol. 35	Irene Lucchitti: Peig Sayers: In Her Own Write ISBN 978-3-0343-0253-1. Forthcoming.
Vol. 36	Eamon Maher and Eugene O'Brien (eds): Breaking the Mould: Literary Representations of Irish Catholicism ISBN 978-3-0343-0232-6. 249 pages. 2011.
Vol. 37	Mícheál Ó hAodha and John O'Callaghan (eds): Narratives of the Occluded Irish Diaspora: Subversive Voices ISBN 978-3-0343-0248-7. 227 pages. 2012.

Vol. 38 Willy Maley and Alison O'Malley-Younger (eds): Celtic Connections: Irish–Scottish Relations and the Politics of Culture
ISBN 978-3-0343-0214-2. 247 pages. 2013.

Vol. 39 Sabine Egger and John McDonagh (eds): Polish–Irish Encounters in the Old and New Europe
ISBN 978-3-0343-0253-1. 322 pages. 2011.

Vol. 40 Elke D'hoker, Raphaël Ingelbien and Hedwig Schwall (eds): Irish Women Writers: New Critical Perspectives
ISBN 978-3-0343-0249-4. 318 pages. 2011.

Vol. 41 Peter James Harris: From Stage to Page: Critical Reception of Irish Plays in the London Theatre, 1925–1996
ISBN 978-3-0343-0266-1. 311 pages. 2011.

Vol. 42 Hedda Friberg-Harnesk, Gerald Porter and Joakim Wrethed (eds): Beyond Ireland: Encounters Across Cultures
ISBN 978-3-0343-0270-8. 342 pages. 2011.

Vol. 43 Irene Gilsenan Nordin and Carmen Zamorano Llena (eds): Urban and Rural Landscapes in Modern Ireland: Language, Literature and Culture
ISBN 978-3-0343-0279-1. 238 pages. 2012.

Vol. 44 Kathleen Costello-Sullivan: Mother/Country: Politics of the Personal in the Fiction of Colm Tóibín
ISBN 978-3-0343-0753-6. 247 pages. 2012.

Vol. 45 Lesley Lelourec and Gráinne O'Keeffe-Vigneron (eds): Ireland and Victims: Confronting the Past, Forging the Future
ISBN 978-3-0343-0792-5. 331 pages. 2012.

Vol. 46 Gerald Dawe, Darryl Jones and Nora Pelizzari (eds): Beautiful Strangers: Ireland and the World of the 1950s
ISBN 978-3-0343-0801-4. 207 pages. 2013.

Vol. 47 Yvonne O'Keeffe and Claudia Reese (eds): New Voices, Inherited Lines: Literary and Cultural Representations of the Irish Family
ISBN 978-3-0343-0799-4. 238 pages. 2013.

Vol. 48   Justin Carville (ed.): Visualizing Dublin: Visual Culture, Modernity
           and the Representation of Urban Space
           ISBN 978-3-0343-0802-1. 326 pages. 2014.

Vol. 49   Gerald Power and Ondřej Pilný (eds): Ireland and the Czech
           Lands: Contacts and Comparisons in History and Culture
           ISBN 978-3-0343-1701-6. 243 pages. 2014.

Vol. 50   Eoghan Smith: John Banville: Art and Authenticity
           ISBN 978-3-0343-0852-6. 199 pages. 2014.

Vol. 51   María Elena Jaime de Pablos and Mary Pierse (eds): George Moore
           and the Quirks of Human Nature
           ISBN 978-3-0343-1752-8. 283 pages. 2014.

Vol. 52   Aidan O'Malley and Eve Patten (eds): Ireland, West to East: Irish
           Cultural Connections with Central and Eastern Europe
           ISBN 978-3-0343-0913-4. 307 pages. 2014.

Vol. 53   Ruben Moi, Brynhildur Boyce and Charles I. Armstrong (eds): The
           Crossings of Art in Ireland
           ISBN 978-3-0343-0983-7. 319 pages. 2014.

Vol. 54   Sylvie Mikowski (ed.): Ireland and Popular Culture
           ISBN 978-3-0343-1717-7. 257 pages. 2014.

Vol. 55   Benjamin Keatinge and Mary Pierse (eds): France and Ireland in the
           Public Imagination
           ISBN 978-3-0343-1747-4. 279 pages. 2014.

Vol. 56   Raymond Mullen, Adam Bargroff and Jennifer Mullen (eds): John
           McGahern: Critical Essays
           ISBN 978-3-0343-1755-9. 253 pages. 2014.

Vol. 57   Máirtín Mac Con Iomaire and Eamon Maher (eds): 'Tickling the
           Palate': Gastronomy in Irish Literature and Culture
           ISBN 978-3-0343-1769-6. 253 pages. 2014.

Vol. 58   Heidi Hansson and James H. Murphy (eds): Fictions of the Irish
           Land War
           ISBN 978-3-0343-0999-8. 237 pages. 2014.

Vol. 59   Fiona McCann: A Poetics of Dissensus: Confronting Violence in Contemporary Prose Writing from the North of Ireland
ISBN 978-3-0343-0979-0. 238 pages. 2014.

Vol. 60   Marguérite Corporaal, Christopher Cusack, Lindsay Janssen and Ruud van den Beuken (eds): Global Legacies of the Great Irish Famine: Transnational and Interdisciplinary Perspectives
ISBN 978-3-0343-0903-5. 357 pages. 2014.

Vol. 61   Katarzyna Ojrzyn'ska: 'Dancing As If Language No Longer Existed': Dance in Contemporary Irish Drama
ISBN 978-3-0343-1813-6. 318 pages. 2015.

Vol. 62   Whitney Standlee: 'Power to Observe': Irish Women Novelists in Britain, 1890–1916
ISBN 978-3-0343-1837-2. 288 pages. 2015.

Vol. 63   Elke D'hoker and Stephanie Eggermont (eds): The Irish Short Story: Traditions and Trends
ISBN 978-3-0343-1753-5. 330 pages. 2015.

Vol. 64   Radvan Markus: Echoes of the Rebellion: The Year 1798 in Twentieth-Century Irish Fiction and Drama
ISBN 978-3-0343-1832-7. 248 pages. 2015.

Vol. 65   B. Mairéad Pratschke: Visions of Ireland: Gael Linn's *Amharc Éireann* Film Series, 1956–1964
ISBN 978-3-0343-1872-3. 301 pages. 2015.

Vol. 66   Una Hunt and Mary Pierse (eds): France and Ireland: Notes and Narratives
ISBN 978-3-0343-1914-0. 272 pages. 2015.

Vol. 67   John Lynch and Katherina Dodou (eds): The Leaving of Ireland: Migration and Belonging in Irish Literature and Film
ISBN 978-3-0343-1896-9. 313 pages. 2015.

Vol. 68   Anne Goarzin (ed.): New Critical Perspectives on Franco-Irish Relations
ISBN 978-3-0343-1781-8. 271 pages. 2015.

Vol. 69	Michel Brunet, Fabienne Gaspari and Mary Pierse (eds): George Moore's Paris and His Ongoing French Connections ISBN 978-3-0343-1973-7. 279 pages. 2015.
Vol. 70	Carine Berbéri and Martine Pelletier (eds): Ireland: Authority and Crisis ISBN 978-3-0343-1939-3. 296 pages. 2015.
Vol. 71	David Doolin: Transnational Revolutionaries: The Fenian Invasion of Canada, 1866 ISBN 978-3-0343-1922-5. 348 pages. 2016.
Vol. 72	Terry Phillips: Irish Literature and the First World War: Culture, Identity and Memory ISBN 978-3-0343-1969-0. 297 pages. 2015.
Vol. 73	Carmen Zamorano Llena and Billy Gray (eds): Authority and Wisdom in the New Ireland: Studies in Literature and Culture ISBN 978-3-0343-1833-4. 263 pages. 2016.
Vol. 74	Flore Coulouma (ed.): New Perspectives on Irish TV Series: Identity and Nostalgia on the Small Screen ISBN 978-3-0343-1977-5. 222 pages. 2016.
Vol. 75	Fergal Lenehan: Stereotypes, Ideology and Foreign Correspondents: German Media Representations of Ireland, 1946–2010 ISBN 978-3-0343-2222-5. 306 pages. 2016.
Vol. 76	Jarlath Killeen and Valeria Cavalli (eds): 'Inspiring a Mysterious Terror': 200 Years of Joseph Sheridan Le Fanu ISBN 978-3-0343-2223-2. 260 pages. 2016.
Vol. 77	Anne Karhio: 'Slight Return': Paul Muldoon's Poetics of Place ISBN 978-3-0343-1986-7. 272 pages. 2017.
Vol. 78	Margaret Eaton: Frank Confessions: Performance in the Life-Writings of Frank McCourt ISBN 978-1-906165-61-1. 294 pages. 2017.

Vol. 79	Marguérite Corporaal, Christopher Cusack and Ruud van den Beuken (eds): Irish Studies and the Dynamics of Memory: Transitions and Transformations ISBN 978-3-0343-2236-2. 360 pages. 2017.	
Vol. 80	Conor Caldwell and Eamon Byers (eds): New Crops, Old Fields: Reimagining Irish Folklore ISBN 978-3-0343-1912-6. 200 pages. 2017.	
Vol. 81	Sinéad Wall: Irish Diasporic Narratives in Argentina: A Reconsideration of Home, Identity and Belonging ISBN 978-1-906165-66-6. 282 pages. 2017.	
Vol. 82	Ute Anna Mittermaier: Images of Spain in Irish Literature, 1922–1975 ISBN 978-3-0343-1993-5. 386 pages. 2017.	
Vol. 83	Lauren Clark: Consuming Irish Children: Advertising and the Art of Independence, 1860–1921 ISBN 978-3-0343-1989-8. 288 pages. 2017.	
Vol. 84	Lisa FitzGerald: Re-Place: Irish Theatre Environments ISBN 978-1-78707-359-3. 222 pages. 2017.	
Vol. 85	Joseph Greenwood: 'Hear My Song': Irish Theatre and Popular Song in the 1950s and 1960s ISBN 978-3-0343-1915-7. 320 pages. 2017.	
Vol. 86	Nils Beese: Writing Slums: Dublin, Dirt and Literature ISBN 978-1-78707-959-5. 250 pages. 2018.	
Vol. 87	Barry Houlihan (ed.): Navigating Ireland's Theatre Archive: Theory, Practice, Performance ISBN 978-1-78707-372-2. 306 pages. 2019.	
Vol. 88	María Elena Jaime de Pablos (ed.): Giving Shape to the Moment: The Art of Mary O'Donnell: Poet, Novelist and Short Story Writer ISBN 978-1-78874-403-4. 228 pages. 2018.	

Vol. 89　Marguérite Corporaal and Peter Gray (eds): The Great Irish Famine and Social Class: Conflicts, Responsibilities, Representations
ISBN 978-1-78874-166-8. 330 pages. 2019.

Vol. 90　Patrick Speight: Irish-Argentine Identity in an Age of Political Challenge and Change, 1875–1983
ISBN 978-1-78874-417-1. 360 pages. 2019.

Vol. 91　Fionna Barber, Heidi Hansson, and Sara Dybris McQuaid (eds): Ireland and the North
ISBN 978-1-78874-289-4. 338 pages. 2019.

Vol. 92　Ruth Sheehy: The Life and Work of Richard King: Religion, Nationalism and Modernism
ISBN 978-1-78707-246-6. 482 pages. 2019.

Vol. 93　Brian Lucey, Eamon Maher and Eugene O'Brien (eds): Recalling the Celtic Tiger
ISBN 978-1-78997-286-3. 386 pages. 2019.

Vol. 94　Melania Terrazas Gallego (ed.): Trauma and Identity in Contemporary Irish Culture
ISBN 978-1-78997-557-4. 302 pages. 2020.

Vol. 95　Patricia Medcalf: Advertising the Black Stuff in Ireland 1959–1999: Increments of Change
ISBN 978-1-78997-345-7. 218 pages. 2020.

Vol. 96　Anne Goarzin and Maria Parsons (eds): New Materialisms
ISBN 978-1-78874-651-9. 204 pages. 2020.

Vol. 97　Hiroko Ikeda and Kazuo Yokouchi (eds): Irish Literature in the British Context and Beyond: New Perspectives from Kyoto
ISBN 978-1-78997-566-6. 250 pages. 2020.

Vol. 98　Catherine Nealy Judd: Travel Narratives of the Irish Famine: Politics, Tourism, and Scandal, 1845–1853
ISBN 978-1-80079-084-1. 468 pages. 2020.

Vol. 99 Lesley Lelourec and Gráinne O'Keeffe-Vigneron (eds): Northern Ireland after the Good Friday Agreement: Building a Shared Future from a Troubled Past?
ISBN 978-1-78997-746-2. 262 pages. 2021

Vol. 100 Eamon Maher and Eugene O'Brien (eds): Reimagining Irish Studies for the Twenty-First Century
ISBN 978-1-80079-191-6. 384 pages. 2021

www.ingramcontent.com/pod-product-compliance
Ingram Content Group UK Ltd.
Pitfield, Milton Keynes, MK11 3LW, UK
UKHW021315180426
11947UKWH00015B/1237